UNDER AN IMPERIAL SUN

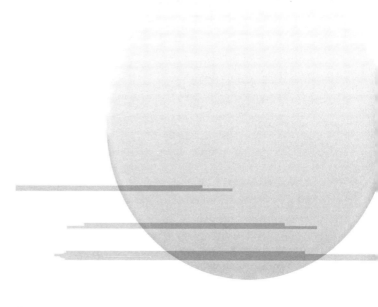

Under an Imperial Sun

JAPANESE COLONIAL LITERATURE OF TAIWAN AND THE SOUTH

Faye Yuan Kleeman

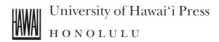 University of Hawai'i Press
HONOLULU

This book has been published with the aid of a subvention from the Eugene M. Kayden fund for the 2002 University of Colorado Faculty Manuscript Award.

Library of Congress Cataloging-in-Publication Data

Kleeman, Faye Yuan.
    Under an imperial sun : Japanese colonial literature of Taiwan and the South / Faye Yuan Kleeman.
        p. cm.
Includes bibliographical references and index.
    ISBN 0-8248-2592-6 (hd. : alk. paper)
    1. Japanese literature—Taiwan—History and criticism.
2. World War, 1939–1945—Literature and the war. 3. Literature and society—Taiwan. I. Title.

    PL889.T282 K57 2003
    895.6'09951249—dc21

                                    2002152995

University of Hawai'i Press books are printed on acid-free paper and meet the guidelines for permanence and durability of the Council on Library Resources

Designed by Josie Herr
Printed by The Maple-Vail Book Manufacturing Group

Contents

Acknowledgments

The researching and writing of this book has taken me to both Japan and Taiwan. It would have been impossible without the help of a variety of friends and colleagues, and without the financial support of both funding sources and institutions.

I first studied Japanese under the direction of Cai Maofeng of Soochow University and continued my studies in Japan under Asai Kiyoshi, Tsutsumi Seiji, and Hirano Yukiko. Coming to Berkeley, I was able to work with Bill and Helen McCullough in classical literature, Francis Motofuji in early modern, and Van Gessel in modern. I have also gained much from interactions with my colleagues over the years, including Barbara Brooks at City College and Laurel Rodd and Steve Snyder at the University of Colorado.

I was first drawn to the field of Japanese colonial literature by Tarumi Chie of Yokohama National University, a former fellow classmate at Ochanomizu University whose study of Japanese language literature opened the discussion of Japanese colonial literature in Japan. Through her I met Fujii Shōzō of Tokyo University, whose history of the last hundred years of Taiwanese literature was an inspiration to me in formulating this work; during my research stay at Tokyo University in 1999–2000, I profited tremendously from conferences and seminars he organized and from frequent personal exchanges of ideas. My deep thanks also go to Kawahara Isao and Nakajima Toshio for their generous advice and assistance in locating materials. In Taiwan I was warmly received by the Institute of Literature and Philosophy of the Academia Sinica and profited much from conversations with Hsiao-yen Peng, Chang Chi-lin, and Chou Wan-yao. I should also thank Douglas Fix of Reed College, who at various points provided me with sources and useful comments. Huang Ying-che of Aichi University helped me understand cultural and literary developments during the transition from colonial to post-colonial Taiwan, and Yomota Inuhiko of Meiji Gakuin University, through his study of the actress Li Xianglan, provides a model study of cultural hybridity.

My research for this book was funded by generous research grants from the National Endowment for the Humanities, the Japan Foundation, and Chiang Ching-kuo Foundation. A publishing subvention from the Kayden Manuscript Award enabled me to add Chinese and Japanese characters. My research was also facilitated by the able staff of the East Asian Library at the University of Colorado as well as by a variety of institutions in Japan and Taiwan. The anonymous readers and editorial staff of the University of Hawai'i Press gave me useful advice on a number of points of both substance and presentation. I am also grateful to my parents, Yuan Fa and Chuang Chiu-yueh, who were born and educated under the Japanese occupation and were living witnesses to the repeated transformations of modern Taiwanese history; this book is really about them and their generation. Finally, thanks to my family, who stoically endured long absences and late nights; without them, this project would never have reached completion.

Introduction:
Imperialism and Textuality

On November 3, 1942, fifteen hundred of the leading writers, editors, and critics from China, Manchuria, Mongolia, Taiwan,[1] Korea, and Japan gathered at the Imperial Hotel in Tokyo to attend the first Greater East Asian Writers Conference (Dai Tōa Bungakusha Taikai 大東亜文学者大会). Before the official opening of their meeting, they first bowed deeply in the direction of the imperial palace. Two days before the conference, these delegates from Japan's colonies and quasicolonies had been taken, in the fog and drizzle, to pay homage to the imperial palace, the Meiji Shrine, and the Yasukuni Shrine. At the conference, the Korean writer Lee Kōshū 李光洙 (b. 1892), the father of modern Korean literature, made a passionate statement on behalf of writers from the colonies:

> The spirit of Greater East Asia must be truth itself; it cannot be a man-made thing, like something created by the League of Nations. We are not here to establish this Greater East Asian spirit but to discover it. To put it in the most easily understood terms, the foundation, the marrow, of this Greater East Asian spirit is the spirit of sacrificing the self. . . . The spirit of offering oneself up, of sacrificing the self, is, I believe, the most elevated of the ways of men and is the path closest to the perfect truth. Why? Because our goal, our goal as Japanese, is not scheming to become a strong nation like America or Great Britain, but to save all the people in the world. . . . However, it will not be us as individuals, but rather the emperor, who accomplishes this goal. Our part is to die singing the praises of the emperor. I firmly believe that the spirit of

sacrificing the self, offering oneself up completely, must be the foundation of the Greater East Asian spirit. [Kawamura Minato 1997a: 10–11]

This zealous speech by Lee, a nationalist writer who later turned collaborator, was well received at the conference, but it would come back to haunt him in the postwar Korean discourse on colonial literature.[2] This type of hyperbolic language, though commonplace at the time among Japanese nationals, still garnered great attention coming from the mouth of a colonial subject. Later, in a private moment, Lee related the difficulties faced by Korean writers to the Japanese authors Kusano Shinpei and Kawakami Tetsutarō.[3]

The Greater East Asian Writers Conference provided an arena where colonized writers could affirm their allegiance to the empire while the empire in turn showcased the cultural and intellectual trophies it had acquired through colonialism. The second conference (August 1943) was again held in Tokyo. The Japanese side mobilized prominent Japanese writers such as Kume Masao, Kikuchi Kan, Takamura Kōtarō, Kobayashi Hideo, Yokomitsu Riichi, and Miyoshi Tatsuji—a veritable Who's Who of modern Japanese literature at the time.[4] The third and final conference was held in Nanjing, China, in November 1944. Again, other than Taiwan, all territories in the Japanese empire sent representatives. The fourth conference was scheduled to be held in Shinkyō (新京), the new capital of Manchukuo, but never came to fruition due to the end of the war.

This series of conferences marked the creation of an East Asian literary sphere that was coterminous with the Japanese empire and centered on the Japanese literary and cultural tradition. Within this sphere, education in the Japanese language, exposure to Japanese-language media, diffusion of Japanese popular culture, and the presence of a Japanese political and legal system all fostered a common worldview and promoted a common literary discourse. Although the empire was built upon military conquest, authoritarian administration, systematic discrimination, and the violent suppression of all dissent—and even though one aspect of colonial administration was the systematic monitoring and censorship of literary production—one must judge the creation of this transnational Asian literary sphere as a significant accomplishment. How, in the short space of a half-century, was Japan able to form from the disparate cultural and historical traditions of East Asia, Southeast Asia, and the South Pacific a single literary space where peoples of diverse nationality and ethnicity could exchange ideas and share their literary creations? What was the effect of this process on the individual cultures and communities subsumed within this new Japanese world? How did the non-Japanese members understand their relationship to the local and national cultural traditions of their ancestors, and how did they justify abandoning their native traditions for those of the Japanese empire?

Although the political and economic aspects of the Japanese empire have been the topic of many studies,[5] the literature of the colonies—including works by Japanese travelers relaying their impressions of the colonies, the creations of Japanese expatriates who made the colonies their home, and the prose and poetry of colonial subjects writing in Japanese—has been largely ignored in the postwar Japanese literary world.[6] It is a sensitive topic because Japan occupies the unique position of having both suffered the impact of Western colonialism, through the unequal treaties of the early Meiji period, and imposed its imperial will on its Asian neighbors. The issue is further complicated by the wartime ideology of a Greater East Asia, which was founded on an insightful analysis of the West's imperialist exploitation of East Asia but in fact was used to justify and legitimate Japan's violent takeover, subjugation, and exploitation of the other peoples of the region.

The publication of Edward Said's *Orientalism* and the rise of (post)colonial studies as an academic discipline—coupled with the passing of the Shōwa emperor, which removed certain taboos concerning the colonial era—has led to reexamination of all aspects of Japan's colonial history. Many studies that appeared in the 1990s focused on cultural aspects of the Japanese colonial enterprise. Oguma Eiji's groundbreaking studies (1995, 1998) have altered our understanding of the Japanese discourse on ethnic identity. Komagome Takeshi's study of the colonial education system, as well as the work of Lee Yeounsuk (1996), Koyasu Nobukuni (1996), Yasuda Toshiaki (1997, 1998, 1999), Shi Gang (1993), and Osa Shizue (1998) on the construction of the modern Japanese language, reveal the mutual influence of the colonial educational apparatus and the education administration of Japan. Cultural critics like Ueno Chizuko (1998) have explored the precarious relationship of gender and nationalism in the colonial period.[7]

Literary studies of the colonial period are a more recent phenomenon. Kawamura Minato's many studies of colonial literature in the colonies, focusing on Korea and Manchuria, paved the way for in-depth examinations of individual authors. Scholars like Leo Ching (1994,

1995, 1998), Yvonne Chang (1997, 1999a), Tarumi Chie (1995a), Kawahara Isao (1997), and Fujii Shōzo (1998) have all examined the literary production of this era from the perspective of postcolonial criticism. The reprinting of many rare and obscure works from this era by Nakajima Toshio and Kawahara Isao (1998, 1999) has greatly facilitated the growth of this field.

This book is divided into three parts covering Japanese visitors to the colonies, a prominent Japanese expatriate author, and the native writers of Taiwan. Part I treats the discursive creation of the empire through the writings of Japanese authors on the colonies and their inhabitants. It looks first at the South as an organizing concept that defined the relationship of Japan to one part of Asia. It was a part of Asia in which Japan saw both its past—in the theories of Yanagita Kunio and others regarding a southern origin of the Japanese people—and its future in the "southward advance" (*nanshin* 南進) that was for many the preferred path of expansion for a Japan bursting at the seams from population pressures and anxious to flex its modern military might. The South provided a space within the Japanese worldview for the primitive and savage, which we see reflected in early tales of idyllic island paradises of the South Seas and later in much more disturbing tales of the savage violence that lurked in the hearts of semi-assimilated Taiwanese aborigines. We see a late conception of the region reflected in the wartime stories and experiences of two Japanese authors, Hayashi Fumiko and Nakajima Atsushi, who lived in these areas briefly and wrote accounts that were widely read in the metropolis. Taiwan, part of the Japanese empire since 1895, was a particularly popular focus for speculation about the South. Satō Haruo's "Devilbird," adapted from a Taiwanese aboriginal myth about scapegoating, functions as a metaphor for the persecution of colonized ethnic minorities within Japan following the Kantō Earthquake of 1923.

Nishikawa Mitsuru, the focus of Part II, provides a more nuanced view of Taiwan and a link to the native literary scene that developed during the colonial period. Having spent most of his life in Taiwan, Nishikawa was intimately familiar with the complex, multiethnic, multilingual society that had developed there. Through his many quasi-ethnographic productions on local Taiwanese culture, Nishikawa advocated not only the assimilation of Taiwan's populace to Japanese language, customs, and beliefs but also the incorporation of Taiwan's distinct heritage into Japan as a new regional variant. Part II concludes with a close, intertextual reading of two stories by Nishikawa that reflect his romanticist appropriation of Taiwan's precolonial past and his genderized relationship to the colonized culture.

Part III, the final section of the book, addresses the literary response to the colonial experience in Taiwan by native Taiwanese authors writing in Japanese. First we examine the linguistic problems associated with Japanese colonial literature. A modern, standard vernacular Japanese (Kokugo) was a necessary precursor to modern Japanese literature, and the transmission of this language to colonial subjects required a new introspection into the structure of Japanese and its relationship to other Asian tongues. The situation in Taiwan was particularly complex because of the lack of a written vernacular Taiwanese, the multiplicity of languages spoken on the island, and the recent development of vernacular literature in Mandarin. The result was a linguistic environment characterized by multilingualism and extreme hybridity.

Despite these obstacles, a robust literature did evolve on Taiwan, though it has yet to find its proper place within the canons of either Japanese or Chinese literary history. The remainder of this introduction focuses on two groups of writers who contributed to this tradition: the nativists and the imperial-subject writers. The first group, flourishing in the 1920s and 1930s, comprised writers who had been educated primarily in Japanese but maintained strong ties to the Chinese literary tradition and were not wholly at ease in identifying with Japanese civilization. Authors like Yang Kui, Zhang Wenhuan, and Lü Heruo were strongly influenced by issues of social justice advocated by the Proletarian Literature movement. In stories like "Newspaper Boy" and "Native Chicks," Yang Kui details the corrosive effect of class and gender-based oppression on the Taiwanese people. Zhang Wenhuan proposes a pastoral utopian response to the onslaught of modernization brought to Taiwan by the Japanese colonial administration. The multitalented Lü Heruo is adept at capturing the human dimension of relations between Japanese and Taiwanese. He is best known for "Oxcart," which tells of a man who is gradually driven into destitution by Japanese colonial appropriations and regulations, but in stories like "Camellia" we see a Japanese photographer who becomes so enthralled by the Taiwanese countryside that he barely escapes with his soul.

The status of the imperial-subject writers is more controversial, and their literary productions have not been the subject of serious scholarly examination. Writing primarily in the last years of the Japanese colonial period, when the pressure for assimilation to Japanese culture reached its peak, authors like Zhou Jinpo, Wang Changxiong, and Chen Huoquan confronted directly the questions of cultural hybridity raised by these pressures. In Zhou Jinpo's earliest works, exemplified by "Water Cancer," we see highly cultivated young men educated in metropolitan Japan who struggle with how to reform traditional Taiwan; but in later works, such as "Weather, Belief, and Chronic Disease," we see a mature convert to Shinto who finds release and a reinvigoration of traditional family life through the time-honored Chinese rituals of his youth. Chen Huoquan's "The Way" features a protagonist who strives to increase production in his factory. When he fails to be rewarded because of his ethnicity, he redoubles his efforts to become Japanese and eventually enlists and fights for the Japanese army. Although the common nationalistic reading of these tales has condemned them as traitorous advocacy of the colonizer's interests, in the context of the time they can be read as an ironic attempt to subvert the oppressor's power by mimicking his language through what Leela Ghandi has called the "Caliban paradigm."

The epilogue to the book considers the continuing production of literature in the Japanese language in postwar, postcolonial Taiwan. Although this literature has been denounced by postcolonial critics and heralded by Japanese nationalists as a type of colonial nostalgia, I argue that it is, in fact, a strategic affirmation of a distinct Taiwanese identity. Taiwan's complex cultural legacy is still evident today in the creolization of the modern language, which mixes Taiwanese, Japanese, and even English elements into the now dominant Mandarin base.

The multicultural, multilingual environment of the Japanese colonial empire raises many questions of naming and terminology. In referring to the indigenous inhabitants of Taiwan, I have used the term "aborigine," which translates the Chinese term "*yuanzhumin*" 原住民, currently the favored designation for these people. In describing the attitudes of the Japanese colonizers and ethnic Chinese population toward these peoples, however, I have employed terms like "barbarian" and "savage" because equivalent terms are used in the discourse of that time. All these terms fail to represent the social, ethnic, and linguistic diversity of the aboriginal peoples of Taiwan during the colonial period.

In referring to the ethnically Chinese inhabitants of Taiwan, who migrated there from China over the last four centuries, I typically use the term "Taiwanese." Taiwan is a Chinese term and was not used to refer to the island before its colonization by the Chinese; moreover,

Taiwanren 台湾人, or "people of Taiwan," is the term used most commonly during both the colonial and postcolonial periods for the ethnically Chinese inhabitants of Taiwan. This is not meant to imply that the aboriginal people are not native inhabitants of the island, and when I use the term "native" I refer to both the aborigines and the Taiwanese.

Generally I have given the personal names of Taiwanese in modern Mandarin pronunciation transcribed in the pinyin romanization system.[8] This practice is somewhat anomalous, since it is unlikely that anyone ever referred to them by these sounds at the time. Japanese would have used the Sino-Japanese *(onyomi)* pronunciation of their Chinese characters or referred to them by their Japanese names (if they had them); locals would have referred to them in some dialect of Taiwanese (Zhangzhou or Quanzhou) or in Hakka, depending on the person's background and the situation. Using the Mandarin reading imposes uniformity on this linguistic mélange and permits readers to refer to other sources on these individuals. Moreover, we still have not advanced far beyond the 1930s in developing a common way of transcribing the Taiwanese language. Where I do have occasion to cite words in Taiwanese, I rely on the transcription in K. T. Tân's *A Chinese-English Dictionary: Taiwan Dialect* (1978).

PART

I

WRITING THE EMPIRE

The Genealogy of the "South"

THE SOUTH, referring to lands and islands to the south of Japan, was the focus of much interest in the decades following the Meiji Restoration and during the establishment of the Japanese colonial empire. The South was a land of untouched, natural beauty and untamed savages, an area where the Japanese imagination could be given free rein, a region into which the burgeoning population of Japan could expand in an Asian version of colonial empires then maintained by all the major European powers. This chapter explores this concept of the South (expressed in Japanese as *nanpō* 南方, *nantō* 南島 , *nanyō* 南洋, and in more literary, romanticized variants, *nankoku* 南国 and *nankai* 南海) and the role it played in Japanese colonialism in general and colonial literature in particular.[1] After examining the portrayal of the South Pacific in early political novels and later popular media, I look at the South close to hand, in Taiwan, analyzing the portrayal of the Taiwanese aborigines in a variety of novels, short stories, popular songs, and films—especially representations of the primitive and the mission of Japanese colonialism to civilize and ultimately assimilate these "savages." Finally, I consider two modern classics that have never been explored from the perspective of colonialism: Nakajima Atsushi's *Light, Wind, and Dreams* (*Hikari to kaze to yume* 光と風と夢, 1942) and Hayashi Fumiko's nostalgic *Drifting Clouds* (*Ukigumo* 浮雲, 1949); both will be shown to illuminate the symbolic meaning and impact of the South in the colonial context.

Japan's encounter with the (barbaric) Other can be traced in early records such as the *Fudoki*. With the sinocentric worldview of the Middle Kingdom as their model, the Japanese developed their own cosmology that placed Japan at the center of the civilized universe and adopted Chinese terms like "*fan*" 蕃 or "*yi*" 夷 that characterized ethnic others on the margins as barbaric. In Japan's earliest poetry collection, the *Manyōshū*, we already read of warriors dispatched to the distant borders to guard against the encroaching barbarians who always hover at the margins of a secure Japan. At this early stage, the barbaric was found within the borders of modern Japan, even on the main island itself.

Japanese colonialism did not begin with Taiwan or Korea. Though the Ainu and Okinawans are often omitted from examinations of Japanese colonialism, Japan as a nation began its modern colonial expansion as early as the mid-nineteenth century by encroaching upon the areas inhabited by these peoples to the north and the south at approximately the same time.[2] With the installation of the expansion envoy (*kaitakushi* 開拓使) in 1869 and the establishment of the Hokkaido Administration 北海道庁 in 1886, Hokkaido was gradually incorporated into the modern nation-state of Japan. The pace accelerated swiftly in subsequent years: full conscription of the islanders into the military (Zendō Chōheirei 全道徴兵令) came in 1898, the Hokkaido Indigenous People Protection Bill (Hokkaidō Dojin Hogohō 北海道土人保護法) was passed the following year, the application of the election bill for the lower house (Shūgiin Senkyohō 衆議院選挙法) came in 1900, and in 1901 the Hokkaido Bill (Hokkaidō Kaihō 北海道会法) regularized the administration of Hokkaido on the model of other prefectural governments. By the turn of the century, Hokkaido had been fully incorporated into the territory of Japan. Natural resources were plundered and the indigenous Ainu people were forced to forsake their own language and customs under policies of forced assimilation.

Meanwhile, on the southern front, the kingdom of Okinawa, though under the indirect control of the Satsuma domain since 1609, was nevertheless able to navigate a course between the Chinese and the Satsuma, surviving as a small trading kingdom. In 1871, the new Meiji government placed Okinawa under the administrative rule of Kagoshima prefecture. In the same year an Okinawan ship ran aground in Taiwan and its crew was murdered by the indigenous people. The next year, Japan granted the king of Okinawa aristocratic status and moved the royal family to Tokyo. In 1874, using the previous incident in Taiwan as an excuse, Japan sent an army to Taiwan, claiming that the interests of Okinawa, its subject state (*Nihon zokumin* 日本国属民), had been trampled on. The conflict is commonly known in the West as the Taiwan Incident. (The Japanese term *"Taiwan shuppei"* 台湾出兵, or "Taiwan invasion," more accurately reflects the military nature of the event.) Japan demanded that Okinawa sever all ties with China and reform its government; when the Okinawans resisted, Japan sent in police and troops to quell the resistance movement and subsequently annexed the kingdom. The formal designation of Okinawa as a prefecture in 1879 marked the beginning of Japanese cultural assimilation and direct administration of the South. Even though domestication of the Okinawans as imperial subjects was, and to a certain degree still is, not an easy task (see Christy 1997). Japanese folklorists and politicians alike, and at times the Okinawans themselves, continue to claim a shared ethnic and culture heritage.[3] Nevertheless, Okinawa anchored Japan's presence in the South. The concept of the South expanded when Japan acquired Taiwan as its first colony in 1895 and later was given a mandate over a group of South Pacific islands by the League of Nations.

The islands of the South Pacific were an early focus of the seagoing Japanese. Iwao Seiichi's studies of early modern Japanese emigrants to the South Seas show that Japanese settlements were established throughout the South Pacific by exiled Japanese Christians and soldiers employed by the Dutch East India Company as early as the beginning of the seventeenth century. (See Iwao Seiichi 1966 and 1987.) Japanese pirates and traders traveled as far as the Straits of Malacca and plundered the eastern coast of China with some regularity. Most of this activity came to a halt with the closing of the country during the Tokugawa period (1600–1867). The Meiji Restoration and the opening to the West, therefore, released a fount of pent-up energy. Masterless samurai and other adventurers with no place in a modern nation-state saw the South Pacific, like the Asian continent, as a place where they could win fame and fortune. Politicians saw it as a possible area of territorial expansion on the heels of Meiji Japan's successful claims to Hokkaido, Sakhalin, the Kuriles, the Ryukyus, and the Bonin Islands—a policy subsumed under the trubric of "southward advance" (*nanshin* 南進).

The idea of "the South" made its way into the public's consciousness during the 1890s, when it became a popular subject for political novels (*seiji shōsetsu* 政治小説).[4] As early as 1887, there were novels such as Gotō Nansui's 後藤南翠 *Sacred Banner of the Rising Sun* (*Hinomihata* 旭章旗), Komiyama Tenkō's 小宮山天香 *Adventurous Enterprise: The King of the Archipelago* (*Bōken kigyō: Rentō daiō* 冒険企業・聯島大王), and Hisamatsu

Yoshinori's 久松義典 *Great Achievements of the South Seas* (*Nanmei iseki* 南溟偉跡), all set in the South Seas and focusing on the development of sparsely populated islands. Soon more famous authors, known for their political novels advocating political reform and civil rights, took up the topic. Tōkai Sanshi 東海散士 (a.k.a. Shiba Shirō, 1852–1922) followed up his novel on the Irish rebellion, *Strange Encounters with Beauties* (*Kajin no kigū* 佳人の奇遇, 1885), with *The Beauty from the Orient* (*Tōyō no kajin* 東洋の佳人, 1888), which was set in Southeast Asia. Yano Ryūkei's 矢野龍渓 (1850–1931) *Epic of the Floating Castle* (*Ukishiro monogatari* 浮城物語, 1890) depicted a group of Meiji patriots who, dissatisfied with the domestic political situation, decided to pursue adventure in the South Seas. There they successfully traded with the barbarians, hijacked a pirate ship which they named "Floating Castle," allied with the natives, and defeated both Dutch and British naval forces. Suehiro Tetchō 末廣鐵腸 (1849–1896) followed suit the next year with two narratives, *The Great Wave of the South Seas* (*Nanyō no daiharan* 南洋の大波瀾) and *The Storm* (*Arashi no nagori* あらしのなごり). The Philippine independence movement provided the backdrop for *The Great Wave of the South Seas*. Authors at this time never visited the locations they wrote about; it was only in the early 1940s, when the Pacific War was raging, that writers were dispatched to Southeast Asia and the Pacific to write and report in support of the war effort. In Meiji, both the authors and audience were aware they were treating an imagined world far removed from their own. The South Seas setting was used primarily as a narrative device in plots really intended to address domestic political concerns. In the introduction to *The Great Wave of the South Seas*, Suehiro remarks: "I do not intend to depict the geography or customs of the South Seas. There is fabrication in truth and truth in fabrication. I constructed on paper a land of miasmal rain and barbarian smoke because it was the only way to release the discontent that has accumulated in my chest" (Yano Tōru 1979: 20–21).

Novels like these, adventures set in the South Seas, were popular enough from the late 1880s to the mid-1890s to warrant identification as a separate subgenre of the political novel: "novels of the southward advance" (*nanshin shōsetsu* 南進小説) or "maritime literature" (*kaiyō shōsetsu* 海洋小説). But with the outbreak of the Sino-Japanese War in 1895 and the tension on the Korean peninsula, the focus of attention shifted to the continent and it was not until the 1930s that the South Seas once again captured the popular imagination.

One of the earlier factual records of the South Pacific and the "barbarians" inhabiting that distant region is found in Suzuki Tsunenori's 鈴

木経勲 *Actual Record of a South Pacific Adventure* (*Nanyō tanken jikki* 南洋
探検実記, 1892). During the early years of the Meiji period, Suzuki and
Gotō Taketarō were sent to the Marshall Islands to investigate an incident in which Japanese pearl divers were attacked and killed by the islanders. Suzuki noted that people living on this island "get along well as
if they are relatives. They rarely fight with each other. They respect, or
rather worship, the head of the island as if he were a god. Once in a while
foreign visitors come bearing rare goods or food; those who receive
them customarily share them with neighbors and friends" (Kawamura
Minato 1994b: 30–31). Despite Suzuki's own on-site observations and
amicable experiences with the natives, he nevertheless perpetuates a stereotypical image of them as lazy, disobedient, amoral, superstitious, pro-
miscuous, and cannibalistic.[5] The discourse of Suzuki Tsunenori and
similar observers had a lasting influence on the Japanese view of the inhabitants of the region, an influence that has not wholly disappeared
even today.

The first formal Japanese trading voyages to the South Pacific began
in the 1890s, and the trade grew over the following decades. Despite opposition from the German colonial administration, which had taken
over certain islands from the Spanish in 1899, Japan soon became the
dominant trader in the region (Peattie 1988: 20–26). Although interest
in imperial expansion continued, the Japanese soon came to the realization that the islands of the South Pacific had been claimed by various
European powers. It was only after the outbreak of World War I that
Japan had a pretense to seize the German colonies in Micronesia. At
Versailles, Japan was given a Class C Mandate over the islands it had occupied and proceeded to integrate them into the empire.

Yano Tōru distinguishes the vision of expansion into the South
during the Meiji and Taishō periods from the realization of that goal
during the Shōwa era. Unlike many historians, he does not see a direct
link between the early concept and the later politicized ideology of a
Greater East Asian Coprosperity Sphere. The earlier vision of the
South resulted in a type of colonial expansion consisting primarily of
private citizens migrating to specific places in Taiwan, the Philippines,
Singapore, and other parts of Southeast Asia to pursue opportunities.
Such people harbored dreams of becoming rich or famous in these
foreign lands but never ceased to regard Japan as their true home. The
colonialism of the 1930s and 1940s, by contrast, featured a comprehensive, state-directed expansion of Japanese territory aimed at creating an enlarged sphere of Japanese control. A typical example of this

approach is the "Plan for the Kwantung Army to Occupy Manchuria and Mongolia" ("Kantōgun Man-Mō ryoyū keikaku," 1929) developed by Ishihara Kanji 石原莞爾 (1889–1949). Yano cites the 1930s as the turning point for this shift from a commercial, entrepreneurial approach toward the colonies to a politicized, imperialistic approach. It was also at this time that the South was first envisioned as part of a Greater East Asian Coprosperity Sphere.

During the first decades after opening to the West, the South was constructed as a complex, multivalent image. It had once been associated with the West (*nanban* 南蛮, "southern barbarian," once referred to Europeans), and even those areas that Japan came to dominate preserved remnants of an earlier, Western colonization. Romantic notions of the South Seas as a land of adventure where a Japanese might make a name and a fortune were particularly appealing during the social and cultural upheaval of the Meiji period, when traditional samurai had lost their feudal masters and enterprising commoners began to dream of greater things. Within the mature Japanese empire of the 1930s and 1940s, the South was the locus of a more mature dream. For Nakajima Atsushi and Hayashi Fumiko, it had already assumed something like its position in the Western imagination: an idyllic land of material bounty and languorous leisure where one might escape the pressures of a modernizing Japanese society. But the hypercolonial context of these realms injected a different layer of meaning. For Nakajima, this was represented by his ideal of an enlightened colonialism inspired by Western reformers like Robert Louis Stevenson. For Hayashi, it was the smart, savvy, and ultracompetent French-Vietnamese woman Mari who presented an ideal to which the Japanese protagonist could not hope to aspire. In both cases the South seemed to offer a utopian escape, but the region's colonial past exposed the limitations of modern Japan. In the next chapter we shall see how Japanese efforts to locate the primitive in the South encountered similar problems of representation—especially in Taiwan, where they came into the most intimate contact with the savage Other.

Taming the Barbaric

AFTER THE INITIAL burst of excitement in the late nineteenth century, interest in the South Seas seems to have waned. It rebounded dramatically in the 1930s, however, when the comic strip *The Adventurous Dankichi* (*Bōken Dankichi* 冒険ダン吉) gained popularity. This narrative by Shimada Keizō was serialized in the popular youth magazine *Shōnen kurabu* 少年倶楽部 from 1933 to 1939. The comical young man Dankichi dozes off one day while fishing and awakes to find himself marooned on a lush tropical jungle island full of coconut trees and savages. With his wisdom and bravery, he soon rules over the various tribes as their chief. To remind us that he came from a civilized society, the cartoonist was careful to draw the perky Dankichi always wearing shoes and a wristwatch. Dankichi's resourcefulness and the advantages of civilization (clothes, shoes, wristwatch) soon gain him the loyalty of the natives, who are referred to as *kuronbō* 黒ん坊, or "blackies." Initially, Dankichi gives his native followers names such as Banana, Pine, and Betelnut, but when this system becomes too complicated, he just writes numbers on their chests and refers to them as "Number 1," "Number 2," and so on. Besides bringing this numerical order to the native population, Dankichi also introduces to the primitive society institutions like schools, hospitals, a military force, a postal service, and the concept of money.[1]

Shimada Keizō spoke of his creation, Dankichi, fulfilling a dream he had harbored since he was a young boy—a dream of traveling to "a warm southern island . . . to become the chief of the uninhabited island, where animals are my subjects and there are neither money worries nor homework." The tropical island of the barbarians was clearly modeled after the South Pacific islands entrusted to Japan by the League of Nations. Shimada later reminisced: "At that time, the South Pacific islands were under Japanese rule. The ideology of a southward advance (*nanshin* 南進) had been realized in the development of the South. All the attention in Japan was on the South, so I thought that would be an ideal setting for Dankichi's adventure."[2]

The Dankichi story fed the public's interest in the exotic South Pacific. The phenomenon has much in common with the West's fascination with tropical islands represented in popular works such as Stevenson's *Treasure Island* or the jungle tales of Burroughs' *Tarzan* series and Kipling's *Jungle Book*. This "Dankichi syndrome," as Yano Tōru calls it, provided a lighthearted, entertaining depiction that reinforced the stereotypical conceptualization of the South in Japan as backward and primitive, full of fearsome headhunters and cannibals. Kawamura Minato points out the inaccuracies that grew out of a lack of firsthand knowledge of the region—reflected in the diverse range of fauna among Dankichi's animal followers, including creatures native to Africa or the desert such as lions, elephants, giraffes, and camels. Kawamura believes that one function of the Dankichi stories was to portray the mature Japanese state, by contrast, as a modern, civilized nation. The uneducated, backward barbarians in the stories highlighted the civilized nature of the Japanese and reaffirmed their cultural superiority. In other words, the Dankichi syndrome was a Japanese version of orientalism by proxy.[3]

Another example culled from the popular consciousness of the same period is the hit song by Ishida Hitomatsu 石田一松, "The Chief's Daughter" ("Shūchō no musume" 酋長の娘).[4] Lyrics include: "My lover is the daughter of the chief. Even though her skin is dark, she is considered a beauty in the South Seas. . . . Just south of the Equator, on the Marshall Islands / She dances alluringly, under the shady coconut trees." Through the new media of radio and record albums, the song spread throughout Japan in the 1930s and fed into the frenzy of interest in the remote, exotic tropics.

These popular representations of the South Seas share certain features common to representations of the foreign and exotic. The location is far away; the inhabitants are often seen as only partially human;

and the social structures and taboos that characterize civilization are absent. Given the pressures in Japanese society to conform to accepted norms and live a conventional life, the world of the South Seas seemed an ideal escape from civilization. In the next chapter we will discuss a person who did just that, Nakajima Atsushi, though not with the expected results. Now let us turn to savages rather closer to hand.

Violent Barbarians or Noble Savages: The Takasagozoku

Once the Ainu of Hokkaido and Sakhalin had been conquered and subdued, the aboriginal tribes of Taiwan took their place in the Japanese imagination as representatives of the primitive Other. Taiwan was unique in the Japanese empire because it encompassed both extremes of colonial experience: illiterate, primitive "savages" and cultivated, highly literate ethnic Chinese. For the moment I want to focus on the aboriginal peoples of Taiwan as a field, represented in literature and film, upon which the Japanese image of the primitive was constructed.

Japan's modern colonial expansion into the South was prefigured by an incident that symbolized the violent encounter with the barbarians. In 1871, four boatloads of Okinawan fishermen ran aground on the southern shore of Taiwan in a typhoon; most (fifty-four of sixty-six) were killed by the Paiwan aborigines. Japan demanded compensation from Qing China for the loss suffered by its subjects. In response, China challenged Japan's claim to Okinawa and disclaimed responsibility for the incident, saying that the aborigines were "beyond the realm of civilization" (*huawai* 化外). To Japan this meant that China, by denying responsibility for their actions, had renounced any claim of suzerainty over the aborigines. In response, Japan dispatched 3,600 troops to Taiwan and the Qing eventually settled the dispute with a payment of half a million taels of gold. The Taiwan Incident stimulated interest in the region and a number of books on this topic, both official and private, were soon published.[5] These early records, though now rarely read, were important in shaping the representation of the Taiwanese aborigines. Consider the opening to the "Document of the Essentials of Managing the Barbarians" ("Shohan shushisho" 処蕃趣旨書), published by the Bureau of Indigenous Peoples Management in 1875: "Alas, the Taiwanese barbarians are vicious, violent, and cruel. It is indeed appropriate that all the nations of the world have since antiquity considered them a country of cannibals. This is a pitfall of the world; we must get rid of them all" (cited in Yano Tōru 1979: 11). This was, to be sure, a self-serving document intended to justify Japan's actions in response to these aborigines, but it set the tone for later accounts of Taiwan as a place of great danger and depictions of its inhabitants as utter savages. Ironically, the natural environment of Taiwan proved more deadly than the aborigines: of the 3,600 soldiers dispatched to Taiwan, 29 were either wounded or died as a result of battle; but 561 died of malaria (Nakazono Eisuke 1996: 44–45). The taming of these "barbaric" people and management of dangerous tropical diseases became one of the empire's biggest challenges (Tomiyama 1997).

The civilizing mission began with the meticulous study of the aborigines. It was in Taiwan that the early ethnologists were first able to apply to actual fieldwork the theory of sameness and difference that is at the heart of the discipline. As early as 1895, the year the Japanese military took over the island, the ethnographer Inō Kanori 伊能嘉矩 (1867–1925) was hired by the colonial government to explore Taiwan.[6] Inō's early interests focused on the investigation of the aboriginal peoples. His harrowing encounters with the barbaric islanders were recorded in his diary and became one of the earliest sources for the systematic documentation of the indigenous people (Inō Kanori 1992). Another early pioneer was Torii Ryūzō 鳥居龍蔵 (1870–1953), who led four expeditions to Taiwan between 1896 and 1900 and also worked primarily on aboriginal culture.[7]

The aborigines whom the Japanese had undertaken to civilize were tribally organized indigenous ethnic groups living throughout the island. The first governor-general, Kabayama, remarked not long after his arrival in Taiwan: "In order to colonize this island, we must first conquer the barbarians" (Shi Gang 1993: 36). These indigenous inhabitants of Taiwan had been referred to by the Chinese since the Ming dynasty (1368–1646) as *"fanren"* 蕃人 (barbarian people) and *"tufan"* 土蕃 (indigenous barbarians). The Japanese inherited the terms and usually referred to these peoples by the same terms in Japanese pronunciation, that is, as *banjin* 蕃人 or *banzoku* 蕃族 (barbarian tribes). Again following the Chinese lead, the tribal people, though culturally and linguistically diverse, were lumped into two groups: "untamed barbarians" (literally raw, uncooked barbarians, *seiban* 生蕃) and "tamed barbarians" (literally ripe, cooked barbarians, *jukuhan* 熟蕃) in accordance with the degree of their civilization. In 1923 a new term, "Takasagozoku" 高砂族, was officially adopted to commemorate the royal visit of the crown prince (the future Shōwa emperor, Hirohito).[8] It encompassed many divergent tribes who spoke different languages, whose lifestyles varied from hunting and gathering to settled agriculture, and who inhabited regions from the coast to the inland plains and the deep mountains.[9] These exotic barbarians, the empire's newest fellow citizens, were the object of great interest among the civilized masses of the metropole.

To feed this exotic desire, many Japanese artists chose to use the Takasago people as subject matter for their films, paintings, and literary works. Edamasa Yoshirō 枝正義郎 made the first such film, *Sad Song* (*Ai no kyoku* 哀の曲, 1919), about a young girl from Tokyo who was abducted and sold to a circus. She eventually showed up as the daughter of a Takasago tribal chief in Taiwan. Shot entirely in Japan, the far-fetched film nevertheless stirred up the curiosity of an audience that was always searching for new stories and had made movies part of their everyday lives just a quarter century after the first moving picture was created in the West.

The abduction theme was a popular plot not only for film but for fiction too. Uno Kōji's 宇野浩二 (1891–1961) "Lullaby" ("Yurikaga no uta no omoide" 揺籃の唄の思ひ出) is typical.[10] A young girl named Ochiyo is abducted by the aborigines when they raid a Japanese pioneer village in the land of the barbarians (*banchi* 蛮地). Fifteen rather uneventful years pass. The barbarians still attack sporadically, but the village is able to fend off the attacks. Ochiyo's old cradle is still hanging in the same place, now occupied by the youngest baby Otsuyu. But lately a band of ferocious barbaric warriors, led by a young woman leader, has been raiding Japanese villages and the village is put on alert. When the young girl leading the attack is captured, rumors soon spread that she is the lost baby Ochiyo. But the girl is defiant, insisting that she was born a barbarian, and refuses to admit her origins. Ochiyo's parents try everything they can think of to revive her lost memory, to no avail, until she hears the mother singing a lullaby to the baby and breaks into tears.

The story is not unlike many early American tales of children abducted by Native American tribes; they represent a struggle between order and chaos, civilization and barbarism. There is in such stories an interesting reversal of the gender relations that typically prevail in colonial tales. Usually it is the colonizer who assumes the dominant (male) role over the colonized (female), but in these tales the forces of barbarism seem to take on the male role, seizing a female in a sort of bride-taking. In this story, a Japanese girl raised as a barbarian takes on a male role, leading the tribe into warfare, but is drawn back to her civilized

Japanese identity by ties to her mother, personified by the lullaby. It is as if the raw, primitive power of barbarism trumps the masculine empire; colonial power is no longer absolute in the face of forces outside the realm of civilization in which empires are constructed and administered. In small, remote pockets of the empire, a dark, unknown energy lived untamed.[11]

An Aboriginal Heart of Darkness: *The Barbarians*

As the nearest and best-known example of the primitive, the Taiwanese aborigines became a symbol of the state of nature where visceral urges long suppressed in polite society were given free rein. In this sense, the aborigines provided a counterpoint to the modern, urban life and its associated constraints, much as in the tales of the Adventurous Dankichi. To some, this suppressed power beckoned, giving rise to stories parallel to London's *Call of the Wild* or Conrad's *Heart of Darkness*. One such tale, by Ōshika Taku, was called simply *The Barbarians*.

Ōshika Taku 大鹿卓 (1898–1959) began his career as poet but was best known for his sensational stories about the Takasagozoku. Ōshika's family moved to Taiwan briefly in 1898, when he was seven years old. After graduating from middle school in Japan, Ōshika wanted to become an artist but was persuaded by his family to attend a professional school for mining in Akita. In 1921, after graduating from the mining school, he studied economics at Kyoto Imperial University for a time but soon dropped out and returned to Tokyo. Through his connection with his older brother, the poet Kaneko Mitsuharu 金子光晴,[12] Ōshika participated in the Paradise Poetry Group (Rakuen Shisha 楽園詩社) and together they founded the poetry magazine *Landscape Painting* (*Fūkeiga* 風景画) in 1924. In 1925 they joined with Hayashi Fumiko and Akamatsu Gessen, as well as other poets who adopted an anti-establishment stance toward traditional poetics, in founding *Lyric Poetry* (*Jojōshi* 抒情詩).

After publishing several poetry collections, Ōshika turned to prose. His first short story, "Tatsutaka Zoo" ("Tatsutaka dōbutsuen" タツタカ動物園, 1931), was introduced by Yokomitsu Riichi in the literary magazine *Sakuhin*. "Tatsutaka Zoo" depicts a wild mountain cat trapped in a cage behind the Tatsutaka guard station deep in the Taiwanese mountains. The caged mountain cat symbolizes the loneliness and suppressed wildness of life in the mountains. This was the first of a series of short stories and novels featuring the aborigines, a genre through which he made his early reputation. He followed with "Barbarian Woman" ("Banfu" 蕃婦, 1931),[13] which depicted a conflict between the members of the Gaogan tribe and colonial police—a scuffle triggered by an affair between a Takasago woman and a Japanese policeman stationed there. The same theme resurfaces in several other narratives. Many of Ōshika's stories frame the conflict between colonial rulers and the barbarians through the trope of an aboriginal woman.

The theme of Japanese/aboriginal relations is further developed in *The Barbarians* (*Yabanjin* 野蛮人, 1935),[14] a novel that is considered to be representative of Ōshika's writing. In the novel Ōshika portrays from an insider's perspective the violent rebellion of the Saramao tribe in 1920.[15] This uprising was the first of several large-scale revolts by the aboriginal peoples of Taiwan. The largest and most shocking was the Musha (Wushe) Incident some ten years later.

It is probably no coincidence that Ōshika's writings on the Takasago people began soon after the Musha Incident, when public interest was at a peak. The novel *The Barbarians* was first written for an award competition sponsored by the literary journal *Chūō kōron* 中央公論. Because of the timeliness of the topic and (for its time) the unusually sexual and violent content, it stood out among the twelve hundred submitted stories and was awarded the prize. Though there is no reference in the text to the Musha Incident, readers no doubt were able to make the connection. Satō Haruo had presented a relatively objective account of a visit to the area shortly after the Saramao Rebellion in an essay called "Musha" 霧社. Ōshika presents an intense dramatization of the bloodshed told, not from the viewpoint of a passing observer, but from that of a fictionalized participant.

The young protagonist, Tazawa, is a new arrival at the White Dog post deep in the mountains among the primitive tribes. Scion of a wealthy family, Tazawa disagreed with the way his father was running the family coal mine, particularly the way he treated his workers, and has been disowned. The novel traces the downward trajectory of this young man's life as he descends into barbarism. Tazawa is at first amazed by the forwardness of the young tribal women, in particular Chief Taimorkaru's daughter, whom Tazawa describes as "wild and unadorned." Although he is attracted to her, Tazawa feels that a barrier separates them. In the course of suppressing the Samarao Rebellion, Tazawa cuts off the head of an aborigine he has just killed, thus crossing the line into savagery. Enthralled by the sense of liberation this act brings him, he embarks resolutely on a journey into barbarism. His wild nature is further aroused when he gazes upon native women who "breathe the naked wildness"; after raping one and making her his wife, he finally feels that for the first time he is tasting "the real wildness." Tazawa resolves to "go native," crossing irrevocably the line between conquerer and conquered (ironically, coercing a woman to perform a sexual act). He joins the woman's family and dresses as a tribesman. Eventually he discovers that even the liberation of the aborigines is insufficient; he asks why "the passion of the conquered is so oppressed" and finds that he still feels like "a caged wild animal pacing back and forth."

Unlike many colonial works in which the protagonist "goes native," Ōshika is unconcerned with the issue of racial contamination. Tazawa's actions are triggered by a taste of the savage way of killing, followed by the temptation of interracial sex, where sexual liaison with the "native" does not mean the defilement of his pure stock but, rather, freedom from familial ties back home. Tazawa soon discovers, however, that the all-liberating "wildness" he has embraced is ultimately as limiting, perhaps more so, than his old life. Like Kurtz in Conrad's *Heart of Darkness*, Tazawa seems to embody a complex sense of vulnerability, primitivism, and horror. The author portrays the tribal people sympathetically. He admires their innate survival instincts, the masculine strength of the men, and the sexual openness of the women. But what really attracts Tazawa, at an unconscious level, is the raw energy of the primitive—a chaotic and enigmatic force. It is precisely this untamed and inexplicable dynamism that draws in Tazawa like a vortex.

The colonial administration was extremely sensitive about any public depiction of aboriginal violence. As a result, both Satō Haruo's essay collection, *Musha*, and Ōshika's *The Barbarians* were banned in the colony.[16] Even in Japan itself, although *The Barbarians* won the *Chūō kōron* award and was published in that magazine, significant portions of the text containing graphic sexual and violent content were blacked out, a practice referred to as "hiding words" (*fuseji* 伏字). In the following quotes, for example, the underlined passages were blacked out when first published.[17] Here is the scene where the protagonist first beheads an enemy:

> Chopping off the dead body's fingers one by one, he then moved to stab its throat. The barbarian's knife (蕃刀) thrust in halfway and then stopped. "Shit! Shit!" He took a rock by the roadside and pounded the knife deeper and deeper. Even that was too much

trouble and he used his muddy feet to push it in harder and harder.

The scene where the protagonist Tazawa rapes the tribal woman was also heavily censored. All the underscored words were blacked out:

> He <u>pulled her into</u> his arms suddenly. The smell of animal skin assaulted his nose. <u>The foul smell numbed his brain; he forgot about all other concerns and turned into a man of violence.</u> He <u>dragged her into</u> the deep woods.
>
> <u>She was surprised by Tazawa's aggressive transformation. Her eyes filled with fear and she wriggled instinctively, but before long the fear turned to excitement and pleasure. She fell on the ground and let her body go.</u> The deep grass <u>surrounding the two bodies rustled.</u>
>
> After a while, Tazawa emerged from the woods alone.

The brutality and sexual violence carried out by the protagonist Tazawa reflect Ōshika's effort to balance the conventional identification of violence and barbarism with only the aboriginal tribes. *The Barbarians* implies that any civilized person can commit such acts once his innate wildness is awakened. There is also an implicit criticism of the colonial administration's actions in this story. If the tribe's practice of headhunting (referred to as *shussō* or *chucao* 出草, "expelling the grass") was cruel, the colonial government's suppression of the rebellion was just as brutal, if not more so. Though the narrative avoids simplistic depictions of the barbarians and presents a young Japanese intellectual gradually drawn away from civilization, it carefully evades any political explanation of the conflict. As a result, the novel eventually suggests the same conclusion that was favored by the colonial rulers: these rebellions were random, irrational eruptions of violence rooted in the barbaric nature of the aborigines. This rationale permitted the empire (including Ōshika) to avoid any self-reflection on the systematic oppression that was part of the structure of colonialism.

Ōshika's depiction of Tazawa's attraction to the barbaric—despite its realistic, graphic representation of violence—is a romanticized version of barbarism. The resulting ambivalence is best exemplified in Tazawa's view of the primitive woman to whom he was attracted. Her unabashed pursuit of Tazawa exuded "wildness" (*yasei* 野生), but Tazawa describes her as someone with an "immaculate heart" (*muku no kokoro* 無垢のこころ). In contrast to his other socialist-leaning writings on the mining industry and the injustice done to the miners, *The Barbarians* was read by metropolitan readers, perhaps rightly so, as just another kind of romantic colonial novel.[18] Ōshika expressed his disappointment that most readers read this novel as a sensationalized portrayal of the barbarism of the Takasago people. In fact he had intended to present a more complex picture of these people and explain what drove them to this drastic act of resistance. His discontent aside, the novel garnered high praise from Satō Haruo, who provided illustrations for the novel when it came out in book form, by which time the story had become Ōshika's signature piece.

A Tale of Assimilation: Wu Feng

Although authors like Ōshika chose to delight in and even defend the barbarism of the aborigines, the primary focus of the colonial period was leading them to civilization and ultimately assimilating them into the empire. The Japanese were not the first to colonize Taiwan and not the first to create assimilation tales. The story of Wu Feng 呉鳳, an ethnic Chinese of the late seventeenth century who dies trying to persuade the aborigines to give up headhunting, predated the Japanese occupation, but it proved useful to both the Japanese and the Nationalists who followed them in ruling Taiwan. In the *Taiwan Prefectural Gazetteer*, Wu Feng is an ambassador to the Alishan aborigines who refuses to send them a vagabond for human sacrifice. Realizing that he himself will soon be killed, he commands his family to make a paper figure of him riding a horse and carrying a sword in one hand and a barbarian's head in the other. When he is killed, his family burns the effigy while chanting, "Wu Feng is entering the mountains." Thereafter the aborigines who see him are stricken by an epidemic disease. Realizing that this is the ghost of Wu Feng, they pledge never again to kill humans in Jiayi county (*Taiwanfu zhi,* pp. 179–180).

The version of the Wu Feng legend that was included in the *Citizen's Reader for Public Schools* of 1914 was edited by the Government General of Taiwan. In this version Wu Feng tries to persuade the Tsuou people of Ali Mountain to give up headhunting by first using the forty heads they had accumulated for their annual rituals of the next forty years. After that, the aborigines agree to forsake the ritual for four years. If at the end of that time they still want a human victim, Wu Feng will supply him. In the forty-fifth year, when the aborigines still demand a sacrifice, Wu Feng presents himself disguised in a red cap and kimono. When the aborigines discover they have killed Wu Feng, they swear to cease head-hunting and begin to worship him as a god. Versions of the story were included in other Taiwanese textbooks as well as the *National Japanese Language Reader* (*Kokutei Kokugo dokuhon* 国定国語読本) used in the Japanese homeland and authoritative reference sources. (See Komagome Takeshi 1996: 166–167.) In 1932, Andō Tarō 安藤太郎 made a film version of the tale titled *The Righteous Man Wu Feng* (*Gijin Go Hō* 義人呉鳳). Komagome Takeshi sees this appropriation of the Wu Feng legend as an effort to mobilize the ethnically Chinese Taiwanese to join in the colonial administration's struggle against the aborigines, making them participants in the colonial discourse of taming the barbarian.[19] Although the story predated the Japanese occupation, the colonial government seems to have played a key role in shaping and propagating the legend, exploiting this figure to further its own consolidation of power.

The Wu Feng story was useful both in the colony and in Japan, though it served rather different purposes. In the colony, it reaffirmed the prejudices of the Taiwanese of Chinese descent against the aborigines and left them grateful for the empire's protection. In Japan, it justified the colonial civilizing mission and portrayed the majority of the colonized populace as willing partners in this project. As the war with China intensified and the imperial-subject movement came to the fore, transforming the islanders' culture, language, and everyday lives, the Wu Feng story exhausted its utility for the Japanese. The textbooks for elementary schools underwent revision in 1940, and the Wu Feng story was removed from texts for Japanese children (though it remained in textbooks used by the native children in the public schools).[20] It was replaced by a newly written, contemporary story of a young Taiwanese boy named Decun who is badly injured in the great earthquake of 1939. Before his death, he sings "Kimigayo," the Japanese national anthem, triumphantly. Clearly the mission at hand in the early 1940s was less to fulfill the exotic fantasies of the metropolis than to demonstrate the empire's ability to win the loyalty of people across the colonies to the emperor and unite them in a sacred quest to fight for and eventually die for the imperial cause.[21]

Violence Explained: Musha and the Mist-Enshrouded Village

The Japanese made a concerted effort throughout the colonial period to civilize the aborigines and transform them into good Japanese. The primary means to this end was an administrative structure that combined education and law enforcement in the person of a single imperial representative who was both policeman and schoolteacher. Originally these individuals were exclusively Japanese, but eventually aborigines were trained to fulfill the lower-level positions in this administration. Beginning in 1910, the colonial authority established a series of five-year plans to eliminate the barbarian threat and bring civilization to the aborigines.[22] For those who willingly assimilated, there was a program that took aboriginal tribal chieftains on trips to the major cities of Taiwan or even to the metropolis itself so they could see for themselves the wonders that awaited them through assimilation. The progress of the program of civilization and Japanization was, however, interrupted periodically by outbreaks of mass violence such as the Saramao Rebellion. None was as far-reaching in its significance, nor did any present such a threat to the colonial mission, as the Musha Incident.

The Musha Incident sent shock waves through both the colony and the metropole. On a fine autumn morning, October 27, 1930, when all the students from the Japanese, Taiwanese, and aboriginal schools had gathered together for an athletic competition, members of the Tayal tribe swooped down on the crowd and killed 136 Japanese in attendance. The surprise was all the greater because the Tayal were among the most thoroughly assimilated of the aborigines. In fact the leader of the Musha rebellion, Mōnarudao, was one of the forty-two tribal chiefs who had toured Japan in 1911.[23] The colonial government invested enormous energy and resources in modernizing this tribe and often held up the Musha community as a model assimilated village. The Japanization process was pursued so aggressively among these tribal people that in many ways they were more fully assimilated than the ethnically Chinese Taiwanese. Unlike the Taiwanese, who often clung to their continental cultural and linguistic roots, reluctant to be absorbed into the Japanese cultural sphere, many aboriginal people were happy to adopt the Japanese language and saw Japanese colonial rule as an alternative to the discrimination they encountered from the Taiwanese.

Two of the best examples of successful assimilation in 1930 were the Hanaoka brothers, Dagis Norbin (a.k.a. Hanaoka Ichirō 花岡一郎) and his brother Dagis Naui (a.k.a. Hanaoka Jirō 花岡次郎), who served as the local policemen and schoolteachers for the Musha community. These assimilated imperial subjects had been educated and even married at the colonial authority's expense and had risen to become respected police officers. The Japanese were caught by surprise when the Hanaoka brothers, in particular, betrayed them.[24] Profoundly different perceptions of the relationship led Japanese to conclude that the aborigines had shown a lack of gratitude whereas the aborigines had in fact acted out of long-pent-up frustration at the colonial authority's harsh policy of forced labor as well as the disrespect shown to traditional tribal leaders. Clearly the myth of an ideal colonial master/subject relationship had been exploded.

Sensational reports by the Japanese media captured the curiosity of the masses and put the authority and reputation of the empire at risk. It took the colonial regime two months, three thousand soldiers, and planes allegedly equipped with poison gas to quell the uprising.[25] The sudden attack caught the government and the public by surprise and threw the colonial government's barbarian management policy (*rihan seisaku* 理蕃政策) into disarray. Investigations into the causes of the incident pointed to issues of ethnic conflict, forced labor, and high-handed colonial rule.[26] But popular analysis tended to see the incident as an unpredictable outbreak of the barbarism lurking deep within the aborigines, who were inexplicably unappreciative of the colonial authority's efforts to civilize them. The colonial administration on Taiwan considered the uprising an embarrassment to imperial rule and sought to regulate media coverage, but the public was both appalled and fascinated by it. According to Kawahara Isao's survey of fifty fictional works featuring the Taiwanese aborigines, forty were related in one way or another to the Musha Incident.[27] One of the more important writers to treat this theme was Nakamura Chihei 中村地平 (1908–1963).[28]

Nakamura Chihei was inspired by Satō Haruo's writings about Taiwan to attend high school there.[29] Returning to Japan, he studied art at the Imperial University of Tokyo and together with Dazai Osamu and Koyama Yūshi joined a coterie under the tutelage of Ibuse Masuji. In 1935 he joined the Japanese romantic school (*Nihon rōmanha* 日本浪漫派) and started writing for literary journals such as *Sakuhin* and *Yonin*. His fascination with the South persisted, and he later wrote many stories set in Taiwan. Two short stories in 1939—"Women of the Barbarian Realm" ("Bankai no onna" 蕃界の女)[30] and "The Mist-Enshrouded Barbarian Village" ("Kiri no bansha" 霧の蕃社)[31]—began a series of writings involving the Takasago people.[32]

"The Mist-Enshrouded Barbarian Village" was the first fictionalized narrative to deal directly with the Musha Incident. Nakamura based his narrative primarily on the official investigative record of the Governor-General's Office and contemporary newspaper reports. Although he did not depart from them significantly in either detail or conclusion, he still was able to provide a unique insight into the massacre by detailing how six of the aboriginal leaders came to participate in the rebellion. By explaining in each case the life incidents that led them to turn to violence, Nakamura put a human face on the uprising.

Whereas Ōshika portrayed the aborigines as succumbing to an inborn feral wildness, Nakamura suggests that a much more complex web of interlocking tensions, growing out of racial, social, and gender-based conflicts, was at the root of the rebellion. For example, Mōnarudao, chief of the Mahebo tribe and leader of the rebellion, opposed his sister's marriage to a Japanese policeman because of the difference in their ethnicities. When his sister was subsequently abandoned by this husband and he himself was treated contemptuously by a Japanese bureaucrat, he vowed revenge against the Japanese. Hipoarise contemplated rebellion because his father had been killed by the Japanese army. But not all the reasons were so political: Hiposatsupo of the Hōgō tribe, who had been cast out by his wife and her family, wanted to headhunt to regain the respect of the villagers and reassert his masculinity.

Like Ōshika, Nakamura is careful to downplay what was perhaps the central issue in the rebellion: the dispute over forced labor. Ultimately he arrived at a physiological explanation, arguing that the pent-up savagery of the Japanicized aborigines, on the verge of extinction as the assimilation project progressed, had burst forth in one final, desperate act of violence rather than submerge into a civilized subconscious:

> At that time, it was not only these three; there must have been many people in similar situations, feeling that if they did not headhunt and thereby change their luck, they could not survive in the community. Due to the success of Japan's civilizing policy, their wild nature had been gradually weakened and subsumed within something called "culture." The ferocity and primitivism of this ethnic group had already declined from its peak, much like a middle-aged woman on the verge of losing her biological functions as a woman. The mist-enshrouded settlement surrounded by beautiful mountains was also showing symptoms of late, terminal disease.
>
> When a woman can see her impending old age, her yearning and obsession for youth, coupled with biological worries, at times drive her to actions outside her normal conduct. Similarly, these barbarians were driven by their evanescent, lingering savageness. They tried one last fight, however ineffectual, against civilization, against a lifestyle that did not suit them. [Nakamura Chihei 1941: 39]

As this passage shows, the Musha Incident was framed as a dichotomy of savage versus civilized. The term "savage" fulfilled an important function in the Japanese colonial ideology of the day. Terms like "primitive," "savage," "tribal," "undeveloped," and "exotic" all take imperial Japan as the norm and define the rest as "inferior, different, deviant, subordinate, and subordinateable" (Torgovnik 1990: 21). All Japanese colonial subjects, but especially the Takasago people, were used by the empire to establish its own superiority as a "civilized" culture shining above the darkness of primitive culture. The Musha Incident, however, revealed a paradoxical aspect of the civilizing mission:

> Since Japan first came into possession of Taiwan to this day, this is not the only attempt of the barbarians to rebel. There have been several similar schemes throughout the island. Usually they were discovered and defused before they could ever take place, however, because there was absolutely no way these pure, simpleminded people could keep any secret as a group. There was always someone who would give away the secret.
>
> This incident is the lone exception. They showed incredible ability in cooperation, detailed planning, and keeping secrets. One reason certainly has to do with the exceptional leadership of Mōnarudao, but it also shows how amazingly the intelligence of the barbarians has advanced. In light of this incident, the Japanese cannot help but lament this ironic consequence of bestowing upon them civilization. [Nakamura Chihei 1941: 42–43]

Nakamura was, however, able to find one redeeming aspect of the event. In the chapter devoted to the (anti-)hero Hanaoka brothers, who after years of nurturing by the colonial authority join their people in rebelling against the Japanese, Hanaoka's participation is described as follows:

> Initially the aboriginal constable Hanaoka Ichirō, in his formal uniform, was one of the participants by the side of the master of ceremonies. Before anyone realized it, he had stripped off his uniform and was now clothed in his primitive attire. It was rare for him to wear native attire. He must have known about the plan beforehand. [p. 9]

Immediately following the incident, the Japanese suspected that the Hanaoka brothers were the instigators—surely only someone trained in the imperial system could carry out such a courageous, intelligently planned operation—and there was various speculation as to why these loyal servants of the empire might have joined the rebellion. In "The Mist-Enshrouded Barbarian Village" the narrator presents the most widely accepted analysis—that the Hanaokas, though graduates of the normal school in Taichū (Taizhong), were denied promotion to supervisory positions because they were not Japanese by birth—but ultimately he settles on a less materialistic interpretation of their participation. He depicts Hanaoka Ichirō as caught between "his love for the people who shared his blood" and "the social obligation (*giri* 義理) he felt toward the Japanese to whom he owed his love and gratitude" (p. 57). As the Japanese army approached and they were about to be captured, the Hanaokas decided to commit suicide. It is in their death that we see the success, if only partial, of the imperial civilizing project:

> November 1. Ichirō and Jirō and their families shed their native costumes and changed into their only Japanese clothes. When they had married, it had been in a Shinto ritual at the Misthill Shrine in Musha, with all the Japanese officials and policemen in attendance. This was the formal wear they had received from the Japanese. When they were ready, all the clan went quietly into the forest southeast of Hōgō village. . . . In a single-layer kimono made with *meisen* fabric,[33] white headband about his head, Ichirō first cut off his children's heads with a foot-and-a-half-long Japanese sword. After that, he cut open his gut and died. His wife, who was also dressed up for her death in a Japanese kimono, laid the children between her and her husband and skillfully struck her own throat, following her husband in death.
>
> Jirō, who was wearing a halfcoat with a plum blossom family crest, and his family all hanged themselves from trees nearby. [p. 60]

Earlier in the novella, a scene describes a friendly visit by Governor Mizukoshi of Taichū province, who is responsible for Musha. After returning to the city, he mobilizes the local Japanese to donate their old clothes for the aborigines and ships a truckload off to the mountains. A week after the incident, Governor Mizukoshi leads a contingent of troops to survey the damage, finally reaching the place where the Hanaoka clan has committed collective suicide. The narrator notes:

> All of them had dressed to meet their final fate in the kimonos given to them by the Japanese, the donated clothes that at the re-

quest of Governor Mizukoshi had been sent in a truck in the spring to placate them. [p. 66]

One cannot help noticing Nakamura's careful descriptions of clothing, how his characters were dressed in various circumstances. External features such as skin color and physical appearance delineate racial difference, but it is clothing that marks the boundary of civilization. In promoting civilization, clothing the naked—or, in this case, trading a scanty, rough loincloth for a kimono (with family crest)—was an obvious advance. Nakamura's dressing and undressing of the barbarians at various critical junctures in the narrative points to the shifting subject positions the native occupied and, as well, gestures toward the constantly changing power dynamic between the domesticating colonial power and its reluctant subjects.

Looking at Hanaoka Ichirō's body, the Japanese are distressed. One comments:

> "Despite how we treated them with affection . . . they are after all nothing but savages. They did not act like us."
>
> However, someone cut him off: "But isn't the way Ichirō died, committing seppuku, a result of education?"
>
> Up until then barbarians had usually committed suicide by hanging. Hanaoka Ichirō was the first in this land of the savages to do so by seppuku. [p. 61]

The highly ritualized suicide scene, conforming in every way to the rite of self-annihilation in traditional Japan, is carried out by imperial subjects who feel indebted to the empire. It is through this highly symbolic act that a barbarian was transformed into a noble savage who understood the lofty purity of high (Japanese) civilization. Nakamura Chihei, in his earnest desire to defend Hanaoka Ichirō from being perceived as simply barbaric, as well as provide a psychological dimension to his characters, is oblivious to the biting irony of the savagery inherent in both headhunting and the death ritual of seppuku.

Nakamura Chihei's story, like Ōshika's *The Barbarians,* tries to present sympathetically the bloody violence perpetrated by the aborigines. Ōshika portrays a dark urge to violence hidden within even the most civilized of men and glorifies the freedom with which it is expressed in aboriginal society. There is implicit here a criticism of the basic program of civilization that is inherent in colonialism. Nakamura understood the aborigines as complex human beings torn by a variety of different impulses and did not hesitate to point out specific ways in which the aborigines were mistreated by the Japanese. As the Hanaokas are about to commit suicide, Hanaoka Jirō writes an epitaph proclaiming: "We must leave this world. It is regrettable that by unreasonably compelling the aborigines to carry lumber, things have turned out this way." Thus both Ōshika and Nakamura faulted specific aspects of the colonial system. Perhaps given the censorship that prevailed in Japan at the time, they could not make more far-reaching criticisms. Still, neither seems willing to confront the complicity of colonialism itself—as opposed to its implementation—in the violence directed by the aborigines toward the Japanese. Instead violence is explained away as a product of contact between the "civilized" and the "barbarian."

Nakamura's "Mist-Enshrouded Barbarian Village" shares with the various formulations of the Wu Feng story an optimistic view of the possibility of assimilating the aborigines into Japanese society. The original Wu Feng story had the ghost of Wu haunting the aborigines, plaguing them with illness, until they gave up killing. In later Japanese versions, the aborigines reform because of their fondness for Wu Feng and their distress at having killed him. Both versions end with the aborigines having mended their ways and forsworn violence. Nakamura's tale addresses a stage further along in the trajectory of assimilation: the aborigines have now reached a portal into civilization. There is resistance against taking that final step through the door into a truly modern, civilized Japanese identity, however, and the resistance is manifested as one horrifying moment of violence. But there is also redemption in the Japanese-style death of Hanaoka Ichirō. And there is the prospect that the assimilation which almost succeeded—perhaps partially succeeded with this group of aborigines—will eventually triumph and that one day these inhabitants of the barbarian village will instead be citizens of the great Japanese empire.

Sayon: Assimilation Achieved?

As the ideology of the Greater East Asian Coprosperity Sphere developed in tandem with the progress of the Pacific War, it became ever more urgent to transform the barbaric yet exotic peoples at the margins of empire into model imperial subjects who would assume their appropriate place in the evolution of Japanese imperialism. The islanders of the South Pacific were no longer viewed as radically different from the Japanese; now they were held to closely resemble the Japanese. In 1942, a Ministry of Health report on "The Development of the South and the Issue of Population," citing extensive research in the field of physical anthropology on the classification of the islanders, concluded:

> It is obvious that the Europeans cannot compare to the Japanese in their ability to adjust to life in the South. Our skin already is the color of the [inhabitants of the] South Seas and the skin pigments are not that different from the current ethnic group. One biologist has studied the sweat glands of the Japanese and proclaimed that our sweat glands are close to those of the people of the South Seas. Japanese eyes are not dazzled by the South Seas sun, and the height of our noses does not stand out as does that of the northern people. Compared to the Europeans, Japanese are superior in adapting to the South and certainly there is no reason why we cannot be active in the South. In terms of physique and temperament, we are people of the South Seas.[34]

There is a clear rhetorical turn from an obsession with distinguishing civilized versus barbarian and superior versus inferior to a stress on the relative similarity of the Japanese to their colonial subjects, an approach that Karatani Kōjin (1993a) believes is characteristic of Japanese colonialism. This "close resemblance" justified Japan's presence in and leadership of the South.

Despite the doubts raised by the Musha Incident, ideology demanded that the Taiwanese aborigines too must be similar to the Japanese and capable of assimilation. Nakamura Chihei had laid the groundwork for a positive interpretation of Musha. The Imperial Subject movement brought a new enthusiasm for taking Japanese culture to the aborigines—including traveling puppet shows that enacted edifying stories of Japanese sacrifice and victory for the mountain dwellers.[35] The same kind of ideological transformation was reflected in popular films. By 1943, as the war intensified, films depicting life in aboriginal villages were colored by the wartime ideology. No longer were the aborigines portrayed as a common threat to the civilized Japanese and Taiwanese; now they were transformed into model examples of the success of the colonizer's benevolent program of civilization. Japan found the perfect representative of this transformation in Sayon, a young aboriginal girl who died in 1938 while carrying the luggage of her Japanese teacher, who had been called to the front in China. Sayon was portrayed in the Japanese and colonial press as an ideal figure: the gentle native girl who gives her life willingly for the Japanese war effort. Shimizu Hiroshi's 清水

広 *Sayon's Bell* (*Sayon no kane* サヨンの鐘, 1943), perhaps the most famous wartime movie made in Taiwan, starred the immensely popular Li Xianglang 李香蘭 (a.k.a. Li Kōran, Yamaguchi Yoshiko, Shirley Yamaguchi, b. 1920) as Sayon.[36] A romantic relationship is established between Sayon and the young Japanese soldier, and her home is portrayed as a model imperial-subject tribal village (Yomota Inuhiko 2000: 106–124). In a perceptive analysis, Leo Ching points out that this tale of "aboriginal redemption and devotion to the Japanese nation through self-annihilation" was popular with both the Japanese and the aborigines because it portrayed an average person, rather than a great hero, who was willing to make a sacrifice for the sake of the empire (Ching 2002: 81off).

All the stories discussed here are grounded in historical events and portray a continuously evolving relationship between the aborigines and civilized society. Such stories are shaped by a dominant ideology which assumed that the mission of Japan as a colonial power was to bring civilization to the savages of Taiwan and demanded that the savages eventually respond to these efforts by willingly assimilating to Japanese culture. Let us now step back to the 1920s and consider the response of the Japanese author and poet Satō Haruo to his encounter with the aborigines. His response was strikingly different from those treated here because it came in a different form: in a reportorial travelogue that is much more openly critical of Japanese efforts at assimilation and in a fable, based on an aboriginal legend, that draws disturbing parallels between the savage violence of the barbarians and the violence inflicted upon its own citizens by the empire.

Satō Haruo's Journey South

In the summer of 1920, Satō Haruo (1892–1964), then a budding writer, traveled to Taiwan and the southern coast of China for a summer. He claimed he was summoned there by "the phantom of the southern lands (*nankoku* 南国) which I have yet to see" (Shimada Kinji 1976: 214). The journey yielded, at various times, about a dozen works ranging from short stories and adaptations of local legends to travelogues. We will discuss this journey—and the story "Strange Tale of the 'Precepts for Women' Fan" later. Here I want to touch on his observations of aboriginal life in his travelogue "Musha" and consider his adaptation of an aboriginal fable, "The Devilbird."

In "Musha,"[37] Satō candidly records what he saw in Musha. He was astonished to see some aborigines with deformed noses, a sign of syphilis, and commented: "In this barbaric place, it is rather surprising to see there are syphilitics, more so that it occurs among the barbarians." He was particularly troubled by fifteen- and sixteen-year-old aboriginal prostitutes who solicited him. Episodes like this seem to have shattered Satō's romantic preconception of the barbaric. He had not expected to encounter among the barbarians the social malaise of modern society. He did have some positive experiences there, such as meeting the chief's son who had graduated from medical school with highest honors. But when the maid in the hotel where he was staying referred to herself as "barbarian" (*banjin* 蕃人), Satō felt a sense of affinity with her, a feeling he describes as similar to what "one feels toward his beloved pet dog." Though Satō tries to avoid sensationalism and tempers his accounts with sympathy, we see here the limitations of his liberality: his master/pet metaphor reveals the innate assumption of superiority that accompanies the hierarchized dominant/subordinate relationship of colonizer and colonized.

Satō saves his most damning criticism for the colonial educational apparatus. While visiting an elementary school, he observed children being taught: "Taipei is the biggest city in Taiwan. Tokyo is the biggest city in Japan. The most powerful man in Japan is the emperor. The most powerful man in Taiwan is the governor-general." When they were later tested on this information, students answered that "Tokyo" was the most powerful man in Taiwan and "the emperor" was the biggest city in Japan. Sato comments:

> The four questions were answered with mismatched answers. This was a review session of something that had already been taught. I know for a fact that the difficulty these pupils were experiencing was not due to their inability to understand Japanese; all were relatively fluent in spoken Japanese. However, they were continuously spoon-fed concepts they cannot possibly imagine in their own world. I sympathized deeply with the effort expended by both the teacher and the students. [Satō Haruo 1936: 150–151]

Compare Satō Haruo's annoyance with the empire's attempts to civilize the barbarians with a similar reaction from another writer, Ishikawa Tatsuzō, who visited a public school on the island of Palau. Ishikawa noted that the principal was from Akita, in the northeastern region of Japan, and spoke with a thick accent. Playing the organ, he tried to teach the native children to sing:

After numerous tries, he was finally able to finish playing the song and the girls started to sing, their high-pitched voices in chorus. I felt a little betrayed when I heard them singing in perfect Japanese. The girls were singing patriotic marching songs, a song for the war god Captain Hirose,[38] and another for Kojima Kōtoku. These native girls, incapable of understanding Japanese tradition, had no chance of understanding the spirit of "eight corners under one heaven" and the concept of "dying to serve one's country." It was a beautiful chorus of parrots.[39]

Both Ishikawa Tatsuzō and Satō Haruo perceived the basic flaw in colonial education. Bound by an ideology requiring them to "civilize" the barbarians, the colonial power drilled the natives in all the imperial and militarist myths. But this intellectual framework, determined in the metropolis thousands of miles away, was meaningless and irrelevant to the lives of children living in small, destitute villages far from the realm of modern urban life. The irony of the situation was more evident to travelers, who came directly from the metropole to these schools in the wilderness, than to the colonial educators and bureaucrats living in the community and seeking to construct there a replica of Japan.

Perhaps one of the most imaginative and subtle uses of the coded signifier of the barbaric can be seen in Satō Haruo's allegorical tale "The Devilbird" ("Machō" 魔鳥, 1923), which was based on a legend current among one of the indigenous peoples of Taiwan.[40] Satō Haruo begins "The Devilbird" with a contemplation of the barbarian and the civilized and, surprisingly, finds many similarities between the two. The prelude to the short story begins:

> The story I am now about to relate has to do with the superstitious beliefs of a certain barbarian tribe. Even barbarians have their superstitions. In this respect, they are no different from civilized people. But compared to the complicated and captious [superstitions] of the civilized, the barbarian's are much more instinctive and fabulous. It is absolutely wrong to assume, as some do, that only the barbarian is superstitious and that the civilized person has nothing like this. Just as the civilized see many superstitions in the customs of the barbarian, so too do the barbarians discover countless superstitions in the arrangements the civilized have made to ensure the survival of their society. They might even think that those things we consider as morality or justice are superstitions,

just as we deem their morality and humanity superstitions. [Kuro-kawa Sō 1996, 1:39]

This excerpt displays a symmetric structure that characterizes the genre of fable writing. Satō forsakes the highly elaborate Sino-Japanese prose style he is known for and opts for a simple, romantic rendering of a local legend. The overall tone is somber. The author purposely deletes all specific place-names and proper names to achieve the generic feel of a fairy tale—but perhaps also to avoid the scrutiny of the authorities, who might be tempted to read politics into the story. Nevertheless, the story is not devoid of political implications. In fact it presents skillfully and subtly, on multiple levels, a critical discourse on Japan's internal and external colonial conditions during the 1920s—in particular the brutal violence that accompanies the need, or rationalized need, for survival. Such a political reading is suggested by the fact that the story is dated December 1923, immediately following the devastating Kantō Earthquake. The implied target of Satō's criticism is the paroxysm of violence directed toward leftists and resident Koreans that followed the earthquake.

The ensuing story consists of two parts. First there is an abstract philosophical meditation on the meaning of the devilbird and the implications of its actions on any given society. As the small white bird with red claws is a harbinger of death, few have ever seen it and lived. It is controlled by human masters (*machōtsukai* 魔鳥使い) who pass their powers down through their family and live hidden among the populace. Much like witches among African tribes, the devilbird masters are despised and feared—upon discovery, the entire family is put to death. Satō gives a detailed description of the way certain members of society, often anomalous individuals who do not get on well with others, are identified as devilbird masters by their telltale glances, ambiguous facial expressions, or the misfortune that strikes one after meeting them. Satō concludes this introduction by mentioning that he has recently observed a "certain civilized country" treating the indigenous peoples of its colony no better than animals. He draws an analogy to the treatment by this country of people who were persecuted and sometimes put to death for maintaining an unconventional viewpoint, even though they desired only to make the world a better place.[41]

This introduction is followed by a tragic narrative related to Satō by two assimilated aborigines who accompanied him on his travels deep in the mountains. Satō understands the tale to be the most recent example of the murder of a devilbird master and his family. The story concerns a family that had been suspected of being devilbird masters because they walked looking at the ground, avoiding the eyes of those they passed on the road, and even the children of the family never smiled. The family had a daughter of fifteen named Pira who, though of marriageable age, had never received the facial tattoo that would mark her new status. It was rumored that she followed the Japanese around, or perhaps had been raped by the Japanese, and this was why she could not undergo the coming-of-age ceremony, which involved a confession to prove one's chastity. The Japanese army at this time was traveling through the region; at each village they would gather together the adult males, seal them in a hut, and burn the hut down. The villagers, hearing that the Japanese were approaching, assumed the devilbird master had placed a curse on the village. They sealed the family in their hut and set it afire; only Pira and her youngest brother, Kōre, escaped into the forest. There they lived for years, confident that their parents were innocent and had indeed entered the sacred realm of the ancestors. When the daughter died, her own transition to that blessed realm was confirmed by the appearance of a rainbow, the bridge between the world of the living and that of the ancestors. Kōre lived on alone, forlornly regretting that he had not followed his sister to that better land. When one day he spied a rainbow, he sped through the forest in pursuit of it. He was seen by a hunting party from another tribe who, after ascertaining that he was not from their tribe, killed him and cut off his head to prove their maturity.

Satō concludes with a comment. When he heard this story, he was traveling toward a spot famous for its exquisite scenery; afterward, with each step he imagined he would see the headless corpse of the young boy. Musing on this violent scene, he concludes that the superstitions of the barbarians and the violence they engender are really no different from those found among civilized society.

The aborigines in this story are not romanticized. They are portrayed sympathetically and there is, perhaps, a certain purity to their actions. Nonetheless, their primary role in this story is as a metaphorical device through which to comment on Japanese society. They are undifferentiated Other, the primitive or uncivilized in human form. Although Satō traveled in Taiwan and visited their villages, he makes no effort to identify the two tribes involved in this story. Nor does he seek to link the myth of the devilbird with any specific ethnic group. It is sufficient that all the action takes place among the Takasagozoku, the primitive barbarians of Japan's colony, because the real message of the story is that the oh-so-civilized Japanese themselves act like barbarians in their treatment of anyone who does not conform to government-ordained orthodoxy. The indigenous inhabitants of Taiwan are an underspecified signifier that can carry this theme. But even if the primary object of Satō's concern is the Japanese leftist intellectual,[42] there is a message of social justice here that explicitly includes the nameless tribes of Taiwan's mountains. By linking injustice and violence, Satō indirectly condemns the colonial enterprise. As we read it together with the comments in Satō's travelogue, we can also perceive a fundamental doubt about the program of civilization at the heart of Japanese colonialism. Finally, the criticism of governmental violence strikes at the heart of the authoritarian social control that came to be identified with the imperial enterprise during the years leading up to the war.

Japan in the early twentieth century was already a densely populated, industrialized nation-state, and social pressures severely curbed individual autonomy. With the acquisition of the Taiwan colony, Japan gained its own savages: blank slates upon which Japanese civilization could be written through education. Many Japanese traveled to Taiwan just to glimpse the primitives. But novelists, on the whole, enlisted them in the service of larger ends. For some this meant using the aborigine as a metaphor for the feral that lives within all of us; for others it meant finding in the aborigines an allegory to the behavior of sophisticated Japan. Nowhere do we really hear the voices of the aborigines themselves. Their subject position within the empire was overdetermined and the meanings attached to them were too diverse to permit their own voices to be heard.

In the next chapter, we will examine the dispatch of writers to the South in support of the war effort and then consider two novels set in the South and their authors who lived in the southern reaches of the empire during the 1940s. They will present us with a mature vision of what life in the colonies could be—and how colonial life would be recollected nostalgically in the wake of Japan's defeat and occupation.

Writers in the South

THE MOBILIZATION OF writers in support of war was characteristic of the modern Japanese nation-state. It occurred first in the Sino-Japanese War of 1894, followed by the Russo-Japanese War of 1905. Neither case compared, however, to the widespread deployment of writers to Southeast Asia and the South Pacific during World War II.[1] Beginning in August 1937, immediately following the outbreak of hostilities with China, publishers and news organizations dispatched established writers to the China front as special correspondents. Yoshikawa Eiji 吉川英治 *(Tokyo Nichinichi shinbun)*, Kobayashi Hideo 小林秀雄 *(Bungei shunjū)*, Hayashi Fusao 林房雄, Ishikawa Tatsuzō 石川達三 *(Chūō kōron)*, Satō Haruo 佐藤春夫, Yasuda Yojūrō 安田与重郎 *(Shin Nippon)*, and Yoshiya Nobuko 吉屋信子 *(Shufu no tomo)* were some of the more famous correspondents sent to China to report on the progress of the war. The following year, the Cabinet Information Bureau held a gathering with a dozen of the most influential writers of the day to persuade them to join the military. This group included writers like Kikuchi Kan 菊池寛, Kume Masao 久米正雄, Yoshikawa Eiji, Yokomitsu Riichi 横光利一, and Satō Haruo; except for Yokomitsu Riichi, who asked to be sent to North China, all were sent off to the South. Since Yokomitsu was allowed to decline the "invitation," it would seem that they were not compelled to enlist, but even Yokomitsu felt compelled to play some sort of role in the Japanese aggression (Kamiya Tadataka and Kimura Kazunobu 1996: 5). The army and navy both organized their own "Pen Brigades" (Penbutai ペン 部隊). Altogether more than seventy writers participated. They did not formally become soldiers or sailors but were dispatched by the military for periods ranging from five months to as long as three years and were paid out of the military budget. There was also a subcategory of "temporary draft" that consisted mostly of women writers. Hayashi Fumiko 林 芙美子, whose experience in the South we will be discussing shortly, was one of the women writers who went to war, as were Sata Ineko 佐多稲子 and Yoshiya Nobuko.[2]

Although writers drew the most attention in this cultural conscription, in fact they constituted only a small portion of the group sent out to represent their country culturally. Great numbers of painters, comic artists, filmmakers, theater people, broadcasters, newspaper reporters, publishers, religious specialists, photographers, and translators were mobilized as well. With the Japanese imperial army taking over more and more territory, the recruitment of elementary school teachers to teach Japanese in the South also increased accordingly. In the preface to Terasaki Hiroshi's *Sensō no yokogao* (Profile of the war, 1944), Ibuse Masuji 井伏鱒二 wrote that in Malaysia alone he counted one hundred and twenty writers and other cultural personnel.

The movement of significant numbers of cultural specialists to the battlefront served three purposes. First and foremost, they conducted public relations activities in the occupied territories. The writers and others were active in the production and dissemination of official propaganda to the civilian population—especially the daunting task of transmitting and expanding the use of the Japanese language. As in earlier colonies, the first step was to establish Japanese-language schools. These were more successful in some areas than in others. The most successful was the Japanese school in Singapore. A month after the British surrendered (February 15, 1942), Japan renamed the island Shōnan (literally "illuminating the south") and founded the famous Shōnan Japanese School (Shōnan Nihon Gakuen 昭南日本学園) to teach a multiracial student body consisting of Chinese, Indians, and Malaysians. Other schools followed. In Java, following its capture from the Dutch, the Chihaya School was instituted. In his *Java Sarasa* ジャワ更紗 (Java chintz, 1944), Takeda Rintarō 武田麟太郎 (1904–1946) told how moved he was when, during a tour of the school, he heard the Indonesian schoolchildren singing Japanese military songs and the national anthem, *Kimigayo*. Burma and the Philippines saw more conflict and, as a consequence, lagged in establishing a program for Japanese education.

Yet even in Rangoon there were two Japanese schools, and in the Philippines, Japanese and Tagalog were both proclaimed official languages.

The cultural brigade's second mission was to educate the imperial soldiers on the meaning of the sacred war and to boost morale. This was done mostly through the publication of newspapers such as the *Shōnan Times* and the *Equatorial Press* (*Sekidōhō* 赤道報), which circulated throughout Indonesia, Burma, and the Pacific Islands, bringing news of victory to all soldiers. The third element of their work involved creating and disseminating propaganda aimed at Japan's enemies. The writers were responsible for drafting the content of all broadcasts to the enemy. Sometimes their impressionistic travelogues of how the Japanese were welcomed into new areas were translated into English and aired.

A new genre of literature developed at this time—*jūgun bungaku* 従軍文学 (accompanying the army literature), which consisted of voluminous reports on military activity and its consequences, fictional works set in the conflict, and critical essays. Kamiya Tadataka and Kimura Kazunobu (1996) have grouped this material into four rough categories according to authorial intent: works that express a genuine faith in the idea of the Greater East Asian Coprosperity Sphere; those that confirm preconceptions about a region by visiting the locale; those that convey an accurate picture of local conditions, involving a modification of one's preconceptions, through active contacts with the local people; and works by authors who expressed their honest emotional responses to their experiences. Kamiya and Kimura (1996: 12–13) consider the last two categories more valuable than the first two, though they admit that some works are not easily classifiable.

For the most part, the writers and other artists were escorted on prearranged tours, so their experiences were limited. Further, writing under the watchful eyes of censors, they could not express themselves freely. Just as in the case of the Greater East Asian Writers Conference, where literature was seen as an instrument for bringing the various colonies together under the unifying code of the Japanese language, the mobilization of cultural workers was considered an effective way to bring the front back home for the domestic population. Through the works of these writers, the masses in Japan were able to learn about the empire.

In the following sections we will look at two authors who wrote about the South but whose creations differed significantly from the typical products of those who were conscripted and dispatched southward under government auspices. Hayashi Fumiko 林芙美子 (1903–1951) was actually one of the conscripted writers sent to the battlefront to report on the ongoing warfare. Nakajima Atsushi 中島敦 (1909–1942), by contrast, went to the South as a different type of cultural representative. He worked as a bureaucrat for the Ministry of the South Pacific and participated in the creation of Japanese textbooks for the native children of the region. Their assignments took these writers a thousand miles away to Southeast Asia and the South Pacific. Although Nakajima Atsushi's *Hikari to kaze to yume* 光と風と夢 (Light, wind, and dreams, 1942) was written before he ever set foot in the South Pacific and Hayashi Fumiko's *Ukigumo* 浮雲 (*Drifting Clouds,* 1949) was completed years after the end of the war, the psychological landscapes of these two distant realms were nevertheless deeply embedded in the two works. Hayashi's novel of the young woman Yukiko's sexual adventure in Vietnam and Nakajima's lyrical account of the British romantic writer Robert Louis Stevenson in the South Pacific were highly nuanced explorations of the individual, and specifically the physical body, in the far-flung southern empire. As we can see from a close reading of these texts, the empire was not constructed solely on the countless bodies of the soldiers who fought and died for it and the corpses of their colonized victims. There were other bodies, not directly engaged in the carnage, that were consummated (in the case of Hayashi) or consumed (in the case of Nakajima) either to valorize the libido of the empire or to prefigure its impending demise. Unlike the utilitarian writings produced by the conscripted writers—the great majority of which were at best superficial documentations of the local scene or at worst active participation in propaganda rhetoric—these two works stand the test of time as literary gems capturing the specific time and place of colonial Japan.

Treasure Islands: Nakajima Atsushi and the South Pacific Islands

It seems odd to talk about Nakajima Atsushi's *Light, Wind, and Dreams* as a colonial text. After all, this is a writer who proclaimed: "War is war. Literature is literature. I deeply believe they are completely different things." He once discussed how writers should conduct themselves at a time when a militarist ideology was the dominant social discourse and censorship hovered over all speeches, written and spoken: "If you are not able to write, then don't write. I don't see any reason to force oneself. . . . Renounce the title of 'writer' and participate as an ordinary citizen, taking care of all the necessary chores that need to be done to carry out the war" (Kawamura Minato 1994b: 150–151). This kind of passive resignation was perhaps as radical a statement as one could make in the unusually harsh environment of the time. By refusing to write, by renouncing the title of "writer," Nakajima affirmed his determination to not become complicit in the war. Fortunately, he was still too young and unknown to be conscripted into military service like his famous colleagues. Nevertheless, he did end up participating in his capacity as a bureaucrat of the South Seas Bureau (Nan'yōchō 南洋庁). Thus he did become involved in the colonial enterprise, though he refused to place his art at the service of the war.

Nakajima Atsushi hailed from a *shitamachi* merchant clan that had made palanquins for twelve generations in the Nihonbashi area of Tokyo. His grandfather, Keitarō, had forsaken the family business to become a Confucian scholar. This tradition was carried on by his sons and grandsons, many of whom became sinologists or were active in the colonial administration in Manchuria. Atsushi's father taught Chinese (*kanbun* 漢文) in high school. In those days a teacher's salary was determined by the principal of the school, and schools in the colonies sometimes paid considerably more than those in Japan in order to attract intellectuals from the homeland. Nakajima Atsushi's father acquired his teaching certificate in classical Chinese through a certifying examination rather than a college degree, and his future career within the hierarchy-bound society of Japan was limited. In 1920, he took a position in Seoul, where Atushi spent his adolescence. It was not unusual for teachers to move from colony to colony in search of higher pay and a better life for the family. When his father took another appointment in Dalian, Atsushi remained behind to finish high school. One of his classmates in Seoul was Yuasa Katsuhiko 湯浅克衛 (1910–1982), who was to become one of the most important writers of the Korean colonial period, publishing "Kannani" カンナニ (1935), "Honō no kiroku" 焔の記録 (Record of the flames, 1935), and various other short stories.[3]

Like his mother, who died of tuberculosis at age thirty-five, Nakajima had persistent health problems and suffered from severe asthma beginning in his late teens. Most readers and critics assume Nakajima to have been a fragile poetic genius, but in fact as a young man he was lively and vibrant. During his college years he was obsessed with ballroom dancing, playing mah-jongg, horseback riding, and girls. In an interesting episode that reflects his youthful exuberance, he once organized a group of dancers from Asakusa to perform in Taiwan. He is said to have written all the scripts and music for the tour. Though the tour was never realized, this incident shows that, at least in his youth, Nakajima was full of energy and ideas.

Health problems never interfered with Nakajima's passion for literature. While he was attending high school in Korea, he started writing fiction about his experiences in the colony.[4] The short story "A Life" ("Aru seikatsu" ある生活, 1927) is about an exotic love affair, set in Manchuria, between a Japanese man and a beautiful young Russian expatriate.[5] "Scenes with Policemen—a Sketch from 1923" ("Junsa no iru fūkei: 1923 nen no hitotsu no suketchi" 巡査のいる風景ー1923年の一つのスケツチ; 1929) depicts the mistreatment the people of colonial Korea suffered at the hands of colonial police.[6] "A Portrayal of D City in July (1)" ("D-shi shichigatsu jōkei (1)," D市七月情景(一); 1930),[7] set in the city of Dalian, exposes the absurdity of colonialism from various angles. These works paid special attention to life in the colonies; the latter two stories, in particular, are told from the viewpoint of the colonized people, which was rather unusual during the prewar period. In this sense Nakajima's depiction of colonialism comes from his own lived experience, not from the imaginings of a bookish bystander. One might say the same thing about two other writers: Abe Kōbō 安部公房, who wrote about Manchuria, and Haniya Yutaka 埴谷雄高, (a.k.a. Hannya Yutaka 般若豊, 1910–1997), who wrote about Taiwan, did not merely write about but also lived the experience. After graduating from Tokyo Imperial University, Nakajima found a position teaching English and Japanese literature at a girl's high school in Yokohama, but he often missed work because of his asthma and eventually, in 1940, he had to take a year off from his job. During this period he established a family but also found time to travel, visiting both the Bonin Islands and China. He even tried graduate school but had to drop out after a year because of his health.

In time Nakajima developed an affinity for the writings of Robert Louis Stevenson that was no doubt based to some degree on significant parallels between their lives. Both were precocious and ambitious writers who were plagued by ill health and died young. By the age of fifteen Stevenson knew he was born to be a writer, though his family wanted him to follow in his father's footsteps as an engineer. In college he studied law. Throughout his career he struggled against the pressures of the British literary marketplace in order to write in the genre he liked and on topics he liked. Nakajima too began writing and publishing when he was fifteen, though the fact that both his father and grandfather were educators may have made a life of scholarship and writing more acceptable to his family. Economic hardship constituted an obstacle for both in pursuing a literary career. Both suffered from a chronic disease that eventually curtailed their careers (tuberculosis for Stevenson, asthma for Nakajima) and sought refuge in the warm, languorous climate of the tropics. Further, Nakajima was intrigued by Stevenson's opposition to colonial policy in Samoa and in the end came to share Stevenson's aversion to colonial authority and its bumbling bureaucracy. During this same period, he also immersed himself in Fraser's *Golden Bough* and Yanagita Kunio's writings on folklore, all of which stimulated his interest in primitive cultures.

Nakajima's fascination with Stevenson was encapsulated in a work that he initially titled *Death of the Storyteller* (*Tsushitara no shi* つしたらの死).[8] Based on the life of Stevenson in Samoa and his battles there with the colonial government, it was written before Nakajima ever saw the South Seas. The storyteller of this tale is Stevenson but represents Nakajima himself, as well, and the death in the title is both Stevenson's tragic end on Samoa and the death that loomed constantly over Nakajima because of his illness. On the recommendation of Fukuda Hisaya, a close friend to whom Nakajima had entrusted the manuscript, the editor of *Bungakukai* agreed to publish it, providing that Nakajima shortened the piece and changed the inauspicious title to something more appealing, *Light, Wind, and Dreams: Excerpts from the Five Rivers Manor Diary* (*Hikari to kaze to yume—Gogashō nikki shō* 光と風と夢—五河荘日記抄, 1942). When the novella finally appeared in *Bungakkai* (May 1942) it was well received and indeed was considered for the Akutagawa literary award.[9] The change of title shifted the attention of the average reader from the act of writing to the exotic locale, setting the course for the dominant reading of the novel to this day: as a lyrical meditation on life in the South Pacific. But this change has obscured the author's original intent to focus the work on the author, Robert Louis Stevenson, and his struggle with writing.

Nakajima's musings on the South were soon to take a more concrete form. For it was at this time, shortly after finishing the manuscript, that Nakajima, through the help of his friend Kugimoto Hisaharu, obtained a position in the South Seas Bureau. With the official title of editorial secretary for the national language (*kokugo henshū shoki* 国語編集書記), Nakajima departed for Palau in the summer of 1941. He was attracted to the position because it offered triple pay and the warm summers, he thought, would be soothing to his asthma.[10] Of course, his appreciation for Stevenson, both as a writer and as a human being, and his yearning to see the South all contributed to this decision.

In his new position with the Department of Regional Internal Affairs, Nakajima was commissioned to create Japanese textbooks to be used by the islanders. Leaving Yokohama on a rainy day in late June 1941, Nakajima made the weeklong journey to Palau alone. Arriving at the island on July 6, he immediately suffered a series of severe asthma attacks, dengue fever, and bouts of malaria. The heat was unbearable and the food unpalatable. Nevertheless Nakajima traveled throughout the region, visiting island after island, surveying the condition of Japanese-language education. In his diary he mentions that his only relief from asthma attacks was while in boats on the open water. His excursion among the islands became "the only time I could feel relaxed amid this despicable, unbearable bureaucratic existence."[11] From July 1941 to March of the next year, during his short nine-month stay, Nakajima wrote home to his wife and sons. The engaging and observant letters he wrote during this period, telling of his experiences on the islands, his illness, his homesickness, and his joy, remain one of the best examples of epistolary writing by a modern Japanese author.[12]

As a mature writer, Nakajima turned his hand to materials familiar to him from his family tradition of Chinese learning. He established a reputation for deep appreciation and training in Chinese and classical literature through a series of allegorical historical tales based on Chinese classical stories.[13] At one point Nakajima was hailed as the second coming of Akutagawa Ryūnosuke precisely because of his familiarity with both Eastern and Western classics and his fluency in retelling them in modern Japanese. His two most famous stories were "Li Ling" ("Ri Ryō" 李陵 , 1943), which retells the famous episode of the Han general Li Ling and the historian Sima Qian 司馬遷, and "Record of the Mountains and Moon" ("Sangetsuki" 山月記 , 1942), based on a Tang-dynasty classical short story (*chuanqi* 傳奇) called "Tale of the Human Tiger" ("Renhuzhuan" 人虎傳). Li Zeng, the protagonist of "Record of the Mountains and Moon," is a talented writer who quits his lowly government position and tries to make his name as a poet. Eventually he is forced to swallow his pride and reenter government service. One night, while on an official mission, he disappears into the darkness and is never seen again. His old friend Yuan Can, now a high official, on his travels encounters a tiger who explains that he is in fact Li, transformed into a beast by his obsession with poetry. He bestows upon Yuan his poetry collection and appeals to him to look after his wife and children. Then, howling at the moon, he springs away into the night, never to be seen again. Each of these stories contains an allegorical message about the difficulties encountered by writers—a theme continued in his master-work, *Light, Wind, and Dreams.*

Although Nakajima Atsushi is best known for his intertextual writings based on Chinese historical tales, his writings on the South Pacific are equally impressive. Other authors, such as Kaneko Mitsuharu 金子光晴, Takami Jun 高見順, and Abe Tomoji 阿部知二, wrote about the South Pacific. But most encountered the area while serving in the military and wrote travelogues or recorded their superficial impressions during their brief stay in the region. Although Nakajima did eventually live in the area, the novel discussed here is not based on his life in the South Seas. It is, rather, a fictional work inspired by the author's insatiable reading of Robert Louis Stevenson, founded on his meticulous research, and augmented by his rich imagination of Stevenson's final days on Samoa. The work does not consist of impressionistic sketches like diaries and travelogues but is in fact a carefully constructed countercolonial discourse set in (and to a certain degree masked by) a lyrical, romantic, and at times exotic southern "paradise."

Light, Wind, and Dreams was based on the life of Robert Louis Stevenson. But as Donald Keene has pointed out: "Nakajima has infused much of his own beliefs into his portrait" (Keene 1984b: 941). There are the inevitable stylistic transformations, as well, so that Stevenson's diary entries as penned by Nakajima reflect Nakajima's pessimism rather than Stevenson's general optimism. More substantial are the critics' objections that Nakajima puts into Stevenson's mouth opinions on colonialism that reflect Nakajima's time (Tierney 2001). Stevenson was a reformer who criticized specific policies and administrators in Samoa and advocated a sort of benevolent colonialism that made the colonizer responsible for the welfare and civilization of the natives under his charge.

Nakajima began to read Stevenson during the summer of 1940.[14] Intrigued by Stevenson's solitary opposition to British colonial policy in Samoa, he read everything he could find of Stevenson's writings and any biographical material he could lay his hands on. The narrative he created interweaves meticulously researched accounts of Stevenson's life with observations and contemplations on topics such as literature and philosophy offered by an anonymous narrator. Often Nakajima, through the narrator, attributes to Stevenson his own views. A deliberation on "plotless fiction" (*suji no nai shōsetsu* 筋のない小説), for example, echoes the famous 1927 debate on this topic between Akutagawa Ryūnosuke and Tanizaki Junichirō. Because of his use of Chinese classical subtexts,

Nakajima is often compared to the early Akutagawa, but here he comes out squarely against Akutagawa's position that plotless fiction is the purest form of fiction; Nakajima insists that the plot is "the backbone" of a story and that contempt for events in fiction is like "a child's forced and unnatural mimetic way of wanting to become a grown-up" (Nakajima 1992: 117–118). Here the author defends Stevenson's romantic adventures from the English critics and the onslaught of Zola's realism, while at the same time defending his own literary creations again the dominant I-novelist tradition in Japan.[15] Through the character Stevenson, Nakajima (1992: 117) relates his thoughts on the relationship between reality and literary work:

> I have heard that the literary scene in Western Europe is rampant with Mr. Zola's tedious realism. Do they think they can represent natural reality by recording everything their eyes can see? The hideousness is laughable. Literature is choice. The eyes of a writer are eyes that choose. To depict the absolute truth? Who can capture the entire reality? Reality is leather. Literary works are shoes. Shoes are made of leather, but they are not just leather.

Through this metanarrative, Nakajima reclaims the novel as his own creation; Stevenson's life is the material (the leather) but the narrative is all his.

When commenting on Stevenson's anticolonial activities, the narrator's presentation of Stevenson's inner thoughts echoes Nakajima's own views. Similarly, the narrator is sympathetic toward Stevenson's complaints about overcoming creative blocks and enduring criticism over his obsession with "those black and brown people of his" (1992: 83, 105). But the subject/object distance is almost obliterated when Nakajima ponders the imminent death awaiting Stevenson (and himself). When Stevenson compares himself to another Scottish poet, Robert Fergusson (1750–1774), recalling their similar youthful passion for poetry, their illness, and later their death, he was foreshadowing his own end and Nakajima's. The relationship between creation and death, which resonates in the original title of the story, is best captured in the following diary entry dated August 1894:

> Stubborn cough and wheezing, arthritic pain, coughing up blood, fatigue. Why should I prolong my life? Since my malady has brought my desire for action to a halt, only literature remains in my life. To create literature. There is neither joy nor agony in it. As

a consequence, my life is neither happy nor unhappy. I am a silk-worm. A silkworm, regardless of whether it is happy or not, cannot help but weave its cocoon. *I am just using the thread of my words to weave the cocoon of my tale. Alas, the pitiful sickly silkworm is about to finish the cocoon. His existence no longer has any purpose whatsoever.* "No, you do have a purpose," a friend said. "You transform. Become a moth, chew through the cocoon, fly away!" It is indeed a well-placed metaphor. But the question is whether my body and my spirit still have any strength left to break through the cocoon. [Nakajima 1992: 124–125; emphasis added]

Notice the shift of viewpoint—from a first-person inner monologue of the character Stevenson to a transitional objective statement on silk-worms and cocoons to the omnipresent narrator looking at Stevenson's existence from the third-person viewpoint. (Stevenson is addressed as "he" in the following sentence.) This shifting point of view makes the ensuing discussion of the meaning of life with an unnamed friend ambiguous. Does it refer to Stevenson, or to the narrator? Examples of the narrating subject intruding upon the consciousness of the protagonist are found throughout the text. *Light, Wind, and Dreams* is thus at once biographical and autobiographical.

The original focus of Nakajima's novel was the storyteller, however, and the work has been read predominately as a lyrical meditation on life in the paradisical islands of the South Pacific. To Nakajima, though, Stevenson's stubborn artistic vision, his heroic sense of social justice, and his empathy for the indigenous people were the central elements of the story. Moreover, the locale is a wholly imaginary landscape; Naka-jima visited the South Seas only after this novel was complete. When Nakajima accepted an assignment to the South Seas, he did so to satisfy his curiosity about the setting of his novel—but also in order to retrace the steps of Stevenson, to pay homage to him, and perhaps to confront the death that stalked him just as it had Stevenson.

Stevenson did find a modicum of relief from his chronic ailment in the tropics. When Nakajima made it to the South Seas, he found a dys-topia that actually aggravated his asthma. Moreover, the setting was de-pressing, the job frustrating, and the populace disaffected. In a letter to his wife Taka he wrote:

It rains every day in Palau. There is never a day that the ground is dry. It's no wonder that the weather is not good for my asthma. Compared to Palau, May to October in Japan is far better. I doubt that I can physically survive in a place like this, fighting asthma, until the end of the war. I am thinking of requesting a transfer to the Tokyo office so that I can use the library in Ueno. My work is not going anywhere at all since I don't have any reference works here. But with things as they are, I have no idea when I will be transferred back to Tokyo. . . . Life here at the bureau is as unpleasant as usual. Every day I feel disgusted.[16]

With his body wracked by chronic illness that the inhospitable environment only exacerbated, Nakajima became disillusioned. The assignment he had come so far to perform seemed pointless. He complained:

From this trip, I can see clearly how meaningless it is to compile textbooks for the natives. There are so many other important things that could be done to improve their lives. Textbooks are trivial and at the very bottom of the list. In the current situation, however, there is no way we can make these people happy. Given the present conditions in the South Pacific, it will slowly but surely become harder and harder to provide them with adequate food and housing. What is the use of improving the textbooks marginally at a time like this! Halfhearted education probably would do more harm than good. I have lost enthusiasm for my editing job, not because I dislike these natives, but because I love them.[17]

Nakajima objected both to the goal of educating the natives and to the means. He was, for example, astonished by the strict military methods used in the local schools.[18] He describes seeing a native boy beating his classmate with a stick, on the instructions of the Japanese teacher, simply because the other lad was unable to pronounce correctly "Ōkuninushi no mikoto," the name of the mythical founding father of Japan. It is unfortunate that Nakajima's critical voice on colonial education was never heard in the metropole.

Confronting the hypercolonial environment of the South Seas, where the Japanese had displaced the Germans, who in turn had taken over from the Spanish, Nakajima developed a certain cynicism regarding relations among the powers. This attitude he expressed metaphorically in a postcard to his son:

Today I was invited to the house of a villager; they served me coconuts, breadfruits, and banana. It was delicious. In the villager's house, there were a dog, a cat, a pig, a goat, and chickens. All of them gathered around when someone threw them coconut meat.

Among them, the dog is the top dog. When the dog is not around, the pig is king. When neither the dog nor the pig is around, the goat gets to be domineering. Isn't it funny that a pig gets to be so pompous![19]

Nakajima Atsushi's life took him from metropolitan Tokyo to Korea, China, and finally to the South Pacific islands. The vast geographical area he traveled overlapped with the burgeoning empire, and his writings reflect his unique colonial experience. Never known for explicit protest or politicizing his literature, Nakajima nevertheless is skillful at allegorical narrative strategies.[20] His Chinese tales adapted classical romances of another time and place but reflected the difficulties he encountered as a modern author. His stories on colonial Korea and his exploration of the South Seas through Stevenson's eyes constitute a subtle yet vivid indictment of the Japanese colonial administration in particular and the colonial enterprise in general.

Colonial Libido in Hayashi Fumiko's *Drifting Clouds*

Hayashi Fumiko (1903–1951), the daughter of an itinerant peddler, experienced privation and want through her early years. Her first novel, *Diary of a Vagabond* (*Hōrōki* 放浪記, 1928), detailing those hardships, won her instant acclaim and remains her signature work. Over the next two decades she became one of the most prominent Japanese female writers, writing often of the downtrodden on the fringes of society but always with an optimism and faith in individual effort that put her at odds with the proletarian writers. Once she achieved fame and started to receive requests for reports from the popular media, she traveled incessantly and saw many parts of East Asia as well as Europe.[21] Her other acclaimed masterpiece was *Drifting Clouds* (*Ukigumo*, 1949),[22] an epic exploration of life at the end of the empire and during the occupation that is characteristic of her "dark period," when military defeat had tempered even Hayashi's indefatigable optimism. *Drifting Clouds* is a massive work, but here we will be focusing on the first portion of the novel, set in Indochina, and its implications for colonialism.

The empire depicted in *Drifting Clouds* is quite different from that portrayed in works by male writers. Although it is a novel about the "loss" of the empire, the colony where the female protagonist, Yukiko, once lived and worked haunts her until her death. It is also a novel about the intertwining interests of the individual and the state that shows us the relationship between human sexuality and colonial libido. Noriko Mizuta calls *Drifting Clouds* Hayashi's "most important work" and "a masterpiece of postwar fiction."[23]

Yukiko, a rather plain and common girl, leaves her provincial hometown after high school to come to Tokyo. There she stays at the home of Iba Sugio, her sister's brother-in-law,[24] and works as a low-level clerk. Sugio rapes her and forces her into a secret sexual relationship. Yukiko detests Sugio but accepts the relationship because she has nowhere else to go and, in a perverted way, she enjoys the unaccustomed attention showered on her. When an opportunity arises for her to take a position in Indochina, which Japan has just seized from the French, she jumps at the chance for a new life. She abandons her dull job and dead-end affair without hesitation.

While the more beautiful and outgoing girls are sent to big cities such as Saigon, where they can enjoy the bustling urban life away from the watchful eyes of the military authorities back home, Yukiko is dispatched to a remote mountain area in the north to assist a forest research team stationed in Dalat, a hill station built by the French. Dalat could not be more different from gloomy, crowded, suffocating Japan. Located in the northern highlands, the town looks to Yukiko like a "mirage in the sky" (p. 251). The Japanese Forestry Office is headquartered in a villa built by the French, surrounded by the forest and facing a lake, with a tennis court and a well-groomed garden, silhouetted against the impressive Lang Bian Mountains in the background.

It is here that Yukiko is transformed into a woman of raw energy, a femme fatale, flirting with one man while attracted to another, establishing a triangular relationship that will alter all their lives. At first she is envious of her more attractive colleagues, who enjoy all the amenities of big city life. But in the colonial outpost of Dalat women are rare and Japanese women in particularly short supply, so Yukiko enjoys the extra attention and soon settles into a comfortable plantation lifestyle. Her life is materially bountiful (compared to her life in Japan) and she is pampered by her attentive Vietnamese maid. The colony provides Yukiko with a radically different life from what she had known; the wage earner enduring unwanted sexual advances becomes a liberated, independent, modern working woman.

Idyll in Dalat

The liberated atmosphere in the colony brings out a feminine strength and passion that Yukiko had never known. The colonial space she attains by leaving the bleak metropolitan Tokyo for a privileged, westernized colonial life casts a dizzying spell on her. The power of empire extends and enhances her sexual potency; for the first time Yukiko assumes control of her own sexual subjectivity and is no longer a passive plaything. With mundane, quotidian life suspended, beyond the reach of family left behind in Japan, and distant from the battlefront, she is fooled into an illusion of love, pursuing and seducing a married man named Tomioka, who in turn enjoys the illusion of conquest, wresting Yukiko from the grip of his colleague, Kano. The false tranquillity of the paradisical setting, the luxurious lifestyle, the distant yet urgent call of the war itself, their temporary isolation from other social bonds—all draw Yukiko and Tomioka together.

The colony depicted in this novel is rather more complex than Taiwan or Korea. Though part of Asia and subsumed under Japan's concept of the South, Vietnam had already been transformed by French colonial rule. Though Eastern in ethnicity and tradition, there is an overlapping layer of Western, specifically French, colonial culture. Consequently the colonial ambivalence is much more complicated than the customary binary relationship of colonizer and colonized. One sees this phenomenon also in the literature on colonial cities such as Harbin (in Manchuria) and Shanghai where the conflicting national interests of the Japanese, the natives, and other Western powers form a tense triangle. When Japanese subjectivity, which sought a dominant position over the natives, encountered a preexisting dominant discourse from the West, it inevitably became disoriented by its own ambiguous positionality. The tangled yet self-reflective stance created in such colonies stimulated postwar discussion, leading to the popularity of stories like *Drifting Clouds* at a time when there was almost no treatment of former colonies such as Taiwan and Korea.

The delicate balance among Western colonizer, Japanese colonizer, and native is demonstrated through a melodramatic configuration of desire and conquest. Young women like Yukiko, in some respects, were similar to the comfort women who were conscripted to serve the sexual needs of Japanese soldiers on the front line; they were not compelled to offer sexual favors, but both types of women were sent to the war to fulfill their assigned gender roles, whether clerical or sexual. As Yukiko herself remarks, there is little to do because most of the office work is performed quite efficiently by a woman of mixed French-Japanese heritage named Mari, while the domestic labor of cooking and washing is the responsibility of a Vietnamese maid named Niu. Marveling at how Mari can effortlessly perform a variety of tasks, including typing, playing piano, and speaking fluently in English, French, and Vietnamese, Yukiko is envious:

> Mari was, it seems, about twenty-four or twenty-five, but she looked older, perhaps because she wore glasses. The story is that she came from a nice, decent family. On her lanky, antelope-like legs she always wore navy blue socks and white shoes. Her waistline was slim and the silhouette from behind was beautiful. Her short, lightly permed golden hair hung to her shoulders, making a torrent of waves. Someone like Yukiko, who did not possess any special talents, felt miserable, racially inferior, whenever she heard Mari playing piano. Mari was fluent in English, French, and Vietnamese. She was so competent at her job. There were times when Yukiko thought there really was no need to bring someone as incompetent as herself all the way to this remote Indochinese highland. [p. 256]

This seems at first sight to be an offhand, descriptive passage introducing the character Mari, but in fact it is all about Yukiko herself. Not long after this, Yukiko gets into an argument with Tomioka at the dinner table when he challenges her claim to have been born in Tokyo (she was in fact from Shizuoka) and guesses her age at twenty-four rather than twenty-two. Yukiko is so upset and embarrassed that she storms out of the dining hall. Her reaction is explained in part by the idea that her youth was her only advantage over the intelligent, talented, and well-bred Mari. To have this stripped away by the object of her affection, Tomioka, was an especially cruel blow. Yukiko's admirer, Kano, catches up with her in the garden, where he makes an advance.

Although Kano consoles her, Yukiko is resolute in her pursuit of Tomioka, goaded by resentment, pride, and above all a desire to conquer him sexually. It is noteworthy that Yukiko feels inadequate in relation to Mari—who is oblivious to this resentment and uninterested in the married Tomioka—but she is not at all threatened by Niu, who has enjoyed a long-term affair with Tomioka and will eventually bear his child. Consider the following passage describing Yukiko's impression of Niu serving dinner when they first meet:

> When Yukiko put her hands on the well-starched white tablecloth, she felt that her yellow hands look dirtier than even the Vietnamese maid's. Petals of bougainvillea flowers floated in the glass finger-bowl. . . . The maid looked like she was in her thirties, but she had

pretty eyes. Her forehead was bare, she wore small green jade earrings, and she spread powder over her flat, colorless face. [p. 252]

Compared to Yukiko's subjective and judgmental observation of Mari, her appraisal of Niu is objective. The initial distress at her working-class hands (dirtier than the maid's) is soon dissipated by her realization that the maid is old(er) and has a typically "oriental" face. Yukiko is confident that she has sized up Niu in one glance. Hayashi Fumiko is remarkably deft in translating the complexity of abstract epistemes of race and class into a concrete, genderized situation. Her writerly eyes see through the veiled female rivalry instantly and enable her to plumb the depths of her characters' unconscious. Yukiko's studied assessments of these two women, Mari and Niu, mirror the positions Japan had assumed in the globalized world since the dawn of its modernity: the West is an imagined construct that is seductive and threatening at the same time; the East is a known entity requiring no scrutiny beyond its "flat" surface. Certainly for Yukiko there is a tacit assumption (incorrect, perhaps) that she herself, as an Asian woman, knows what lies behind that flat face. The hasty dismissal of Niu makes Yukiko concentrate all her sexual competitiveness on Mari: to be like Mari and to be better than Mari.

Ultimately Yukiko emerges triumphant in the competition for Tomioka's affections. Physically Yukiko reminds Tomioka of his wife Kuniko, and "most of all, Tomioka's heart was resonant with an odd discovery: that they understood the nuances of words when they spoke to each other. The casual familiarity of life and words only click between men and women of the same race; and here is one right here, Kōda Yukiko, who confirmed that [for Tomioka]" (pp. 262–263). We see this choice foreshadowed in the their first kiss while on an outing in the jungle:

> Tomioka pulled Yukiko's face away from his chest, gazing vacantly at her lips. He felt grateful for this woman of the same race, with whom he could communicate fully. He discovered something that was totally different from the kiss he had had with Niu the night before. Not holding anything back, feeling relaxed and dazed, he stared into Yukiko's flushed face. With her eyes closed and trying hard to suppress her heavy breathing, Yukiko's face looked awfully like his wife's. In reality, he was holding Yukiko's heavy face yet the coursing of his numbed heart wandered aimlessly a thousand miles away. His heart eagerly desired something else and Tomioka could do nothing about it. [p. 268]

The familiarity comes not only from Yukiko's being Japanese but also from Yukiko's resemblance to his wife; this provides Tomioka with a certain reassurance he cannot obtain through his frantic search for sexual satisfaction. The long, deep kisses excite Yukiko so much that she "impatiently dug into Tomioka's shoulders with her nails" while Tomioka "gradually felt his ardor cool; his passion to take further action to parallel Yukiko's urgency had already dissipated" (p. 268).

It is ironic that Tomioka, known among his colleagues as a model husband who writes to his wife faithfully and frequently, is later proved to be a frivolous lout who abandons his marital obligations and his ailing wife after the war (as well as an illegitimate baby in Dalat). Kano, the third member of the romantic triangle, when confronted by Tomioka, admits inadvertently that he does have someone he loves back in Japan. In a conversation after Tomioka had just returned from a trip, the two men carry on an oblique yet suggestive chat:

> "Tomioka-san, anything interesting happen in Saigon?"
> "How could there be anything like that?"
> "Really? . . . I don't believe you."
> "Before you go back to Trangbom, you should make a trip to Saigon and refresh yourself."
> "Saigon, huh? . . . Haven't been there for a while." [p. 261]

Right after this libidinous exchange, Kano flashes back to his earlier tour of duty with the troops in Nanjing:

> That gloomy war cast a shadow in his mind. What was that lake called? The recollection of a hasty sport with a woman on a boat, hidden in the dark of night, crept over him like a silhouette on his eyelids. [p. 262]

As sexual tensions build, the men are constantly pursuing their next sexual encounter; as often as not, they feel let down afterward. From China to Southeast Asia, each hasty sexual interlude is followed by another, as if these men are grasping for proof they are still alive, still sexually potent. The wives and lovers left behind are no longer on the map; the men have left Japan and its social constraints far behind. But as the sexual escapades proceed, these men seem to feel more and more confused and weak. Yukiko, by contrast, grows bolder and more demanding. And Niu, with "her womanly vigor that never knows fatigue" (p. 264), makes Tomioka somewhat desperate. For a metaphor that captures both the personal frustration of these colonial men and, in a larger sense, the colonial enterprise as a whole, Tomioka turns to the management of flora:

> "Plants do not do well unless they are native to the place. Just look at the Japanese cypress trees that were planted in front of the Forestry Office here in Dalat," Tomioka thought to himself. "The differences in races are like these plants. Plants are rooted in the land of specific ethnic groups. . . . According to the distribution map, there are 35,000 hectares of pine trees around Dalat. In the confusion of the moment, a dull-witted Japanese forestry officer arrives. How is he going to be able to decipher these statistics of a foreign land? . . . Just because we think that the shape of the tree, the grain of the wood, are magnificent, where are we going to sell this great forest of pines? Aren't we just outsiders who suddenly marched in here to raid someone else's treasure, these pine trees that someone nurtured over so many years?" . . . "Kano and I are in love with something that is not love. Both of us have lost the robust spirit we had back in Japan. Gradually we are turning into the Japanese cypress tree, which after being transplanted to the highlands of Dalat is about to wither away. We have somehow," Tomioka murmured, "fallen victim to the listlessness of the South Seas (*nan'yōboke* 南洋呆け)." [p. 264]

These Japanese men are lost in the foreign forests of Southeast Asia, staggered by the immensity of the mission they have taken on, worried they will not be able to survive away from their accustomed environment. The listlessness of the South is on the point of overcoming their imperial purpose—the spirit that led them to venture beyond Japan's borders and take a hand in creating a greater Japanese empire. It is tempting to read into this account the dawning realization that the fortunes of war have turned against the empire; certainly Hayashi, writing in 1949, must have seen the hubris of Japan trying to administer such distant lands and rule over such vastly different societies. Whatever the political implications of the story, the theme of overreaching, followed by failure and continuing misfortune, is compelling when portrayed on the personal level, in the figure of Tomioka, whose life deteriorates at an accelerating pace.

The fate of Japan's women is somewhat different. Yukiko goes south in search of excitement and adventure, too, and for her the experience is disturbing but also liberating. For the first time in her life she is able to transcend the gendered hierarchical structure of Japan; instead of serving as a sort of sexual slave for her in-law, Sugio, she is now served by Niu, a woman of a different ethnicity and class. In Japan, she would have been nothing more than a young office lady unlikely to associate socially with bureaucrats like Tomioka or Kano; but in the colonies she takes on a different social identity as one of the colonizers. From this position of privilege as "a woman of their own race," armed with her Japanese female sexuality, Yukiko is able to manipulate both men into submitting to her. Niu's sexuality, though potent enough to captivate Tomioka for a time, is inherently inferior to Yukiko's because it belongs to a native body.

Perhaps not all Japanese women in Vietnam enjoyed such a comfortable situation, but for Yukiko the change in lifestyle is profound. In fact, most of *Drifting Clouds* deals with Yukiko's life after she returns to Japan and must resume her lowly and forlorn position in Japanese society. Perhaps because her life in the South differed so markedly from her existence in Japan, Yukiko is troubled by the leisure and luxury she enjoyed in Dalat; soon, she fears, the good life will prove ephemeral. This fear is foreshadowed upon Yukiko's arrival in Dalat, when her superior, Makita, asks her:

> "I hear that life in Japan is getting harder and harder. That sure makes this place look like paradise, doesn't it?"
>
> Paradise? Yukiko had never lived a life like this before; she felt that this was even better than paradise, but that in turn made her uneasy. Her heart was overshadowed by an anxious emptiness, as if she had wandered into a rich man's mansion when no one was at home." [pp. 254–255]

The intoxicating but always tentative feeling of living a life too good to be true brings with it a distorted sense of time and place that frustrates Yukiko's desire to accelerate her sexual adventure—to seize the day and live life while it lasts. Her exhilaration is always accompanied by a sense of unease and displacement similar to that felt by Tomioka, the sense of being a Japanese cypress in a Vietnamese rainforest.

Back in the Homeland

Japan's defeat challenged the masculinity of its men. Yukiko, now back in Japan, cannot rid herself of a lingering fondness for the sweet memories of Dalat, but she sees for the first time the weakness of the man she thought she was madly in love with. In a dirty little hotel room amidst the rabble of black marketers in Ikebukuro, Yukiko looks at Tomioka and thinks to herself: "Why have the men around me fallen so low and become so miserable? . . . This man, so full of energy and life in Indochina, has suddenly shriveled since his return to Japan" (p. 291).

While maintaining her occasional trysts with Tomioka, Yukiko has a brief affair with an American soldier but then returns to her relationship with her in-law, Sugio, largely for economic reasons. Hayashi displays her mastery of irony in the character of Sugio, who transforms himself from a lowly businessman before the war to a position of power and wealth in the postwar world of new religions. The fanaticism of fascist militarism is replaced by a fervid hunger for instant salvation and quick profits. Sugio finds a job in the church for Yukiko and buys her a house so that he can rendezvous with her without his wife knowing it.

In *Drifting Clouds*, Hayashi gives us a masterful portrayal of a woman adjusting her ever-changing identity to shifting circumstances while the men about her become jaded or get lost in the shuffle of political and economic transformation. Typical of many female characters created by this author, Yukiko relies on her survival instincts. She never becomes unduly sentimental, nor does she intellectualize her situation. As a contemporary saying put it: "Women and stockings got stronger after the war."

Tomioka does not fare so well and can only marvel at Yukiko's tenacious desire for life (and love). While Yukiko continues to savor the sweet madness of Dalat, Tomioka admonishes her that, with Japan defeated, they will never live like that again. The loss of empire translated into a loss of self-confidence, even sexual desire, for men like Tomioka. He resents Yukiko's dogged determination to make a living in bleak circumstances while he himself, saddled with the extra burden of a family, approaches financial ruin.

Now sober and somber, with no illusion of romance between them, Tomioka and Yukiko cling to their fading memories of the colonial past, the only thing that still connects them. The author emphasizes their changed circumstances through a New Year's trip together to a hot spring that parallels their journey into the Vietnamese highlands. Yukiko begs Tomioka to go away with her, and at the hot spring they contemplate a double suicide. The gloomy, rainy sky, the miserable, cheap inn, and the suspicious innkeeper are in stark contrast to the warm, languorous trip through the clear, bright highlands not so long ago. In the end, they are unable to resolve to commit suicide. Instead Tomioka strikes up an affair with the wife of the owner of a bar at the hot springs. When she follows him back to Tokyo, the irate husband pursues them, murders his wife, then kills himself.

Yukiko becomes pregnant with Tomioka's child and aborts it—suffering, it would seem, the karmic retribution due Tomioka for abandoning Niu and her baby. This series of incidents weighs heavily on

Tomioka, who decides to take an assignment to distant Yakushima at the far southern end of Japan. Yukiko embezzles funds from Sugio's church and flees south with Tomioka, hoping to recreate in southern Japan the excitement of their former life in Dalat. The long journey takes its toll on Yukiko, however, who has never completely recovered from the abortion and is battling consumption. Soon after their arrival on the remote southern island, far from the metropolis, Yukiko dies. Kawamura Minato argues that this ending indicates that Hayashi Fumiko, not unlike her character Yukiko, is confused. For Kawamura the ending disrupts the entire narrative. In his own words: "The narrative would have made more sense if Tomioka and all the men had died while Yukiko survived, living resiliently in the postwar world. . . . I think the way the narrative was constructed shows that Hayashi Fumiko was influenced by the chaos of the postwar period" (Kawamura 1998a: 152).

Through the different responses of Tomioka and Yukiko to misfortune, Hayashi does draw upon a common theme in the postwar fiction of female writers: the adaptability and resilience of the postwar liberated woman. But the unexpected ending, culminating in Yukiko's death, reveals an important truth about gender roles and the colonial experience: although the colonies provided a liberating environment for many women, this freedom was temporary and did not outlast the empire. Just as Rosie the Riveter went back to the kitchen when the American men came home, so loss of empire meant loss of opportunity for Japanese women. When they were folded back into Japanese society, the old gender hierarchy was reestablished and Yukiko resumed her subordinate position.[25]

The tenacity that Yukiko displays immediately after repatriation is merely a residual effect of colonial life. It disappears just as completely as the empire itself. The illusion of love and the physical passion—or, as Yukiko calls it, "madness"—between herself and Tomioka exists, and can only exist, because they are away from Japan in an exotic foreign land. The illusory nature of the romance between Yukiko and Tomioka, possible only outside of Japan, is not unlike the delusion of the empire itself. The outward expansion of Japan proves to be as capricious as the bond between Yukiko and Tomioka.

Life in a Hypercolonial Arena

Both Nakajima Atsushi's experiences in the South Seas and the sojourn of Hayashi Fumiko's Yukiko occur in a hypercolonial arena—in places where Japanese colonization was constantly encountering the remnants of previous colonial enterprises. Leo Ching (1998: 66) points out the ambiguity such an environment introduces into the dichotomies that are supposed to characterize relations between colonizer and colonized in a typical colonial context:

> Caught in between the contradictory positionality of non-white, not-quite and yet-alike, Japan's domineering gaze towards its colonial subjects in the East must always invariably redirect itself, somewhat ambivalently, to the imperialist glare of the West. What characterizes Japanese colonial discourse, then, is this uneasy oscillation between being both the seeing subject and the object being seen.[26]

Nakajima Atsushi and Hayashi Fumiko had different relations to this ambiguous colonial context and it shaped their writing in different ways.

Nakajima Atsushi, raised by a father who spent much of his life as an educator in the Japanese empire, grew up in the colonies. His first literary creations focused on the injustices perpetrated by the colonial system upon its native subjects. In the stultifying intellectual environment of wartime Japan, he retreated to historical novels about the distant past, using a foreign setting and characters to disguise his anguish at being unable to write the stories he wished. He found a kindred soul in Robert Louis Stevenson, a man of precocious talent and failing health, who was forced to write in clichéd genres but found escape in the lush tropical beauty of the South Seas. Stevenson also shared Nakajima's vision of a benevolent colonialism that would actually benefit its colonial subjects.

After completing his paean to Stevenson, Nakajima went off to the South Pacific hoping to find his utopia, a natural wonderland that would heal his tortured body and provide a place for him to express his altruistic tendencies. He found, instead, a dystopia. The natural environment tortured him and exacerbated his illness. The natives, dependent on their colonial master for the basics of existence, lived in deprivation and squalor. Moreover, Nakajima discovered that his mission—to revise textbooks that would teach these natives a language of no practical use in their environment while no attempt was made to ameliorate the circumstances of their lives—was a charade. Disillusioned he returned to Japan where his tale of Stevenson's tragic fate was now, ironically, winning him recognition; but true to the tragic arc of his fate, he died almost immediately. For Nakajima, Western colonialism, as depicted in the writings of Stevenson, affirmed his misgivings about its effect on the colonized. But Stevenson's life also presented a model of how to resolve some of these concerns through a firsthand encounter with the South Seas Other and the advocacy of a program of benevolent colonialism. When Nakajima's dreams of reform proved unrealizable, the colonial experience of Stevenson, captured in *Light, Wind, and Dreams*, provided him with fame.

Hayashi Fumiko was not a stranger to colonialism. She had traveled to Taiwan, China, Korea, Manchuria, and Indochina and seen various aspects of the colonial condition. And as the first Japanese woman to enter Nanjing after the massacre,[27] she had even witnessed the empire's naked aggression. Susanna Fessler notes two changes in her postwar writing that grew out of her wartime experiences: her attitude toward warfare itself became strongly negative, and she came to believe that the distribution of fortune and misfortune was random.[28]

In *Drifting Clouds*, Hayashi studiously avoids direct mention of war, but fate does seem to strike the players at random. Still, the primary message of this postwar rumination is the liberating influence of the colonial environment on the colonizers. Tomioka and Kano are freed from the constraints of lovers back home to pursue the urges of their male libidos through various sexual conquests. Yukiko is freed from the limitations of class, education, and region to pursue the men she desires. Noriko Mizuta notes: "Now that Yukiko has isolated herself from the Japanese social system, she can display her intrinsic sexuality and vitality toward men and be on an equal footing with them."[29] She also lives a life of material comfort unlike anything she has ever known and a privileged status (both legal and social) she could never attain in Japan. Personal freedom and physical comfort are both perquisites of being a colonizer woman. For Yukiko colonialism was a utopia, and after returning to Japan she spends the rest of her short life trying to recapture that joy.[30]

Although colonialism is liberating for Yukiko, this was not true for colonized women like Niu. She is forced into a sexual relationship with Tomioka, impregnated and abandoned, a victim of the colonial male libido. Yukiko is largely oblivious to her maid and, at least initially, unaware of Niu's relationship with Tomioka. But she does notice Niu occasionally, if only to gloat over her superiority to the dark-skinned, thirtyish woman with the "flat, colorless face." Niu occupies the position of a colonial subject, a subject with little control over her own life in the face of demands from her colonial masters.

The character Mari reflects the complexity of human relations in the colonial context. Mari is half-Vietnamese, half-French. As part-colonial subject and part-hypercolonial power, Mari deconstructs the dichotomy of master/subject with her liminal, transgressive identity. Her personal power and influence are amplified by her general competence and advanced skill in clerical tasks, music, and languages. Mari is too well connected, too well informed, and too self-assured to fall victim to intimidation by a representative of the current colonial power in Indochina. In this sense, Mari confounds the traditional genderized structure of colonial power, which would subjugate her to the colonizer male.

Bodies are central to both these stories. Nakajima Atsushi's body, which doubles with Robert Louis Stevenson's body, is a source of pain, sorrow, and anxiety to him. It suffers unusually from the environment of the South Seas colonies and is unable to recover. Symbolically the wasting of Nakajima's body foretells the demise of the empire. Yukiko's body is traded to Sugio, Tomioka, and an American serviceman for shelter and compassion, but in Indochina it is liberated—able to serve as a weapon in hunting what she wants. The bodies of the Asian girls seduced by Tomioka and Kano mark the progress of Japanese imperialism across the face of Asia. Niu's swelling body represents the legacy of colonialism to the colonized people, who are mistreated, abandoned, but fertilized and ready to grow beyond their colonial situation. Mari's tall body with antelope legs is the unattainable Other: a symbol of the status of senior colonial power to which Japan can never attain. Finally, Yukiko's still-young body, battered by worries, financial hardship, and emotional turmoil, victim of a botched abortion, comes to an inglorious end alone, in a hotel room, at the southernmost tip of Japan.

PART

II

COLONIAL DESIRE AND
AMBIVALENCE

Nishikawa Mitsuru and *Bungei Taiwan*

In his "Japanese Imperialism: Later Meiji Perspectives," Marius Jansen characterizes Japan's drive for colonial control during the late Meiji period as "an entirely reasonable approach" to security considering the geopolitical circumstances of that era when the Western powers had divided up most of Asia if not the world (Peattie and Myers 1984: 61–79). He further compares Japanese imperialism with that of the West and argues that "imperialism never became a very important part of the national consciousness. There were no Japanese Kiplings, there was little popular mystique about Japanese overlordship and relatively little national self-congratulation" (p. 76). We have seen that there were travelers, like Satō Haruo and Nakamura Chihei, who visited the South, often only briefly, and brought back tales of exotic wonder and untamed savages that were quite popular back in the metropole. There were also Japanese expatriates who lived, even grew up, in the colonies and made them their homes, and who then wrote about them with deep insight. If they did not make the same impression on the Japanese reading public, perhaps it was because everyday life in Japan's main colonies, Taiwan and Korea, was not that exotic, not that different from everyday life in rural Japan. Whereas the British were successful in mobilizing their nation domestically with an imperialist mandate portrayed as a shared social mission, Japanese imperialism, in comparison, seems fragmented and ill articulated. The grand vision that seemed absent at the inception of Japan's imperial enterprise was eventually supplied in an attempt to justify imperial expansion retroactively. Slogans such as *naigai ichijo* 内外一如 ("Japan and the colonies are as one"), *naisen ittai* 内鮮一体 ("Japan and Korean are one body"), and *gozoku kyōwa* 五族協和 ("five races living in harmony"), which pepper Japanese colonial discourse, were nothing more than ideological afterthoughts catching up with military and political reality.

Jansen may be correct that there was no Japanese author who conveyed life in the colonies back to the metropolis in the compelling way in which Kipling did. But the Japanese empire did produce a generation of expatriates whose homes were in the colonies and who tried to capture that experience in literature. Nishikawa Mitsuru 西川満 (1908–1999), an eminent author and editor based in the colony of Taiwan, was one who tried to convey in words and images the culture of Taiwan and his experiences as a Japanese resident of the island.[1] Nishikawa was born in 1908 to an adventurous family from Aizu Wakamatsu. His father was a veteran of the Russo-Japanese War and remained in Manchuria after its end. Nishikawa's given name, Mitsuru 満 ("*man*" in Sino-Japanese pronunciation), was in fact meant to commemorate his father's ties to Manchuria 満州.

Nishikawa's family moved to Taiwan when he was two years old, joining relatives who were already there in the management of a family-owned coal mine. Except for six years at prep school and Waseda University in Tokyo, Nishikawa lived in Taiwan until the end of World War II. After Japanese rule had become established on the island, and especially after the Xilaian uprising of 1915, Taiwan entered a period of peace and calm.[2] Nishikawa enjoyed a privileged childhood: his father was a prominent local entrepreneur and politician and the family was considered rather well off even among the ranks of the colonial ruling class.[3] Surrounded by loving parents, Nishikawa was given freedom and financial support to pursue his interests—especially his precocious interest in literature and art. He created his own illustrated magazine when he was only in second grade.

Like many modern Japanese writers, Nishikawa began his career as a poet. In 1920, he entered Taipei Premier High School and established a journal called *Poet in the Woods* (*Mori no shijin* 森の詩人). This publication, printed by lithography, was the first of many literary journals Nishikawa created during his life. He showed his mastery as a book designer and bookbinder with his early handbound poetry collections, *The Illusion of Love* (*Ai no gen'ei* 愛の幻影) and *The Ivory Boat* (*Zōge no fune* 象牙の船).

Nishikawa later was known for combining art and literature in exquisitely fashioned books. It is also during this time that Nishikawa began to experiment with fiction. His first short story, "Swine" ("Buta" 豚, 1923), was awarded first place in a competition sponsored by the *Taiwan News*. He was also a frequent contributor to the colonial government's official newspaper, the *Taiwan Daily News* (*Taiwan nichinichi shinpō* 台湾日々新聞). When he was later appointed editor of the Cultural Affairs Department, he created a literature and arts section (*gakugeiran* 学芸欄) that provided a venue for local (Japanese and Taiwanese) writers.

From 1927 to 1933, Nishikawa lived in Japan, studying at the Waseda Secondary Preparatory School and later majoring in French literature at Waseda University, where he studied with famous scholars such as Yoshie Takamatsu 吉江喬松 (1880–1940), Yamauchi Yoshio 山内義雄 (1894–1973), and Saijō Yaso 西条八十 (1892–1970). His inclination toward romanticism was influenced, no doubt, by his personality and family background, but it must have been shaped as well by these three teachers of French romantic literature. During his five-year stay in Tokyo, the ever-prolific Nishikawa produced six poetry collections and founded the journal *La Poésie*.[4]

After his graduation, Nishikawa was undecided about whether to stay in Tokyo or go back to Taiwan. At the urging of his mentor Yoshie Takamatsu, he returned to Taiwan in 1933. Later Nishikawa recalled that Yoshie had instructed him to "devote my whole life to regional literature," which "made me make up my mind to return to Taiwan."[5] Yoshie composed a poem for him upon his return to the island (Shimomura et al. 1995: 408–409):

Nanpō wa hikari no minamoto	The South,
wareware ni chitsujo to	source of light.
kanki to karei to wo ataeru	give us order, joy, and splendor.

The word "*karei*" 華麗, meaning "splendorous beauty," is a translation of the term coined by the Portuguese to refer to the island, *Formosa*, "the beautiful." It came to be a poetic name for the island and Nishikawa used it often, as in the poetry journal *Kareitō* 華麗島 (Beautiful island), which he founded in 1939, and a collection of Taiwanese folktales titled *Kareitō minwashū* 華麗島民話集 (1942). The term was revived, with a slight variation, in the postwar Taiwanese struggle against the authoritarian rule of the Nationalist government during the 1970s and 1980s.[6]

Nishikawa's activities were multifaceted—he was a poet, novelist, playwright, and publisher, the founder of the Taiwanese Poetry Society and, later, the Taiwanese Writers Association. Nishikawa is now best known for his role in running the journal *Literary Taiwan* (*Bungei Taiwan* 文芸台湾, 1940–1944), the official publication of the Taiwanese Writers Association. Though the magazine was published for only five years, it had a great impact on the literary scene at the time and occupies a pivotal place in the history of colonial literature in Taiwan. The rapid spread of literacy in Japanese during the colonial period (by 1941, some 57 percent of the island's six million inhabitants were considered literate in Japanese) and the suppression of the Chinese language in print, and eventually in public speech, facilitated the development of a Japanese-language press.[7] A new mass market for ideas competed for a sizable readership now capable of understanding Japanese and reading demanding material in that language. Under these favorable circumstances, an astonishing array of literary, poetic, and cultural magazines flourished (Fujii Shōzō 1998: 25–45). Nishikawa's *Bungei Taiwan*, together with Zhang Wenhuan's *Taiwanese Literature* (*Taiwan bungaku* 台湾文学, 1941–1943), were the main pillars of a robust, competitive literary scene in Taipei.[8]

In 1942, Nishikawa's career as a cultural arbiter reached its pinnacle. He quit his job at the newspaper to become a full-time writer. In October he and several other writers attended the first Greater East Asian Writers Conference (Dai Tōa Bungakusha Taikai 大東亜文学者大会) in Tokyo as delegates representing Taiwan. The next year, his "Record of the Red Fort" ("Sekikanki" 赤嵌記, 1942) was awarded the Taiwanese Culture Award.[9] He also began work on his epic novel *The Taiwan Cross-Island Railway* (*Taiwan sōkan tetsudō* 台湾縦貫鉄道). In January 1945, following his father's death, Nishikawa succeeded to the position of head of the Shōwa Mining Company. In August of that same year, Japan surrendered. In its list of potential war criminals, the colonial government named Nishikawa Mitsuru and Hamada Hayao as the two principal leaders of the Taiwanese culture scene. Ordered to wait for further investigation, he was never formally tried as a war criminal.

Nishikawa was repatriated to Japan in the spring of 1946 and died in 1999. Most bibliographies of Nishikawa's works end in 1945, but Nishikawa continued his career as a writer—primarily for publications geared toward the masses, such as *Ōru yomimono* オール読物 (All reading material), *Goraku sekai* 娯楽世界 (Entertainment world), and *Hōseki* 宝石 (Jewels). His novel *Kaishinki* 会真記 (Record of meetings with the perfected) was awarded the Natsume Sōseki Award in 1948,[10] and another novel, *Nisshoku* 日蝕 (Eclipse), was nominated for the prestigious Akutagawa Award. But Nishikawa was never to regain the stature as a writer that he held while in Taiwan, and at one point he was even forced to work as a fortune teller to support his family.

During his career in Taiwan, Nishikawa founded and edited eighteen magazines and published numerous novels, collections of short stories, and poetry collections. His articles on such topics as Taiwanese folklore, religion, customs, architecture, and art number in the hundreds. Back in Japan, Nishikawa continued his prolific literary activities: he ran a publishing house, edited the journal *Andromeda* アンドロメダ, wrote fiction and nonfiction works, reprinted some of his previous books, compiled bibliographies, composed an operatic biography of the medieval monk Nichiren (with a score by Marubeni Toshio), wrote popular books on fortune telling, and published two personal memoirs. He was never able to fully recuperate his status as an aesthete, literatus, and connoisseur of culture, however, and remained an outsider to the Japanese literary scene, largely unknown to the public.

Colonial-Period Criticism of Nishikawa

Nishikawa's status as a cultural trendsetter in the elite circles of Taipei was firmly established by the late 1930s and early 1940s. The semi-official newspaper he worked for provided a forum for his literary and cultural endeavors, and his family's financial backing enabled him to publish exclusive, expensive artistic monographs without worrying about the realities of the marketplace. This privileged colonialist position has played a significant role in the formation of critical opinion concerning Nishikawa. Here I want to retrace some of the debates surrounding his life and work in order to show how the discourse on one particular colonial writer took shape and to understand its implications for our view of prewar Taiwanese literature as colonial literature.

Colonial-period studies of Nishikawa's writings by his contemporaries render a mixed verdict. Most positive reviews of his work as a writer and leader of the cultural scene derive from his colleagues, that is, members of his own camp. Nakamura Tetsu 中村哲 (b. 1912) was acknowledged informally as the literary theoretician among the *Bungei Taiwan* writers.[11] In an article titled "The Issues of Colonial Literature" ("Gaichi bungaku no kadai" 外地文学の課題),[12] Nakamura points out the limitations imposed on colonial literature by its isolation from the metropolitan culture. In response to the question "How can literature created in the cultural apex take on different forms and be reborn in a wild colony devoid of culture?" he suggests two courses of action: One is to adopt a totally different orientation from that of the metropolitan literature, writing about issues that are unique to the colony. The other is to absorb the metropolitan culture as fully as possible and create a colonial literature that follows as closely as possible that of the metropolis. Nakamura does not, however, offer much hope for the creation of a colonial literature that would match the standards in Japan:

> Emotional sensitivity must always be guided by intellect. Unfortunately, those who live in the colonies possess neither such intellect nor sensitivity. The colonial life and customs cloud their intellectual perception. One could even say that intellectual perception and consciousness can be found only among those immigrants to the colony who were educated outside the colony or among travelers who visited the colony. Perhaps in a sense, only strangers [*étrangers*, those "foreign" to the colony] are capable of creating colonial literature. The consciousness of the stranger is drawn to things that are unique, eccentric, and abnormal; they are surprised by and suspicious of them. The surprise turns into the literature of exoticism and romanticism; the suspicion leads to the literature of satire and social criticism. Merimée's "Colomba" and Satō Haruo's "Strange Tales of the 'Precepts for Women' Fan" belong to the former and Gogol's "The Nose" and Gide's "Travels in the Congo" are in the latter category. . . . However, since only those strangers who are distant from the colony can recognize the special qualities of the colony, conversely the danger becomes that in dealing with everything the stranger focuses overmuch on difference. This hypersensitivity toward difference easily leads to a literature of exoticism. . . . In this way, the literature of the stranger provides an important lesson for literature created by the expatriate Japanese. The colonial literature created by second-generation Japanese should not put too much emphasis on difference but rather on depicting the reality of the natives' lives.[13]

Nakamura's delineation of the relationship between colonial literature and metropolitan literature is problematic and certainly chauvinistic in its cultural outlook. In just a few sentences, he erases the native from the picture of colonial literature and designates colonial literature as by nature both exoticizing and cynical. Nakamura suggests that only a "stranger," someone who maintains a certain distance, can capture the true essence of Taiwan; the natives are intellectually incapable of doing so. Yet he also cautions against overemphasizing the colony's unique qualities. To negotiate between the exotic "surprise" of the stranger and the "suspicion" of excessive exoticization, Nakamura prescribes the tool of realism. Although Nakamura did not explicitly mention Nishikawa in this definitive article, Nishikawa was the most famous and powerful second-generation writer and no doubt he had him in mind. This advocacy of realism foreshadows their later conflict.

In contrast to the writings of Gogol, Gide, and Kipling, social satire never came to fruition in Japanese colonial literature. Romantic, exotic writings, however, became an important part of this body of literature. Some might point out that by the late 1930s and early 1940s, colonial literature was becoming increasingly politicized and propagandistic. But as I argue later in this chapter, these writings represent a mutation of the same romantic, exotic writing couched in a different rhetoric to serve a specific purpose.

Nishikawa's reputation as the quintessential writer of the exotic and romantic was established early on. His own publishing houses, Nikkō Sanbō and Maso Shobō, supported the publication of many poetry anthologies and ethnographic monographs while various journals founded and edited by Nishikawa provide a literary arena for himself and his colleagues. Nishikawa's literary endeavors were supported economically by his family's fortune, but he also enjoyed academic support from the most prestigious local institution of higher education. Shimada Kinji and Yano Hachito, professors at Taipei Imperial University, lent their intellectual imprimatur to Nishikawa's literary venture and frequently contributed articles to his magazine. After the war, Shimada Kinji taught at the University of Tokyo and founded the first comparative literature department in Japan. His study of Taiwanese literature was the first academic attempt at a systematic study of colonial literature (*gaichi bungaku* 外地文学) (Shimada 1995; 1976: 112–295). Accepting Nakamura Tetsu's definition of *gaichi bungaku*, Shimada's studies of colonial literature deal only with expatriate and visiting Japanese writers; he excludes all native authors.

Nishikawa's leadership of the local literary scene was not always appreciated. In fact, his dictatorial editorial stance bruised some writers' feelings and led to defections from his camp. Moreover, he did not garner support from everyone in academia, and dissident voices arose among the community of Japanese expatriate writers as well. One of his most vocal critics was Kudō Yoshimi 工藤好美 (1898–?), who also taught at Taipei Imperial University. Like Nakamura Tetsu, he chose to publish most of his critical writings in *Taiwan bungaku*—a rival journal created by Zhang Wenhuan after he left *Bungei Taiwan* over personal and editorial disagreements with Nishikawa.[14]

If direct criticism from native Taiwanese writers was rare, this is hardly surprising: within the colonial context of the master/subject relationship, they had to exercise more caution than their Japanese counterparts. In memoirs, recollections, and interviews that came out after the war, we see simmering discontent among some of the natives who worked with him.[15] Prewar criticism from fellow Japanese expatriates was vocal but not unified. In his study of prewar criticism of Nishikawa Mitsuru, Nakajima Toshio cites three critical approaches arising from three distinct groups: the Academic school, the Taizhong school, and the *Taiwan bungaku* faction (Shimomura et al. 1995: 407–432). The Academic faction is best represented by Kudō Yoshimi and Nakamura Tetsu. The Taizhong school centered on Tanaka Yasuo 田中保男, literary editor for the *Taiwan News* in the central Taiwan town of Taizhong (Taichung). The *Taiwan bungaku* faction centered on Nishikawa's former high school classmate Nakayama Susumu 中山侑, who later joined the rival *Taiwan bungaku* and wrote scathing criticisms of Nishikawa.

Rivalry within the expatriate community was intense. Tanaka Yasuo, for example, in one of his criticisms of Nishikawa and his associates, suggested: "If they really wish to become a wing of Japanese literature, they should not only purge from their marrow the special characteristics of colonial literature, but also abandon literary indulgence and the feebleness that derives from an emphasis on empty form and lofty posturing" (Shimomura et al. 1995: 412–413). Even taking into account Tanaka's position as editor of a rival newspaper, these are stern remarks. Regionalism too played a part in this conflict. The cultural centers of the island before the occupation were mostly in southern or central Taiwan. It was not until the colonial government settled in the northern city of Taipei (Taihoku) that this sleepy, backwater town was transformed into a modern city. As the new political and commercial center of the island, Taipei became the zone of cultural contact with metropolitan Japan. Quickly Taipei came to be identified as the (colonial) metropolis outside the home metropolis and became associated with colonial policymaking. Local politics also had a role in the antagonism between the two most important literary journals, *Bungei Taiwan* and *Taiwan bungaku*: the former was a metropolitan, elitist publication, whereas the latter had a more rural and bucolic leaning.

The two competing journals were the standard bearers of literary culture at the time. *Bungei Taiwan* was the bastion of "pure" literature and devoted itself to romantic poetry, novels, art, and folklore; *Taiwan bungaku* advocated realistic representations that reflected the harsh realities of life for peasants and the downtrodden. Recent studies, especially those done by Taiwanese researchers, tend to emphasize the ideological chasm between the two groups—pitting *Bungei Taiwan* as a procolonial publication run primarily by Japanese versus *Taiwan bungaku* as the magazine for native resistance. This juxtaposition appears convincing but is simplistic. In fact, both camps were racially mixed; both had active members drawn from the Taiwanese and Japanese communities; and both were genuinely trying to open up the magazines to new young writers. One of *Bungei Taiwan*'s missions, as stated in every issue, was to "stalwartly open up space to newcomers and to elevate the island's culture, making the journal a genuine literary training ground." As a monthly general magazine, *Bungei Taiwan* put a lot of effort into securing readership and searching out new writers; at one point it chastised the quarterly *Taiwan bungaku* and said it should "try harder to recruit Taiwanese writers."[16]

The reputed disparity of content in the two magazines—romanticism versus realism—is equally exaggerated. *Taiwan bungaku* had no monopoly on realism. Hamada Hayao's 浜田隼雄 (1909–1973) epic *Southern Immigrant Village* (*Nanpō iminson* 南方移民村, 1942), which documented the harsh life of Japanese immigrants in eastern Taiwan, is a case in point: it is a model narrative of social realism. Nishikawa Mitsuru's only historical novel, *Taiwan Cross-Island Railway*, encapsulated the history of post-1895 Taiwan through a metaphorical account of the construction of the transisland railroad. *Bungei Taiwan* was often accused of being a hotbed of imperial-subject literature. We will discuss this literature in detail later, but certainly these narratives by Taiwanese authors, writing about sometimes unabashed but most often ambivalent feelings about becoming Japanese, are grounded in the tradition of realism.

Another criticism often directed toward *Bungei Taiwan*—in particular toward Nishikawa Mitsuru—is the magazine's cozy relationship with the metropolitan literary scene *(chūō bundan)*. In fact, eighty well-known intellectuals, including such writers as Kawabata Yasunari and Yokomitsu Riichi, were listed as honorary members and sometimes commented on the journal in a column called "Fragrant Missives from Various Masters" ("Shoka hōshin" 諸家芳信). Nishikawa Mitsuru proved to be a savvy master of public relations; by sending beautifully produced poetry collections and magazines to these metropolitan writers, he was able to marshal encouraging messages from them. Nishikawa was not alone in these efforts. *Taiwan bungaku* too boasted of its metropolitan connections. In the column "Correspondence on the Literary Art" ("Gakugei ōrai" 学芸往来), they proudly presented symposiums and dialogues *(taidan)* held with writers who passed through Taiwan on their way to official assignments in South China. Even Yang Kui, one of the most ardently nationalistic writers, when he started his journal *New Taiwan Literature (Taiwan shinbungaku* 台湾新文学), highlighted his close relationship with members of the Proletarian Literature movement which was at the time the center of the literary scene.[17] For literary magazines in the colony, whatever their political position, any connection with the literary establishment in Japan was a plus in the fierce competition for readership. Ideological differences aside, claims of association with the metropolitan culture enhanced the legitimacy and stature of a magazine. To be sure, ideological chasms existed. But immediate concerns for survival often outweighed ideological and philosophical divergence.[18]

The various critical voices on Nishikawa Mitsuru can be subsumed into two main categories, each of which included representatives from among Japanese expatriates and Taiwanese natives. The first type of criticism centered on Nishikawa's willful appropriation of Taiwanese culture, which they considered mere exoticizing and romanticizing of the island. The other focused on the issues of realism and representation. In fact, the two issues can be seen as two sides of the same coin. This cursory outline of the criticism directed at Nishikawa by his contemporaries reveals the controversies that swirled through the literary scene in Taipei during the late 1930s and early 1940s. The rivalry between the two major literary magazines was waged on frequently shifting ground. The two camps do not fit into neat ethnic categories; alliances zigzagged across social, economic, ideological, and regional boundaries; even generic and stylistic oppositions did not remain constant. We can see, however, that by the early 1940s the Japanese language had established itself as the shared intellectual language and that the readership for Japanese-language publications was sufficiently broad to prompt spirited competition.[19] Whatever one's final appraisal of Nishikawa's literary endeavors, his efforts certainly contributed to the rapid maturation of Taiwanese colonial literature.

Postwar Assessment of Nishikawa

Postwar study of Nishikawa Mitsuru began as early as 1948,[20] but it did not reach full speed until well into the 1970s.[21] Though he garnered an entry in Kōdansha's *Nihon kindai bungaku daijiten* (Encyclopedia of modern Japanese literature), critics and researchers in Japan largely ignored Nishikawa—initially because of a preoccupation with postwar reconstruction, ultimately because of a self-imposed silence on their colonial past. As a consequence, the production of criticism, limited as it may be, has come primarily from Taiwan. Most of the postwar studies on Nishikawa in Japan can be found in the literary magazine *Androm-eda*, which was created and funded by Nishikawa himself.

A debate between Zhang Liangze and the writer Chen Yingzhen in 1980 demonstrates the degree to which the evaluation of Nishikawa's oeuvre as a colonial writer has been politicized. Zhang Liangze spear-headed the postwar reevaluation of Nishikawa Mitsuru in many of his articles, proposing that the affection for Taiwan expressed in his writ-ings should be considered a positive contribution to the formation of a Taiwanese consciousness (*Taiwan yishi* 台湾意識).[22] Chen Yingzhen made a fierce rebuttal in the journal *Wenji*.[23] Emphasizing the funda-mental differences between Nishikawa Mitsuru and Taiwanese colonial writers such as Lai He, Yang Kui, and Wu Zhuoliu, Chen concluded:

> In each colony, there always exist two standards for culture. From the cultural point of view of the colonizers, all the stories, legends, and customs of the colony are nothing but vulgarity. But from the perspective of the colonized, these stories, legends, and customs are considered most beautiful and are the basis of their pride. From an even more radical standpoint, when those resistant intel-lectuals in the colony noted the deficiency, the backwardness, of their own culture and were extremely critical of its benightedness, they did so with the intention of strengthening it. This is very dif-ferent from the Japanese, whose detached attitude toward the col-ony enabled them to love the mystical, exotic side of the colony. They even went so far as to praise the corrupted and decadent. The significance of these two standpoints is completely different. [Chen Yingzhen 1988: 55–56]

The debate between Zhang and Chen can be interpreted as a dispute be-tween nativism and nationalism. In most (post)colonial contexts, the two overlap. But within the context of the postwar Taiwanese political scene, the two are not necessarily the same. Chen Yingzhen argues that the ro-mantic colonialism of Nishikawa and his compatriots arose only be-cause they had no real emotional investment in the colony. A colonialist who criticizes the native culture does so out of cultural chauvinism; a native does it out of patriotism. Conversely he dismisses as pure exoticism the colonialist's love for the native culture, whereas similar feelings on the part of the colonized are an expression of genuine appreciation and pride. Chen thus makes ethnicity a key factor in the interpretation of attitudes toward culture.

At the root of this debate about Nishikawa was a conflict between Zhang Liangze's localized politics, centering on the recovery of a "Taiwanese consciousness," and Chen Yingzhen's insistence on a grand discourse founded upon a totalizing, unified national (that is, Chinese) identity. Moreover, this dispute occurs against the backdrop of the much larger, louder debate over the nativist literary movement *(xiangtu wenxue yundong)*.[24] At this critical moment in the conflict between those seeking to reaffirm a local, native identity (an indigenous Taiwanese identity) and their opponents—represented by writers such as Chen, Wang Wenxing, and Yu Guangzhong—Nishikawa Mitsuru and his discourse on indigenous Taiwan were viewed nostalgically by the nativist movement as the point of departure for the creation of a new local identity whereas the nationalists considered it nothing more than a rehashing of the memories of colonial oppression and a threat to national unity.

Nishikawa's Definition of Colonial Literature

We have been examining critical conceptions of colonial literature, especially Nishikawa Mitsuru's kind of colonial literature, espoused by his contemporaries during the colonial period and by younger scholars during the postwar era. Here we turn to Nishikawa's own assessment of this issue. As the (self-appointed) spokesman for the Japanese literary establishment *(bundan)* in Taipei during the 1930s and 1940s, Nishikawa Mitsuru frequently expounded upon the state of literature in Taiwan. A close examination of his exegesis reveals an ambivalent and at times contradictory discourse that echoes the same hesitancy and confusion we see in the critical positions described earlier.

The taxonomy of the colonial literature written in Japanese has recently been the subject of vigorous debate—specifically, whether it should be considered part of modern Japanese literary history or part of the native literary tradition of the colonized land. (See, for example, Kawamura Minato 1989: 92–97 and Komori Yōichi: 1998.) For Nishikawa, such ambiguity does not exist. Like a horse with blinders, he never wavers from his conviction that the literature of colonial Taiwan is part of the larger world of Japanese literature. Nishikawa was aware of the marginalization of Taiwanese literature within the prevailing Japanese worldview, but he fought to secure its legitimate place. In an overview of literary production in Taiwan, published in 1937, Nishikawa expressed his expectations for the newly appointed head of the Ministry of Culture (Bunkabu 文化部), Kishida Kunio, and his hopes for recognition from the central government.[25] He begins by acknowledging the geographic remoteness of Taiwan, which he characterizes as "a lonely island in the desolate southern sea" (*nanpō zekkai no kodō* 南方絶海の孤島), but argues that in the expanding Japanese empire Taiwan will one day occupy a more prominent position: "South is South and North is North. What good will it do to yearn constantly for the snowy sky of the northern state while we are in the bright, clear country of light? Eventually, with Taiwan at its center, Japan will extend further to the South." He concludes:

> Examining these achievements, I came to the conclusion that this nascent period of Taiwanese literature must follow its own unique course of development. It cannot be subordinated to nor be inferior to the literature of the metropole. Just as Frédéric Mistral created exquisite poems in the Provençal language that surpassed the urban literature of Paris, thus establishing a brilliant provincial literature that rivaled the great palace and garnered praise from thoughtful people, just so do we expect that our beautiful isle in the South Seas shall give birth to a literature that will live up to its reputation and occupy a unique place in the history of Japanese literature. [Nakajima Toshio and Kawahara Isao 1998, 1:467]

One cannot help noticing the north/south juxtaposition (dark, snowy sky versus clear, bright light) and the parallels drawn between the literatures of southern France and Taiwan. Clearly Nishikawa took seriously the mission entrusted to him by his mentor, Yoshie Takamatsu, to cultivate Taiwanese literature as a species of regional Japanese literature.

Orientalism and Art: Yanagi Muneyoshi and Nishikawa Mitsuru

Another of Nishikawa's contemporaries, Yanagi Muneyoshi 柳宗悦 (a.k.a. Yanagi Sōetsu, 1889–1961), traversed a parallel route to an orientalist aestheticism. Yanagi was a renowned art critic credited with creating the Arts and Crafts movement (*mingei undō* 民芸運動) and promoting Japanese culture overseas. Yanagi's father was a rear admiral in the navy, but his own interests lay elsewhere. While studying psychology at the

University of Tokyo, he became a member of the romantic literary coterie known as the White Birch or Shirakaba school 白樺派. Associating with fellow members such as Mushanokōji Saneatsu 武者小路実篤 (1885–1976) and Shiga Naoya 志賀直哉 (1883–1971), he was drawn to Western art, philosophy, and religion. Early on he established a reputation for his studies of such poets as Walt Whitman and William Blake. His lifelong friendship with the British sculptor Bernard Leach (1887–1979) opened his eyes to French impressionism, Rodin, and Matisse. Two trips to Korea in 1916 and 1920 had a far-reaching effect in shifting Yanagi's focus from Europe to Asia. His fascination with Yi-dynasty art and architecture, for example, led him to write a series of articles on Korea. He was also the founder of the Korean Ethnic Art Museum (Chōsen Minzoku Bijutsukan 朝鮮民族美術館), which opened in Seoul in 1924.

In 1922, Yanagi became involved in a controversy. The colonial government planned to tear down a Yi-dynasty city gate to make way for a modern office building for the administration. In an essay titled "For the Sake of One Piece of Korean Architecture About to Be Lost" ("Ushinawaren to suru ichi Chōsen kenchiku no tame ni" 失われんとする一朝鮮建築のために),[26] Yanagi praised the gate as "pure oriental art," condemned the planned structure as "Western-style, lacking creativity or aesthetic merit," and pleaded with the colonial government to "love pure Eastern beauty for the sake of your own honor." Yanagi saw this example of Yi-dynasty art as a last vestige of traditional East Asian art, threatened by the onslaught of Western culture and westernized Japanese civilization. For Yanagi, the Yi-dynasty artworks preserved a purity that was gradually disappearing from Japan.

Yanagi also raved about the folk art of the Ainu and Taiwanese aborigines, characterizing these works as "honest," "unadorned," and "untainted by civilization."[27] What attracted Yanagi to these folk traditions was a "purity" that was imperiled and yet resisted Western modernity. In 1926, Yanagi took a trip around Japan and discovered there, as well, the "pure beauty of the East" (*jun tōyō no bi* 純東洋の美) that he thought had already been lost to westernization (*bunmeika* 文明化). This discovery led Yanagi to refocus his attention on Japanese *mingei*—literally "people's crafts" (*minshūteki kōgei* 民衆的工芸). It is interesting that Yanagi's rejection of Western art and his consequent rediscovery of the traditional Japanese aesthetic required a detour through colonial Korea and forays into the authentic folk art of the Ainu and Taiwan.[28]

Yanagi's attitude toward primitive art, animated by a distaste for civilization, is typically orientalist. He praised the beauty of Ainu folk art as "not hypocritical, not dishonest. Can we find this awesome phenomenon in works of contemporary artists?" Commenting on the costume of the South Pacific islanders, he noted that "those ethnic groups that are denigrated as uncivilized primitives in fact possess the most overwhelming beauty. The products of the so-called civilized nations . . . have no way of avoiding the dishonesty of production." His appraisal of Taiwanese aboriginal textiles was also in this vein: "In the history of textiles, the further back we go in time, the truer the beauty is. Since the fabric woven by the barbarians (*hanbu* 蕃布) was outside the flow of time, it unquestionably possesses beauty" (Oguma Eiji 1998: 396–397).

Yanagi's primary criterion for aesthetic authenticity was the remoteness of the creator from civilization in terms of temporal distance and physical distance. Thus true beauty—or in Yanagi's term "honesty" 誠実さ—can be found only where there has been no pollution from civilization, specifically the civilizations of the Western nations and modern Japan. Any interaction with the civilized leads inevitably to defilement. Yanagi once complained that contact between the Ainu and the Japanese had led to the debasement of traditional Ainu arts and crafts. Pure Ainu art could still be found among the Ainu of the northern Kurile islands, but objects produced by the Hokkaido Ainu were altered through long-term contact with the Japanese. Yanagi leveled similar complaints against the ethnic artifacts of the Taiwanese, cautioning that they could remain authentic only so long as there were no Japanese influence.[29]

Although Yanagi maintained that authenticity demands a pure, unadulterated expression of indigenous aesthetics in the process of producing art, at the stage of aesthetic appreciation and appropriation a mediator is necessary. Commenting on Chinese folk art, he remarked: "I think it is the Japanese more than the Chinese who can best understand the value of Chinese folk art. Nevertheless the Chinese indeed possess, even to this day, a fertile energy in making things. Therefore, if the Japanese viewer/aficionado and the Chinese creator (見る日本人と作る支那人) can work together, a fine result is attainable" (Oguma Eiji 1998: 397). Or, similarly, commenting on Ainu and Taiwanese aboriginal arts: "They cannot tell good art from the bad. It will take the Japanese to discern the beauty [for them]. . . . Therefore, it is the duty of Japanese to raise their consciousness of beauty first by recognizing and respecting their own art as something worthy."[30] Consciously or unconsciously, Yanagi is reappropriating the discourse of the "noble savage" who can instinctively produce the most exquisite objet d'art yet possesses no language to articulate its beauty. Despite his opposition to civilization, Yanagi believed that civilized eyes were necessary for these savages to perceive true, essential beauty. The roles of producer and consumer of art in this scheme mirror the colonial power structure.

A discourse like Yanagi Muneyoshi's, on the aesthetics of ethnic art both in Japan and in Japan's colonies, is helpful in understanding Nishikawa's literary and artistic endeavors in Taiwan. There are many similarities between Yanagi and Nishikawa: the Western influence in their formative years, the dramatic return to Eastern tastes, their acknowledged positions as aesthetes, and their focus on folk arts and crafts rather than the traditional high arts. Nishikawa adhered to Yanagi's idea of yō 用 (utilitarian value) as a key aesthetic standard and was particularly interested in local bamboo crafts, architecture, customs, and folk religion rather than the rarefied realms of high culture. There are significant contrasts, as well, between the two contemporaries. Yanagi at times found himself in an antagonistic relationship with the government, but Nishikawa maintained good relations with the authorities. Yanagi repeatedly asserted that his concerns were artistic, not political, but Nishikawa at times served as a mouthpiece for the colonial authority's cultural policies.

Both Yanagi and Nishikawa imbued their surrogate homelands with an allegorical romantic significance. Yanagi remarked that Korean art was characterized by a "beauty of sadness" growing out of their historical experience of invasion by external forces: "There is a certain forlorn sadness unknown to outsiders in Korean art that comes from a lengthy Korean history filled with pain and brutality." He proclaimed: "There is no other art that expects and yearns so strongly for love." Yanagi criticized the tendency of the colonial administration to respond to Korea's needs with money and military force: "What the Koreans hunger for, more than money, politics, and military force, is a sliver of human consideration (ninjō 人情)." Yanagi asked: "When is Japan going to send its love?"[31]

Echoing Yanagi's sentimentalization of Korean art, Nishikawa's orientalist gaze on Taiwan focused on the beauty of the dilapidated (haikyo no bi 廃虚の美). He treasured the old Taiwan that was disappearing under the onslaught of modernity imposed by colonialism. Nishikawa's many ethnographic writings can be seen as an attempt to counter this force of modernization, a last-ditch effort to record the old, since time could not be stopped altogether. Like Yanagi Muneyoshi, Nishikawa directed his attention to folksy, local events such as everyday religious practices and produced various works that were ethnographic yet poetic. For Nishikawa, the turning point in his journey from abstract, French symbolist poetry to an aesthetic centered on local culture was around 1935. As part of his quest to "recover" the past for the "Taiwan that has no history," he set out to capture the magic of the native culture. This project was first manifest in poetry collections such as *Maso Festival* (*Maso matsuri* 媽祖祭, 1935), *Opium* (*Ahen* 亜片, 1937), and *Paean to the Beautiful Island* (*Kareitō shōka* 華麗島頌歌, 1940). *Maso Festival* includes a dozen narrative poem sequences depicting local festivals to deities such as Mazu, the patron goddess of sailors, and the city god (Chenghuang 城隍爺). One sequence, "After Decadence" ("Taitō igo" 頹唐以後), was later included in the *Anthology of Japanese Lyrical Poems* edited by Natsume Kōnosuke.

Besides these ethnopoetic writings, Nishikawa produced prosaic works that hewed closely to an anthropological or folkloristic approach. His *Records of the Land and Customs of Taiwan* (*Taiwan fudoki* 台湾風土記, 1940) and *Records of Famous Taiwanese Customs* (*Taiwan kenpūroku* 台湾顕風録 1935–1937) were illustrated with drawings and photos of local Taoist rituals, annual religious ceremonies, holidays, and celebrations. *Records of the Land and Customs* even included a collection of aboriginal songs, a rare example of Nishikawa's venture into non-Chinese cultural terrain. He not only rewrote and published traditional Japanese folktales such as *The Peach Boy* but also collected native folktales and children's stories. *The Weaver Maiden* (*Qiniangmasheng* 七娘媽生) includes the love story of the weaver maiden and the herding boy's ill-fated love affair and many other traditional folktales of continental origin. *The Anthology of Formosan Folktales* (*Kareitō minwashū* 華麗島民話集, 1942), by contrast, focuses on Taiwanese fairy tales. He also translated into Japanese many native historical tales such as *A Brief Record of the Jiading-Period Massacre* (*Jiading tucheng lueji* 嘉定屠城略記, 1939), a genre extremely popular among native readers, and the famous *Journey to the West* (*Xiyouji* 西遊記, 1943). Nishikawa expended prodigious amounts of time, energy, and money producing these monographs, which he published himself. For the bindings he sought out expensive, handmade materials, including distinctive items symbolic of local culture (hemp, temple talismans, bamboo paper), as well as artwork that would harmonize with the contents.[32] These books were in every sense artistic productions.

Yanagi collected objets d'art of Korea and other Japanese colonies; Nishikawa collected the indigenous narratives of Taiwan.[33] Yanagi's sizable collection enabled him to establish the Japanese Folk Art Museum, still open to the public in Komaba, near Tokyo. Nishikawa's collection of narratives is mediated through language, recorded in translations (both cultural and linguistic), and viewed through the prism of authorial subjectivity; thus it is less transparent and less accessible to the general public. Like Yanagi, Nishikawa assumed the role of cultural arbiter—a sophisticated (and civilized) connoisseur who appreciated, appropriated, and consumed indigenous cultural artifacts. Yanagi's collecting was itself a creative act, but Nishikawa implicated himself much more deeply in the act of cultural production. Nishikawa participated in transcribing, transmitting, and transforming the native information into objects of desire for himself and his readers. For Yanagi, any colonial intervention into the art rendered it inauthentic; for Nishikawa, the preservation through narration was a poetic act.

Nishikawa's publications on Taiwanese culture do not reflect an impartial, academic discourse on the culture of the Other. Nishikawa is a poet first and foremost, and he injects into every object he sees his own subjective, poeticized interpretations. Each object, each festival, each deity, in turn, acts as a catalyst that allows the imagination to soar. Thus Nishikawa's presentation of folk art and customs is not grounded in historical development or practical functionality; instead it fuses to these native artifacts a discourse that has its roots in authorial subjectivity and represents the aesthetic viewpoint of the colonial romanticism of the 1930s.

Gender, Historiography, and Romantic Colonialism

AT THIS POINT let us turn from Nishikawa's work as an editor and patron of the arts to look at Nishikawa the writer. During his years in Taiwan, Nishikawa produced an impressive oeuvre of short stories on a variety of topics, as well as one epic novel and many essays. Here we will focus on two short stories that highlight different aspects of his literature, his romanticism, and his concern for history. The first story, "Spring on the Rice River," illuminates gender relations within the colonial context. The second, "Record of the Red Fort," demonstrates how the modernity of the colonizer must negotiate with the traditions of the colonized in creating a shared present. But first let us begin by examining one of the most famous stories about Taiwan. A story by Satō Haruo, who traveled to Taiwan and wrote stories based on his experiences, sets the stage for these two tales of Nishikawa and provides some interesting contrasts.

Satō Haruo's "Tale of the Fan"

Satō Haruo (1892–1964) was one of Japan's most prominent writers and poets of the first half of the twentieth century. (See Hata Kōhei 1997: 22–26, 32–35; Keene 1984b: 631–644; Oketani Hideaki 1987: 248–309; Satō Haruo 1944.) Heir to a family tradition of sinological scholarship, he gained a wide familiarity with Western literature and published translations from a variety of foreign languages. In the summer of 1920, he traveled to Taiwan and the southern coastal area of China. Much has been written about Satō's reasons for taking the trip, above all his affair with Tanizaki Junichirō's wife.[1] In his travelogue "A Record of That One Summer" ("Kano ichinatsu no ki" かの一夏の記), he glossed over the affair and attributed his motivation to "some depressing matters," "the friendship of an old buddy," and "the phantom of the southern country (*nankoku* 南国), which I have yet to see" (Satō Haruo 1936: 253). After his return to Japan he wrote various pieces, fiction, essays, and travelogues, based on his experiences. The most famous work to come out of this was a short story titled "A Strange Tale of the 'Precepts for Women' Fan" ("Jokaisen kidan" 女誡扇奇譚, hereafter referred to as "Tale of the Fan"). It is often cited as an exemplary piece of exotic writing, and Satō himself proclaimed the story to be one of his five favorites. As an established writer of the Taishō romantic movement, Satō Haruo's writings surely drew attention to the colony.

Satō Haruo's writings on colonial Taiwan were not in the form of a casual travel journal like the famous "Here and There in Manchuria and Korea" ("Mankan tokorodokoro" 満韓ところどころ) by Natsume Sōseki or "Record of a Trip to China" ("Shina yūki" 支那遊記) by Akutagawa Ryūnosuke.[2] The first to appear was Satō's account of a two-week side trip to Southeast China (Amoy and Zhangzhou) titled *Record of a Journey to the South* (*Nanpō kikō* 南方紀行). Satō's harshly critical attitude toward China was revealed in his complaints about the sloppiness of the bellboys, the filth and odor of the cities, and the anti-Japanese posters plastered throughout the city of Amoy. He also published some short stories inspired by his experiences in China, such as "Star" ("Hoshi" 星),[3] but they are far outnumbered by works growing out of his stay in Taiwan, including travelogues, essays, and short stories. Compared to the critical and, at times, contemptuous gaze he directed at China, his depictions of the colony are more complex, studied, and subtle; often they reveal a sympathetic attitude toward the aboriginal peoples and native Taiwanese intellectuals.

There was a sizable temporal gap between the publication of Satō's writings on China, a foreign state and former and future enemy, and those on Taiwan—reflecting the political sensitivity of writings relating to Japan's colony. His first publications on Taiwan adapted local tales such as "Eagle Claw Blossom" ("Takatsumebana" 鷹爪花),[4] the children's story "The Locust's Great Journey" ("Inago no dairyokō" 蝗の大旅行),[5] and the aboriginal legend, "The Devilbird" ("Machō" 魔鳥), discussed in Chapter 2. His travel journal, which one might have expected to be the first product of the trip to see the light of day, did not appear for five years. The potential sensitivity of this material is evident in his record of his visit to the aboriginal village called Wushe 霧社 (Jpn.: Musha).[6] He visited shortly after the Saramao Incident, a small-scale armed uprising by the indigenous people that foreshadowed a much larger, more brutal mutiny a decade later: the so-called Musha Incident. Though rumors claimed that more than one hundred Japanese had been killed, Satō's sympathies clearly lie with the aborigines. He notes the economic hardship suffered by the village and projects a sense of ambivalence and regret upon seeing aboriginal schoolchildren struggling to grasp remote concepts such as metropolitan Tokyo and the emperor. It is no wonder that when this travel account was reissued in book form in 1936, it was promptly banned.

In 1932, a full twelve years after his journey and a year after the Manchuria Incident, Satō published another travel account, "Journey to the Colony" ("Shokuminchi no tabi" 植民地の旅),[7] in which he recalls the various local elites he has met and his many conversations with them concerning issues such as modernity, colonization, and cultural identity. Satō tried to maintain his position as a detached observer who would listen and provide a forum for the natives to express their views on various subjects. The careful selection of memories and the array of characters give this piece the feel of social science—as if he were laying out a taxonomy of the colonized, from the passive resistance of an old poet who refused to meet him to members of the younger generation who aggressively pursued news of all new cultural trends in Japan. Satō felt the need to tell the full story of the colony, not just to satisfy the metropolitan readers' insatiable curiosity about the aborigines, but to offer a more nuanced account that would depict his encounters with Taiwanese intellectuals.[8]

Of the dozen works that resulted from Satō's journey to the colony, "Tale of the Fan" is the best known and artistically most accomplished piece. Structurally "Tale of the Fan" uses a more straightforward narrative structure than the story-within-a-story of the Nishikawa tale discussed later. Nonetheless, complex issues of class, gender, and colonial historiography are concealed under the seemingly simplistic, linear narrative trajectory.

The protagonist, a Japanese journalist stationed in the colony, has befriended a native youth called Segaimin 世外民,[9] a poet who composes in classical Chinese. The two go on an excursion to see the famous Red Fort (Chikanlou; Jpn.: Sekikanrō 赤嵌楼). On their way back, they wander into a desolate fishing village where the narrator, a journalist with a sense of modern poetic sensibility, expounds upon his conception of the "beauty of the ruined" (*kōhai no bi* 荒廃の美) (Satō 1966: 247). Although the complex, multilayered history of the fort and the seaport surrounding it is not lost on the narrator, he insists: "The reason I was so moved by the beauty of Anping seaport was not necessarily its rich history. No matter who the person is or how much they know about this place, all one needs to do is set foot here to see the deterioration of this town. Anyone who has a heart would be aware of its melancholy beauty" (p. 227). Segaimin's enthusiastic commentary on prominent landmarks and historic sites falls on deaf ears: "In fact, I was so young at the time that I was totally uninterested in history. When I saw my friend Segaimin, who was, like me, an unattached young man, relating the past with such reverence, I could only come to the conclusion that a poet infused with Chinese blood is indeed a different breed" (p. 229).

The two wander into an abandoned mansion. Though it is old and dilapidated, the vestiges of past glory and extravagant luxuriance still captivate the narrator. The locals inform them that it had been the mansion of a local merchant named Shen, reputed to be the richest man in southern Taiwan. Although the gold and vermilion posts are tarnished with time, its original splendor can easily be seen:

> Were I a true connoisseur, I probably would have jeered at the dubious taste of this colonial nouveau riche. But exposure to wind and rain had given the place a rustic air and saved it from distasteful vulgarity. Further, since only a portion of the structure remained, it freed the imagination; before lamenting the elements of disharmony, one should delight in the exotic atmosphere. [p. 236]

The pair are astonished to hear a woman's voice from upstairs. Having been stationed in the colony for three years, the narrator has acquired some familiarity with the native language, but this is clearly not the Amoy dialect spoken by most. His native companion, who hesitantly identifies it as Quanzhou dialect, thinks the voice is saying something like, "Why? Why could you not have come earlier?"

Startled, the two quickly leave the ruins. An old lady, after hearing of their bizarre encounter, tells them the haunting story of the old manor. Shen, the last owner, was a fourth-generation immigrant from the southeastern coast of China. His family had amassed great wealth through various devious and cunning methods, including cheating others out of their land. In karmic retribution for their outrageous behavior, the merchant fleet that had brought them handsome profit and an opulent mansion was destroyed overnight in a thundering storm. Then misfortune continued as death claimed one member of the family after another. Eventually Shen's daughter was left alone, impoverished, and dependent on the charity of her neighbors for food. She grew despondent and then deranged, waiting for a fiancé whose ship never arrived. The locals often saw her dressed in gorgeous wedding attire, talking to herself and to her imagined future husband.

The narrator and his native friend disagree on how to interpret their spine-chilling encounter. While Segaimin genuinely believes they have experienced something supernatural, the narrator dismisses it as superstition:

> It seems that Segaimin truly feels there is something uncanny about the dilapidated mansion in Bald Alley. Come to think of it, the story sounds so Chinese. A beautiful woman's spirit left behind in an old abandoned house is a clichéd motif in Chinese literature. The Chinese people must feel a particular affinity for this kind of story, but for me it just won't do. If I were attracted to anything in that house, it would be that everything was large in scale with garish colors. If I could really convey what about it appealed to me, it might be something like a toned-down version of Ukiyoe master Yoshitoshi's frenzied painting. The characters in his paintings are of the robust continental type, and there is a certain modernity in its barbaric character, in which the beauty of the subject coexists with ugliness. A ghost tale is usually set either on a moonless night or under the bright moon; that this one happened in daylight, under the bright hot sun, is its only redeeming feature. Still, it is totally unpersuasive as a ghost story. In spite of this, Segaimin is totally fascinated by it. No, rather he is actually terrified by it! Perhaps he thinks he really had a conversation with a ghost. [p. 245]

The journalist narrator puts on his detective's hat and argues, over the protests of Segaimin, that the voice they heard must have come from a living woman and was directed toward someone other than them.[10]

> "But what about all those people in the village who heard the same words uttered by the same voice all these years?"
> "I don't know," I said. "Because I did not hear what they heard. It was probably people like you, who are fond of ghosts, who heard it. But for me, I don't care a hoot about things that happened in a

past that has nothing to do with me personally. . . . Segaimin, you are just too much of a poet. It's one thing for you to immerse yourself in old traditions. But remember that in the moonlight things reveal themselves vaguely. I can't tell if it is beautiful or ugly, but one can see clearly under the sun!" [pp. 246–247]

Here a casual conversation about apparitions between a Japanese journalist with a modernist bent and a traditionalist native poet turns into a critical discourse on national culture and aestheticism. Contrasts are made, mostly by the narrator, between the old (belief in the old ghost tale) and the new (scientific reasoning against it). By placing this seemingly innocent story within the colonial context, the text exposes its deep implications for imperialism and the colonial process. Thus a discussion of whether an ancient ghost exists suddenly takes an unexpected turn from a casual conversation about the uncanny into a discursive explication of a much larger subject: the historiography of the past. Ghost stories are narratives bound by an unresolved past and a troubled present. Reading ghosts and specters as codified symbols gesturing to the past (history), the narrator (the colonizer) rejects, or perhaps is incapable of hearing, a voice from the past that spoke to the native people long before Japanese colonialists set foot on the island. Repeatedly the narrator averts his eyes from the relics of the past (in this case, the ghost story and the dilapidated ruins) and attempts to neutralize history by redirecting his gaze to an apolitical, universalized aestheticism. The disparate perceptions of the ruins—what the narrator sees and what the native youth Segaimin sees—reflect a disparity in the interpretation of history, in this case the precolonial history of Taiwan:

> The aesthetic conception that something spiritual continues to live on in perished ruins is something rather traditionally Chinese. If I may say so, and don't get angry with me, it seems the taste of a state that has perished (bōkokuteki shumi 亡国的趣味). How can something that has already perished still go on forever? Don't we say it has perished precisely because it is no longer there? [p. 247]

Segaimin protests loudly against this view:

> To have perished and to be in ruins are not the same, are they? Sure, something that has perished is indeed gone. But there remains a living spirit in ruins that are on the verge of perishing. [p. 247]

At this point the discussion of aesthetics turns ontological, revealing an epistemological gap between the narrator and the native youth. Of course, the narrator and the native are both creations of the author, and Segaimin has been set up as a straw man to counter, however feebly, the narrator's self-assured discourse on the history and culture of a conquered other. Satō is careful not to create in the role of colonizer an insensitive, arrogant character. Instead he portrays a modern young man attuned to an unusual aesthetic and impatient with the past. The protagonist repeatedly shifts the focus of his conversation with Segaimin from history to aesthetics—as when he dismisses the supernatural historiography of the site as an anachronistic feature of Chinese culture—and links the garish luxury of the abandoned mansion to the animated paintings of the pop artist Yoshitoshi. The question, then, is whether this erasure—or, to be more precise, eliding of history—by the narrator is an intentional act or an indication that he is incapable of perceiving a past that does not belong to him.

A scene at the beginning of the narrative prefigures the impenetrability of the Other. When the two men first arrive at the dilapidated Red Fort and the history buff Segaimin is busily consulting an ancient map in order to identify various historically significant sites, the narrator, indifferent to the man-made architecture, gazes instead into the ocean:

> Spreading out before my eyes was the muddy sea. It was yellowish brown in color and countless small waves rolled in, one row after another. There are words such as "ten-layered" and "twenty-layered" (*toe hatae* 十重二十重), but nothing in our vocabulary could describe the layer upon layer of waves that rushed in and drew back. These waves stretched out to the horizon, and all were pushing in to the place where we stood. . . . Even the tropical sun just before noon would not reflect off the mucky surface of the waves. This strange sea without reflection . . . Burning white beneath the bright noon sun. A sea that absorbs all the light . . . Amidst this landscape of violent movement not a single sound reverberated. From time to time, a humid, dull breeze like the breath of a malaria patient would brush through. All these images congealed into an inner landscape. The symbols multiplied, filling me with an uneasy feeling like that aroused by a nightmare. No, it was not just the scene. After coming into contact with this seascape, there were two or three times when, recovering from a hard night of drinking, I was frightened by nightmares of dreary seashores. [pp. 229–230]

This is not a casual observation by a random tourist. The disturbing seascape is inhospitable and foreign to this stranger in a strange land. The dark water swallows up the light of the sun and a pall of silence hangs over the constant movement of the waves. The alien landscape of the colonial Other summons nightmarish visions of a terrifying inner landscape. On a conscious level, the narrator is able to dismiss the uncanny remnants of the past by resorting to his modern, rational worldview; but on a more visceral level they impact upon his unconscious and surface in his dreams.

As it turns out, the narrator was correct in identifying the voice they heard as belonging to a living woman, who was using the abandoned manor to rendezvous with her lover. He exults in the triumph of science and rationalism over irrational superstition, but his euphoria is short-lived. The story quickly shifts into a complicated detective novel full of intrigue and mystery. The narrator, to prove his theory to Segaimin, drags him back to the manor. This time they resolutely proceed upstairs and there find an ivory fan upon which is inscribed a chapter of Ban Zhao's "Precepts for Women" 女誡 .[11] This discovery leads the narrator to speculate on the original owner of the fan and its more recent use:

> The elaborate design was appropriate for something that a parent might give his beloved daughter when she was becoming a bride—it must have been from the Shen family, that fan. Then I imagined that reckless, ignorant girl from a poor family in Bald Alley. Guided by her instincts, she had no fear of a house associated with such gruesome legends. Oblivious to what sort of person had experienced what sort of death on it, she lay upon that stately bed, grasping that fan with its inscription on wifely virtues, playing with it, using it to blow cool air on her sweat-drenched lover. [p. 256]

The narrator is quite taken with the idea of an amorous couple using this dilapidated mansion for their illicit trysts. The juxtaposition of modern, lower-class lovers occupying the same bed in which the elite Shen maiden had passed her days upholding the dictates of feudal ethics appealed to his modernist aesthetic. And while he did not believe in the ghost stories surrounding the manor, he enjoyed the air of eerie danger they imparted to the deserted building.

Not long after, a young man is found to have committed suicide in the abandoned manor. The narrator imposes upon Segaimin to investigate. He finds that the body was discovered by the maid of a local merchant, and further investigation reveals that the maid was in fact the lover of the deceased. Her employer had betrothed her against her will to a

Japanese national, and her native lover, out of desperation, had hanged himself above the ancient bed they had shared. It was this maid they had heard in the upper room, several days earlier, awaiting her tardy lover. She is distraught to have been discovered, and a few days later follows him in death.

This story reveals a fundamental truth about the oppressed status of women within the colonial context. In the patriarchal system of traditional Taiwanese society, women seldom had the freedom to determine their own fate. This tale of a maid who can only respond with suicide to the imposition of an undesired marriage could easily be cast as a modern protest against the feudalistic disenfranchisement of women. By placing the events in a colonial context, with the unwanted suitor a Japanese and the true love a native Taiwanese, Satō Haruo adds a new layer of meaning. It is now a Japanese colonizer who would steal the lover of a colonized native, a man who is driven to suicide in order to protest the appropriation of his chosen mate.

Colonial Desire and Colonial Patronage: "Spring on the Rice River"

The interaction of native women and colonizing men is also the theme of a short story by Nishikawa Mitsuru, "Spring on the Rice River," which tells of a romantic relationship between the narrator (a Japanese man) and a Taiwanese prostitute.

The story begins with a Japanese man meeting a Taiwanese *geidan* 芸姐,[12] Mari (her professional name), whom he has been seeing for about a year. It is the evening of the Lantern Festival, and Mari suggests they visit the temple of the Lord of the Dark Altar, the god of wealth.[13] The protagonist's romantic sentiment is dampened a bit when he hears Mari pray to the god for money. Later they visit Mari's simple but tidy apartment atop a tea merchant's house by the river, where the protagonist happens to find a photograph of a teenaged boy. Forced to reassess his estimation of Mari, he now sees her actions as driven by the altruistic love of a mother for a son. But he also decides, without informing Mari, that he will not see her again so that she can be a strong mother to her son. Two months later a young boy appears, begging him to go see his mother. Realizing that this must be Mari's son, he accompanies him and finds Mari on her deathbed. Before she loses consciousness for the last time, they share a sentimental moment gazing at the mountain across the river that represents Mari's unfulfilled dream for a better life.

This tale has all the trademarks of Nishikawa's romantic touch. The setting is not accidental. The Rice River is a poetic name for the Tamsui (Danshui 淡水) River that flows south to north along the border of Taipei. The city developed along the river, and certain areas on its banks are among the oldest districts. Most Japanese lived in the central and southern parts of the city, but Nishikawa felt a particular affection for the northern area, called Daitōtei, where traditional Taiwanese buildings mixed with the Western-style residential houses of foreign merchants. In his autobiography Nishikawa later reminisced about the various neighborhoods of Taipei:

> Of all the various old sections of town, I have very little interest in Banka because it is a purely Chinese-style (Shinafū 支那風) neighborhood.[14] Because foreigners (ikokujin 異国人) lived in Daitōtei, it had a good mixture of East and West that was very attractive to me. . . . There was hardly a day when I did not walk through its streets at least once. [Shimomura et al. 1995: 418]

This passage captures Nishikawa's romantic view of Taiwan. He is fascinated with Taiwan, but on his own terms. Despite his often proclaimed affection for the land, he is not really interested in the most traditional, purely "Chinese," mode of beauty. What interests him is the exotic amalgamation of East and West. It is within this exotic hybrid landscape that Nishikawa anchors his border-crossing romance.

Nishikawa's taste for the exotic is evident in his description of the temple festival. The vivid sights and sounds of the local festival—the firecrackers, a noisy percussion band, a dancing palanquin that carries the statue of the god, the colorful flickering of the lanterns—typify Nishikawa's ethnographic narration, lively, richly textured representations that assault the reader's senses. But the narrator is disenchanted by the utilitarian aspect of the festival—requesting monetary benefit from the gods. Indeed Nishikawa's treatment of the festival reveals a key limitation of colonial texts: they are characterized by an inability to see beyond surface phenomena and understand the full cultural significance of objects and events. One advantage of a postcolonial reading of literary works is that it uncovers the blind spots of colonial authors. The bustle of activity surrounding the festival has a purpose and a meaning in the context of Taiwanese society; by ignoring or consciously rejecting this cultural import, Nishikawa is committing an act of violence—ripping attractive bits of culture from their context and serving them up to a Japanese audience as tasty exotica. Colonial romanticism both reveals (the surface beauty) and conceals (the social significance) at the same time.

From the hustle and bustle of the street, we are led to Mari's quiet attic room with its view of the beautiful villas belonging to foreigners (Westerners) built on the slopes of Mount Datun across the Tamsui River. A pleasing fragrance of tea wafts through the room from the teashop downstairs while Mari recites traditional poems written for her by the famous poet Lian Yatang,[15] creating a spellbinding moment of repose for the protagonist. The tranquillity is broken, however, when he happens upon the photo of an adolescent who turns out to be Mari's son. Mari explains that her husband died many years ago when she was only eighteen. Her parents advised her to sell the baby and re-marry, but she chose to support him herself by becoming a courtesan. Mari is proud of the fact that she has been able to support her son through middle school, and now he is about to graduate.

Moved by her devotion, the protagonist sees her in a new light—as a "strong mother" doing her best for her son—and is forced to recon-sider the disdain he felt hearing her prayers for good fortune. Since the boy is about to graduate from middle school, he resolves to buy him a watch as a graduation gift. As he is leaving, she gives him a book of poetry by Lian Yatang and he ponders briefly the distinguished old gentleman who would visit courtesans and teach them traditional po-etry. He then muses on his relationship with Mari: "If at this point I were to go on meeting frequently with this woman, I don't know how deep a relationship we might fall into, and that certainly would not bring her happiness. I have to let her live her life as a strong mother." The protagonist portrays his decision to sever relations with Mari as a benevolent act of self-sacrifice. The bleak financial and emotional con-sequences for Mari are only hinted at in the text.

Nishikawa's portrayal of Mari is not simply that of a native subaltern female signifier. Mari has a past, though an unfortunate one, and she looks forward to her son's future with hope. The narrator, by contrast, is an enigmatic cipher about whom we know next to nothing. Although this makes the viewed object, Mari, accessible to the reader, it establishes an unbalanced power relationship between the two. The lack of meaningful dialogue between Mari and the narrator leads to various misunderstand-ings. Looking out the window of Mari's apartment, the narrator sees only a misty river and setting sun; Mari sees beyond the river to the villas of the foreign merchants on the mountainside that represent her aspirations for a better life and social mobility. The colonial narrator, perpetually a visitor in the colonized landscape, has the luxury of appreciating it in a purely aesthetic fashion; to Mari, the landscape is inscribed with all the limitations and potentialities of her life. When Mari reveals the private details of her past and present, the narrator is impressed, even moved, but he reciprocates only with a watch for her son and, because he cannot envision a future for the two of them, decides not to see her again. Colonial patronage and colonial desire are withdrawn at the same time.

By avoiding the formulaic structure of a romance between colonizer man and subaltern woman, bounded by erotic desire and domination, Nishikawa produces an innovative story. But the theme of motherhood draws him into a different ideological trap. Maternal images were exploited during the war to exhort women to contribute to the war effort by giving birth, supporting the government's domestic agenda, and enthusiastically sacrificing their older sons to the military.[16] The death of Mari's first husband and father of her child can be read symbolically as the loss of the fatherland, China. When Mari reveals to the narrator her role as a mother, he can no longer see her as merely a sexual object to be enjoyed and appreciated; a historical link with the past is added to Mari's sexualized body. Once the narrator knows Mari to be a mother, his relationship to her takes on new meaning and responsibilities. Wary of a role in raising the next generation, the narrator retreats. Ironically, with her death he is left alone to deal with the boy.

Another provocative element of the story is the relationship of Lian Yatang, the native historian, to the amateur history buff-cum-narrator. These two—one a native poet, the other a colonial literatus—are connected only through the body of the subaltern female. The narrator is at first bemused by the idea of this aged scholar visiting courtesans, but his respect is renewed when he later discovers that Lian's visits were to teach Mari poetry. It is Lian's lyrics that Mari sings wistfully while gazing off to Mount Datun; they encapsulate her melancholy and her dreams. This is not the only story of Nishikawa's in which Lian Yatang plays a role. His name surfaces again in the next story we will discuss, "Record of the Red Fort," a story with obvious ties to Satō Haruo's "Tale of the Fan," where the theme of history, its reliability, and its relation to modernity again comes to the forefront.

"Record of the Red Fort"

"Sekikanki" 赤嵌記 ("Record of the Red Fort") was written in 1940, the same year as "Spring on the Rice River." It too was published in *Bungei*

Taiwan, but the two stories could not be more different in terms of style, atmosphere, and content.[17] Nevertheless they share an underlying anxiety that is common to much of colonial literature. At first glance, "Spring on the Rice River" seems a quiet reflection on a brief encounter between a Japanese man and a native woman, whereas "Record of the Red Fort" is an ambitious treatment of Taiwanese history and colonial politics. Reading these stories together with "Tale of the Fan" allows us to locate Nishikawa in the larger discourse of a distinct brand of colonial romanticism which claims Satō as one of its founding fathers while, at the same time, illustrating the conceptual gap that separates the traveler Satō, who visited Taiwan only briefly, from the expatriate Nishikawa.

Nishikawa is known for poems and short stories infused with romantic sentimentality. His interest in history is not so often discussed, but it sheds light on the psychological components of Nishikawa as a colonial writer. Although Nishikawa had lived in Taiwan since age two, his interest in Taiwanese history began only after his return from a six-year stay in Tokyo (1927–1933). In an essay published in the magazine *Taiwan jihō* 台湾時報 (February 1938) he confessed:

> I was fifteen when I first set foot in Japan (*naichi*) and was embraced by its mountains and rivers. It was then, for the first time, that I was able to understand the indescribable sadness I have always felt toward the place called Taiwan. That is a sadness which came from, perhaps I am using the wrong words, not having a history. . . . For several years after I came back to Taiwan, I was obsessed with discovering the history of Taiwan. . . . I came to understand the absurdity of my childlike opinion that Taiwan had no history; I could not help but be angry with myself. But then, on further reflection, I realized that the situation is not my fault alone. When we were young, how much were we taught about the history of Taiwan before it came into our possession? Only about Hamada Yahei,[18] Zheng Chenggong, and Wu Feng. After that, it was nothing but Japanese history.

Nishikawa's displeasure at being shortchanged on Taiwanese history led him to make use of historical materials in his fiction. His guide was Lian Yatang's *Taiwan tongshi* 台湾通史 ("Comprehensive history of Taiwan"), the first systematic history of Taiwan written from a native's point of view. In addition to being the preeminent historian of his day, Lian was also a renowned poet and, as we have seen in "Spring on the Rice River," Nishikawa often quotes bits and pieces of Lian's poetry and essays in his stories. Nishikawa's respect and fondness for Lian's writings is evident in his various essays and stories. Lian was a pioneering poet and historian who felt the need to record Taiwanese history for posterity. In the preface to his history of Taiwan, Lian pointed out the pressing need for a detailed and correct record of the island's history. His impulse to record the Taiwanese past through historical narrative coincides with Nishikawa's passion in discovering Taiwanese history. In his usual hyperbolic way, Nishikawa exclaims:

> Oh, Taiwan! You are the limitless treasure house of history; the gallery of blooming religions; the unpolished daemon of historical studies. Oh, Taiwan, you are the glorious island where cultures of the West and the East come together. I am delighted to live here. My enthusiasm overflows for the history that ought to be discovered.[19]

"Record of the Red Fort" is Nishikawa's attempt to create a fictional historical tale that will relate to an important past event. In this tale, full of minute details drawn from historical sources, we see a struggle playing out between the author's urge to romanticize exotic Taiwan and his desire to treat Taiwan's history faithfully. The Red Fort of the title refers to Fort Provintia, constructed by the Dutch in what was to become Tainan city. When Zheng Chenggong (Koxinga) drove out the Dutch in 1661, he renamed the city Chengtianfu (Inheriting Heaven prefecture) and used the fort as his headquarters. From the continent Zheng brought his family, his private army, and their families, who settled and cultivated the lands around the castle. When Zheng and his army were defeated by the Manchu Qing regime in 1683, locals reverted to using the aboriginal term for the area, "Cha-ka-mu," which was pronounced "chhiah-kham" in the local Southern Min dialect; because the fort was built of brick, characters with this pronunciation meaning "red fort" 赤嵌 were used to transcribe the sound. This was then read "sekikan" in Japanese and "chikan" in Mandarin. The various names for this spot—from Cha-ka-mu to Provintia to Chengtianfu to Chhiah-kham to Sekikan to Chikan—parallel the course of Taiwan's colonial history over the last four hundred years. The Red Fort occupied the cultural and political center of the island until the Japanese colonial government established the modern capital in the northern city Taipei at the end of the nineteenth century. Renovated many times, it is still an important landmark and tourist site.

What piqued Nishikawa's curiosity about this historical edifice, an old fort, fallen into disrepair in a desolate part of town? Although Nishikawa had lived in Taiwan since the age of two, he rarely visited the south. For him, the southern part of the island, in particular Tainan, represented the old Taiwan. Relying primarily on voluminous historical sources, Nishikawa produced a vivid, detailed portrayal of the fort and its neighborhood as it existed both in his day and in the seventeenth century.

The story has a dual structure: a frame story set in the contemporary period introduces a tale from three hundred years earlier. As the story begins, the narrator, a famous Japanese author who has come to Tainan to lecture on the preservation of Taiwanese culture, visits the Red Fort about which he has heard so much. There he encounters a Taiwanese youth, Chen, and they strike up a conversation. The young man had been present at the public talk the day before, where the narrator mentioned that he had not yet visited the famous castle. Hoping to speak to him in private, Chen has waited there the whole day on the chance that the writer might decide to pay a visit to the famous spot. Chen urges him to write about the history of the fort, but the narrator says he is not interested in history. He does, however, indicate that he would consider writing a romantic tale about young lovers rendezvousing there under the moonlight. Chen promises to take the narrator to a pleasure house that evening to help him find inspiration for the love story.

At first the writer is suspicious of the young man's intentions, but then he decides to go on the adventure after all. Before meeting the young man that evening, he wanders into a frame shop selling old folk prints and is intrigued by an ink painting depicting a young couple accompanied by a passage from a popular folksong indicating that the figures in the drawing were the daughter of Lord Wenzheng (a.k.a. Chen Yonghua 陳永華) and her husband.[20] Charmed by the artless folk depictions, the narrator is willing to pay a handsome sum for the painting, but the shop owner's mother stubbornly objects to the sale.

Chen appears—now dressed in traditional Chinese garb rather than a Western suit—and takes the narrator to several spots of historical interest, finally arriving at an elegant abode where they meet a beautiful woman. The evening is filled with delightful delicacies, exquisite tea, and lively discussions of poetry. In the course of the evening, the young couple tells the author a tale of Zheng Chenggong's heirs quite at variance with that recorded in Lian Yatang's authoritative history. In this version, the succession within the Zheng family was surrounded by bloody intrigues. The eldest grandson of Zheng Chenggong and designated heir, Kezang, aided by his father-in-law, Lord Wenzheng, thought to pursue Chenggong's unachieved goals in restoring the overthrown Ming empire and reestablishing the maritime dominance in the South Seas and Southeast Asia that China had enjoyed during the early years of the Ming dynasty. Kezang's uncles, however, were enamored of the easy life of plenty they had established on Taiwan and wanted nothing of their nephew's grand plans. They spread rumors that he was illegitimate, murdered him and his family, then set his younger brother Keshuang in his place.

The narrator leaves the house doubting the reliability of this version of events, but several days later he receives from the young man a book called *Unofficial Record of Taiwan* (*Taiwan waiji* 台湾外記) that, like the painting the old lady in the print shop refused to sell, supports this alternative account.[21] Perusing this book, the writer is intrigued and decides to pay another call on the young man. But in tracing the return address on the package he comes to an old, dilapidated temple, a memorial hall of the Chen clan with plaques of generations of the deceased:

> These are the spirit tablets of Chen Yonghua and his wife. . . . So this old temple was the official Chen residence during the reign of Zheng Chenggong. . . . It was in this mansion that Yonghua died his anguished death. I felt the furious power of history overtake me and could hardly breathe. . . .
>
> The temple turned darker. The inner courtyard was dead silent. Except for the giant candle stands, now covered with spiderwebs, there was not a shadow of another human being. I was immobilized before the spirit tablets, terrified by the power of the invisible spirits who had summoned me here. Perhaps the young man Chen and the beautiful woman were the ghosts of Kezang and his wife the Lady Chen, daughter of Wenzheng, that people of old had often seen. . . . Certainly I have to maintain my composure. There is just no way, in this day and age, that ghosts only fit to trick small children would appear. The young man must be a descendant of the Chen clan whose fate is tied up with this ancestral temple. Nevertheless, can we not assume that it was indeed the influence of Kezang and his wife that led the young man to go to the trouble of wresting it out of the hands of historians and imparting to me, over my protests, the true story of the third-generation descendants of Lord Yanping [Zheng Chenggong]? Spirits, rest in peace! I will most likely not meet the young man again. I will stop trying to figure out the old song of Lord Wenzheng and his daugh-

ter. Precisely by leaving the song ambiguous, I can give the tale a deeper resonance. I tried to drag my heavy feet away from the hundred generations of the Chen ancestral tablets. [Nakajima Toshio and Kawahara Isao 1998, 1:234–235]

Colonial Power vs. Native Resistance

Gender and history intersect in these tales. The courtesan Mari in "Spring on the Rice River" is symbolic mediator between two men: a colonizing intellectual and a colonized poet/historian. Knowledge of Mari's history leads the narrator to withdraw his colonial desire and patronage from her. In "Tale of the Fan," the focus is on a dialogue about the aesthetics and interpretation of history as mediated by different modern cultures. Gender becomes an important theme of the second half of the book. The inscription on the fan is an ancient code defining proper conduct for women. Both the Shen maiden—determined to wait for her betrothed year after year—and the young maid—refusing to accept an arranged marriage because she had already given herself to another—can be said to be following the spirit of the "Precepts for Women," if not their letter. The influence of this morality is evident in "Record of the Red Fort," as well. One of the sites on the protagonist's guided tour of the old city is the palace of the Southern Ming emperor in exile; one of the most famous features is a giant rafter from which five courtesans of this ill-fated emperor hanged themselves following his defeat. After Kezang's assassination, his wife, née Chen, was granted permission to follow her husband to the other world.

A traditional conception of female virtues—chastity, for example, and loyalty to male relations—links these three tales. Both Satō Haruo and Nishikawa Mitsuru inscribe into their texts a conventional, Confucian view of gender. Although colonial subjects like Segaimin have undergone a profound transformation in their thinking (witness Segaimin's feeble defense when faced with the protagonist's contempt for Chinese culture and history), gender dynamics remain unchanged. In fact, were the standard for women applied to native men in the colonial situation, the dictum that "a chaste woman does not serve two husbands" (*zhennü bugeng erfu* 貞女不更二夫) would indicate that the menfolk must choose the ethnic, cultural, and linguistic identities of their birth culture rather than those of the colonizing power, or at least choose between the two.[22]

Nishikawa's "Record of the Red Fort" takes Satō Haruo's "Tale of the

Fan" as its pretext and shares several similarities in both subject matter and narrative structure.[23] All three stories revolve around issues of gender, historiography, and romantic colonialism. "Tale of the Fan" was hailed as a masterpiece representing the best of *ikoku bungaku* and remains the most famous piece of fiction about Taiwan in Japanese.[24] Fifteen years after its first publication, Nishikawa felt the need to update the story—to give it a fresh rendering that fit into the political and social context of the colony in the 1940s. By reading these two narratives closely side by side, one sees subtle differences that reflect the different stages of coloniality and the different positionalities of the two romantic writers. Satō's trip to the island occurred after the armed rebellions had been quelled and the colony had settled into a relatively calm period of Japanese rule. Nishikawa's tale is set in the early 1940s, when the Pacific War was intensifying and total mobilization was in effect throughout the empire.

Both texts employ reluctant narrators who at first refuse to become embroiled in the history of the natives. They elide the history that the natives call to their attention with aestheticism (in "Tale of the Fan") and romanticism (in "Record of the Red Fort"). While the historical connection with the past in "Tale of the Fan" is symbolically represented by a haunting ghost story, Nishikawa seems determined to bring in the real history. His bookish side shows itself in his meticulous research on Zheng Chenggong—drawing not only on the standard version by Lian Yatang but also on earlier, more anecdotal, sources.

By 1940, when Nishikawa's "Record of the Red Fort" was written, the ideological apparatus of the Greater East Asian Coprosperity Sphere was in place. The Red Fort, which represents the multilayered history of the island, was again turned into a symbol that served its particular time and historical moment. In a poem by Nishikawa titled "Attacking the Red Fort" ("Sekikan kōryaku no uta" 赤嵌攻略の歌),[25] it represents the conflict between East and West:

> Defeat the Dutch! Head off Koiette!
> The twenty-five thousand soldiers roared excitedly.
> A will that reached into the sky, Koxinga.

The poem begins with the introduction of the two pivotal figures in the battle between the Chinese and the Dutch: Koxinga (a.k.a. Zheng Chenggong) and the Dutch commander. It then proceeds to describe, scene by scene, the actual battle, with the Red Fort burned by the escaping Dutch soldiers. The final stanza is a shout of victory:

East is East. West is West.
We had driven those blue-eyed, red-haired urchins to the end of
    the West.
Now the great enterprise of restoring the mandate has succeeded.
He smiles, Koxinga.

In this poem the Red Fort and Zheng Chenggong become icons for the resistance to Western colonialism. A Ming loyalist's action—capturing an island from which to resist the Manchus who had conquered China—was refashioned into a triumph of East over West in the context of 1940s Japanese colonial discourse.

There is further evidence that Nishikawa's appropriation of the Zheng Chenggong segment of native history was intended to serve other ends. In rejecting Lian Yatang's official version of history and opting for an alternative account, Nishikawa is subverting the position he granted Lian in "Spring on the Rice River," where Lian functions as a sort of gatekeeper for traditional Taiwanese poetry. Why, then, would he turn to the obscure account in Jiang Risheng's *Taiwan waiji* for this particular narrative? The key would seem to be the issue of the legitimate succession after the death of Zheng Jing. By casting doubt on the legitimacy of Zheng Keshuang and promoting the position of Zheng Kezang instead, Nishikawa is arguing for the legitimacy of Kezang's plan to expand Chinese rule to Southeast Asia and the South Pacific—a plan with obvious parallels to the contemporary Japanese doctrine of advancing southward and expanding the Greater East Asian Coprosperity Sphere. "Record of the Red Fort" is a tightly constructed narrative full of historical characters and events taken from historical sources. Here and there, however, one can detect the contemporary ideological idioms seeping through the veneer of the historical past. Before he is murdered by his political rivals, Kezang lays out his scheme for governance:

> Once Kezang was made regent, he quickly consulted with Lord Wenzheng and immediately embarked on the implementation of a *new order* (*shintaisei* 新体制) and the reform of social customs. He renewed the internal political structure, putting public interest first. Even close relatives were no longer given favors. [Nakajima Toshio and Kawahara Isao 1988, 1:218; emphasis added]

The term "new order," anachronous in this context, refers to the New Order movement of 1940, which tried to centralize power and improve bureaucratic control of local affairs throughout the empire. At another point, we read a description of the long-term plans of Kezang and Lord Wencheng:

> Kezang strategized with Lord Wencheng. Hoping to salvage something from his father's failed attack on the continental coast, he thought of giving up on China. Instead, someday, by *enriching the state and strengthening the military* (*fukoku kyōhei* 富国強兵), they might make alliance with Spain, conquer Vietnam and Burma, and rebuild the Great Ming Dynasty with Taiwan as its base. [p. 218; emphasis added]

The concept of "enriching the state and strengthening the military," a common phrase in the modernization movements of both China and Japan and a notion circulated by the Japanese in the late 1930s, is anachronistic in the seventeenth century. Kezang's aspirations for a southern empire are jarring in the context of the tale's setting as well, but dovetailed with current Japanese strategy. After the initial focus on Taiwan as Japan's first colony and later the fascination with the aborigines, Taiwan had receded in the minds of the public as the empire's attention turned to North China, Manchuria, and Mongolia. As the Pacific War approached and the concept of a Greater East Asian Coprosperity Sphere was promoted more vigorously, popular discourse focused again on Taiwan as the gateway to the South. Nishikawa welcomed this new attention and promoted this idea through an organization called the Southern Culture Club (Nampō Bunka Kurabu 南方文化クラブ), a research body that set out to compile the massive eight-volume *History of Taiwanese Culture* (*Taiwan bunkashi* 台湾文化史). Nishikawa's editorial strategy was not, however, without its risks. Criticism of the complacent regime of Zheng Keshuang could be interpreted as a hidden criticism of the colonial authority's lack of enthusiasm in promoting the southern advance strategy.

Fujii Shōzō, in his intertextual reading of "Record of the Red Fort" and "Tale of the Fan," suggests that Nishikawa borrowed the narrative structure of Satō's exotic tale, which he believes is essentially an expression of Taiwanese nationalism, and retold it as a romantic historical narrative that mirrored the official ideology of his day concerning the South (Fujii 1998: 123). Fujii also notes with irony that only seven years after the assassination of Kezang, Zheng family rule came to an end in Taiwan and wonders why Japanese intellectuals of the day could not foresee that five years later the empire would collapse. And this raises larger questions: "Can any colonizer truly understand the history of the native Other and participate in its future? Can the disruption of history caused by colonial intervention be mended? Satō evades native history by focusing on grand aesthetic theories; Nishikawa recuperates the past in order to serve the present.

Yasuda Yojūrō 保田与重郎 (1910–1981) articulated this dilemma of competing histories in his travelogue *Mōkyō* 蒙彊 (Mongolia and Xinjiang, 1938), which recorded a trip he took with a group of Japanese writers to North China and the far-flung regions of Mongolia and Xinjiang. As the leading advocate of the increasingly nationalistic Japanese romantic school (*Nihon rōman ha* 日本浪漫派), he was opposed to left-leaning, progressive intellectuals who thought Japan should take a more tolerant stance toward interpreting China's history:

> From a purely speculative standpoint: this modern intellectualism has clearly proved ineffectual in dealing with the human world. It is possible for a fleeting moment *(shunkan)* for our thoughts to take the "Japan" position as Japanese people. This is not to speak and act with the presumption that we are Japanese. We speak from those fleeting moments when we are bearers of our ancestors, history, classics, and traditions. In all those fleeting moments, we and our heritage stand in the midst of limitless history. . . . We are the Japanese people who lived through the Taika Reform, Minamoto no Yoritomo, the Tokugawa period, and the personal administration of the Meiji emperor. When we speak of looking at things from the standpoint of the Chinese people, is it really possible for us to think in the mode of a people who have gone through the early Ming dynasty, late Ming dynasty, early Qing dynasty, and late Qing dynasty? To think of putting oneself in the place of the Chinese, whether through conjecture or spontaneously, this is perhaps the current trend of intellectual purists, but for me it is total nonsense.[26]

Colonial power inevitably contends with native resistance to control the history of the colonized nation. In the case of Taiwan, Japan thought first to efface its Chinese history and replace it with Japanese history, just as it worked to eliminate the local language and replace it with standard Japanese. Nishikawa, educated in Taiwan, had learned so little about Taiwanese history that at one time he suspected Taiwan had no history. With a little research, however, he discovered Taiwan's long, colorful history and, digging a bit deeper, found an indigenous alternative view of the past that could both subvert the traditional understanding and further the interests of the Japanese empire. But just as the protagonist of "Tale of the Fan" stares into the sea, seeing only the impenetrability of the past, Nishikawa was oblivious to the significance of the parallels he was drawing between the policies of the Japanese empire and actions of the doomed last ruler of a perished state. Ultimately both authors resort to the uncanny to invoke an aporia that will elide the differences in historical vision growing out of the master/subject dichotomy.

Romanticizing History

Satō Haruo was a member of the Japanese romantic school and Nishikawa Mitsuru was strongly influenced by it.[27] From the mid-1930s to the early 1940s, this school filled the void left by the collapse of the Proletarian Literature movement. Riding the tide of a literary and cultural renaissance (*bungei fukkō* 文芸復興), the Japanese romantic school rose to prominence in 1935.[28] Drawing together such writers as Kamei Katsuichirō 亀井勝一郎 (1907–1966), Nakatani Takao 中谷孝雄 (1901–?), and Yasuda Yojūrō, the group sought to create a new romanticism that could articulate, from an indigenous ethnic point of view, a past that could capture the rapidly waning difference between Japanese and Western culture.

One of the early missions of the Japanese romantic school was to reevaluate the accomplishments of the Meiji era in prose and poetry, which they considered significant, and use it as a counterweight to westernization. It sought to make a distinction between a nationalist discourse by the nation-state and one articulated by the ethnic masses *(minzoku; minshū)*. Karatani Kōjin points out a subtle difference between Meiji romanticism, which saw "nature" as represented in the *Manyōshū* as the true origin of romanticism, and the Japanese romantic school of the mid-1930s, which valorized the artificial and the beauty of decadence (Karatani 1997b: 168–170). This retrogressive search for an illusive past led the group toward a reevaluation of the Japanese classics and other artifacts of antiquity. The cultural identity crisis felt by the intellectuals of the time led them to search for cultural uniqueness (*bunkateki tokushushugi* 文化的特殊主義) (Doak 1994; 1999: 31). In this sense, Yanagita's development of a Japanese national ethnology and the essentialization of a "common folk" (*jōmin* 常民), Watsuji Tetsurō's discourse on the Japanese landscape (*fūdo* 風土), or Tanizaki Junichirō's return to the classics (though he was less interested in nationalism) can all be seen as related to the Japanese romantic school's program.

The school also was heavily influenced by German romanticism, particularly in its view of history. The German romantics believed that time—past, present, and future—can only be conceptualized through memory and unified through the imagination. In a sense, the Japanese romantic school was striving to reach a new romantic language via realism and to exoticize history in order to emphasize cultural differences.[29] In their historical tales, therefore, Satō and Nishikawa were not historicizing romance but romanticizing history.

This leads us back to the characterization of Nishikawa Mitsuru's literature by his contemporaries, both Japanese expatriates and Taiwanese, as romantic. His activities in the colony have to be viewed within the larger cultural discourse of the time. His romantic tendency in poetry and prose, his collecting of objets d'art, his interests in folklore and ethnography—all were part and parcel of this search for the lost (colonial) past. In Nishikawa we see both trafficking and cross-fertilization between the metropolitan culture and the colony.

FIGURE 1. Prince Kitashirakawa arrives in Taiwan to take possession for Japan in 1895. [He Kaozhu, *Photo Chronicle of Taiwan (1895–1945)*, p. 101]

FIGURE 2. Editorial cartoon from 1923 depicting major events of that year. The pair of Shinto gods are Takasago, whose name was bestowed upon the Taiwanese aborigines then in commemoration of the visit of the future Emperor Hirohito. [Dai Baocun, *Manhua Taiwan nianshi* (Taipei: Qianwei, 2000): 76]

FIGURE 3. *(Right)* Nakajima Atsushi.
[Nakajima Atsuhi 1962: ii]

FIGURE 4. *(Below)* Taiwanese girls were
trained in Japanese culture. Here they
learn tea ceremony, ikebana, kendo,
and archery. [n.a., *Witness—the Colonial
Taiwan 1895–1945*, v. 1, p. 199]

FIGURE 5. *(Left)* Nishikawa Mitsuru. [Nakajima Toshio and Kawahara Isao 1999: v. 1, p. 7]

FIGURE 6. *(Below)* The coterie of *Bungei Taiwan* in 1941. Nishikawa Mitsuru is the second from the right in the front row. [Nakajima and Kawahara 1998: v. 1, frontispiece]

FIGURE 7. Lü Heruo as a young man. [Nakajima and Kawahara 1999: v. 2, p. 7]

FIGURE 8. *(Right)* Zhang Wenhuan. [Nakajima and Kawahara 1999: v. 4, p. 7]

FIGURE 9. *(Below)* Poster warning against letting water buffalo graze freely. The conflict between water buffalo and modern transportation is a theme in Lü Heruo's story, "Oxcart." [n.a., *Witness—the Colonial Taiwan 1895–1945*, v. 2, p. 113]

FIGURE 10. Hijikata Hisao painting of South Seas women. [Minami-Taiheiyò ni roman wo motometa Hijikata Hisao ten, image 6]

FIGURE 11. Three aborigines. The English caption identifies them as head hunters. [n.a., *Witness—the Colonial Taiwan 1895–1945*, v. 2, p. 20]

FIGURE 12. Aborigine hunters from the Alishan region. [He Kaozhu, *Photo Chronicle of Taiwan (1895–1945)*, p. 115]

Figure 13. Civilized or "cooked" aborigines. [He Kaozhu, *Photo Chronicle of Taiwan (1895–1945)*, p. 101]

Figure 14. Hayashi Fumiko and friends travel in Taiwan. Some of the younger women have elected to "go native."

PART III

THE EMPIRE WRITES
BACK

Language Policy and Cultural Identity

IN THE PRECEEDING CHAPTERS I have concentrated on the vicissitudes of the native informant as a figure in literary representations by Japanese colonial writers. Now I turn to works written by the native writers themselves and would remind the reader of a point made earlier: not all colonial literature is, or should be, anticolonial. In the Taiwanese literary tradition we see the full gamut of positions ranging from complete rejection of the colonizing culture to willing acceptance and assimilation.

In Part III, after exploring language as a vehicle for literature in Japan's oldest colony, I deal with Japanese texts written by native Taiwanese writers during the colonial period. The term "native" warrants clarification since the authors I treat are all descendants of immigrants who came from the mainland over the last four hundred years. Before their arrival, various tribes of indigenous peoples lived throughout the island.[1] The infusion of Han Chinese from the Fujian and Guangdong areas into Taiwan was a kind of migrant colonization not dissimilar to the British colonization of North America and other parts of the world. The Han ethnic group in Taiwan consists mainly of immigrants from Quanzhou and Zhangzhou in Fujian province and Hakka people from the Guangdong area. In addition to conflicts between these Han immigrants and indigenous peoples, there were schisms among the Chinese resulting from regionalism and disputes over land and water rights. Before the Japanese took over, violence among various armed, clan-based groups was not unusual (Tsurumi 1977: 7). The Japanese colonial authorities were well aware of these internal conflicts and often exploited them to their own advantage. Nonetheless, in relation to Japanese colonial administrators and settlers, as well as the later influx of mainlanders after World War II, this earlier wave of Han Chinese immigrants can be considered indigenized natives.

The following chapters look at the literary creations of two groups of native writers who were historically considered to be on opposite sides of the spectrum: the nativist writers asserted, however subtly, a cultural identity that was different from the dominant imperial discourse; the *Kōmin,* or imperial-subject writers, submitted to that imperial ideology and participated in that discourse. My analysis focuses primarily on texts in which the cultures of the colonizer and the colonized intersect. Among nativist writers I consider Yang Kui and Lü Heruo. For the second group, the imperial-subject writers, I examine stories by Zhou Jinpo and Chen Huoquan.

The polarized reading of these two bodies of literature usually occurs along lines of national identity and is deeply entangled with the issue of colonial agency and individual subjectivity. As we shall see, however, the lines are often less clear-cut than one might think. While there is a distinct difference in the stances of these two groups of writers, there are also significant similarities. All belonged to the intellectual elite of the native society, and all shared the exile experience of being separated from their cultural and ethnic origins. They are of a new generation—an in-between class of colonially educated natives. They were placed in situations that required them to negotiate their positions between the newly acquired social and cultural practices of the colonizer and the old traditions of their native land.

The issues of agency, subaltern subjectivity, ethnic and cultural identity, and the entanglement of native traditionalism and (colonial) modernism are concerns shared by nativist and imperial-subject writers alike. Literary texts do not simply reflect dominant ideologies; they also militate against them or contain elements that cannot be reconciled with them. As we shall see shortly, the texts of both the nativist and imperial-subject writers demonstrate a complex articulation between the individual and his sociopolitical context that resulted in a rich cross-fertilization of multilingual literary imaginations.

Linguistic and Cultural Identity in Colonial Taiwan

Before taking up Japanese colonial literature in Taiwan, we must first consider issues of colonial language policy, the educational apparatus, and various socioeconomic factors that created an environment which nurtured a common intellectual language. In the following sections we will look at the promotion (from the colonizers' perspective) or formation (from the vantage point of the colonized) of linguistic and cultural identity to provide a context for understanding Taiwan's colonial literary production.

Language is both a primary vehicle for the transmission of group culture and a badge of national identification; it possesses the power to signal ethnicity and express national identity. Since language plays a crucial role in defining an individual, an ethnic group, and a nation, a culture molded by a language is an incubator that fosters a shared identity. Languages, like cultures, are constantly impinging upon each other's territories, transforming the Other and being transformed at the same time. The transformations transpire through peaceful interactions and adaptations; migrations and diasporas; and, of course, forced domination through warfare and other political processes.

Colonial language encounters, like many other aspects of colonialism, are characterized by an asymmetric power relationship—in this case, between the languages of the colonizer and the colonized. For the Japanese, there is no more sensitive issue than the purity and spirituality of their language. The *kotodama* 言霊, the ancient belief that words carry potent mystic power, was a central part of Japanese linguistic identity as early as the time of the *Kojiki* and *Manyōshū* (eighth century).[2] In his famed preface (*jo* 序) to the first imperial *waka* anthology, the *Kokinshū* (Collection of ancient and modern poems; 905 A.D.), Ki no Tsurayuki delineated a distinctive Japanese poetic spirit that distinguishes Japanese poems from the Chinese poetic tradition, which has had such a dominant influence in East Asia. The process of essentializing the national language was continued by scholars of the nativist National Learning (*kokugaku*) movement and reached its zenith when the ideology of a supreme imperial subjectivity, as encoded in the Imperial Rescript on Education (*Kyōiku chokugo* 教育勅語, 1890), was applied to Japan's colonial expansions. The Japanese language became the primary tool for the administration of its colonies.

The Japanese language was also employed to promote the assimilation of colonial subjects to Japanese culture. It has been claimed that

Japanese colonialism is more closely related to the French variety than to the British. As early as 1937, the scholar of colonialism Yanaihara Tadao pointed out several similarities. First, both France and Japan administered their colonies through a centralized bureaucratic system—indicated in French by the term "*rattachements*" and in Japanese by metropole extensionism (*naichi enchō shugi* 内地延長主義). Second, both adopted a radical assimilation policy with compulsory language education at its core (Kurokawa Sō 1998a: 175–177). Yanaihara was quick to point out, however, the divergent historical conditions that led to these apparently similar policies.[3] In the French context, he argued, the policy of assimilation was a result of the Enlightenment and the subsequent French Revolution, which gave rise to a belief, based on the idea of natural law, in universality, that is, affirming the "sameness" of all citizens of the empire. Japanese assimilation policy, by contrast, was founded on the conviction that the Japanese citizen was spiritually superior. As the premier thinker of the liberal faction (*jiyūshugi* 自由主義) of colonial studies, Yanaihara was critical of the imposition of the Japanese language. Citing Ireland as an example of linguistic assimilation that had not led to the realization of spiritual assimilation, he thought the propagation of Japanese language into the colonies would not achieve the desired results.[4] Nevertheless, linguistic colonialism was pursued aggressively on all fronts. And Taiwan was one of its key proving grounds.[5]

For the Taiwanese, adopting a new language was a complex proposition. They inhabited a multilingual environment, negotiating among a number of dialects of the southern coastal Min family as well as the distinctive Hakka dialect of the Yue group, none of which possessed an accepted orthographic system. From the beginning of Chinese settlement, the dominant mode of expression was literary Chinese, a purely written language that could be read and comprehended in a variety of dialects but did not provide a means of oral communication except in very restricted contexts. The prestige dialect for vernacular fiction, Mandarin, was the lingua franca of the official class but was not widely spoken on the island. During the Japanese occupation, there were efforts to promote the continental Vernacular Language movement *(baihua yundong),* which was based on northern Mandarin, and counterefforts to develop a writing system that would legitimate the local Min dialect (that is, Taiwanese). Writers such as Lai He, who was educated in Japan as a physician and is sometimes called the father of Taiwanese literature, wrote only in Chinese.

The backdrop to these actions was a continuing determination on the part of the colonial government to accelerate the linguistic assimilation of the Taiwanese. Taiwanese linguistic identity during this period shifted through different stages. During the early years of the occupation, when ties with China were still strong and the colonial government had not yet implemented an aggressive policy of language assimilation, the linguistic preference of most intellectuals was for some form of Chinese. Gradually, as ties to the continent weakened with the advance of colonization, they began to wrestle with the choice between Taiwanese, which reinforced a newly localized, indigenous ethnic identity, and Japanese, the language of the colonizers, which promised participation in a rising empire. The second generation of Taiwanese writers, men such as Yang Kui, Zhang Wenhuan, and Lü Heruo, came of age just at this juncture and their literature reflects the prevailing ambivalence regarding these linguistic paths. In the latter half of the occupation, a new breed of writer, the "imperial-subject writer," emerged. To most of these authors, China was but a distant and irrelevant memory of their grandfathers and they had only a limited familiarity with written Chinese.

In the following pages we will consider the promotion of Japanese language supremacy and the subjugation of the native languages by the cultural designers of the Japanese empire, on the one hand, and the struggles for autonomy and sovereignty on the Taiwanese side. Only by considering both sides of this linguistic encounter can we assess its full effect. Though the experience was not fully reciprocal, both sides were profoundly transformed by this cultural contact. Through their colonial expansion, the Japanese for the first time were forced to consider the role of their language in a globalized context. Taiwan's postcolonial identity was, and to some extent still is, shaped by the contestations and uncertainties of this period as diverse ethnic voices struggle for position in the post–Cold War East Asian geopolitical landscape.

Between Kokugo and Nihongo

Modern Japanese encounters with the Other were fraught with anxiety and uncertainty. Initial encounters with the West in the sixteenth century, through European missionaries and traders, brought Christianity and guns, which the powers-that-be found so disruptive that Christianity was violently suppressed, guns were confiscated, and the country was closed to external contact for two hundred and fifty years. Commodore Perry's black ships forced Japan to open to the outside world, which occasioned the Meiji Restoration, in which a mass mobilization of its people transformed Japan into a modern nation-state and a major Asian power. In both cases, Japan responded to external pressure with an internal transformation. The dynamic changed when Japan found itself, for the first time, on the other end of the power structure. The first Sino-Japanese war brought to the Japanese the pleasant realization that their continental giant next door, which had long cast a shadow over Japan culturally and politically, was no longer a superpower. The Russo-Japanese War further confirmed that Japan's military superiority was not limited to Asia but could overcome a sovereign European state. These triumphs in flexing Japan's military muscles led to a reaffirmation of Japanese cultural identity and a search for a self-narrative that incorporated Japan's changing relationship with the world at large.

The drastic change in collective Japanese self-identity engendered by these new circumstances has been documented most thoroughly by Oguma Eiji in *The Myth of the Homogeneous Nation* (*Tan'itsu minzoku shinwa no kigen* 単一民族神話の起源, 1995). Having pored through the vast amounts of primary and secondary materials on "Japaneseness" (*Nihonjin ron* 日本人論) that circulated during the prewar and postwar periods, Oguma discerns a prewar mixed-race theory and a postwar single-race theory, both legitimized as "national traditions" (*minzoku no dentō* 民族の伝統).[6] The prewar mixed-race theory, invented to shore up the colonial expansion of the Japanese empire, promoted the idea that Japan had since antiquity consisted of "different racial groups living in harmony" (*izoku kyōwa* 異族協和) and supported it with historical evidence drawn from Japan's earliest histories, the *Kojiki* and *Nihon shoki*.[7] Thus a new national myth was fashioned that emphasized homogeneity (*dōshitsusei* 同質性) and a shared group mentality (*shūdan shikō* 集団志向) among ethnically diverse groups.

In a dramatic reversal of the prewar identity discourse, the postwar period saw the promotion of an exclusionary single-race theory which argued that the inhabitants of the Japanese islands had always been and remained today a single, unitary, ethnic group. In this discourse, the imperial lineage was reinvented as an unbroken continuity from the archaic age; this view was encapsulated in the ideology of "a single lineage for ten thousand generations" (*bansei ikkei* 万世一系). The irony, of course, lies in the fact that the single-race theory, which has become widely accepted as the primary characteristic of Japanese racial identity, was never a mainstream theory during the time when Japan was consolidating its multiethnic empire before and during the war. The theory really gained acceptance only after Japan had lost all its oversea colonies. Thus Oguma demystified the prewar/postwar construction of an essentialist discourse of Japanese identity by relocating it in a post-colonial context.[8] These theories of Japanese identity were inextricably entangled with conceptions of the Japanese language. Was it a unique reflection of Japanese society, or was it potentially a lingua franca for a Japanese-led East Asia? This debate had profound ramifications for Japan's colonial empire, at the time, and for the diffusion of Japanese language and culture after the war.

The terminology used in relation to a language often reveals attitudes that are not normally made explicit. Certainly this is the case with Japanese, which is referred to in Japanese as either "Kokugo" (national language) or "Nihongo" (Japanese language). In 1994, the journal *Gekkan Nihongo Ron* published a special issue titled "Kokugo or Nihongo?" ("'Kokugo' ka 'Nihongo' ka" 国語か日本語か).[9] The issue alleges the decline of the discipline called "Kokugo." One article points out, for example, that in 1953 only 19 percent of the departments in Japanese universities and colleges focusing on the study of Japanese literature and language used the terms "Nihongo" or *"Nihon bungaku"* (Japanese literature) in their titles as opposed to the predominant "Kokugo" or *"kokubungaku"* (national literature).[10] By 1993, however, departments using "Nihongo" or *"Nihon bungaku"* had increased to 48 percent. In fact, none of the new departments instituted during the last ten years chose to use the term *"kokubungaku."* Most of the contributors to this issue of the journal attempted to decipher the difference between Kokugo (国語) and Nihongo (日本語) through various forms of linguistic taxonomy. The rhetorician Toyama Shigehiko, for example, found a shift in the usage of these two terms over the years. He notes that "Kokugo" has been used since the beginning of the Meiji period but "Nihongo" was used most often from the mid-1960s on, when a new interest developed in the mother tongue *(bokokugo)*. The linguist Koizumi Tamotsu, the only participant to consider the political implications of these terms, defines Kokugo as "the language of the nation-state of Japan *(Nihon kokka)*" whereas Nihongo is the "language of the Japanese ethnic group *(Nihon minzoku)*." He argues that "Kokugo" is closely tied to national policy, whereas "Nihongo" does not serve such political purposes inasmuch as it refers merely to one of the many languages in the world. Koizumi was alone in insisting on a clear semantic distinction between the terms.

Recent years have seen a surge of interest in Japanese attitudes toward their language, as studies that break new ground have placed the issue in the context of Japanese colonial language and cultural policy.

This younger generation of scholars, including Shi Gang (1993), Komagome Takeshi (1996), Lee Yeounsuk (1996), Koyasu Nobukuni (1996), Osa Shizue (1998), and, most recently, Yasuda Toshiaki (1999), has re-examined the Kokugo/Nihongo debate that took place among many educators, linguists, and colonial policymakers during the 1930s and 1940s. Their research sheds light on the impact of colonialism on the conceptual evolution of the national language. Essentially these studies reveal that the demarcation between Kokugo and Nihongo can be located on the boundary of Japaneseness. Kokugo was the language (some might argue a highly politicized entity constructed since the Meiji period) shared by the community of native speakers in mainland Japan *(naichi)*. Nihongo, by contrast, was considered a "potential" common language for Greater East Asia (*Tōa kyōtsūgo* 東亜共通語) within the context of the pan-Asiatic sphere of the 1930s and 1940s.

Kokugo is inward looking and self-content. It is taken as a given—an inalienable birthright of the Japanese people. Wartime Japan (and to a certain degree this mode of thinking continues into the postwar era, constituting an essential part of the postwar discourse on Japaneseness) emphasized the symbiotic trinity of Japanese language, Japanese spirit *(Nihon seishin)*, and Japanese culture. The linguist and creator of the Yamada grammar *(Yamada bunpō)*, Yamada Yoshio 山田孝雄 (1873–1958), describes the national language in the article "What Is Kokugo" ("Kokugo to wa nanzo ya?" 国語とは何そや) in this way:

> What we regard as the national language is a tool that the Yamato people, the core of the empire, have used to express their thoughts and to communicate since the archaic era. It is a language they use now and no doubt will be the one language that will carry them into the future. Kokugo was developed among the Yamato people as their shared language and, simply put, shall become the standard language for the Great Japanese Empire. [Koyasu Nobukuni 1996: 127]

As the father of modern Kokugo, Ueda Kazutoshi 上田万年 (1867–1937), so eloquently stated it, Kokugo is "the protecting fence of the imperial house; the nurturing mother of the citizen."[11] He further linked the Japanese language to the notion of the nation as an organic body (national polity, *kokutai* 国体) and referred to language as "the spiritual blood" of the Japanese:

> Just as blood in a body shows blood relationships, the language that the people speak indicates their spiritual compatriots. In the

case of the Japanese language, it is the spiritual blood of the Japanese people. The national polity of Japan has been maintained primarily through this spiritual blood. It is the strongest and longest lasting key to the preservation of the Japanese race and it is because of it that this race has not fallen into chaos. . . . This language is not merely a symbol of the national polity; at the same time, it is also an educator, what we might call "a compassionate mother." As soon as we are born, this mother sits us on her lap and earnestly teaches us how to think and how to feel as a citizen of Japan. For this reason, the compassion of the mother is truly like the sun in the sky. [Ueda Kazutoshi 1968: 110–111]

This discourse personified the language as a living entity existing within a complex system of hierarchical human relations (mother/child; teacher/pupil). Ueda's organic conceptualization of Kokugo was crystallized in a series of public speeches given immediately following his return from a three-year period of study in Europe. His ultranationalistic rhetoric, invoking the national polity, seemed to hark back to Motoori Norinaga's "national learning" (*kokugaku* 国学) ideology of an earlier age. As Lee Yeounsuk points out, however, Ueda in fact looked at Motoori's traditional scholarship as rather archaic—a hindrance to the development of a scientific approach to language. Ueda's theories were influenced more deeply by German linguists such as Wilhelm von Humboldt, who conceived of language as an organism linking the modern citizen and the nation-state.[12] Notice that Ueda uses a maternal allegory here, not a paternal one. In this case, the imperial structure positions the emperor as the head of the family, the people as the (infant) child, and the Japanese language as the mother. Through the marriage of the imperial throne and the national language, Kokugo was elevated to the highest political stratum and imbued with a sacred character.

Ueda's disciple, Tokieda Motoki 時枝誠記 (1900–1967), followed Ueda's lead in privileging Kokugo; he argued that respect and love for Kokugo should consitute "a religion," prompting Koyasu Nobukuni to cynically label this line of thought "national language theology" (*kokugo shingaku* 国語神学). It was on the basis of this theology—an ironclad trinity of Japanese state, Japanese ethnicity, and Japanese language *(Nihon kokka, Nihon minzoku,* and *Nihongo)*—that the exalted status of Kokugo was secured. Extending the kinship analogy, Tokieda built upon his teacher's emotionally charged metaphors of the corporeal and maternal. He talked about the blissful period of the pure Kokugo moment as a time when "a family consisting of parents, brother, and sister live harmoniously in their own house. The time when there is still no brother-in-law or sister-in-law" (Koyasu Nobukuni 1996: 130). But as a linguist teaching at Keijō Imperial University in Seoul who had spent much of his youth in the colony, Tokieda realized that the tranquillity of the nuclear family was no longer attainable. Fully aware of the problems inherent in applying the concept of Kokugo to a group of people ethnically and linguistically different from the Japanese,[13] he felt the need to modify Ueda's concept:

> If one looks at the current structure of the Japanese state and its place in the international world, one feels the need to rethink Doctor [Ueda]'s claim for our mother tongue (*bogo* 母語). I have been having second thoughts about this in my heart ever since I came to my job in Korea. If we accept Doctor Ueda's conception as is, we would lose half of the reasons why we would disseminate Kokugo to the Koreans, who have a different language. This is because for the Korean people, Korean is their mother tongue, their living language, and their spiritual blood. But if the proliferation of Kokugo is a vital policy and, in reality, a necessity in order to rule Korea, how shall we resolve the conflict of the two? [Koyasu Nobukuni 1996: 131]

While theorists within Japan proper were settling on a totalizing linguistic theology that centered on the emperor, outside the Japanese homeland educators and linguists were struggling to cope with the disruptive contradictions that arose when this philosophy was applied to the colonies. Tokieda's experience in the colony exemplifies the clash between the unsullied purity of national language theory and the realities of the colonial condition. The xenophobic, self-contained boundary of Kokugo confronted the multiracial, multilingual reality of the Japanese empire, which threatened to destabilize the established position of the national language.

This debate pitted the ideological absolutism of Kokugo hardliners against the pragmatism of educators in the field, whose job it was to spread the Japanese language as quickly as possible among the colonized. Ando Masaji, for example, was first put in charge of education policy in Taiwan; after the war, he became the education minister and was at the center of the postwar Kokugo reform movement. Ando argued against the call of many colonial educators to reform and simplify Kokugo to suit pedagogical purposes in the colonies. He insisted:

"Kokugo is the language we inherited from our distant ancestors and belongs to all citizens *(kokumin)*. . . . To revamp and reform Kokugo and Kokuji [the national orthography], paying attention only to convenience, in order to teach the foreigners and to spread it overseas, is to damage the *sacred character* of Kokugo (*kokugo no shinsei* 国語の神聖)" (Koyasu Nobukuni 1996: 122-123; emphasis added). This quasi-linguistic theology was, in a sense, parallel to the nationalistic discourse of ethnic purity that drove the wartime ideology and later fueled the postwar *Nihonjinron* (discourse on Japaneseness) boom. Eventually an accommodation was reached: Kokugo as a concept should not be extended beyond the boundary of the Japanese archipelago, or *naichi*, while Nihongo was designated as the language to be spoken in the colonies, or *gaichi*.[14]

Domestic theorists and colonial educators alike insisted that only through the Japanese language could one become a real Japanese. The forced adoption of the Japanese language wrought havoc in the everyday lives of the colonized and disrupted their cultural and ethnic identities. Moreover, Japan itself was for the first time faced with the daunting pedagogical task of disseminating its own language to other parts of Asia. This new urgency prompted a searching examination of just what a national language is and, for the first time in history, the Japanese were compelled to take a comparatively objective look at their language as a foreign language. Some critics have noted that, in comparison with European colonialism, the Japanese never articulated a coherent, systematic vision for their empire. Territorial expansionism came first; then rhetoric was fashioned to justify the act. In any case, language education was always at the center of Japan's colonial cultural policy. At the same time the ideology of Kokugo was being formulated in the homeland, pragmatic pedagogical considerations were forcing redefinitions and improvised understandings of the Japanese language as it was being taught in the colonies.

Postwar discussions of the national language have sidestepped the impact of Japanese imperialism and colonialism on the linguistic identity of the Japanese themselves. Compared to the restrained discussion seen in most postwar sources, debates during the colonial period were straightforward and highly politicized. Revisiting these debates, Shi Gang (1993) and others have revealed the impact of colonialism on native cultures in the Japanese colonies, as well as its impact on the conceptual evolution of the national language in Japan itself. As we shall see, the effects of colonial language policy were not confined to that tumultuous historical period. Indeed they rippled through the intellectual history of the half-century following the end of the war.

The reform of the Japanese language *(kokugo kaikaku)* that was implemented after the war resulted in the language we know as modern Japanese. Outside Japan, in former colonies like Taiwan, the consequences of the colonial language policy were deeply entangled in the postcolonial, post–Cold War politics of identity. Many studies have addressed the economic, military, and political strategies of Japan's ex-colonies. In contrast to this focus on the "hardware" of Japanese imperialism, comparatively little has been done on the impact of cultural policies—in particular, education and language policies. Because of the close relationship between identity and language, these colonial policies, at the core of Japanese colonialism, may have had the greatest and most long-lasting psychological influence.

Language Reform and Educating the New Citizen

Since Taiwan was Japan's first colony, it was the proving ground for aspects of colonial policy, including language. The institutionalization of the Japanese language in Taiwan began almost immediately.[15] Three months after the Qing court handed over Taiwan to Japan in accordance with the Shimonoseki Treaty (signed by both sides on April 17, 1895), the first Japanese-language school was opened on the outskirts of Taipei, in Zhishanyan 芝山巖. Enrolling only six students, this modest endeavor was the brainchild of the colonial educator Izawa Shūji 伊沢修二 (1851–1917).[16] It is worthy of special mention because, as the first Japanese-language school outside of Japan, it provided a blueprint for the ensuing half-century of Japan's colonial language apparatus. Izawa reminisced fondly about his early days spent establishing Japanese language education on the newly acquired island amidst the still ongoing battles between the Japanese army and a hastily assembled Taiwanese civilian resistance force:

> This couple of days, when I went upstairs and looked out, I could see villages such as Sanjiaoyong, Erjiajiu, and Ankeng, where the bandits had gathered, being attacked and burned down by the imperial army. At times, the blasts of the cannon could be heard clearly, and I felt quite pleased. It is indeed interesting that amidst all this, more and more students showed up and we did not cancel even one day of class.[17]

While Izawa was gleefully watching the Japanese imperial army disman-
tling the island's remaining native opposition, an ominous event
awaited him. Less than six months after the school opened, on New
Year's Day of the following year (1886), a group of local armed fighters
led by Jian Dashi attacked the Zhishanyan School and killed all six of
Izawa's teachers in the so-called Zhishanyan Incident.[18] Izawa and the
colonial government used this incident to promote the "Zhishanyan
spirit" touting the sacrifice of the Japanese educators as a symbol of the
mission to promote Japanese language education in the colony. A
Shinto shrine called Taiwan Jinja, the first on the island, was built on
the site and elaborate annual rituals commemorating these cultural
warriors were conducted until the end of World War II. The incident
was incorporated into the textbooks for local schoolchildren, as well,
and a yearly pilgrimage to the shrine became de rigueur; the shrine
was often the first stop for visitors from Japan.

After the Zhishanyan Incident

Izawa was not the first to marry imperialism, the Shinto religion, and the
Japanese language. Compared to many fundamentalist Japanese linguists he was open to a more liberal interpretation of what role the Japanese language should play in the colonial context. As one of the most
influential theorists on colonial language education in the early period,[19] Izawa adopted the egalitarian position that the colony should be
treated equally as part of the greater empire.[20] His position was similar
to that of policymakers who insisted that colonies should not be discriminated against institutionally but should be treated as an extension of
the homeland, or *naichi*, the so-called metropole extensionism (*naichi
enchō shugi* 内地延長主義). Izawa firmly believed that it was only through
education that the colony could be transformed into part of the empire
and its subjects into true Japanese. He noted: "So far, Taiwan had been
conquered with military force. However, it is still a big question whether
we can make them obedient from the bottom of their hearts and truly
become part of Japan for ten million years" (Shi Gang 1993: 30).

For Izawa, the purpose of educating the Taiwanese was to "truly
make Taiwan part of Japan" and "to truly Japanize the Taiwanese from
the bottom of their hearts."[21] As the first head of the Education Department (*gakumu buchō* 学務部長) of the colonial government, Izawa was
in an excellent position to see firsthand how the acculturization process worked and also to experiment with various ideas on how to advance his educational philosophy. It was not, however, a smooth ride

for him. He expressed his bewilderment at having to deal with the native Taiwanese dialect, a variant of Southern Min, and not the Mandarin Chinese he had expected:

> This island is located at the southernmost end of China proper and its language differs greatly from that of the north. The interpreters, usually well versed in Mandarin, are totally ineffective here, as was evident in the battlefront experience not too long ago. Very few Japanese understand the native language (*dogo* 土語) and as for natives (*dojin* 土人) who know Japanese, they are nonexistent.[22]

But this initial frustration did not stop Izawa from confronting the difficult task. Just a year after the occupation, he sponsored two Japanese-Taiwanese reference books: the *New Japanese Dictionary* (*Shin Nihongo genshū* 新日本語言集, 1896) and *Detailed Explanations of Fifteen Taiwanese Consonants* (*Taiwan jyūgo'on jibo shōkai* 台湾十五音字母詳解, 1896). The *New Japanese Dictionary* was a concise Japanese-Taiwanese conversation dictionary consisting of vocabulary items for daily life tailored to the colonial context as well as special terms related to the army and police. Thus Izawa implicitly recognized the importance of knowing the native language for effectively teaching the target language to the native.

After the Zhishanyan Incident, the tiny school that Izawa had set up to teach children of the native gentry class was revamped into several separate institutions. Izawa clearly had both long-term and immediate goals for his national language project. The Japanese school was renamed the National Language Learning Center (*Kokugo Denshūjo* 国語伝習所): one part was set up as a six-month intensive course in interpreting (for individuals from fifteen to thirty years old), while youths from eight to fifteen could enroll in a four-year course in the Japanese language. Looking toward long-term goals, he instituted two separate, professionally oriented institutions. The Colonial Government Normal School (*Sōtokufu Shihan Gakkō* 総督府師範学校) trained Japanese nationals to become Japanese-language teachers. The Colonial Government National Language School (*Sōtokufu Kokugo Gakkō* 総督府国語学校) trained professional interpreters and included a Japanese Course (*honkokugoka* 本国語課), which enrolled indigenous people, as well as a Local Language Course (*dogoka* 土語課), which taught the native Taiwanese dialect to the Japanese.[23]

Initially the use of a romanized system to teach Japanese was explored. In 1860, when the Presbyterian Church began its missionary activities in Taiwan, it also developed a system for representing the local dialect in a roman alphabet and began translating the Bible into Taiwanese. In light of the relative success the missionaries enjoyed in proselytizing the natives in Taiwanese after they switched from teaching them English to learning Taiwanese themselves, the Scottish missionary Thomas Barclay (1849–1935) advised Izawa to do the same: using the natives' own language to teach them about Japan.[24]

Use of the roman alphabet (*rōmaji hyōkihō* ローマ字表記法) had been hotly debated in Japan two decades earlier.[25] Anticipating rapid westernization throughout Meiji society, the enlightenment group Meirokusha 明六社,[26] and its magazine *Meiroku zasshi* 明六雑誌 (1874–1875), became the forum for those who advocated a romanized orthographic system. In the first issue of *Meiroku zasshi* (July 1874), Nishi Amane (西周 1829–1897) argued in the article "A Thesis on Using the Western Alphabet to Write the National Language" ("Yōji o motte kokugo o shosuru no ron" 洋字ヲ以テ国語ヲ書スルノ論) that Japan should forsake the kana syllabary and adopt the roman alphabet in place of its traditional orthographic system. Among ten advantages suggested for this plan, Nishi insisted that academic terms should be kept in the original when translating Western books into Japanese so that "using this method [romanization] we can make all European things our own" (Lee 1996: 33–34). Underlying this proposed orthographic reform was a deep desire not only to master Western civilization but to become part of it.

Shimizu Usaburō advocated a reform based on the Japanese syllabary (kana) in the article "A Theory on Hiragana" ("Hiragana no setsu" 平仮名ノ説), which appeared in *Meiroku zasshi* in May 1874. Shimizu believed that the key to the high level of Western civilization was the unity of spoken and written languages. The best way to achieve this in Japan, he argued, was a system based on hiragana alone. After all, it had a long tradition in Japan, was well known by its people, and could achieve the goal of consolidating the spoken and written languages. Shimizu's kana-only theory encountered two problems in implementation: composition in kana alone tended, consciously or unconsciously, to emulate a traditional, quasi-classical style (*gikotai* 擬古体), and it posed great difficulties in the translation of Western terms. Scientific terms, such as chemical elements, proved particularly troublesome.[27]

Whether through romanization, intended to increase access to Western civilization, or through the Japanese syllabary, which sought continuity with the traditional orthographic system, these reforms shared a common purpose—to purge Chinese characters (kanji) from the written language—reflecting a shared desire to break away from the Chinese cultural sphere.[28] Maejima Hisoka 前島密 (1835–1919) and Inoue Tetsujirō 井上哲次郎 (1855–1944) were the most vocal in advocating the elimination of kanji from the Japanese language. Maejima was known for his "Proposal for Abolishing Kanji" ("Kanji haishi no gi" 漢字廃止の議), which he submitted to the fifteenth shogun, Tokugawa Keiki 慶喜, in 1866 while serving as his interpreter.[29] He later served as director of the Imperial Education's Association National Orthography Reform Section 帝国教育会国字改良部長 and as chair of the National Language Research Council 国語調査委員会. Maejima took a utilitarian approach to language, seeing it not as an end in itself, but rather an instrument for conveying knowledge. In order to take advantage of "ten thousand people pronouncing consistent sounds," he believed that the orthography should represent the sounds of the spoken language in a consistent, unambiguous fashion (Lee 1996: 30). He linked this idea to a larger theory of civilization and orthography. Establishing a correspondence between civil (Western) societies that used phonetic systems, on the one hand, and backward (Eastern) societies that depended on ideographic orthographies, on the other, he concluded that the stagnant state of Japanese politics and culture was due to its continued use of "inconvenient, useless ideographs."

Three decades after Maejima's proposal for the abandonment of kanji, Inoue Tetsujirō took up his thesis. But whereas Maejima's argument was pragmatic, seeing kanji as an impediment to progress, Inoue's position was distinctly anti-Chinese, arguing that the eradication of kanji was necessary to safeguard Japanese national identity. Inoue was known as the official interpreter of the Imperial Rescript on Education 教育勅語 (Inoue 1891: 1–5) and a promoter of the concept of "national polity," which touted a familialized nation-state founded upon a paternal relationship between the emperor and his subjects. Inoue took an uncompromising position on the question of Japan's emerging national identity.[30] In a piece on the unification of written and oral language (*genbun itchi* 言文一致), he characterized the Chinese language as backward and inflexible because its lack of suffixes, inflections, and verb conjugations impeded the expression of complex thoughts. The Chinese language, he claimed, would never be able to deal with Western ideas of logic, economics, and philosophy.[31] Escaping from the dominance of Chinese compounds (*kango* 漢語) and subscribing to the principles of *genbun itchi*, whether through kana or romanization, would be the first step toward the independence of the national language (Yoshida Sumio and Inoguchi Yūichi 1964: 317–330).

Inoue's focus on *genbun itchi* reflected a wider concern with the problem at the turn of the century. In 1901, the Imperial Education Association formally petitioned both the House of Peers and House of Representatives: "We believe that the independence, proliferation, and development of the national language is the best method to assure the unity of the state, augment its influence, and hasten its progress, and that to do so, we must unify speech and written expression." They cited European nations that had attained the highest level of civilization because they had abandoned the crutch of Latin three hundred years earlier and, as counterexamples, countries like Korea, Manchuria, and Mongolia, which had suffered decline because of their failure to implement a modern written language that recorded the spoken vernacular. The petition concluded: "A National Language Research Council (Kokugo Chōsa Iinkai 国語調査委員会) should be set up immediately to implement *genbun itchi* as a national enterprise."[32] A sense of urgency, founded on something like social Darwinism, seems to have driven the request. The petition quickly passed both houses, and in 1902 the council was formally established as a governmental organization by the Ministry of Education. The president of Tokyo Imperial University, Katō Hiroyuki, was formally appointed as chair of the committee, and he dispatched Ueda Kazutoshi to study in Europe in order to introduce Western linguistics into Japan. The council quickly designated a "standard language" (*hyōjungo* 標準語); rules were issued for *genbun itchi* restrictions of kanji usage; and the modern Japanese language, as we know it, was born (Komagome Takeshi 1996: 53).

The arguments concerning the elimination of Chinese characters would have remained an internal debate over the trajectory of the spoken language and its orthography if not for the fact that both the major colonies of Japan, Taiwan and Korea, made use of Chinese ideographs. Ruling over newly acquired cultural territory while using numerous elements of the colonized people's language was problematic to the nationalist linguists. The turn of the century, 1900, is often cited as a pivotal period in the transformation from Meiji Japan to Imperial Japan. Lee Yeounsuk sees a parallel shift of consciousness to what she calls "Imperial Japanese" 帝国日本語 at approximately the same time. This shift of direction is typified by a speech given by Ishitsuka Eizō 石塚英蔵, minister of general affairs in the Taiwan colonial administration. Ishitsuka lamented that it was widely believed that "the prosperity or decline of a nation's national language reflects the nation's prowess," yet compared to English "the national language of our Japan is spoken by almost no one outside of our national boundary." He concluded that Japanese should be quickly taught to the native children as part of the imperial assimilation process.[33]

The difficulties inherent in constructing a modern national language were exacerbated by the need to begin teaching this nascent language to Japan's colonial subjects immediately. Under the auspices of the National Language Research Council, the modernization and imperialization of the Japanese language were undertaken by a diverse group of scholars including linguists (such as Ueda Kazutoshi), philosophers (such as Inoue Tetsujirō), bureaucrats from both the central government and the colonial administration (such as Ishitsuka Eizō), as well as domestic and colonial educators (such as Izawa Shūji); eventually the effort would impact upon millions of language learners both inside and outside Japan proper. Through rigorous debates, groups competed for the attention of the central government and its support. The theoretical framework instituted in the metropolis could not be applied without modification in the colonies and the two groups were often at odds with each other—as is evident in Tokieda Matoki's experiences in Korea discussed earlier.

The modern linguistic transformation of Japan was wrenching for everyone both in Japan and in the colonies. As Karatani Kōjin has pointed out, with the adoption of *genbun itchi* and, subsequently, modern theater and literature, the privileged status of kanji was undermined "through advocating an ideology of phonetic speech" (Karatani Kōjin 1980: 53–65). Nonetheless, it is clear that the pedagogical demands of the colonies accelerated the agenda—often faster than nationalist scholars were willing to proceed. The evolving ideology of the national language, tested in the colonies, encountered both successes and failures in its mission to incorporate the colonial subjects into the empire. Often colonial policies were more daring, more progressive, than their metropolitan counterparts, and the results were applied to education in the homeland. Recent studies of the British colonial enterprise have shown that the discipline of English literature as we now know it was shaped, in part, by the need to present to the colonized Indians a coherent body of culture and humanities that would represent the quintessential Englishness" (Trivedi 1995). Japanese colonial language policy had a similar relationship to Japanese linguistics in the homeland: the colonial need to define and efficiently disseminate Japanese language and culture contributed to the modernization of the national language in Japan.

Izawa's Pragmatic Approach to Education

Izawa Shūji was not a liberal. Having studied education in the United States in 1875, he was one of the first educators to introduce music, in particular chorus, into the normal-school curriculum, but he advocated the creation of a category of national music (*kokugaku* 国楽), paralleling the national learning (*kokugaku* 国学), that would "create songs transcending the boundaries of noble and mean, elegant and vulgar, tunes that everyone can share and that will promote the shared qualities (*kyōdōsei* 共同性) of Japanese citizens" (Osa Shizue 1998: 16–19). In fact, before he arrived in Taiwan, Izawa supported ideas of the purity of the Japanese bloodline and the notion of "national polity." Following the lead of Inoue Tetsujirō and Ueda Kazutoshi, he was also a purist regarding Kokugo and before leaving for Taiwan proclaimed that he would "import Japanese to replace the troublesome kanji with katakana."[34] As in the case of Tokieda, experiences in the colony prompted him to rethink some of his theories. Working with Taiwanese students persuaded him to retain kanji and even kanbun 漢文 (composition in Chinese) in the curriculum, using kana only as a supplement. Izawa came to criticize the National Language Research Council's demand that only kana be taught. Pointing out the similarity of the Sino-Japanese pronunciations of kanji to Korean, Mandarin, and Taiwanese, he reversed his position by suggesting that kanji were a "useful tool for communicating the thoughts of the five to six hundred million people in East Asia."[35]

Izawa also revised his ideas concerning the content of the curriculum. In the speech just cited, made before he was assigned to Taiwan, he faulted traditional Chinese education for overemphasizing impractical works like the Four Books and Five Classics 四書五経.[36] The Chinese people, he remarked, "though not barbarians lacking a written language, have, from the standpoint of modern education, sunk into the realm of dumb animals."[37] He later toned down this criticism, acknowledging that "the Four Books and Five Classics are something that every Taiwanese should know about."[38]

The curriculum he eventually implemented combined Japanese kana with a limited number of kanji (Osa Shizue 1998: 201–204). He opted for a curriculum that included both the Japanese language and elements of the traditional Chinese education (pp. 196–199). The compromises he made are preserved in the twelve volumes of the *Citizen's Reader of Taiwan Textbooks* 台湾教科用書国民読本, issued at Izawa's direction from 1901 to 1903. All textbooks were in the kana phonetic script; volumes one to six also included Taiwanese text with katakana pronunciations. In their reading class, in addition to the Education Ministry–approved *Elementary School Reader* 小学読本 (1889), Taiwanese students studied traditional Chinese classics like the *Three Character Classic* (*Sanzijing* 三字経), *Classic of Filial Piety* (*Xiaojing* 孝経), *Greater Learning* (*Daxue* 大学), *Doctrine of the Mean* (*Zhongyong* 中庸), and *Analects of Confucius* (*Lunyu* 論語).[39] The Kokugo class was devoted solely to learning how to speak the Japanese language. Taiwanese parents who could afford it normally sent their children to private village schools, called *shufang* 書房 or *xuetang* 学堂, where they would be tutored in the *Three Character Classic*, the *Four Books* and *Five Classics*, and classical poetry—all the types of literature necessary to pass the traditional civil service examinations.[40] Izawa understood that in order to compete with the traditional schools for students, it was essential to incorporate instruction in the texts that most parents deemed vital to their children's future career. Juxtaposing Chinese and Japanese texts side by side, in a sense, used Chinese classical texts to teach the Japanese language. This holistic approach to reading and language was not adopted in Japan until several years later, when a new Kokugo curriculum that combined reading, writing, and calligraphy was installed in 1900.

The traditional Chinese classics were subject to censorship. For example, Izawa commissioned Shigeno Yasueki 重野安繹 (who was also the Chinese translator of the Imperial Rescript on Education) to edit out all mention of the Qing dynasty in the textbook on the *Three Character Classic*. *Mencius*, an even more central text, was excluded because it justified the overthrow of an unworthy ruler and the assumption of rule by individuals with no ties to the ruling house solely on the basis of their moral qualities. This notion was at variance with the Japanese insistence on a single, unbroken imperial line from the dawn of history (*bansei ikkei* 万世一系)—an idea central to the concept of Japan's distinctive "national polity." In fact, *Mencius* had already been condemned during the Tokugawa period by members of the Mito school, whose theories had inspired the Meiji Restoration.

The content and design of the textbooks proved controversial as well. Concrete guidelines were issued to the editor, Ōya Tōru 大矢透, such as "treat local customs with care," "include unique local characteristics," "provide illustrations that the students can identify with," and "give fictional characters native names." Cultural misunderstandings were inevitable. One, cited by Izawa in a speech about whether the Imperial Constitution could be fully implemented in Taiwan, concerned the glorification of militarism that was standard in Meiji textbooks. When a mother overheard her son reciting war accounts from the text at home, she was shocked, fearing that the Japanese were teaching the child the Japanese language just so they could draft him into the army; she refused to let the child attend school anymore.[41] Though Izawa used the episode to argue against subjecting the islanders to military conscription, it nevertheless epitomizes the disruptive potential of the wholesale transplantation of cultural content—particularly when it is out of sync with the local cultural context.

Japanese colonialism vacillated between a desire to assimilate the colonized and a countervailing need to subjugate and discriminate against them. Izawa coined three terms to characterize the different approaches Japanese colonialism could adopt in its colonies: self-determism (*jishu shugi* 自主主義), referring to a policy of assimilation; relying on the other (*kata shugi* 仮他主義), meaning a policy of discrimination; and a mixed policy (*kongō shugi* 混合主義), which he saw as the only appropriate choice for the new colony (Shi Gang 1993: 38–44).

The term "self-determinism" is deceptive, because "self" refers here to the Japanese colonialists' authority to make autonomous decisions concerning the role that Japanese culture and language would play in the lives of the colonized. According to Izawa, the application of this ethnocentric educational policy would mean that there would be no difference between the content of education in the metropolitan homeland and in the colonies. Izawa noted that the application of such a policy to the Alsace-Lorraine region by Prussia had resulted in an undesired outcome—leading the inhabitants to "yearn to escape German rule and return to France as quickly as possible." He cited America's annexation of Hawaii as a successful example of self-determinism.

The "other" (他 in "relying on the other") refers to elements of native culture—in this case, Confucianism, the Chinese written language *(kanbun),* and Chinese characters. This approach recognizes a certain value inherent in the native culture and attempts to use it as a means of achieving the final goal: incorporation of the native into the imperial culture. Izawa sees French policy in Vietnam and Dutch policy in Indonesia as two examples of this school of colonial thought. Initially France imposed French on the Vietnamese, but after encountering native resistance it changed direction in 1891 and required all colonial bureaucrats to learn the local language. The Dutch went even further in this regard by prohibiting the natives from learning Dutch. By keeping the natives ignorant and maintaining a clear linguistic demarcation between the dominator and the dominated, the power dynamic could be preserved forever. Izawa gave another example, from his personal experience, of the full implementation of this policy: in the Fukuyama domain (later Matsumae) that ruled over the local Ainu from the seventeenth century until 1807, it was illegal for the Ainu to learn Japanese and Izawa had met a native who had been severely punished for doing so.

These two ideas—centrifugal assimilation versus centripetal ethnocentric dominance—seem diametrically opposed, yet they share a sense of nationalistic entitlement. Izawa was certainly no anticolonial libertarian, but compared to fundamentalist educators such as Hashimoto Takeshi, Takaoka Takeaki, and Hirai Matahachi or politicians such as Nogi Maresuke, Gotō Shinpei, and Mochiji Rokusaburō, Izawa tried to navigate a moderate course.[42]

Izawa's mixed policy, his preference, tempered the absolutism of the Imperial Rescript on Education with the pragmatism of Confucianism. The goal was a gradual penetration of Japanese into Taiwanese life on an analogy with the infiltration of English into the former French colonies of Canada, which Izawa thought had succeeded without overt strife. He cited several reasons why he thought such a policy appropriate and likely to succeed: Taiwan is geographically a continuation of the Japanese archipelago; Japanese have a long historic relationship with Taiwan, including immigration to Taiwan since ancient times; Zheng Chenggong (Koxinga), who had played a key role in Chinese colonization of the island, was half Japanese; the Taiwanese and Japanese peoples are closely related ethnically; despite differences in their spoken languages, they share the use of kanji; and the Taiwanese people are nearly a match for the Japanese in terms of intelligence and virtue.[43]

Izawa's progressive ideas—Japanese teachers should learn the native language, for example, and native students should learn Japanese while continuing to study classical Chinese—were the product of his personal flexibility and his desire to see the cultural and linguistic transition period go smoothly. His attempt to implement the Imperial Rescript on Education without alteration, however, encountered opposition that resulted in the promulgation of a Taiwanese version of the Education Rescript (Taiwanban Kyōiku Chokugo 台湾版教育勅語) in the 1910s. Another demand—that the colonial education be equivalent to that in Japan with six years of compulsory education—was never realized in Korea and was only implemented in Taiwan in 1943, forty-some years after Izawa's initial proposal (Komagome Takeshi 1996: 363–364).

Soon after Izawa was fired from his position and left Taiwan, a debate arose between Hashimoto Takeshi and Hirai Matahachi on abandoning the teaching of Chinese in schools completely. In the 1902 debate, Hashimoto argued from a utilitarian viewpoint that the premise of the study of Chinese was to prepare students for the traditional Chinese civil examination system; thus he considered such study useless in a modern context. By teaching Chinese in the public schools, he argued, the colonial government was endorsing loyalty to the Chinese empire and its emperor. He also attacked the notion from the pedagogical point of view: "I wonder about teaching two languages from completely different language families simultaneously in public school. There is also the issue of the impact the teaching of Chinese will have on teaching Kokugo. . . . So long as the Taiwanese keep applying the grammar of an isolating language in speaking Japanese [an agglutinative language], they will never be able to speak authentic Japanese" (Osa Shizue 1998: 204–206).

Hirai, his colleague at the Association of Kokugo Research, countered that "the reason Chinese people love the Four Books and Five Classics is not just a simple desire to acquire knowledge through the language; they truly admire and desire to be immersed in the teachings of Confucius and Mencius. . . . If we look at the totality of the pace of governing Taiwan, it seems to me that only in regard to education are we leaping ahead by abandoning the classical canons and relying solely on Kokugo to achieve the goals of education and cultivation."[44] Hirai also pointed to pressing practical matters: how would they deal with all the unemployed Chinese teachers, for example, who at that time still constituted the bulk of the public school faculty, and how would they respond to native students' lack of enthusiasm toward Kokugo education? He concluded that Hashimoto's proposal, though commendable in its ideals, was too radical to be implemented. This debate led to the revision of the curriculum in 1904. Article 13 of the Public School Regulations, issued in March of that year, established *kanbun* as a "special course"; Chinese characters and language would be taught for use in daily affairs, but classical texts such as the Four Books, the *Three Character Classic,* and the *Classic of Filial Piety* were forbidden. Starting from first grade, ten hours per week would be devoted to studying Kokugo and five hours to Chinese (Osa Shizue 1998: 222).

Despite this early experimentation and changes in policy, as well as the departure of Izawa and his successor, Mochiji Rokusaburō (he too was demoted), the colonial language policy proceeded. In 1905, ten years after Japan took over the colony and one year after the implementation of the Public School Regulations, the estimated number of Taiwanese people who could comprehend Japanese (officially designated as *Kokugo kaisha* 国語解者) was 11,270—just 0.38 percent of the total population of three million. By 1941, three years before Japan turned Taiwan over to the Nationalist government, 57 percent of the total population was being or had been educated in Japanese. In three and a half decades, the Japanese-language population had increased fifty-sevenfold. In particular, a rapid 20 percent growth can be seen from 1937 onward, after the Imperial Subject movement was launched. In a short four years, from 1937 to 1941, the Japanese-language population grew from 37.8 percent to 57 percent of the total population (Fujii Shōzō 1998: 31–34).

Considering the modest beginnings and various false starts, the outcome was indeed dramatic. Taiwan achieved the highest rate of Japanese literacy of any colony. These statistics do not, however, reveal the role the language played in daily life and we cannot be certain that all those counted as literate in Japanese actually used it in everyday situations. Taiwanese fiction of the period often portrays a generation gap: older family members communicating in Taiwanese while younger members of the same family accept Japanese as the dominant intellectual language, even at home.[45] Still, the propagation of Japanese had begun to impact the everyday lives of the natives.

From the Japanese point of view, however, too many Taiwanese were still incompetent and, worse, lacked the proper enthusiasm for mastering the language. In his *Reader for Imperial Subjects* (1939), Ueda Mitsuaki 上田光輝 lamented:

> Nowadays, one reads articles in the newspaper almost every day reporting the graduation ceremony of Kokugo classes; it is indeed a blissful sight to see the great improvement achieved in all areas. But if one goes inside the home of a native family, be it in a big city, small town, or village, one almost never hears Japanese spoken inside the family. It saddens me to see the students in public school study every day in Japanese but, once they leave the school gate, they revert back to speaking in Taiwanese as if they had forgotten all their Japanese. [Osa Shizue 1998: 46]

A teacher who went to Taiwan wrote that the everyday Japanese used by the children was debased (*kitanai* 汚い, literally "dirty"). He described an incident when he felt proud of the superb performance of students who had been selected to give speeches in a Japanese speech contest. Later, when he overheard them talking to each other in their native language, he was extremely disappointed to discover that to these students "Kokugo is a mere toy for performances."[46]

Beginning with the Manchuria Incident (1931), and increasingly as conflicts with China intensified and a second Sino-Japanese war seemed imminent, the Japanese colonial government was eager to sever Taiwanese ties with the continent. Abandoning the Chinese language was a logical step in this process and Japan's colonial language policy came to focus on making the use of Japanese the norm (*jōyō* 常用) in the natives' daily life. The Taiwan colonial government employed a carrot and stick approach by punishing those who did not use Japanese and rewarding handsomely those who did. They adopted a variety of punitive measures—from fining those who refused to learn Japanese to firing anyone who used Taiwanese in the conduct of official business—culminating in shrill threats that anyone caught using Taiwanese or learning classical Chinese would be deported to China (Shi Gang 1993: 47). In 1934, for example, the governor-general's office took the lead by issuing a decree that all employees were forbidden to speak Taiwanese or risk heavy fines.[47] But widespread acceptance of Japanese was not achieved until the mid-1930s and received a big boost with the inauguration of the Imperial Subject movement. As part of this program, the colonial government honored certain families with the designation "Official Kokugo Family" (*kokugo jōyō katei* 国語常用家庭), which entitled the family to a plaque on their front door and extra rations.

These drastic measures testify to the problems Japan encountered in trying to make Japanese the lingua franca of East Asia (*dai Tōa kyōtsūgo* 大東亜共通語 or *Tōago* 東亜語)—a concept that was an implicit part of the Japanese colonial enterprise from the beginning but came to be ardently promoted in the early 1940s in tandem with the political idea of a Greater East Asian sphere. The modernization of the Japanese language, like any other modernization process, was prompted by an internal dynamic among the Japanese people themselves and by demands from outside Japan proper. It occurred through a rather chaotic process of consolidation represented by the movement to unify speech and writing (*genbun itchi*) and the movement to reform the national orthography. It entailed a process of selection that purged local dialects and accents in order to privilege the middle-class Tokyo Yamanote diction as its nation's standard dialect. Japanese evolved from a grammatically and phonologically diverse, multivocal vernacular into a unitary, prescriptive language that embodied the spirit of the modern nation-state of Japan. It is, then, somewhat ironic to see this newly emergent idea of a single, unifying language so quickly challenged by another multiethnic, multicultural reality: the world of the Japanese empire that was produced as a by-product of colonialism. In this sense, the modern Japanese empire accords well with what Benedict Anderson has called "imagined communities," in which a community is unified by a shared language.[48]

The influence of colonial language policy did not end with conclusion of the war; it rippled through the postwar Kokugo reform movement and continues to influence pedagogical strategies in overseas language teaching. The National Language Research Council (Kokugo Chōsa Iinkai 国語調査委員会, 1902–1913) and its successor, the Interim National Language Research Council (Rinji Kokugo Chōsakai 臨時国語調査会, 1921–1934), were charged with adopting a phonetic script and, later, a program of script reform that in 1923 limited the number of Chinese characters in wide use to 1,962. The interim council was replaced in 1934 with the National Language Council (Kokugo Shingikai 国語審議会), which to this date remains Japan's primary organ for the formulation of language policy. In 1948 a research body, the National Language Research Institute (Kokugo Kenkyūjo 国語研究所), was established to help with the postwar mandate for language reform. The council further pared down the number of Chinese characters to 1,850 (with a subset of 881 characters to be taught during the six years of compulsory education) and implemented "modern kana usage" (*gendai kanazukai* 現代仮名遣い), a spelling reform that adjusted use of the kana syllabaries so they conformed to modern rather than historical phonology (except for a few remnants of the old system).[49]

The national language of Japan, now commonly referred to as Nihongo (Japanese language) rather than Kokugo (national language), for many still remains central to Japanese identity—as evidenced by the key role it plays in the plethora of works published in the postwar era on Japaneseness (*Nihonjin-ron*).[50] The impact of Japanese colonial language policy in its former colonies is gradually fading as the older generation ages and dies off. Yet there are geographical areas where Japanese continues to be used either as an alternative vehicle for daily communication or as a literary language for creative writing.[51] Japan's economic ascendancy, beginning in the mid-1970s, ushered in a global frenzy for learning Japanese—in response to which the Japanese government has invested heavily in promoting Japanese-language education with an eye toward shaping the manner in which the language is taught outside Japan. In the context of a neocolonial Asia, the propagation of the Japanese language as a commodity (and the larger issue of the commodification of Japanese culture through phenomena such as *manga*, Japanimation, pop music, and fashion) suggests the possibility of a postcolonial allegorical reading of the prewar Greater East Asian Cultural Sphere.[52] In the former colonies of Japan, in particular, the problem of linguistic imperialism and colonial linguistic inheritance raised by Robert Phillipson still is a pertinent issue.[53]

So far we have focused on the modernizing of Japan's national language and how this process was influenced by the burgeoning imperial expansion and colonial language policy. While leading Japanese thinkers, linguists, and colonial educators were striving to balance pedagogical and ideological aspects of teaching Japanese overseas, the colonized natives were faced with the equally daunting, and even more urgent, task of resisting this linguistic imperialism and preserving their own native language. Let us turn, then, to the native perspective: their resistance to this linguistic and cultural invasion and the strategies they developed to find a common ground that could simultaneously sustain the traditional Chinese written language, the local native dialect, and the new imperial language.

"My Hand Writes My Heart": Multilingual Culture and Hybridity

The struggle of Taiwanese writers for a unique cultural and linguistic identity during the Japanese occupation entailed more than a simple contest between an indigenous Taiwanese language and the colonizer's Japanese. Preoccupation Taiwan was home to multiple ethnic groups and linguistic communities. The Chinese population was divided primarily among immigrants from Quanzhou and Zhangzhou in Fujian province and Hakka people from the Guangdong area, with an admixture of peoples from other areas of Southeast China (Kerr 1974: 8–9). For the most part they lived in separate villages that coexisted peacefully, but disputes over land and water rights could erupt into paroxysms of violence that sometimes evolved into long-standing blood feuds.[54] All these ethnically Chinese peoples were separated by a greater ethnic and cultural gulf from the indigenous peoples of Taiwan—speakers of Austronesian languages who by the twentieth century had either been assimilated into Han society or driven into isolated communities in the central and eastern parts of the island. The Chinese ethnic groups were united by a shared literary language, classical Chinese, and a common cultural heritage expressed through the literary canons of traditional China. It was only after a quarter century of Japanese rule that the first truly hybrid generation emerged. Hailing from middle-class families, these young people were educated in Japanese and often had attended institutions of higher education in Japan or mainland China.

In this section we will examine the intricate political and cultural negotiations conducted by generations of Taiwanese intellectuals in pursuit of a linguistic and literary expression to represent their hybrid identity. This search by Taiwanese for a modern representation of their distinct identity had two stages. Beginning in the mid-1920s, the New Literature movement (*xinwenxue yundong* 新文學運動) was an echo in Taiwan of the Vernacular Literature movement (*baihua wenxue yundong* 白話文学運動) that had transformed China a few years earlier. Like its continental counterpart, this movement rejected the classical Chinese tradition and promoted in its place an innovative, transgressive new literature couched in a colloquial form of Northern Mandarin and responding dynamically to a modern, rapidly changing world.[55] In the early 1930s, the Taiwanese Language debate (*Taiwan huawen lunzhan* 臺灣話文論戰) and the closely related Nativist Literature debate (*xiangtu wenxue lunzhan* 鄉土文學論戰) sought an effective way to create an indigenous, vernacular written language and employ it in creating an indigenous literary tradition that would give full expression to the unique, hybrid Taiwanese identity.

A political agenda was implicit in both these movements. There was a general recognition, as there had been in China's May Fourth movement (*Wusi yundong* 五四運動), of the danger to modernization posed by "the cultural sediments of the neo-Confucianist moralism and the feudalist social orders as the reactionary forces" (Chang 1999a: 264–265). Moreover, the principle of self-determination enunciated by Woodrow Wilson and example of the communist revolution in Russia both inspired Taiwanese intellectuals to speak up for their rights and their identity as Taiwanese. The result in Taiwan was a fourfold contestation: between classical Chinese and vernacular Mandarin; between vernacular Mandarin and vernacular Taiwanese; between classical Chinese and modern Japanese; and between vernacular Taiwanese and modern Japanese. Japan played a key role in all these interactions. The colonial administration watched carefully all ties to the continent and potential challenges to its authority. Ironically, Japan itself provided a nurturing environment for reformers: language reform in Taiwan was inaugurated by a group of Taiwanese students studying in Tokyo.[56]

The Debate on New and Old Literature in the 1920s

Literary and cultural movements promoting a new Taiwanese literature began in the 1920s. Prior to 1920, classical Chinese remained the dominant form of expression and education was centered on the classics and the composition of traditional poetry. A younger generation of intellectuals who had studied abroad was exposed to the modernization of the Japanese language (especially the *genbun itchi* movement discussed earlier) in the metropole of Tokyo and the modern vernacular reform espoused by the May Fourth movement in China. These young men brought home a sense of pride and an urgency to modernize their own mother tongue. In 1920, Taiwanese expatriates in Tokyo organized the New People's Society (Xinminhui 新民會) and the student-based Taiwanese Youth Association (Taiwan Qingnianhui 台湾青年會).[57] The two groups founded a journal called *Taiwan Youth (Taiwan qingnian),* published half in Japanese and half in Chinese, to promote progressive ideas on the island. The journal caught the attention of young Taiwanese in both Japan and Taiwan; soon the wave of cultural reform reached the colony itself and the Taiwanese Cultural Association was founded to enlighten and educate the masses. To avoid the scrutiny of the governor-general's office, the association claimed blandly that its purpose was "to promote the development of Taiwanese culture" (Kawahara Isao 1997: 139). With one thousand members drawn from the upper echelons of the native society (doctors, teachers, lawyers, students, landlords), the association published a newsletter, provided the public with newspaper and magazines, showed movies, produced plays, and above all sponsored lectures on various cultural issues. From 1923 to 1927, the association's most active period, they sponsored eight hundred lectures that reached a total audience of 300,000.[58]

The issue of Taiwanese language reform appeared as early as 1922 in an article by a Taiwanese student studying in Tokyo. Inspired by both the vernacular-literature movement in China and the *genbun itchi* movement in Japan, Chen Duanming 陳端明 set forth the advantages of replacing the classical written system with a colloquial vernacular in an article titled "A Treatise on Promoting Daily Language."[59] Because this article was published in Tokyo and only circulated among a small group of people, however, it had little influence on the colony. These ideas finally reached Taiwan—and met with an enthusiastic reception—through two articles published in 1923 in the Chinese-language section of the journal *Taiwan*: Huang Chengcong's 黄呈聰 "Discourse on the New Mission of Popularizing Colloquial Vernacular" examined the history of colloquial vernacular, comparing literary and colloquial works, and argued that the vernacular language should be used to enlighten Taiwanese society and promote literacy.[60] Huang Chaoqin's 黄朝琴 "Discourse on Reforming Chinese" advanced this thesis by proposing pragmatic steps to rid the common language of classical formalism and encourage authors to write as they think and speak.[61] These early discussions paved the way for Zhang Wojun 張我軍 (1902–1955), who ignited the New and Old Literature debate (*xinjiu wenxue lunzhan* 新舊文學論戰, 1924–1926) and launched the Taiwanese New Literature movement.

The debate echoed the Literary Revolution (*wenxue geming* 文学革命, 1917–1925) that had begun in China less than a decade earlier, pitting those who wanted to adopt vernacular Chinese as the new literary medium against the traditionalist poets. Drawing on Hu Shi's historic "Preliminary Propositions for a Literary Reform" ("Wenxue gailiang chuyi" 文學改良芻議)—which criticized parallelism, imitation of ancient writers, clichés, and classical allusions while advocating the use of modern grammar and colloquialisms—the vernacular movement attacked "conservative and reactionary" poets who adhered to the classical poetic tradition.

Of all the advocates of the Mandarin vernacular in Taiwan, Zhang Wojun was the most aggressive. Born in Taiwan, while studying at National Peiping Normal University he published a series of articles attacking the conservative literary environment that prevailed in Taiwan. He later moved to Tokyo and continued his activities working for the weekly *Taiwanese People's Newspaper* (*Taiwan minbao* 台湾民報).[62] Zhang differed from later promoters of literary and language reform of the 1930s in that he firmly situated the literature of the colony within the larger Chinese literary tradition. In an article with the sort of hyperbolic title that Zhang was inclined to give to all his writings, "Let Us Please Cooperate in Tearing Down This Dilapidated Palace Overgrown with Weeds," he wrote:

> Taiwanese literature is a tributary of Chinese literature. It is natural
> to expect that when something impacts upon and changes the main-

stream, the tributary will also be impacted upon and changed. But ever since the Japanese took over, the access to Chinese books has been greatly hindered. As a consequence the two places seem to be on different planets and the chasm separating them seems to grow deeper every day. If we look back ten years ago, a great revolution occurred in the world of Chinese literature. The debate between the new and the old literature reached a peak. Did this old literature, which was on the brink of extinction, truly "lack the power to counterattack, possessing only the power to defend itself?" No, it did not even have the power to defend itself. The herd of stubborn old scholars has already slunk away in defeat. The ruins of the old palace, the palace of the old literature, has, after a violent storm, been completely wiped away, leaving not a trace.[63]

Zhang, continuing the analogy, exhorts the colony to rid itself of the old literary establishment as well.

In a follow-up article in the next issue of *Taiwan minbao* titled "Meaning of the Unique *Jiboyin*,"[64] he attacked the poetry composition game *jiboyin* 擊鉢吟, which was extremely popular on the island. *Jiboyin*—literally "reciting while striking a bowl"—was a traditional poetic competition in which poets were given specific topics and rhymes and had to compose a certain number of poems in a set amount of time. Contrasting this practice with Goethe's ideas about the function and goal of poetry, Zhang admits that the practice may be good for developing a certain facility with poetic composition but maintains it has nothing to do with true literature. Pointing out the practice's social role of introducing the author to people of wealth and influence, Zhang blasts the association of literature with social and political power.

Zhang's polemic did not go unnoticed. The rival daily newspaper *Taiwan nichinichi shinpō* 台湾日々新報, sponsored by the colonial government, served as the main arena for the traditionalists' counterargument. In one typical rebuttal to Zhang's advocacy of the new literature, the author cites the difficulty of representing the colloquial language in written form, the dangerous radicalism of Hu Shi and Chen Duxiu in China, and, finally, the example of Japan, where despite a modernization process Japanese literature still relies heavily on Chinese characters and allusions to classical Chinese literature.[65] In all these arguments it is fascinating to notice the role played by the colonial government. Though concerned about the traditional ties to China, the colonial government tacitly aligned itself with the old school in attacking the New

Literature movement. Because of their familiarity with Chinese poetry, colonial administrators felt more secure with traditional Chinese literature and resistant toward the New Literature movement, which implicitly promoted a radical antifeudalistic and anticolonial agenda.

Zhang Wojun's position eventually evolved from a cantankerous opposition to the older literature into more constructive discourse on how to build the new. In "The Liberation of the Poetic Form,"[66] he offers guidelines for the creation of a new poetry; a full presentation of his reformist ideas is to be found in the famous article "The Meaning of the New Literature Movement."[67] Essentially Zhang took a two-pronged approach to reform: constructing a vernacular literature that would stand in opposition to traditional classical writings while reforming the Taiwanese language so that it would accord more closely with standard Chinese, that is, Mandarin. His position was uncompromising. Alternatives proposed by others, such as a mixed style of vernacular and literary Chinese or writing in the Taiwanese dialect, were flatly rejected. He saw the vernacular as a vehicle that could disseminate knowledge to all people and serve as a social equalizer. To those who asked how the Taiwanese could use vernacular Mandarin to write when they do not speak that language, Zhang asked: "Can Taiwanese be expressed in written language? Is there any literary value in Taiwanese? Is Taiwanese a logical language?" For Zhang the answer to all three questions was no. He insisted that the Taiwanese dialect should be reformed along the lines of Mandarin and eventually unified with this "standard" form of Chinese.

This historic article effectively settled the debate on literary reform. Various native writers responded to Zhang's call and attempted to write in the new vernacular. The most prominent of them was the author Lai He 賴和, often called the father of Taiwanese literature. Lai He, who studied medicine and was said to be fluent in Japanese, wrote many stories over a long life working as a physician. Like many of his contemporaries in the New Literature movement, Lai chose the Chinese vernacular as his creative language and refused to write in Japanese. Another active native writer was Yang Yunping 楊雲萍 (1906–?), whose short vignettes such as "Arrival" (1926),[68] "Twilight at the Sugarcane Plantation" (1926),[69] and "Curry Rice" (1927)[70] shed light on how the writer grappled with a new mode of expression both linguistically and thematically. Native writers like Yang Shouyu 楊守愚 (1905–1959) and Cai Qiutong 蔡秋桐 (1900–?), who had no firsthand experience with China, experimented with a style that mingled vocabulary items and expressions drawn from Taiwanese and Japanese in a Mandarin syntax.

Zhang Wojun, having attended university in Beijing, strove to write in standard Mandarin style. He published the first collection of vernacular lyrical poetry, titled *Love in the Labyrinth City* (*Luandu zhi lian* 亂都之戀), in 1925.[71] He also published short stories and novels and translated Japanese works such as plays by the Taishō White Birch school writer Mushanokōji Saneatsu and the novels of Tokuda Shūsei and Shimazaki Tōson. In the pages of the journal he edited, *Taiwan minbao* 臺灣民報, he presented creative works by local writers, translated works by contemporary Japanese writers, and introduced to his readers Chinese writers such as Lu Xun and Guo Moruo. His treatment of Hu Shi's "Eight-Don't-Ism" (*babu zhuyi* 八不主義) and Chen Duxiu's "Three Great Principles" (*sanda zhuyi* 三大主義) was a formidable attempt to theorize Taiwanese literature based on a Chinese model.[72] In his short two-and-a-half-year tenure as the editor of *Taiwan minbao*, Zhang published more than fifty critical articles, essays, short stories, travelogues, and translations of Japanese literature. In this sense, Zhang and his publication served as a conduit linking the regional literary endeavors in Taiwan, China, and Japan.

In 1926, Zhang left for China again, this time with his newly wed wife. He studied Chinese literature at Peiping Normal University and later became a lecturer in Japanese at both the University of China and Peiping University.[73] He served as a member of the Chinese delegation (not the Taiwanese delegation) to the first and second Greater East Asian Writers Conferences held in Tokyo in 1942 and 1943, respectively. His participation in the first conference invited some criticism. Noting his long-held anticolonial stance, some questioned his decision to take part in gatherings that glorified Japanese imperialism. Years later his good friend Hong Yanqiu defended him: by the time Zhang was selected as the delegate, he explained, he was already the most famous professor of Japanese language and literature in Beijing but had yet to set foot in Japan. He took this opportunity in order to visit some of the Japanese writers he so greatly admired. In Japan he met with Mushanokōji Saneatsu and Shimazaki Tōson and eventually translated Mushanokōji's *Dawn* (*Akatsuki* 曉) and Shimazaki's *Before Dawn Breaks* (*Yoake mae* 夜明け前).

Although some accused Zhang of abandoning his native Taiwan, it seems that he never really forgot his roots and was frustrated by China's seeming lack of concern for Taiwan. In 1926 he met with Lu Xun 魯迅, the most influential Chinese writer of the time, and spoke of Taiwan's plight. Lu Xun later recalled the visit (though he misremembered his name as Zhang Wochuan 張我權), especially Zhang's accusation: "The Chinese people have completely forgotten the Taiwanese people. No one is making an issue [of their suffering]." Lu countered: "We feel the pain as if we ourselves had been cut. . . . No, we certainly are not ignoring you. It just that our country is in chaos, too. Internal strife and external assaults keep our hands full. For the time being, we just have to let it go."[74] The mistrust and lack of understanding between China, the former overlord, and the now colonized Taiwan ran deep and fostered a mutual sense of resentment and betrayal. Guo Moruo 郭沫若, another major Chinese writer and playwright, once wrote: "We have heard about an independence movement in Korea and the noncooperation alliance in India, but we have never heard of any history of revolution in Taiwan. The Taiwanese people are our closest compatriots (*tongbao* 同胞), and yet ever since the cession of the territory they have acted as if they have forgotten their motherland. This is a common question we all have toward our Taiwanese compatriots."[75] The isolationist policy the colonial government imposed on the island had effectively limited communication with the continent. Although scholars in China were aware of colonial resistance in other parts of Asia, they were ignorant of the early armed resistance to the Japanese and the continuing effort to establish a linguistic and cultural identity that might counter Japan's assimilation efforts. A wave of hope swept over Taiwan in 1911, when the Nationalists overthrew the three-century-old Manchurian regime (Kawahara Isao 1997: 190–191). But as time passed, China took no action on the Taiwan issue, the Japanese colonial regime became more deeply entrenched, and the Taiwanese felt abandoned and disillusioned.[76]

In 1945, when the war ended, Zhang organized the Association of Taiwanese Expatriates in Beijing to assist the return of many Taiwanese to the former colony. He himself returned to the island in 1946 after twenty years of self-imposed exile in China. Of all the writers from the Japanese colony of Taiwan, Zhang had the closest ties to China. He was frustrated that Taiwanese writers did not heed his warning that they must write in a pure Chinese style or risk being absorbed into the Japanese literary realm, where they would end up expressing their creative impulses in a foreign language. Nonetheless, his attitude toward China was not one of pure adulation. The stories he wrote while in Beijing vividly captured the corrupt and immoral aspects of life in China. One of his best-known stories, "The Tragic History of Mrs. Bai" ("Baitaitai de aishi" 白太太哀史, 1927), depicts a Japanese woman's unhappy marriage to a Chinese man. She suffers through his philandering, but her pure love cannot overcome an archaic, feudalistic family system that sees her as an outsider. The story concludes with the tragic end of the female protagonist's life amidst illness, opium, and a broken heart. "Buying a Lottery Ticket" ("Mai cai-piao" 買彩票, 1926) and "Temptation" ("Youhuo" 誘惑, 1929) tell of the isolated, lonely life of Taiwanese expatriates living in China who some-times are treated like outsiders by their Chinese compatriots.[77]

Zhang Wojun's advocacy of a new literature focused on the use of language and fell short of articulating a systematic theoretical structure for the literary form. Still, his active involvement played a significant role in the movement's development and contributed to the awareness among native Taiwanese writers of an alternative to the colonial lan-guage for their literary creations. The debate in Taiwan peaked around 1925 and diminished after Zhang left for Beijing. Interestingly, though, the traditional poetry societies 詩會, which were subjected to relentless attack by Zhang and other advocates of the New Literature, did not re-treat into oblivion. Indeed with the colonial government's implicit en-couragement they thrived, increasing from 66 societies in 1924 to double that number a decade later. A 1936 survey found there were 183 such organizations (Kawahara Isao 1997: 168). These poetry societies continued to serve as centers of social and cultural interaction for the islanders. They sponsored frequent poetry competitions and group compositions (*lianyinhui* 連吟會) that drew thousands of enthusiasts.

The debate over the creation of a new literature based on vernacular Mandarin continued through the rest of the colonial period. For advo-cates of the New Literature, it was a cultural movement intended to maintain their ethnic identity and an anticolonial resistance movement that sought to counter Japan's attempts to cut the colony's ties with China. Their criticism of traditional writers included an implicit criti-cism of their complicity in colonial rule. The traditional schools, under attack, held their ground and continued to offer a refuge for islanders who wanted to escape the pervasive presence of the Japanese language. The debate, by clarifying the positions of the two camps, resulted in two distinct outlets for the creative energy of Taiwanese writers. Literary pro-duction in the Japanese language, however, would have to wait another decade before a generation of native writers had matured in the Japa-nese educational system and began to write in their master's language.

The Nativist Literature Debate in the 1930s

The New Literature movement firmly established the status of collo-quial Mandarin as the standard modern Chinese vernacular—in oppo-sition to literary Chinese—and launched a new body of literature using this modern language. During the 1930s, however, questions were raised concerning whether this movement really reflected Taiwan's unique circumstances. The cultural affinities to China claimed by Zhang Wojun attenuated as the colonial experience continued.[78] The debate in the 1920s pitted a Chinese identity against an encroaching Japanese one; the 1930s, however, saw a distinct Taiwanese identity emerge as a counter to the imposed colonial identity. To some extent this was the result of the increasing isolation of Taiwan from China. In the early days of colonial rule, Japan had allowed the islanders to leave for China if they so chose in hope of weakening ties to the continent. Later, strict prohibitions on communication and trade between the island and the continent were rigorously enforced.

Taiwanese was a spoken language with no systematic written representation.[79] Zhang Wojun's proposal for unifying the Taiwanese dialect with Mandarin, as set out in "The Meaning of the New Literature Movement," was never really practicable. The rejection of the literary language, a lingua franca that unified China's many vernacular languages and could be read in a variety of regional pronunciations, left the Taiwanese without a written language with which to express themselves other than the foreign languages of Mandarin and Japanese they might learn in school. In these circumstances, many natives confronted the fear that the Japanese colonial assimilation project and the Chinese vernacularization movement would lead to the disappearance of their mother tongue. Arguing that every society has the right to preserve its own language and the obligation to defend itself from the linguistic hegemony of an alien language,[80] Lian Wenqing 連溫卿 inaugurated the Taiwanese Language Preservation movement (*Taiwanyu baocun yundong* 臺灣語保存運動). Together with Cai Peihuo's 蔡培火 Romanization movement (*Luomazi yundong* 羅馬字運動), which sought to popularize an alphabetic representation system for the indigenous language, he was the first to consider the local vernacular not as a mere dialect of Chinese but a full-fledged language of its own. The sense of urgency found expression again in two articles published in 1929 by the famous poet Lian Yatang 連雅堂 in which he condemns the oppressive colonial policy that threatened to eradicate the native language.[81]

The key figures in this second wave of reaction against Japanization, paralleling Zhang Wojun's role in the New Literature debate, were Huang Shihui 黃石輝 and, to a lesser degree, Guo Qiusheng 郭秋生 (1904–1980).[82] Huang Shihui's "How Could We Not Advocate Nativist Literature?" laid the foundation for an indigenous language reform movement that sought to foster a separatist native identity not only during the colonial period but well into the postwar era.[83] The article articulated the core principles of the campaign. Huang insisted that native writers should write about familiar subjects: "You are a Taiwanese. The Taiwanese sky hangs over you and your feet tread on Taiwanese ground. What you see are conditions unique to Taiwan and what you hear is news about Taiwan. The time you experience is Taiwanese time and the language you speak is Taiwanese. Therefore, your powerful pen and your colorful paintbrush should also be depicting Taiwan." As for the language to be used in creating literature suited to this specific locale, he insists: "One should compose in Taiwanese, write poetry in Taiwanese, create fiction in Taiwanese, and fashion song lyrics in Taiwanese."[84] This process involved three elements: eschewing Mandarin colloquialisms with no counterpart in Taiwanese; employing local idioms from the Taiwanese language; and reading the written language in the local pronunciation.[86]

The word "*xiangtu*" in "*xiangtu* literature," which I normally translate as "nativist," literally means "homeland" and was originally taken from such terms as "Heimat Kunst" (local art), which was coined by the nineteenth-century German writer F. Lonhard (see Xu 1997a: 157). In its original German manifestation, it refers to a literary art form devoted to the depiction of a bucolic, pastoral landscape and the simple, rustic ways of its people. Huang Shihui's use of the term imparts a more politicized meaning that seeks to distinguish this new literature from that written in literary Chinese, vernacular Mandarin, or Japanese. Such literature he deemed elitist, since the great majority of the working class was illiterate in all three languages. He advocated, instead, a literature written for the masses, concerning subjects they could identify with, in a language they shared and understood. The colonial government found Huang's proletarian bent so disquieting that his writings were frequently banned. In fact, the forums in which Huang published most frequently during his early career—*Wurenbao* 伍人報, *Taiwan zhanxien* 台湾戰線, and *Hongshuibao* 洪水報 —were suppressed so regularly for their socialist content that few copies survive.[86]

Although there was widespread agreement with the basic tenets of Huang's concept of *xiangtu* literature—that it should be a localized, native literature reflecting the colony's everyday concerns and reality—not everyone agreed that it should be written in the Taiwanese language. Liao Yuwen 廖毓文 and Zhu Dianren 朱點人 opposed using the Taiwanese vernacular for literary creation, claiming that this isolationist stance would hamper the colony's connections with China. Other objections as well were raised by the opposing camp—that the Taiwanese dialect is crude and hence unsuitable for writing; that the island and the continent are linked culturally and should remain so; and that, rather than writing in Taiwanese, all Taiwanese should master and write in vernacular Mandarin so that mainland Chinese could appreciate Taiwanese literature. The split occurred along the fault line of Chinese nationalism versus native Taiwanese nationalism (or nativism). Despite Huang's proletarian position—gesturing toward a literature to which the working masses could relate—his initiative was also opposed by radical Marxists. Lai Minghong, for example, faults Huang and Guo's reformism not for promoting isolation from the continent but for isolating Taiwanese literature from a global proletarian literature: "The reason for promoting *xiangtu* literature is to benefit the Taiwanese proletarian class. For the [experiences of the] Taiwanese proletarian masses should be meaningful as well to the proletarian class around the world."[87] Therefore, he argues, the newly constructed Taiwanese orthography, though designed for the masses, would in fact cut them off from an alliance with their compatriots around the world.

Huang Shihui agonized over assuring equality of access for the working class to literacy and literary production. But for much of the Taiwanese educated class during this period, their goal was to find and eventually master a means of expression that fulfilled their basic needs. This sentiment was summed up in a slogan: "My hand writes what my mouth speaks" (*woshou xie wokou* 我手寫我口) or its variant, "My hand writes my heart" (*woshou xie woxin* 我手寫我心).

Guo Qiusheng laid out concrete steps to establish a system of representation for the Taiwanese vernacular in articles and a weekly column.[88] Coming from a poor, working-class background (he managed a restaurant for a living), Guo further chastised the elitist posture of the debate, which focused on high literature at the expense of popular culture.[89] He set out to collect folk literature, including jokes, and simple folktales in the Taiwanese dialect. These provided examples of "pure Taiwanese" that would win favor with the illiterate masses and guide them to literacy. There was, however, in Guo's conception of this process the idea that the intellectual elite, having collected this raw Taiwanese literature and used it to universalize literacy, would continue to refine and improve the literature until it attained the sophistication and complexity of a world literature.[90]

Although most of the politicized discussions published in the political journals cited here have been lost, we do have access to material published in the biweekly literary journal *Southern Accent* (*Nanyin* 南音). This journal of the literary group of the same name provided fertile ground for native writers to debate the merits of writing in one's spoken language and to experiment creatively with nativist literature. *Nanyin* served as a forum for teasing out the various problems associated with creating a Taiwanese written vernacular. Together with the Chinese-Japanese mixed journal *Taiwan xinminbao* 台湾新民報 and the Japanese-language journal *Formosa* フォルモサ (published in Tokyo by a group of Taiwanese expatriate intellectuals), the three literary journals filled the diverse needs of the multilingual reading environment.[91]

Despite the opposition within the native community to writing in the Taiwanese language and despite constant censorship and suppression by the colonial government, the practice gradually gained favor among writers. By early 1937, when the colonial government banned writing in all languages other than Japanese, Taiwanese had become an established medium for creative writing second only to Japanese. The drive to achieve native language representation was not without its complications and internal strife (Huang 1995: 63–66). Through a process of trial and error, two stylistic formats evolved. One attempted to express the work entirely in Taiwanese. One of the most accomplished works in this category is Lai He's "Letter from a comrade," in which he adheres resolutely to Taiwanese vocabulary and syntax.[92] It is said that Lai He had to write his works in classical Chinese first, then translate them into the Chinese vernacular, and finally revise them with authentic colloquialisms (Rubinstein 1999: 268). This laborious process—not unlike that employed by postcolonial writers such as Zhong Zaozheng and Wu Zhuoliu, who first composed their novels in Japanese, then translated them into their mother tongue (in this case Hakka), and finally retranslated them into standard Mandarin—took its toll on writers. Lai He quit writing altogether not long after the publication of "Letter from a comrade."[93] The other stylistic format was an amalgam of Mandarin and Taiwanese that largely followed Mandarin syntax and vocabulary but inserted distinctively Taiwanese elements—such as modal suffixes (the exclamatory *"la"* 啦, for example, and diminutive *"á"* 仔) and pronouns (such as the first-person pronouns *"goán"* 阮 [I] and *"lán"* 咱 [we]—and often peppered the text with Japanese vocabulary items that had become part of the indigenous lexicon.[94]

Toward a Golden Age

The *genbun itchi* movement in Japan spanned the period from 1866 to 1922 and achieved a modern colloquial vernacular whose adaptability and subtlety is evident in the works of such writers as Akutagawa Ryūnosuke, Nagai Kafū, Tanizaki Jun'ichirō, and the members of the White Birch school (Hisamatsu and Yoshida 1954: 286–288). The New Literature movement in colonial Taiwan began a half-century after the inception of the *genbun itchi* movement, but it shared the goal of creating a modern written language that reflected the spoken vernacular and could form the foundation for a new literary and cultural identity. Although the Taiwanese movement arose from a desire to maintain an identity distinct from Japan, it took its cues from the Japanese movement. The counternarrative to the dominant, encroaching forces of colonial assimilation took a page from the language modernization campaign of the metropole. Two early advocates of vernacular reform, Huang Chengcong and Huang Chaoqin, in fact appropriated the Japanese term "*genbun itchi*" *(yanwen yizhi)* to characterize the need to close the gap between spoken Taiwanese and written Chinese.

The New Literature movement led by Zhang Wojun sought to resolve the conflict between literary Chinese and modern vernacular Chinese; the nativist-literature movement focused on creating a distinctively Taiwanese written vernacular that could supplant the continental Mandarin. Taiwan's continuing separation from China, as well as Japan's active program of education and cultural assimilation, resulted in a diminution of interest in a vernacular literature based on the speech of the North China plain. In the 1930s, there was a concerted effort to create a written vernacular language that captured the distinctive features of the local language and a vernacular literature, written in this new orthography, that could express the unique aspects of Taiwanese life and culture. Huang Shihui articulated a socially progressive rationale for this literature, which was to give voice to uneducated masses who had no access to the privileged realms of Japanese and Mandarin fiction. Guo Qiusheng made substantial contributions to the practical task of achieving a coherent orthography for this literature.

After the Manchuria Incident of 1931, which increased tension with China, experiments with any sort of Chinese-related language were viewed with new suspicion—and when the Sino-Japanese War erupted in 1937, they were terminated by the colonial government. The ban on all publications in Chinese or Taiwanese and the interdiction against speaking these languages in public places interrupted the development of Taiwanese-language literature. The issue would be revisited in a postcolonial context in the 1970s, when the second Nativist Literature debate would again pit a nativist cultural identity against the politically dominant, sinocentric ideal. The immediate consequence, however, was the emergence of a new generation of native writers whose first intellectual language was Japanese. Together with an active circle of expatriate Japanese writers, they ushered in a short but prolific period of robust literary activity, a period that some would come to refer to as the golden age of Taiwanese colonial literature.

The Nativist Response

In November 1934, *Literary Review* (*Bungaku hyōron* 文学評論) published a reader's letter titled "Let Us Guide Colonial Literature" ("Shokuminchi bungaku wo shidōseyo" 植民地文学を指導せよ！). In it the writer, a student in Tokyo, expressed his excitement about an award given by the magazine to Yang Kui's 楊逵 (1905–1985) short story "Newspaper Boy" 新聞配達夫 the previous month:[1]

> After countless struggles, one year after a Korean, our Taiwanese writer finally enters the Japanese literary establishment (*bundan* 文壇). My heart was filled with joy when I saw my friend and rival Yang Kui's name in *Literary Review*. First let us celebrate this new development of Taiwanese literature. Of course, we Taiwanese writers are not satisfied just simply to be recognized as Japanese writers. As a new work, one cannot deny that "Newspaper Boy" is immature. The creative style is childish and certainly not up to the level of Chō Kakuchū 張赫宙 [a Korean writer]. But Chō's work does not deal with the historical reality of the colonies as authentically as Yang's. It is precisely in this realism that the value of "Newspaper Boy" lies. We must observe the island with proletarian eyes, dig deeper, and continue to achieve high-quality artistic works.[2]

This assessment of the event by the letter writer, Lai Minghong,[3] captures the literary climate of the 1930s and gives us a glimpse into the delicate relations not only between Japan and its colony, Taiwan, but also between its two major colonies, Taiwan and Korea. Lai rejoiced that for the first time a Taiwanese had been recognized and published in a major literary journal, but he also cautioned Taiwanese writers not to think of this as an ultimate goal and subordinate themselves to Japanese literature. Instead he regarded this as an auspicious beginning for the development of Taiwanese literature, a chance to catch up with Korean writers who also wrote in Japanese.[4] Lai took comfort in the fact that while Yang's story was immature as a literary work, it excelled in its accurate depiction of the situation in the colonies, an element he found lacking in the Korean Chō Kakuchū's work. This short paragraph not only hints at the underlying competitiveness between segments of the colonized but also indicates the power dynamic between the colonized and the colonizer: the colonial power should be emulated and resisted at the same time.

This pattern of simultaneous inclusion and exclusion defines the controlling tension between Taiwanese writers and their master culture during the colonial period. The other issue that determined the trajectory of Taiwanese colonial literature was proletarian/socialist realism. We have seen in the debates between Nishikawa's *Bungei Taiwan* and Zhang Wenhuan's *Taiwan bungaku* the ideological gulf that separated romanticism (associated with Nishikawa) and realism (Zhang). Most native writers insisted that only realistic representations of life on the island were true literature; they rejected other forms of literary representation as mere exoticized games that satisfied only those who did not truly love or see the real Taiwan (that is, the Japanese and their cronies). The tradition that native literature was synonymous with realism had been established by Yang's "Newspaper Boy," and its influence continued even after the war and helped to shape a native literary vision. The second Nativist Literature *(xiangtu wenxue)* movement in the latter half of the 1970s was a revitalization movement that grew out of opposition to the ideology-bound anticommunist literature *(fangong wenxue)* of the 1950s and the dominant modernist trend of the 1960s *(xiandai wenxue)*. Beyond the core debates on the necessity and methodology of establishing a native Taiwanese identity, the issue of how to represent this newly uncovered identity began to surface. The nativist movement called for authentic realism, which would include using the local Taiwanese dialect as the primary mode of expression in a medium dominated by Mandarin.[5] There was no writer of the colonial period more adamant than Yang Kui in achieving this social realism.

Socialist Idealism and Colonial Reality: Yang Kui

Yang Kui was both a proletarian writer and a social activist. Often his social message and sense of mission take precedence over artistic expression. The urgency of his pleas for social justice, a common theme through all of Yang's works, is closely related to the details of his life. Of the writers I discuss in this chapter, Yang was the earliest. He was born into a working-class family in Tainan in 1905 at a time when Japanese colonial rule was gradually getting on track after years of suppressing armed resistance. All armed rebellions had been quelled by 1902, in fact, and by 1905 the island had achieved economic self-sufficiency to the point that the colonial government was able to sustain itself financially with no support from the central government (Yamaguchi Mamoru 1992: 130). Under a restrictive educational system set up solely for the natives, Yang Kui was able to get into public elementary school.[6] In 1915, Yang's outlook on life was altered by a dramatic incident. Inspired by the armed uprisings that led to the fall of the Chinese empire in 1911, anticolonial Taiwanese sought to topple the colonial government by organizing the armed rebellion now known as the Xilaian 西来庵 Incident. Xilaian was near the town where Yang grew up. His brother was conscripted by the Japanese to fight the rebels and Yang recalled his shock when he saw Japanese cannon being paraded in front of his house. As a result of this last major uprising against Japanese rule, more than two thousand people were arrested and over half of them executed. After this incident, Taiwanese dissidents realized that the only way to advance their cause was through organization. Various social and cultural bodies came and went. Then, in 1921, while Yang was in middle school, the Taiwanese Cultural Association (Taiwan Bunka Kyōkai) was founded; it would become a base for a transformation of the national consciousness.[7]

As a student Yang was not particularly enthusiastic about his schoolwork; he was, however, absorbed in reading Japanese books on literature and thought. In the following passage we see not only his taste for contemporary Japanese literature but also his appetite for the wide variety of world literature he was exposed to through Japanese:

> I did not read much classical Japanese but read everything that was available by Natsume Sōseki, Akutagawa Ryūnosuke, and the White Birch school. At that time, translations of foreign literature were very popular in Japan. In the beginning I relied on dictionaries and read

foreign literature in English. But then it was so much more efficient to read the Japanese translation. I loved Russian literature, particularly the nineteenth-century works. Tolstoy, Turgenev, Gogol, Dostoevsky. I also liked works written around the French Revolution. For English literature, I preferred Dickens. I was quite moved by Hugo's *Les Misérables*. On the whole, I was most moved by works that resisted or protested against old customs and social vices and those that depicted the difficult lives of people at the bottom of society.[8]

Yang's hero was the civil rights activist Ōsugi Sakae, and his assassination by the fascist government in 1923 had a great impact on him. Longing for a place where he could write and publish, he left high school in 1924.[9] In Tokyo he sought an outlet for his creative energy but also an escape from the increasingly oppressive environment of the island (and perhaps an escape from a marriage arranged by his parents). Yang enrolled in the art department at Nihon University. Unlike many of his contemporaries, who came from the bourgeois landlord class and were supported in their studies in Tokyo, Yang's family was not well off. Rather than devoting himself to study, Yang spent most of his time working to support himself and immersed himself in the student movement and various social causes. He associated with proletarian writers, studied Marxist theory, worked as paper deliveryman and day laborer, and was active in the labor movement. Japan was in a recession, however, and Yang was barely able to eke out a living.[10] In 1927, he was arrested for participating in a protest by Korean farmers and thrown into jail for three days. This marked the first of his many arrests by the authorities. By the time the occupation ended, Yang had been arrested ten times.

Returning to Taiwan in 1927, Yang became involved in local union activities for farmers and was active in the left-leaning Taiwanese Cultural Association. In 1928, he left the association and formed his own People's Party of Taiwan (Taiwan Minshūtō 台湾民衆党), which concentrated on organizing unions for peasants and laborers. In 1930, the crackdown on leftist movements intensified—and with the Manchuria Incident the next year all activities were suppressed. Yang was frustrated by the crumbling of the movement. Abandoning activism, he devoted himself to literary pursuits.

The story "Newspaper Boy," which grew out of Yang Kui's personal experiences, was first published in the newspaper *Taiwan xinminbao*. Only the first half, however, made it into the paper; the second half was banned from publication. The full text was made known to the world when Yang submitted it to a contest at *Bungaku hyōron* and won second place (though no first place was awarded). Told by a first-person narrator, the story is about a Taiwanese youth who goes to Japan to study under conditions of extreme financial difficulty. He suffers inhumane treatment from a newspaper distributor and is eventually fired for failing to sign up more subscribers. On top of that, the seizure of his family's land by a sugar factory leads to his father's death and his mother's suicide. The young protagonist decides to organize his fellow newsboys to fight against their ruthless boss.

"Newspaper Boy" was translated into Chinese by Hu Feng in 1936 with the title "Songbaofu" 送報伕 and was included in two anthologies.[11] This was the first Taiwanese literary work ever translated and published in China and is an example of the early interaction between the two locations.[12] While most critics credit "Newspaper Boy" with blazing the trail for Taiwanese colonial literature to break into the Japanese literary scene, all agree that it is rather pedantic and flat as a piece of literature. The colonial oppressors in Taiwan who persecute his family are caricatures of corruption and immorality, as is the newspaper distributor for whom the protagonist worked in Tokyo. Yang's goal was to convey a message, and he did not expend a great effort in dressing up the messenger.

"Newspaper Boy" is framed in terms of class conflict and does not venture beyond this analysis to explore other elements of his people's pain and suffering. The economic misery of the protagonist is rooted in a simplistic structure of oppressor and oppressed, and the narrator implies, somewhat naively, that the peasants who work on the sugar plantations in Taiwan and the urban laborers in Tokyo, once united, can turn the world into a utopian paradise. The story does, however, manage to avoid a simplistic nationalism: it does not condemn all Japanese and it does not let colonial collaborators go blameless. The friendship the protagonist forms with Tanaka, who helped him when he was desperate, is depicted with great warmth, whereas his own brother is portrayed as a heartless blackguard who works as a policeman for the colonial regime. In the end, the protagonist feels closer to Tanaka than to his own blood relative and comes to realize that there are good people and bad people in both communities. The story ends on a hopeful note. After learning that the paperboys have organized themselves against the merciless boss and won better working conditions, the protagonist decides to go back to Taiwan to do the same thing.

The selection committee that awarded Yang the prize was split over the merit of the work. Comments on the story's artistic merit included: "as a novel, it is not very good" (Tokunaga Sunao); "it has not fulfilled the form of a novel yet" (Kubokawa Ineko); and "on the whole, it is subjective and childish" (Takeda Rintarō). Some opinions, however, expressed sympathy for the author's struggle. Comments praised the sincerity expressed by the author: "the story is devoid of ill-intentioned artificiality; the straightforward feeling (*chokujō* 直情) that he had no choice but to write about it is well conveyed" (Kamei Katsuichirō); "I have never read anything so full of true feeling (*shinjō* 真情)" (Nakajō Yuriko). Fujimori Seikichi was most supportive in his evaluation, though it might sound patronizing to today's readers. He valued the work's historic significance in breaking new ground for colonial literature, saying: "We must be compassionate to works by peasants and working people, particularly those from the colonies" (Kawamura Minato 2000a: 210–211).

The most intriguing aspect of "Newspaper Boy" was that it raised the possibility of forming alliances across ethnic and class lines. The protagonist responds to the tragedy that befalls his family by forging ties with members of his own working class in Japan. In order to change the system in Taiwan, it is necessary to initiate the change from within Japan. Yang's efforts to create an alliance with the Japanese left continued after he had returned to Taiwan and founded his own literary magazine, *New Taiwan Literature* (*Taiwan shinbungaku* 台湾新文学, 1935). Though interest was by then beginning to flag, Japanese proletarian literature was still a force to be reckoned with. One would think that if anyone were going to be sympathetic to colonial literature, it would be the members of the proletarian literary group.

Yang Kui and the Proletarian Literature Movement

Yang Kui's relationship with the proletarian writers cannot be characterized as affectionate. That his story was published in the proletarian magazine *Literary Review* demonstrates that Yang had cultivated his relationship with the group, particularly with Tokunaga Sunao (徳永直 1899–1958), whose strong recommendation played a major role in getting Yang's story published and awarded a prize. Yang was conscientious in maintaining ideological, and financial, connections with Japanese proletarian writers, and he revisited Japan in 1937 to renew his friendship with the group. But Japanese proletarian writers at times were harshly critical of the state of proletarian literature in Taiwan. They failed to understand the financial burdens, the problems posed by the paper shortage, and the political dangers associated with publishing a proletarian magazine under the watchful eye of the colonial administration.

In two issues of his *New Taiwan Literature* (2(1) and 2(2), January/February 1937), Yang published contributions he had solicited from Japanese writers, addressing questions such as the path that colonial literature should take, the mission for Taiwanese writers in particular, and general advice for Taiwanese writers and editors. Among those who responded were Tokunaga, Hayama Yoshiki 葉山嘉樹 (1894–1945), Ishikawa Tatsuzō 石川達三 (b. 1905), Chō Kakuchū 張赫宙 (b. 1905), Hirabayashi Taiko 平林たい子 (1905–1972), and many other writers from the proletarian movement. Tokunaga emphasized that only colonized people themselves can depict the realities of the poor and convert them into artistic works. Hirabayashi Taiko and Hashimoto Eikichi 橋本英吉 (1898–1978) both indicated that Taiwanese literature was unsophisticated. Hayashi Fusao (1903–1975) went further, saying that "the novels, either in Taiwanese or Japanese, are extremely childish" and "the mission for Taiwanese writers is to become cultured people *(kyōyōjin)*. If they don't work toward this goal, it will be useless no matter what they write."[13] Thus even among the proletarian writers of Japan, from whom one might have expected some degree of empathy toward their colonized colleagues, this sort of cultural chauvinism was prevalent. Yang's firm belief in international solidarity with his Japanese counterparts kept him blind to the racial overtones of the criticism. He reflected on these comments and vowed to work harder to live up to the various expectations of the Japanese writers.

It is rather ironic that Yang came onto the Japanese proletarian scene at a time when the movement had already lost much of its momentum. Indeed many of its writers would soon renounce their beliefs and rechart their artistic direction, becoming victims of the so-called reorientation (*tenkō* 転向). If his literary career had blossomed just a few years earlier, he might have been able to publish more frequently and garner more attention in Japan. The birth of Japanese proletarian literature can be traced as far back as 1916 to works depicting the miseries of the working class and their resistance to social injustice—such as Nakajō (later Miyamoto) Yuriko's *The Impoverished (Mazushiki hitobito no mure)*. Another genre of writing, referred to as laborers' literature (*rōdōsha bungaku*) and represented by such writers as Miyaji Karoku and Hirazawa Keishichi, was considered kindred to the proletarian literature. The term "proletarian literature," however, was officially used only after the Russian Revolution in 1917.[14]

The Russian Revolution shocked the world, and the subsequent whirlwind that swept through Germany and France quickly became a global movement. Japan was no exception. The leftist movement began with the journal *The Sower* (*Tanemaku hito* 種蒔く人, 1921), which became the base for early proletarian writers. After the Kantō Earthquake in 1923, *Tanemaku hito* folded but another journal, *Literary Battlefront* (*Bungei sensen* 文芸戦線), took its place in 1924. *Bungei sensen*, proclaiming its mission to create "an artistic shared battlefront based on the proletarian liberation movement," featured writers such as Hayama Yoshiki, who published his well-known short stories "Prostitute" ("Inbaifu" 淫売婦, 1925) and "People Who Live with the Sea" ("Umi ni ikuru hitobito" 海に生くるひとびと, 1925) there. The proletarian movement began to gather momentum at the end of 1925 with the founding of the Japan Proletarian Literary Alliance (Nihon Puroretaria Bungei Renmei; that is, Puroren プロ聯), followed by the Japan Proletarian Art Alliance (Nihon Puroretaria Geijutsu Renmei; that is, Purogei プロ芸) the next year. The following year saw the inauguration of Nakano Shigeharu and Hayashi Fusao's Marxist Art Association (Marukusu Shugi Geijutsu Kenkyūkai; that is, Marugei マル芸), Labor Peasant Artist Alliance (Rōnō Geijutsuka Renmei; that is, Rōgei 労芸), and the Avante-Garde Artist Alliance (Zen'ei Geijutsuka Dōmei; that is, Zengei 全芸). In 1928, perhaps the apex of the Japanese proletarian movement, all these fractious groups were consolidated into the Federation of Japanese Proletarian Art (Zen Nippon Musankaikyū Geijutsu Renmei; that is, Nappu ナップ),[15] and its journal *Battle Flag* (*Senki* 戦旗) became a vital breeding ground for Japanese proletarian literature. It published, among many other works, Kobayashi Takiji's 小林多喜二 "Crab Factory" ("Kani kōsen" 蟹工船)[16] and Tokunaga Sunao's "Street Without Sunlight" ("Taiyō no nai machi" 太陽のない街).[17]

The following years constituted the golden age of Japanese proletarian literature. It occupied a central position in the literary world and attracted many mainstream writers who were sympathetic to the cause. In 1930 another journal, *Nappu*, was formed to focus on literature and *Battle Flag* became a general educational instrument. Nappu as an organization was disbanded in November 1930, replaced by the Federation of Japanese Proletarian Culture (Nihon Puroretaria Bunka Renmei; that is, Koppu コップ). With the Manchuria Incident of 1931, however, the movement came under mounting attack and many writers were arrested. In 1933, the police killed one of the major proletarian writers, Kobayashi Takiji, and the next year saw the complete dissolution of both

Narupu (March) and Koppu (September). The movement was battered, but some continued to struggle. The magazine *Bungei hyōron*, for example, which published Yang Kui's "Newspaper Boy," was founded in 1934, after Narupu folded. Despite these efforts, proletarian literature was finished as an organized movement after the second Sino-Japanese war exploded in 1937.

If the situation in Japan was intolerant of social activism, conditions were even harsher for Taiwanese writers engaged in proletarian literary and social activities. Certainly there were Japanese activists who lived in the colony, such as Fujiwara Kiyosaburō, who established connections with Nappu. Inspired by *Battle Flag*, Fujiwara and several of his compatriots started the short-lived journal *Mukidō jidai* 無軌道時代 (Off-track age). Most proletarian publications of the time, however, were founded by Taiwanese.[18] The indigenous Taiwanese proletarian movement faced a number of limiting factors not shared by the movement in Japan. First, a modern, educated class did not really take form until late in the colonial period. Second, the colonial government was far more severe than the administration in Japan in suppressing budding organizations. Third, Japanese-language education was still in its formative stages during the period from the mid-1920s to the mid-1930s—the height of the Japanese proletarian movement—and there was little cross-fertilization between the two places. Nevertheless, early activities can be traced back as early as the founding in 1923 of *Taiwan minbao* 台湾民報, which advocated the political, social, and cultural awareness of the masses. In the late 1920s, anarchism and communism slipped into the island. And in 1927, the communist activist Lian Wenqing was successful in reorganizing the only cultural educational organization of that time, the Taiwan Cultural Association (Taiwan Bunka Kyōkai 台湾文化協会), into a communist organization.[19]

Before Yang Kui's literary debut in Japan in 1934 and the subsequent founding of his own journal, *Taiwan shinbungaku* 台湾新文学 (*New Taiwan literature*), in Taiwan in 1935, there were heroic attempts by native intellectuals to start several organization-based publications. But on the whole they were short-lived, and most issues were banned shortly after they appeared. In August 1930, for example, the monthly magazine *Taiwan sensen* 台湾戦線 (Taiwan battlefront) was inaugurated with writers such as Xie Xuehong 謝雪紅 and Lai He 頼和 as its core members. The magazine published a total of four issues; each was banned immediately upon its appearance and the magazine was ordered to disband only four months after its founding. Although it tried to resurrect itself by joining forces with *Gojinhō* 伍人報 (Squad report), it was eventually crushed again. Another example was *Taiwan bungei* 台湾文芸 (*Taiwan Literary Arts,* not to be confused with Nishikawa Mitsuru's *Bungei Taiwan,* which appeared several years later), the official magazine of the Taiwan Bungei Sakka Kyōkai (Association of Taiwanese Writers). As the first literary magazine for the whole island, *Taiwan bungei* lasted about a year and a half (November 1934 to August 1936) before it was banned. Several other journals followed, such as *Nanyin* 南音 (Southern accent) and *Forumosa* フォルモサ (Formosa), emphasizing the literary expression of the social movement in the early 1930s.

Yang Kui's contact with left-leaning literary works no doubt began during his stay in Japan, from 1924 to 1927, when he enrolled in the night school of Nihon University's art department while working at various menial jobs during the day. After his return to Taiwan, Yang served on the editorial board of *Taiwan bungei* and was the editor in charge of the Japanese section. In 1935, he left the magazine due to differences with its editorial policy and started his own journal, *Taiwan shinbungaku* 台湾新文学. Despite his straitened financial circumstances, Yang supported it with his own funds and was able to publish a number of special issues on Gorky and compositions in Chinese. Several issues were banned and the magazine itself was ordered to cease publication in April 1937.

Yang Kui's Fiction

If Yang's fiction tends toward the polemical, his observations on social and economic conditions in the colony are razor sharp. In the short story "Water Buffalo" ("Suigyū" 水牛),[20] Yang points out the contradictions inherent in the colonial policy of confiscating thousands of domestic water buffalo, typically the most important possession of Taiwanese peasants, and sending them to help with the development of the South Pacific. A young girl named A-yu, who once tended her family's water buffalo, stops her daily trips to the riverside, where she has been socializing with the young narrator, a student who has returned to the village for the summer. The narrator had grown fond of the girl, and the river that once gave him such pleasure now seems forlorn with so many buffalo and their caretakers gone. Worse, the young girl's family has been deprived of its livelihood; after her father fails to make a living as a road construction worker, he resolves to sell his daughter to the narrator's father. The narrator tells us angrily that he is sure the girl he loves will become his father's newest sexual playmate, as he has already bought two girls in the past. The background of this story is a traditional local practice of child marriage in which a preteen girl called a *shinbua* 媳婦仔 is adopted into the family and serves initially as a household servant. When mature, she usually becomes the wife of one of the sons of that family, but here the patriarch is usurping his son's position. Yang was always troubled by this ancient practice, and one of the reasons he fled to Japan in 1924 was to avoid his family's imposition of a *shinbua* on him.

Inherent in this story is an economic critique. Within the empire, arbitrary decisions are made to develop one colony at the expense of another. These policies subvert the traditional farming community in Taiwan, but the modernization that is supposed to replace the farm economy, in the form of road building and other state-directed public works projects, is unable to provide a living wage. Yang also directs his criticism toward the inhumane aspects of the traditional economic system as embodied in the practice of *shinbua* child marriage. Thus beneath the empire's obvious macroeconomic oppression there is underlying anxiety and frustration toward the indigenous microeconomic system that has ensnared the object of the narrator's desire, the young girl A-yu, whom he will have to cede to his own father.

The economic relationship between the colonizer and the colonized, an intertwined yet asymmetric power relation, is again addressed in the story "Native Chicks" ("Fan'age" 蕃仔鶏).[21] The title is a sexually derogatory term referring to native women who work as maids for the Japanese. Mingda has seen his job in a factory reduced to half time. His wife, Suzhu, works as a housemaid for a Japanese family. Mingda's underemployment has a big impact on the family's livelihood, because he is still trying to pay off the loan he took out to pay for the dowry when he married Suzhu. Suzhu is caught between her family's financial exigencies and her desire to quit her job in order avoid her employer's sexual advances. When she does become pregnant by her employer—unable to tell her husband and unable to quit her job—she chooses to hang herself.

The predicament in which Mingda and Suzhu find themselves is similar to that in "Water Buffalo." The protagonists are caught in an inescapable net of social and economic pressures rooted both in discriminatory economic policies (government confiscations, factory layoffs, underpaid workers) that can be related to colonialism and in oppressive social traditions like child marriage and the dowry system. Thus they are sandwiched between, on the one hand, a modernizing capitalist colonial economy in which the colonized are less human beings than cogs in the machine of production and, on the other, a traditional feudalistic economy in which marriage is chiefly a financial transaction.

Yang's fictional creations are primarily vehicles for social criticism, and the characters are not well developed. Compared to such writers as Zhang Wenhuan and Lü Heruo, for example, Yang's characters demonstrate less complex psychological dimensions. They reflect the role of class in a capitalistic colonial society; seldom do they express the entangled cultural elements of individual identity and modernity. Yang's antipathy for capitalism, as seen in "Newspaper Boy," is both experiential and instinctive.[22]

Yang Kui's visceral aversion to capitalism has its origins in Marxist ideology, to be sure, but also in the traditional ideals of the literati. In the short story "Clay Dolls" ("Doroningyō" 泥人形),[23] which is closely modeled on aspects of Yang's own life, the protagonist expresses open contempt for his friend Liu (who has recently changed his name to Tomioka). Liu has come to borrow some money before he leaves for Japan to participate in a get-rich-quick scheme. The impoverished protagonist lives a meager life working as a flower farmer to support a wife and four children. Though his life is hard, he devotes his free time to writing, and his children, though materially deprived, play contentedly with the clay dolls their father makes for them. The protagonist steadfastly believes that the poor but virtuous lifestyle he has chosen is correct and places his hopes in his son, who wants to become an aeronautical engineer. He is sustained in his determination, not merely by the socialist, anticapitalistic philosophy that shaped many of Yang's choices in life, but also by the traditional Chinese ideal of a literate gentleman who endures material hardship without acquiescing to injustice.[24] Thus the protagonist's contempt for his friend's materialism is rooted both in imported Western ideology and in a traditional ideal of conduct.

Most critics, when discussing Yang's works, focus solely on his defiant stance against the empire and imperialism. From these texts it is clear that Yang Kui was disturbed by the internal paternalistic feudal system as much as the external imperial hegemony imposed by Japan. As a writer and thinker, Yang Kui was attentive to the contradictions caused by class in the classic Marxist sense and by those endemic to the indigenous feudalism. He drew inspiration from these two sources and carefully wove the two strains of discourse into his narrative. His at times polemical, radically Marxist, discourse of liberation was consistently tempered by his ambivalent attitude toward the merits and deficiencies of his own native culture.

Yang's participation in the Japanese proletarian literary movement was limited by his late arrival on the scene and by the unspoken ethnic tension that existed between Japanese writers and those from the colonies.[25] The private friendships he later cultivated with left-leaning Japanese expatriates, in contrast, developed into fruitful alliances between Taiwanese and Japanese socialists. Yang credited two Japanese with changing the course of his life: Numakawa Sadao 沼川定雄 and Nyūta Haruhiko 入田晴彦.[26] Numakawa Sadao was a teacher at the public school (*kōgakkō* 公学校 as opposed to primary school, *shōgakkō* 小学校, for Japanese children) who was fond of Yang and attentively nurtured his budding interest in literature. Numakawa made his private library collection available to Yang, and it was at Numakawa's house that he had the opportunity to read Japanese modern literature and translations of Western literature. Numakawa's generosity opened Yang's eyes to the outside world and expanded his intellectual horizons during his critical formative years.

Nyūta Haruhiko was an idealistic leftist student who loved literature. After his reorientation *(tenkō)*, he moved to Taiwan and took a position as a policeman in the village where Yang had his flower farm. Soon they became the best of friends, sharing their passion for books. Nyūta visited Yang and his family almost daily, and on various occasions he offered financial help. An aspiring writer himself when young, Nyūta was a loner who did not socialize with his fellow colonial bureaucrats and was privately critical of the colonial policy. When forced to quit his job and ordered to return to Japan, Nyūta committed suicide. To Yang Kui he bequeathed his own collection of books, which the impoverished Yang could never have afforded. In particular, the collected works of the father of modern Chinese literature, Lu Xun, served as a portal to Chinese literature for Yang. Lu Xun's work had a great impact on him, shaping his anticolonial stance and encouraging his critical view of the decaying feudal tradition. The fact is that Yang's knowledge of world literature—first Japanese modern literature, then Western literature through Japanese translation, and later Chinese literature—was mediated through colonial patronage at various stages of his life. Schoolteachers, policemen, and low-level bureaucrats (directors of train stations, post offices, and the like) constituted the foundation of the empire. Unlike the policymakers sitting in their offices at the headquarters of the colonial administration or the central government, they were on the front line dealing with the colonial subjects on a day-to-day basis. Yang's associations with Numakawa and Nyūta are also indicative of the relations between knowledge and power in the colonial context.

Kawamura Minato (2000a: 194–216) makes an interesting comparison between Yang and Haniwa Yutaka 埴輪雄高, (1910–1999), the eminent postwar abstract writer who was born and raised in colonial Taiwan. Both were born at about the same time, part of the second generation of colonizer and colonized. Both awakened early in life to the inequities of colonialism, both were later involved in one way or another with the proletarian movement, and both were arrested several times. Tracing the similarities of their life journeys, Kawamura discusses how these life experiences have been manifested in their respective works "Newspaper Boy" and *Dead Spirit* (*Shiryō* 死霊). In Kawamura's view, *Shiryō* is a masterpiece that could not have been written without Haniwa's Taiwan experience—which, he insists, formed the basis for Haniwa's literature. Haniwa relates how the colonial experience left him with a schizophrenic "gap" between two languages and two identities; Kawamura sees this "gap" as a key concept in reading *Shiryō*. Despite the similarities in life story and in the presence of a shared enemy—Japanese imperialism—Kawamura sees a contrast in their treatment of the relationship between colonizer and subject: whereas Haniwa avoids any meaningful encounter between colonial subject and Japanese, Yang's "Newspaper Boy" falls into the easy trap of universalism, naively portraying an unproblematic union between the two.

It could be argued, however, that it is precisely Yang Kui's stubborn optimism that allowed him to persevere through both political and financial hardships. It is also this hopefulness (naive though it may be in Kawamura's eyes) that kept Yang in the vanguard of writers of social conscience. Many writers who were active during the colonial period gave up writing after the war. The postwar political situation in Taiwan was no doubt one reason for this development, but the difficulty of adapting to Mandarin, now the dominant mode of expression, was likely more important. Yang Kui admitted that he experienced great difficulty in writing in Chinese, but he continued to write for the impoverished and the oppressed. He was imprisoned by the Nationalist government for twelve years (1950–1962) on Green Island, where most political prisoners were kept until the dissolution of martial law in 1986.[27] Most writers from the occupation period were able to keep out of trouble with the new regime because they either kept silent or advocated a distinct native cultural identity to which the Nationalist government at first paid little heed. After a prolonged and bloody war with the Communists on the mainland, the Nationalist government's first concern was to purge leftists. Yang's trouble arose from his outspoken opposition to capitalism and the leftist tendencies expressed in his socialist writings, which he refused to forswear. Yang was, for the most part, ignored, and his literature was taboo until the late 1970s when martial law was lifted and certain native writers gradually regained their stature. Yang lived a difficult life, mired in poverty, and devoted whatever he could afford to his cause. No matter how one regards Yang Kui's literary accomplishments, his faith in the union of art and action and his determination in pursuing his convictions throughout his life are indeed admirable. In the early 1970s, his works began to be reissued in Chinese translation. In 1976, his short story "The Rose That Cannot Be Trampled" ("Ya bubian de meigui hua" 压不扁的玫瑰花), written in jail and published in 1957 with the original title ("Can't Keep Out the Spring" ("Chunguang guanbuzhu" 春光関不住), was included in a junior high school textbook. The rehabilitation of Yang Kui continues, and a fourteen-volume official collection of his complete works has been published.[28]

The Colonial Encounter and Memory: Lü Heruo

Lü Heruo (1914–1951) is the most skillful and mature of the prewar nativist writers. Lü was able to encompass Yang Kui's social mission and Zhang Wenhuan's native realism yet still create a sophisticated, highly personal literature. Whereas Yang Kui's passion for social causes sometimes overwhelms his narrative and Zhang Wenhuan seems too sentimental at times, Lü Heruo's stories are consistently well constructed, told in an authoritative voice, and populated with subtly depicted characters for whom the author expresses genuine empathy. Moreover, Lü's talents were not limited to fiction: he was a prominent critic with the best command of Japanese among his peers; he was intimately involved in the Taiwanese new-drama movement and wrote many stage plays and radio dramas; and he played an important role in the popularization of modern Western-style music. In his short and tempestuous life, the multifaceted Lü participated energetically in the cultural life of the colony. Indeed, his dedication won him the endearing nickname "premier genius of Taiwan" (Taiwan diyi caizi 台湾第一才子) (Lü 1995: 11).

The publication of Lü Heruo's short story "The Oxcart" ("Gyūsha" 牛車, 1935) in the left-leaning Japanese literary journal Literary Critic (Bungaku hyōron 文学評論) marked his debut in metropolitan literary circles.[29] In this story, an oxcart driver has suffered fierce competition from trucks and motorized carts ever since a modern highway to his village was opened. Even with his wife working at the new pineapple factory, they still cannot eke out a living. His wife turns to prostitution in order to raise the down payment on a piece of land he can farm. The tale ends with him being fined for driving his oxcart on the modern road and the goods on his cart being stolen. The story, similar to Yang Kui's "Newspaper Boy," is a seething indictment of the disastrous effect of colonial economic policy on the working class. The same journal had just published Yang Kui's "Newspaper Boy" the previous year and was happy to follow up with another story by a writer from the colony. "The Oxcart" is, in fact, rather atypical of Lü's writing. Most of his later stories veer away from direct engagement with politics and focus on the condition of people living in oppressed and inhumane circumstances.

To a certain degree, all native writers of the colonial period—whether "nationalists" who stressed cultural ties to China, "nativists" who advocated a distinctive Taiwanese identity, or "imperial-subject" writers who sought to assimilate to Japanese civilization—confronted this issue of how to navigate between their native Chinese/Taiwanese cultural heritage and the vision of modernity promoted by the Japanese colonial establishment. But to Lü Heruo there is an urgency to this issue and many of his stories convey an acute sense of loss. Frequently his compositions, though expressed in elegant Japanese, deal with strictly native issues and feature no Japanese characters or Japan-related events.

"Fengshui" ("Fūsui" 風水, 1942) is a prime example of this type of story.[30] It tells of a conflict between a pair of brothers—one trendy, successful, and calculating, the other filial and modest. The impatient brother claims that his recent misfortune has been caused by the bad *fengshui* (geomantic influence) of their mother's tomb and insists on performing the "washing bones" reburial ritual prematurely to improve his fortune. "Fortune, Children, and Longevity" ("Sai, shi, ju" 財子寿, 1942),[31] "A Happy Family" ("Gōke heian" 合家平安, 1943),[32] and "Pomegranate" ("Zakuro" 石榴, 1943)[33] all deal with old-fashioned domestic issues complicated by such factors as marriage, kinship relations, and economic worries within the feudalistic familial institution. Lü shows particular concern for the status and circumstances of women during his day. "Being a Woman" ("Onna no baai" 女の場合, 1936)[34] and "The Temple Courtyard" ("Byōtei" 廟庭, 1942)[35] depict the harsh reality faced by young women left on their own through betrayal by their lovers or an unsuccessful marriage. All these narratives are set in Taiwan; the characters are Taiwanese, the problems are those inherent in Taiwanese society, and there is almost no interaction with the Japanese.

In "Clear Autumn" ("Seishū" 清秋, 1944),[36] the protagonist is a young doctor named Xie who has just finished his training in Tokyo and returns to his hometown ready to start his own practice. The family is ecstatic about the prospect of their son opening a clinic in town and reversing the family's declining fortunes. Forced to wait for the colonial authority to issue him a license, Xie meets the only doctor in town and is taken aback by the cutthroat way he runs his profitable practice. Moreover, he discovers that the building his father wants to convert into his clinic is still occupied by a small businessman who faces financial ruin if he is evicted. These events lead the idealistic youth to question the commercial nature of his own practice. When Xie travels to Taipei to visit his younger brother, who works for a pharmaceutical company and has just been transferred to Southeast Asia, he returns resolved to give up the practice of medicine and turn his attentions to medical research—but discovers, ironically, that all his problems have been resolved. His license has been approved, his potential competitor, the town doctor, has been drafted, and the businessman has volunteered to fight in the South Pacific.

Compared to "Fengshui," which juxtaposes the traditional versus the modern, self-interest versus familial benefit, "Clear Autumn" triangulates among the Japanese colonial bureaucracy, the privileged Taiwanese gentry class, and the working class in a complex and understated deliberation on the meaning of life. While some critics have deemed "Clear Autumn" a failure among Lü's works because of its flat, subdued storytelling and its rather abrupt ending, Tarumi Chie has come to its defense (Tarumi 1995b: 157–162). In her analysis of Lü's narrative strategy she identifies a technique she calls "delaying" (*enchi* 延遲), which sheds light on the deliberate noneventfulness the author brings to the piece. Tarumi argues that it is precisely these delays and deferrals that prompt the protagonist Xie to question the purpose of his life—which was imposed through the traditional family value system and the imperial educational apparatus—thus allowing him to shift directions and embark on the new life implied at the end of the story. Lü deftly captures the subtle changes in the young man's state of mind during the long and aimless wait as he progresses from exhilaration to despair to confusion trapped in a cultural and professional limbo. Xie represents many young intellectuals of the day who were ambivalent about giving up life in the metropolis to return to a small town. In one way or another, each grappled with the guilt of privilege and the economic gap that existed in the colony.

Perhaps because he spent more time in Japan, studying music theory and voice at Tokyo University of the Arts and later performing as a professional singer with the musical troupe Tōhō Kagekidan, Lü seems to have enjoyed a wider range of contacts with the Japanese. Consequently, the characters he creates are complex figures with subtle emotions. Although stories like "The Oxcart" directly address political issues, most do not. In "Clear Autumn," for example, the colonial administration hovers in the background of the narrative, delaying and redirecting the trajectory of the young man's life.

Now let us turn to two short stories that do shed light on the colonial encounter—without, however, resorting to the language of cultural nationalism or plots involving bureaucratic politics: "Neighbor" ("Rinkyo" 隣居, 1942)[37] and "Magnolia" ("Yülanhua" 玉蘭花, 1943).[38] These stories have attracted little critical attention, perhaps because they are comparatively late works, written during a period of intense warfare, when censorship and the mechanisms for ideological control were so strict that freedom of expression was severely curtailed. Compared to his earlier stories, these tales contain little in the way of overt social or economic criticism. For this reason, they have sometimes been dismissed as echoing current slogans about the unity of Japan and Taiwan. They deserve consideration, however, for two reasons. First, Lü is by this point a much more mature artist; his command of Japanese is superior and his storytelling is more refined, judicious yet profound. Second, by locating the conflicts inherent in the colonial condition at the personal level he is able to reveal the impossibility—whatever goodwill might exist—of two divergent ethnic and cultural traditions ever truly coming together.

"Neighbor": Friendly Affections, Motherhood, and Benevolent Colonialism

"Neighbor" is told from the viewpoint of a third-person narrator, Mr. Chen, a young Taiwanese man who has moved from a provincial town to the city to take up a teaching position. When he rents a room in the house of a Japanese couple named Tanaka, Chen is puzzled why they are living in such a poor working-class neighborhood, mixing with the natives, far from the expatriate Japanese community. But gradually they come to know each other. The Tanakas are gentle people whose marriage is marred by the lack of a child, a fault attributed to Mrs. Tanaka's weak physical condition. One day the Tanakas bring home a three-year-old boy, whom they at first try to pass off as their own child who has been living elsewhere. When Chen points out that the boy is dressed like a typical Taiwanese infant and looks just like a Taiwanese child, the Tanakas admit that he is Min, the youngest of five sons of their neighbors, the Lis. Mrs. Tanaka has befriended Mrs. Li and gradually come to care for Min more and more. At first both Min and his parents are reluctant, but each time the Tanakas bring the Lis more and more gifts, asking that the boy be allowed to stay with them. Under the fawning, indulgent care of Mrs. Tanaka the boy settles into his new home and begins to call her mother. The Tanakas ask that the Lis not come to visit for a time, so that the boy will not feel homesick. When Mrs. Li comes after a month to bring the boy home, he no longer remembers his birth name, Min, and answers only to his new Japanese name, Tamio. Chen notices several occasions when the two mothers would compete, half-jokingly, to entice the boy to their side; he is pleased to see so much maternal love and attention being showered on the small child.

One day, the boy falls seriously ill and the mothers get into a heated dispute over how to treat him. Mrs. Tanaka is adamantly opposed to Mrs. Li's suggestion that they take him to a local temple and give him Chinese herbal medicine. Instead the child is hospitalized and the Tanakas attend upon him night and day, frantically nursing him back to health. Again Chen is moved by the devotion the Tanakas show to a child not of their own blood. The situation comes to a head when the Tanakas are transferred back to Taipei. They ask Chen, a teacher respected by the locals, to serve as go-between to the Li family in negotiating formal adoption of the boy. Chen is willing—he feels it is the least he can do for this devoted, loving couple—but his busy schedule keeps him from attending to it right away and soon the morning of the Tanakas' departure is upon them. Chen and the Li family all come to see the Tanakas off. The boy, dressed in fancy clothes, has completely taken to his new parents and does not even acknowledge his birth parents. Mrs. Li is distraught, shedding tears when she is rejected by Min, but her other children are quite excited about the chance to visit the big city in the future. As the train pulls out of the station, the narrator asks Mr. Li if the child has been adopted:

> Standing there, stunned, Mr. Li answered: "Not yet." His eyes never left the train as it gradually receded into the distance. When I raised my eyes, the train had already disappeared into the shadows of the jungle of tall buildings that pepper the cityscape. [Lü 1991: 206]

Among Lü's various short stories, "Neighbor" has received almost no critical attention—perhaps because the story is simple and told in a linear fashion with no plot twists to complicate the storytelling. Xu Junya is the only scholar to have discussed the story at length (Xu 1994: 273–320). Xu rejects a simplistic reading of the story that sees it merely as a response to the dominant propaganda of the day extolling "Japan and Taiwan as one" 内台一如 and "goodwill between Japan and Taiwan" 内台親善. Her further claim is more problematic. Xu argues that by portraying the Tanakas as living in a poverty-stricken neighborhood and loving someone else's child, Lü Heruo is drawing upon his socialist background and gesturing toward a classless society that transcends the ethnic divide between Taiwanese and Japanese. Thus, in Xu's reading, Lü affirms that the two people, colonizer and the colonized, can come together. Xu also praises Lü for creating an ideal maternal figure in Mrs. Tanaka without detracting from the image of the child's native mother. Both women, that is, are portrayed sympathetically; both are equally fit as mothers and exude a "maternal aura so beautiful" that the narrator is profoundly moved.

Xu's reading, however, misses the fundamental problem posed by the text. If the two women are indeed equally qualified as mothers, why does one deserve the child while the other is left without? The premise that the Lis and the Tanakas are comrades of the same class (inherently unattainable, I think, in a colonial society) seems to collapse when the Tanakas move out of the neighborhood, taking the boy away. The straightforward storytelling and warm human exchanges give way under closer analysis to a far darker and more disturbing message—an understanding of colonialism that is confirmed by Lü's postwar compositions in Chinese.[39] Here I want to focus on two aspects not treated by Xu Junya: the position of the narrator, Chen, who is not in fact a neutral, objective observer, and the maternal economy portrayed in this tale, which has implications far beyond that of a woman altruistically accepting and loving a child not her own.

The narrator of the tale, Mr. Chen, is initially distrustful of the Japanese couple but comes to accept them as basically kind. He is particularly taken with the gentleness of Mrs. Tanaka. The Tanakas are so deeply in love, and so demonstrative about it, that sometimes he, a single man, has to be careful to avert his eyes during their intimate moments. Mrs. Tanaka is portrayed as a quintessentially maternal figure:

Every time I see her, I lower my eyes and say the usual things, such as "Good morning," or "Good evening," to her. But she is always so very kind. Perhaps because I am single, she often brings me tea or water and asks me whether I need her to do my laundry. She is so solicitous that sometimes I don't know what to do. . . . She never puts on makeup, and that makes her look older than her real age. She seldom wears dresses; she is always in a kimono with a sash casually tied. She bundles up her reddish hair unassumingly. But she projects a maternal aura to the extent that at times I would even have mistaken her for my own mother. [Lü 1991: 190–192]

Since even an adult has a hard time resisting the maternal force of Mrs. Tanaka, the effect on a little child who is showered with attention and goodies can be imagined.

Although the Tanakas are, on the whole, blessed with conjugal happiness, the question of fertility is a source of continuing disharmony. Chen recalls that he once happened to observe an argument between the two centering on Mrs. Tanaka's failure to conceive. To Chen's consternation, Mr. Tanaka asked him to take sides:

"Well, Mr. Chen, who can say for sure if the problem is the seeds or the field? Naturally, both sides should share the responsibility. Don't you agree?" [p. 191]

Anne McClintock has pointed out the key role of female fertility in empire building. The empire invests in its women because "controlling women's sexuality, exalting maternity, and breeding a virile race of empire-builders was widely perceived as the paramount means for controlling the health and wealth of the male imperial body" (McClintock 1995: 47–50). Within the Japanese colonial context, the body of Japanese women was not only a site for reproduction of future soldiers and colonialists; as part of the total mobilized national workforce, they worked in the fields and factories, some volunteered to serve as nurses and clerks on the front, and some actually took up arms by joining the Women's Defense Brigade (Joshi Teishintai 女子挺身隊).

A flurry of recent studies by feminist scholars have reevaluated the role of Japanese women during the war.[40] Suzuki Yūko's study of feminist wartime activities reveals the complicity, even collaboration, of leaders of the women's movement like Takara Tomi, Ichikawa Fusae, and Yamataka Shigeri in the imperial project (Suzuki 1997a; 1997b). The tacit understanding was that in exchange for their support of the war effort and its associated ideology, women's liberation would be achieved after the war. Instead of focusing on elite women, Kanō Mikiyo has depicted the daily life of ordinary women during the war and examined how they participated in and facilitated a wartime discourse that sanctified motherhood so fanatically that Kanō coins the term "maternal fascism" (*bosei fashizumu* 母性ファシズム) to describe it (Kanō 1987; 1995a; 1995b; 2000). Wakakuwa Midori's work on wartime motherhood uses the Yasukuni Shrine to illustrate the deification of not only soldiers who died on the battlefield but also their mothers, who were called "mothers of the army gods" (*gunshin no haha* 軍神の母)."[41] One striking contemporary image cited by Wakakuwa shows a dignified young widow (who had just lost her husband in battle) carrying a young boy in her arms; this image parallels the structure of a genre painting of the Madonna and baby Jesus discussed in Ueno Chizuko (1998: 36–37).

Earlier feminist scholarship tended to lump Japanese women with all other Asian women as victims of patriarchal imperialism and the colonial war. These recent studies, however, treat women as active participants in the imperial enterprise, assessing in detail their roles and degrees of complicity. Ueno Chizuko refers to this change of paradigm—from regarding Japanese women as victims of the war, rather like Japan's colonial subjects, to seeing women as perpetrators—as a shift from victimized historical view (*higaisha shikan* 被害者史観) to a victimizer historical view (*kagaisha shikan* 加害者史観). Any attempt to reclaim female historical agency brings with it the responsibility to acknowledge its consequences (Ueno 1998: 29–30). Under wartime mobilization, everyone was supposed to be engaged in both the physical and ideological aspects of warfare. As a consequence, the public and private spheres became blurred. Even women's wombs were mobilized, and the natural biological function of reproduction took on a political and ideological significance. Similarly the child was no longer just a child of the parents but rather property of the nation-state.

The stakes are high for the Tanakas, who must fulfill their imperial mission by giving birth to the next generation of empire builders. In this sense, Mrs. Tanaka's barrenness represents a double threat: it undermines the empire's mission and undercuts the symbolic masculinity of the empire, which is articulated through Mr. Tanaka's "brawny" (*takumashii* 逞しい) physique. As intimated in the metaphor posed to the narrator by Mr. Tanaka, neither the seed nor the field is fertile in this land of the Other. A subtle irony is implicit here—especially when the tale is read within the larger context of colonial discourse: no matter how masculinely endowed Mr. Tanaka is, in the end he must "adopt" an offspring from the (dominated) Other.

What, then, is the role of the narrator in this transaction? A school-teacher responsible for educating the native children for the empire, he is a cultural mediator between the empire and its subjects. In fact, he is the teacher of one of the Li's children, through whom he learns many details concerning the little boy. In a sense, the narrator is as much implicated in the affair as the Tanakas, since he views matters only through the Tanakas' point of view. It does not dawn on him how the Li family might feel until the last scene when, for the first time, he comes face to face with Mr. Li and sees in his eyes the deep sorrow of the traumatic loss. Chen's willingness to act as a comprador, negotiating between the Tanakas and the Lis, is based on his assessment that the Tanakas are kind and generous people. As a comprador, the narrator's gaze is aligned with that of the colonizer: he sees the object of desire through the eyes of the Tanakas. The consequences of this action upon the Lis are never considered. It is precisely this blindness of the narrator, turning his back on the pleas of his own people, that makes this heart-wrenching story even more troubling.

One of the reasons why this story is so often misread, I think, is that Lü Heruo has installed an unreliable narrator as the only conduit of information to the reader. His take on the situation is based on his personal observations and interactions with the Tanakas while sharing their home. Of the Li family he knows little except for his relations with one of their children, who is his student, and he has no direct source of information concerning the relationship of the Tanaka and Li families or what sort of agreement they have reached. As his friendship with the Tanakas grows, based on a shared residence and a similar class background, he comes to see the situation more and more from their point of view. This bias sometimes interferes with his ability to assess matters objectively. Consider the following two scenes.

At first Min stays only for a day or two at a time and cries the whole night through. After he gets used to the Tanakas and can stay in their home, Mrs. Tanaka asks the Lis not to visit the boy for a month in order to allow him to get over his homesickness and settle in. When the Li family is allowed to visit the little boy Min again, he has become totally attached to the Tanakas. Min's brother comes and tries to take the toddler home to play. Realizing Min is the baby brother of his student, the narrator asks him about the situation in detail and discovers: "It wasn't that they had given the boy to the Tanakas. On the contrary, Mrs. Tanaka had taken a liking to the boy and insisted on taking him away. . . . Min is the Lis' fifth son, which is why Mrs. Tanaka thought to adopt him. Min's mother, Mrs. Li, must have thought the same; that is why she agreed" (Lü 1991: 198).

Later, when the Tanakas finally confide the truth to Chen, Mrs. Tanaka insists: "But now he has become my child. Yes, Min is my child. . . . See, Sensei, he does not want anyone but me. Mrs. Li now is nothing but a nanny to him." The narrator comments on how loving and tender a mother Mrs. Tanaka is and how happy she looks. That afternoon, Mrs. Li comes to visit and after that shows up every few days. Each time there is a sort of contest between the two women for the boy's affection which is observed repeatedly by the narrator:

> Mrs. Tanaka embraced him tightly and would not let go. The boy Min, surprisingly, showed no reaction when he saw Mrs. Li. On the contrary, he stayed clinging to Mrs. Tanaka. There was a forlorn look in Mrs. Li's eyes and she tried all sorts of ways to get close to the child. Afterward, every time she came, she would bring something nice to eat for the baby, just to please him.
>
> "Min, it's Mommy!" Mrs. Li held out her hands, but Min paid no attention to her. Mrs. Tanaka was quite pleased: "Look, Little Min, she is not your mother. Is she your nanny?" "This is horrible, he does not recognize his own mother," Mrs. Li sighed, trying to grab the child. Mrs. Tanaka held onto Min tightly, avoiding Mrs. Li's reach, laughing. [p. 199]

This quotation is pivotal to the narrative's development. We learn that the child the Tanakas now call their own was obtained from Mrs. Li through insistent persuasion. The mother/child relationship has been recast. The boy is now Tamio 民雄, a Japanese, not a Chinese boy named Min 民, and his birth mother has become his nanny. The superficial goodwill and laughter surrounding this transformation of identity cannot disguise the hurt felt by Mrs. Li, who finds her own son estranged from her.

One must marvel at Lü Heruo's dexterity in crafting this scene. It is lighthearted, yet beneath the surface lie unspoken tensions and suppressed emotional turmoil. As I noted earlier, the narrator is an unreliable guide in this situation and conveys a different message from the author. Right after this heart-wrenching scene, for example, the narrator observes: "I personally have seen them half seriously and half jokingly teasing and jostling with each other at various times. I felt an indescribable joy when I saw both women bursting with warm motherly love for the same boy" (p. 199). The narrator consistently puts a positive spin on events. He ignores the disparity in power between the two women and is oblivious to the anguish felt by Min's birth mother as she loses the affections of her son. The author, however, allows the reader to see through this veil of positivist interpretation to the raw nerve of pain felt by Mrs. Li and to experience revulsion at Mrs. Tanaka's gloating victory, which can only intensify Mrs. Li's sense of loss. The reader is free to decide whether to follow the narrator's interpretation or to read more into the story. But even the narrator must confront the Li family's loss at the end. There are, moreover, several hints that might lead the reader to draw a very different conclusion.

One doubt raised by the story concerns the Tanakas' motivation. The narrator wonders repeatedly why they are living in this run-down neighborhood, which he describes as "dirty and crowded, populated by rickshaw-pullers, food cart operators, convenience store owners, craftsmen, and farmers" (p. 185). When asked directly about this, Mr. Tanaka is evasive. Could it be they feared social pressure from their fellow Japanese because of their childless status? It seems that this lack of offspring has long been a source of disharmony between the Tanakas. Might their move into this neighborhood even be a Machiavellian ploy to obtain an offspring not of their own birth? In this case the title "Neighbor" takes on a sinister connotation. At the very least, they are so infatuated with the idea of parenthood that they lose sight of everything else. It is not that they have no empathy for others. Their warm friendship with the Taiwanese narrator disproves this, and no one can deny they are loving parents for the little boy. But the sympathetic portrayal of these two characters, presented through the eyes of the narrator, highlights the cynicism of their ultimately self-interested actions.

In Xu Junya's reading, Lü Heruo seeks in this story to transcend the class distinction between the Tanakas and the natives by having the Tanakas move voluntarily into a working-class Taiwanese neighborhood. I would argue, on the contrary, that the intermingled issues of class and race are at the forefront of the story. The author skillfully masquerades his true message by couching the narrative in understated, nonaccusatory language; it might remain hidden without a contrapuntal reading that enables the colonial implications of the story to emerge. Read as a short, sweet vignette depicting a rare friendship between Japanese and Taiwanese, in accord with the dominant ideological requirement of that tense time, one might miss the class and racial implications altogether.

Colonial cultural hegemony operates on all levels: through violent oppression, through an invisible network of filiative connections, through an internalized psychology, and through unconsciously complicit associations. Many of these elements are implicit in the narrative, which also problematizes the claim that benevolent colonialism brings civilization with all its modern trappings such as technology, medical care, sanitation, railroads, and education. This claim ignores the price the colonized must pay in exchange for these colonial niceties: submission of their culture, their language, their subjectivity, even their own children. The maternal compassion that Mrs. Tanaka exudes is so dangerously comforting that both the Lis and the narrator indulge in it until, too late, they realize the consequences. The Tanakas are lovely people doing a horrible thing. Through gentle persuasion and indirect coercion, these intimate, friendly raiders take possession of a child.

The position of the Li family is ambiguous. They no doubt see this adoption as a way for their son to attain a better life. Through Min's adoption, he can ascend racially into the ranks of the colonizers and live a life of material well-being and opportunity that will be forever denied his parents and even the educated Mr. Chen. But the pain felt by his parents is real, and it is the injustice of the colonial condition that forces them to make this sacrifice. As for the young boy, he is stripped of his own identity so that, by the time he is ready to leave for his new life, he can no longer recognize his own birth mother.

After almost half a century of the colonization process, Lü Heruo sees a generation that is gradually disconnecting from its indigenous roots and becoming assimilated into the colonial culture—as attested by the little boy's siblings, who are preoccupied and excited about a future trip to Taipei rather than the loss of one of their own brothers. The displaced child becomes the site of multiple contentions seeking to resolve the maternal rivalry between the two mothers, to reinvent motherhood for the imperial body, and, most important, to restore the imperial "manliness" of the empire. Through Lü Heruo's quiet storytelling, the narrative ultimately questions the legitimacy of the colonial enterprise.

"Magnolia": Images, Scents, and Colonial Memory

"Magnolia" ("Yülanhua" 玉蘭花, 1943) is a touching story relating an intimate friendship between a Japanese visitor to the colony and a native boy.[42] The serene, warmhearted story is unique in that it portrays an intensely personal interaction between a Japanese and a colonial native that is, in fact, quite rare in the body of Japanese colonial literature. To avoid the political implications of colonialism, Lü adopts the point of view of a seven-year-old boy who is barely able to leave his mother and grandmother's side. The boy's eyes serve as an innocent observer of the Japanese with no judgments and no preconceptions.

The story begins with the adult narrator looking at some old faded photographs of his childhood:

> To this day, I still have some twenty photographs of my family when I was a young boy. Every one of them has turned brown and begun to fade; in some the contours have blurred and the images are disappearing. But just a glance at them brings back the ambiance of my family when I was little. Most of the pictures are of my grandmother, aunties, and mother; all of them have since passed on. Dressed in their skirts and tops trimmed with chunky five-colored cords, with deck chairs and potted plants as the background, they look stiff. In most of those photos, the child me would either be standing by my grandmother or clinging to my mother's side. Though my grandmother and mother were holding my hands, they were staring stiffly and nervously into the camera as if there was not a moment to spare to pay attention to me. [Nakajima Toshio and Kawahara Isao 1999, 2:263]

We are told that the locals were not keen on being photographed, believing that it would make one thinner with each picture taken. The reason these pictures were taken was because during that particular year a Japanese houseguest and photographer, one Suzuki Zenbei, was staying with the family. The boy remembers that his first encounter with Suzuki was filled with fear and confusion. Suzuki had gotten to know the boy's uncle in Tokyo and during his visit to Taiwan, staying in the family's home, a traditional residential compound of the elite, comprising some forty rooms.

The first meeting was impressed with images and scents of native plants and flowers:

> Amidst the hearty longan, guava, hibiscus trees filling the courtyard, there was a giant magnolia tree by the bamboo fence. The yellowish green leaves of the giant tree, which towers nearly twenty feet tall in front of the evenly cropped bamboo bushes, rustled when the wind blew. We kids often used to climb up the tree when our parents weren't watching. Under the magnolia tree, the person who was the focus of our curiosity, Suzuki Zenbei, was standing, looking at us with a smile on his face. I remember that he was wearing a kimono. His long hair blew in the breeze; he seemed to

be captivated by the rare fragrance of the white magnolia flowers. ... When he realized he was being observed closely (by the children), to show that he was not someone scary he gazed at us in a friendly manner and smiled. ... It must have been a strange scene, with us facing each other silently. Just a minute ago we were as noisy as a bunch of chickens in a fight. Perhaps realizing that this wouldn't do, Suzuki Zenbei at last took the black object hanging on his shoulder and aimed it at us. Now I know that it was a camera, but at that time we thought only that it was something frightening and when it was aimed at us we all screamed and scattered, as the saying goes, like little spiders." [p. 266]

The young narrator was, at least initially, particularly afraid of the newcomer. Too young to tell truth from fiction, all he could think of was his mother and grandmother telling him when he cried that the Japanese police would come and punish him. Eventually this initial fear gave way to familiarity with the visitor. The amiable Suzuki soon endeared himself to the entire family, particularly the children. Throughout the story, the boy narrator and his family (mostly the women, since the older boys were now in school and beginning to learn Japanese) were unable to communicate with Suzuki verbally. Yet a deep bond developed between them, a bond felt by the reader.

This initial scene deftly frames the first encounter between a Japanese and the natives. Both are curious about the other, but as they gaze at each other, the experience is not identical. Suzuki's gaze is indirect, mediated by a camera, a piece of modern technology that empowers the Japanese and alienates the native. The device serves a double function for Suzuki: it is powerful technology that can capture the illusory, everchanging world and give it a momentary permanency; but it also separates the photographer from his subjects, the natives, whom he can see only through his filtered lenses. It traps him perpetually in the representational trap of the Other.

Suzuki develops a deep attachment to the tranquil, easy life and shows no sign of homesickness. He spends long days walking around the countryside, taking pictures, fishing, or just napping by the river. At night he helps the children with their homework and tells them old Japanese folktales. Even the young narrator, though unable to understand any Japanese at all, establishes a relationship with him. Instead of calling him uncle, he chooses to call him "Ki" while Suzuki playfully addresses the boy as "Tiger." The two spend almost every lazy afternoon idly by the riverside.

One day Suzuki comes down with a fever. Since the small village has only one Chinese doctor, the family goes to the neighboring village for a Western doctor to treat him. Despite the physician's efforts, his illness seems to worsen day by day; he grows thinner and thinner, with no sign of recovery. With Suzuki in critical condition, the grandmother asks the child to lead her to the spot where they usually fish. The grandmother tucks one of Suzuki's jackets under her arm; then, with incense and spirit money in her hands,[43] she prays and performs an exorcistic ritual by swirling Suzuki's jacket through the smoke of the burning incense and paper money and sprinkling it with water from the river. She continues the ritual until the sun has set and the stars have begun to peek out from behind the bamboo bushes. On their way back, having warned the boy not to talk to her or utter a sound, she tucks the coat into the bosom of her kimono and gently calls out, "Mr. Suzuki. Please come back . . . Mr. Suzuki, come back" repeatedly. Even the boy knows that she is performing a common ritual to call back a soul that has been captured by the river goddess. He remembers his mother once did the same thing for him when he was sick, so he imitates his grandmother by quietly calling out, "Ki, let's go home. Let's go."

After few days Suzuki, who had been on the verge of pneumonia, has miraculously recovered. The family rejoices, relieved that this visitor who came from afar did not die here, but soon they are saddened by his imminent return to Japan. On the day of departure, all the children clamber up the magnolia tree to watch Suzuki and their uncle disappear into the rice field. Only the little narrator, too young to climb fast enough or high enough, is left behind again by the older children, and out of frustration he begins to cry.

In this brief coming together between two individuals, Lü depicts an experience that is uniquely personal and intimate yet encompasses all the features of a classic colonial encounter. The two protagonists are not equals—one is grown, the other a child—and they share no language with which to communicate. By adopting the point of view of a young, naive child and describing only Suzuki's interactions with the womenfolk and children, Lü strips the encounter of political implications. The asymmetric power relationship is diluted by the banality of mundane, tranquil, everyday life. The little boy Tiger is so young that he still belongs to the maternal world of mother, aunts, and grandmothers; he is still excluded from the paternal world of father, uncles, and brothers. The photographs taken by Suzuki are all of women and the narrator as a young boy. The boy's interaction takes on special significance because it marks his initiation into the privileged world of men. Excitedly he recalls the first time Suzuki took him outside the confines of the family compound to the other side of the river: "I felt the desire to come into contact with a world I did not know and something joyful went through me" (p. 270).

In this new world, Suzuki plays the role of surrogate father. The bonding between the boy and Suzuki echoes that of the young boy and his surrogate parents in the previous story, "Neighbor." After a half-century of colonization, in the author Lü's view, the paternalistic connection between Japan and the colony's younger generation seems to be an inevitable fact of life. As seen in both these stories, the pattern of surrogate paternity takes shape naturally, without overt coercion, but whereas the association of colonizer and native in "Neighbor" results in harm to the indigenous culture (represented by the biological parents), the bonds established in "Magnolia" seem natural and benign.

Although the relationship between Suzuki and Tiger is not exploitative, it is ultimately doomed. The gap between the two cultures can be bridged only temporarily. Suzuki captures the island, its scenery, and its people through the mechanical eyes of the camera he brought with him from Japan, but his soul is instead being captivated by the indigenous landscape. He is saved through the ritual activity of the family matriarch, who knows how to tame the local spirits and retrieve his soul in a rite with ancient analogs (*zhaohun* 招魂).[44] For Suzuki, a longhaired, bohemian artist who escapes from the metropolis, the colony is a place where he can pursue his art while being pampered by the native women and admired by the native children. His respite from civilization in this pastoral utopia is, however, temporary. In a trope recalling Mr. Tanaka's transfer to Taipei, which puts an end to their brief but intense encounter with the natives, Suzuki goes back to Japan at the appointed time, never to return.

Time and memory are an important theme in this story. The narrative present of "Magnolia" is toward the end of the colonial period with the narrator, now grown up, describing a colonial encounter in the distant past. Most of the people in the photographs, grandmother, aunts, and mother, had by that time passed on and memories of them, like the photographs themselves, were fading. Lü Heruo successfully captures this elusive memory of a special encounter—between the dominant (technology) and the dominated (magic ritual)—but most of all between a man and a boy. The memory is nonverbal because the two are barely able to communicate in language. Rather, it is etched in the fading images of old photos, the scent of magnolia blossoms, the quiet river, the warm sun, and the slowly moving clouds that greeted the two on their various outings. Suzuki, the one who took the pictures, does not appear in any of the photos himself, and the boy admits that he forgot Suzuki's face shortly after he had left. The absence of Suzuki from photos again illuminates the subject and object positions of the seer and the seen. Suzuki's knowledge of Taiwan, always enigmatic because never verbalized, is now fading like the discolored photographs. Lü seems here to be foreshadowing the coming demise of the empire, prophetically gesturing toward the end of colonialism.

A deep sense of loss pervades both "Magnolia" and "Neighbor." In both stories the native and the colonial come together, are profoundly transformed in some way, but in due course part with regret, nostalgia, and a haunting sense of anxiety. The absence of Suzuki from the pictures, paralleling his absence from the native landscape, denotes the transience of the visitor; his sojourn leaves no trace. Suzuki happens upon a transitory moment of bliss, created through a confluence of lush nature and kind people, but that moment disappears.

The luxuriant magnolia tree, however, is invested with a sense of eternity. It is under this tree that the boy sees Suzuki for the first time, and it is nestled among its branches that he sees him off. With its roots deep in the earth and its canopy of leaves stretching for the sky, the tree is much like a multigenerational extended family. This nurturing entity at the center of communal life stands in stark contrast to the feeble loner Suzuki.

A similar image is prominent in the story "Mountains, Rivers, Grass, Trees" ("Shan, chuan, cao, mu" 山川草木).[45] Here the female protagonist Baolian returns to the colony after her dreams of studying art in Tokyo have been shattered by a blow to her family's financial situation. She now works on a farm deep in the mountains, finding solace and hope for the future in the natural environment of her youth: "This lianwu tree has been here for more than twenty years. During these twenty years, it never moves. Every year the green and fresh leaves renew themselves. In my opinion, this kind of existence is beautiful" (Lü 1995: 496). Thus the indigenous flora of Taiwan, exemplified by the deeply rooted trees, provides a metaphor for Lü's nativist convictions. The Japanese occupation washed over the island like a tidal wave, but the basic elements of Taiwanese life remained unchanged. Despite the active program of assimilation being pursued by the colonial administration when these stories were written, Lü believes that an incompatibility of natural environment and culture (concepts linked in the term "*fūdo*" 風土) doomed the relationship.[46]

The fundamental disharmony of colonizer and colonized, reflected even in nature, extends to the realm of language as well. One cannot help noticing Lü's assured command of the Japanese language—especially when compared to Yang Kui's agitated, polemic style. Lü is an exemplary product of Japan's colonial language policy; he writes about deeply personal sentiments not in his native tongue but in Japanese. Nonetheless, a certain melancholy permeates his stories deriving from his awareness that this mode of expression he has mastered is not his own. In a now famous episode, Lü once asked a Japanese friend how to describe what in Taiwanese is called "*kalúnsún*" 加忍損, the shiver men experience when they relieve themselves. He was distressed to discover that no equivalent word exists in Japanese (Kurokawa Sō 1996, 1:3). Mastering the master's language did not allow Lü to express himself fully. And the tension this engendered between Japanese, his intellectual language, and his native identity permitted him to create a literature that was uniquely his own yet captured the universal experience of colonial Taiwan.

In 1944, both Yang Kui and Lü Heruo were part of a government-sponsored program intended to involve writers in the war effort. The Southern Conscripted Writers, discussed in Chapter 3, were Japanese who had been sent throughout Southeast Asia to write about the war on the southern front; now thirteen of the most prominent writers in Taiwan were dispatched to sites around the island to investigate popular support for the war.[47] Lü visited the Xieqing farm in Taizhong from June to early July and produced in response a short story depicting the extreme hardship of a peasant family, "At the Wind's Head and the Water's Tail" ("Fengtou shuiwei" 風頭水尾).[48] Xu Hua and his family relocated to a village by the sea to start farming. The farm, a collective, was located in a place where strong winds blow and fresh water is hard to get (thus the title). The land was high in salt content, moreover, and not suitable for farming. The story depicts the first day the Xu family arrived in their new home. The bleak living conditions and the harsh natural environment were somewhat ameliorated by the kindness, perseverance, and practicality of the landowner and head of the collective. The story ends with Xu's upbeat anticipation of going to work the next morning. Though the story is couched in the genre of investigative journalism, Lü avoids slogans touting the war effort. Instead he approaches the assignment from his usual personal vantage point—telling the story mostly from the internal thoughts, the fears and hopes, of the protagonist Xu and his casual conversation with the landlord and other tenants. The ongoing war on the far-off fronts recedes into the background. These salt flat farmers are fighting a different war, with nature, a constant battle to reclaim farmland from the sea. This sort of contest with nature was a feature of the ethnic Chinese settlement of Taiwan from the beginning. The communal camaraderie that made living in a harsh land physically possible and mentally bearable is all that matters. Ye Shitao, who describes Lü's detached yet compassionate writing style as "socialist realism," credits him with being "from beginning to end an objective observer and not a compromiser."[49]

Lü Heruo's most active period as a writer began in 1942 when he returned from Japan.[50] Pulmonary edema had left him unable to continue performing with the Tōhō Musical Revenue Theater Group, and Lü turned his hand to writing fiction and plays. During the next few years, Lü played an active role in the Taiwanese cultural scene. He participated actively in Zhang Wenhuan's literary coterie, *Taiwan bungaku*, engaging in a series of lengthy and cantankerous debates over merits and demerits of romanticism and social realism with members of Nishikawa Mitsuru's *Bungei Taiwan*. In 1943, Lü Heruo, Zhang Wenhuan, the musician Lü Quansheng, and several others founded the theater group Kōsei Engeki Kenkyūkai 厚生演劇研究会. In the same year his short story "Fortune, Children, and Longevity" was awarded the first Taiwanese Literary Award (*Taiwan bungakushō* 台湾文学賞). The following year, his short story collection *Clear Autumn* (*Seishū* 清秋) was published.[51] This was a rare event. Most short stories by Taiwanese writers during the colonial period were published in newspapers and journals; Lü's *Clear Autumn* and Chen Huoquan's short story collection *The Way*, published later in the same year in Nishikawa Mitsuru's Imperial Subject Series 皇民叢書, seem to be the only two examples during the half-century of colonial rule.

Lü Heruo's increasingly active role in politics landed him a position as the only Taiwanese on the five-member board of the executive committee of the Taiwan Bungaku Hōkōkai 台湾文学奉公会, the Taiwan branch of the Society for Japanese Patriotic Literature (Nihon Bungaku Hōkōkai 日本文学奉公会) and the cultural wing of the powerful central office for the Imperial Subject movement, the Imperial-Subject Patriotic Association 皇民奉公会.[52] He also worked as an editor for the quarterly magazine *Junkan Taishin* 旬刊台新, published by the newspaper *Taiwan shinpō* 台湾新報.[53]

When the war ended in 1945, Lü joined the Chinese Communist Party and embraced the idea of writing in Mandarin Chinese. He published several short stories in Chinese after the war, taking sarcastic jabs at the Japanese occupation. His barbed criticism was aimed both at colonial rule and at the absurdity of natives who still were enslaved to a colonial mentality. In a series of short vignettes, "The Warfare of My Country" ("Guxiang de zhanshi" 故鄉的戰事, 1946), he depicts the confusion and chaos that characterize the period at the end of the war.[54] In "Bright Moonlight: Before the Restoration" ("Yue guangguang— guangfu qian" 月光光一光復前, 1946),[55] the protagonist Zhuang, to avoid the American bombing that was increasing in intensity day by day, seeks to rent a place for his family outside the city. He must pretend that his family is a national-language family (*kokugo katei* 国語家庭) even though his children are too young, and his aged mother too old, to speak Japanese. After half a century of indoctrination, the Japanese language had come to represent a certain social status and was the language of choice for social interactions. Zhuang warns his mother and children to stay inside the house most of the time to avoid interaction with the landlord and other tenants. One day, however, they reveal themselves when the family happily sings the folk tune "Bright Moonlight" in the courtyard under the moon. Lü's postwar treatment of the colonial condition is understandably more direct and overtly critical than his writings during the colonial period. Although his command of the Chinese language in these short stories does not compare to his mature works in Japanese, his distinctive style, involving detached, thoughtful observations and a finely honed though somewhat dark sense of humor, is still evident in these postcolonial stories. It is not mere speculation to assert that Lü had the potential to become an important writer in the postwar Taiwanese literary scene. But Lü's passion for politics took him further and further from creative writing.

While serving as director of the Taizhong branch of the Communist Party's Youth Group, Lü worked as a reporter for the *People's Report News* (*Renmin daopao* 人民導報) and was involved in peasant protests in Takao (Gaoxiong). The paper was soon banned, however, and the editorial board reorganized by the Nationalists. Lü and several other reporters founded the Taiwanese Culture Promotion Association (Taiwan Wenhua Xiejinhui 台湾文化協進会), which promoted musical activities throughout the island. Lü was not directly involved in the February 28 Incident of 1947, but he helped to save his friend and former colleague Wang Tiandong. He also drafted several articles to the commission established to investigate the disturbance and for radio broadcast.

The short story "Winter Night" ("Dongye" 冬夜, 1947) captures the intense emotions surrounding the Nationalist persecution of left-wing intellectuals, called the "white terror."[56] It tells the story of a Taiwanese woman, Caifeng, whose life is, in a sense, a metaphor for the fate of Taiwan. Her first husband was drafted by the Japanese and dispatched to fight in the Philippines, where he was killed. Once his fate became known, her husband's family disowned her and she returned to her natal family, working as a prostitute in a bar to support her parents. A wealthy businessman from Zhejiang province became enamored of her, married her, then gave her a sexually transmitted disease and abandoned her. She went back to prostituting herself and took up with a Taiwanese man who had, like her first husband, been sent to the Philippines. There he had surrendered to the Americans, gone briefly to the United States, and come back to Taiwan as an agent of the Nationalists. Unbeknownst to her, he was involved in the white terror. One night, while visiting her, he receives a message, grabs his gun, warns her to stay inside, and runs out to kill some "bandits." Shocked to discover his true identity, she runs screaming into the night.

Caifeng's life is determined by the men she is with—much as the colony's fate was determined by its succession of rulers. Like her first husband, Taiwan was used as a tool of war and sacrificed in the Pacific War. Left destitute, Taiwan was taken in by a powerful, continental presence but was ultimately betrayed and poisoned with its disease. Turning back to its native sons, Taiwan found that they had sold it out and now act as agents of the mainland. It is a bleak, depressing story—written prophetically on the eve of the February 28 Incident—giving voice to the disillusionment that so many Taiwanese felt with first the Japanese and then the Nationalists. It has become common in postcolonial discourse to see the relationship of colonizer to colonized as gendered; here a representative of the colonized, writing in the midst of his oppression, employs the same potent metaphor of exploited women and predatory men to express the nature of the relationship.

The next year, Lü became chief editor of an underground paper for left-wing activists, *Guangmingbao* 光明報, while supporting himself as a high school music teacher. When the Nationalist government led by Chiang Kai-shek retreated to Taiwan at the end of 1949, the crackdown on Communist Party members in Taiwan intensified. Many of Lü's comrades were arrested one after another; Lü and several remaining colleagues went underground, setting up a short-wave radio base outside Taipei. In 1951, he was found dead in a mountain cave. To this day, the mystery surrounding Lü's death still has not been resolved. The official version claims he was bitten by a poisonous snake, but many still believe that his death was the result of persecution by the right-wing Nationalist government. With Lü's death at the age of thirty-seven, Taiwan lost one of its native sons and one of the most talented writers of the colonial period.

Legacy of the Japanese-Language Generation

Both Yang Kui and Lü Heruo lived in Tokyo while they were young; there they gained firsthand knowledge of how metropolitan society functioned and what it was like to live as a colonial subject in the colonizer's country. Differences in their experiences in Japan shaped their view of the empire and led to different literary strategies. Yang Kui put his faith in an alliance with the Japanese proletarian movement. Lü Heruo was more successful in integrating into the metropolitan cultural apparatus; yet despite his doubts concerning traditional society, he was ambivalent about modernity. By moving to the metropolitan center of the empire, these writers escaped the marginalization inherent in life in colonial Taiwan. But for the most part they found life in Japan simultaneously inspiring and dispiriting. The unremitting frustration this tension engendered became a source of creative energy.

For the nativist writers, their willing geographic dislocation (to Tokyo) was accompanied by a reluctant cultural and social dislocation as they were incorporated into a hierarchical worldview that subordinates their native culture and displaces its institutions and values in favor of those of the colonizing culture. And yet, upon returning to their native land, both had to readjust to their native identity. Yang Kui could envision a socialist utopia in Taiwan's future. Unlike the imperial-subject writers, who endorse a positivist modern vision that is closely associated with Japanese colonial rule, Lü Heruo's attitude toward modernity is at best ambivalent. Lü chooses not to confront colonialism directly in his writings—that would have been at best a perilous and perhaps fruitless task given the level of censorship and social control which prevailed at the time—but he does indict colonialism indirectly in his understated, subtly worded tales. Coloniality looms in the background of his texts, but it never comes to center stage.

Much the same can be said for many of Lü's contemporaries. The

Romanticist Long Yingzong 龍瑛宗 (1911–1998?), perhaps the most widely published Taiwanese writer in prewar Japan, won the *Kaizō* literary award with "The Town with Papayas" ("Papaya no aru machi" パパヤのある街), the sentimental tale of a young man with unfulfilled ambitions trapped in a small town and a dead-end job.[57] The modernist Weng Nao (1908–1940), heavily influenced by neosensualist literature *(shinkankakuha),* was the only major writer during that period to eschew realism and opt for an avant-garde mode of artistic expression. Weng wrote about everyday life in a traditional Taiwanese family, a common theme among Taiwanese writers of the time, but his passionate rendering of love and desire, crafted in the modernist lexicon, sets him apart from all other writers of the colonial period. Weng's modernist sensibility, employing symbolism and psychoanalytic terms to convey an unabashed craving for both physical and spiritual love, stands out among more politically charged literature.[58]

Compared to the first generation of Japanese-language writers, such as Yang Kui and Zhang Wenhuan, this second generation was more adroit in its use of the Japanese language and less interested in a direct confrontation with Japanese colonialism. These differences were to some extent the result of the colonial government's policies of linguistic and cultural assimilation, but they also reflected a different conception of literature and the functions it can fulfill. At the other end of the spectrum, writers such as Lü Heruo are to be distinguished from the imperial-subject writers treated in the following chapter by their strong native consciousness and their unwavering conviction that Taiwanese culture—though in some respects backward, even feudalistic—is central to the identity of the islanders and will remain so despite colonial efforts at assimilation.

Imperial-Subject Literature and Its Discontents

IN THE AUGUST 1940 issue of *Taiwanese Education (Taiwan kyōiku)*, a monthly journal on education issues put out by the office of the governor-general, an article titled "Policies and Practicality of Citizens' Total Spiritual Mobilization" ("Kokumin seishin sōdōin jikkō seisaku" 国民精神総動員実行政策) put forward four major goals for the spiritual education for the Taiwanese: express reverence for the emperor; show deference to Japanese gods *(kami)*; reject selfishness and contribute to the public; and love and use Kokugo at all times.

The article was part of the campaign called the Imperial Subject movement (*kōminka undō* 皇民化運動), which took as its goal the conversion of colonial subjects into imperial subjects.[1] Beginning in 1937, immediately after the outbreak of the second Sino-Japanese war, efforts to convert colonial subjects into true Japanese were intensified. One of the three basic guiding principles of the newly arrived governor-general, Kobayashi Seizō, along with industrialization and the fortification of Taiwan as a base for the empire's advance to the south, the Imperial Subject movement quickly accelerated the pace of cultural assimilation in the colony. Kobayashi immediately disbanded the Taiwan Self-Governing Alliance (Taiwan Jichi Renmei 台湾自治連盟), established a Headquarters for Total Mobilization of the Citizens' Spirit (Kokumin Seishin Sōdōin Honbu 国民精神総動員本部), and restricted the entry of foreigners into the island. The use of Chinese was banned in all public media, pilgrimages to Japanese Shinto shrines became compulsory, and local inhabitants were required to adopt Japanese family names (Tani Yasuyo 2000: 72–86). In many respects, the same basic policies were applied to both Taiwan and Korea. But some practices were specific to Taiwan, such as the unbinding of women's bound feet and the cutting off of men's queues (*bianzi* 辮子).[2] The implementation of these measures gained urgency as the war intensified in the early 1940s.

In response to this frenzied social and cultural environment, a group of new writers emerged to chronicle the slow but sure assimilative process. Mixing fervor with anxiety, they differed from writers like Yang Kui and Zhang Wenhuan, for whom the greatest challenge was, faced with a choice between Japanese and Taiwanese culture, finding a mode of conciliation between the two. The ethnic and cultural identities of this previous generation were in a precarious balance that sought to avoid the overpowering of one side by the other. This newer group of writers was less concerned with these transethnic and transcultural conflicts. They ignored the question of whether they should become Japanese and focused instead on *how* they might attain this goal: how they could become imperial subjects. This unquestioning loyalty to Japan, its emperor, its gods, its language, and its culture earned for them the collective sobriquet of "imperial-subject" (*kōmin* 皇民) writers.

Imperial-subject writers have been poorly treated in the postwar era. With the nationalist discourse of "resistance" dominating the postcolonial interpretation of colonial texts, the typical reception of this body of literature has been unsympathetic and disapproving. Deemed to have betrayed their own national identity and sold out to the enemy, these writers have been accorded no place in the discourse on colonialism. Critics have favored texts endorsing an anti-Japanese nationalism either overtly, as in the case of Yang Kui, or subtly as with Zhang Wenhuan. Realistic stories that promoted working-class or agrarian values have been particularly singled out for valorization.

This critical assessment of the imperial-subject writers does not, however, take cognizance of the changed circumstances in which they lived. As Japanese colonization progressed, a certain structural transformation occurred within colonial society—shaped, in part, by the evolving educational system. The imperial-subject writers had been endowed by this society and educational system with a highly hybrid cultural identity and an impressive linguistic agility. Moreover, they were younger than those writers discussed previously; they had been more thoroughly educated in Japanese and felt more comfortable with it. Entirely cut off from the continental Chinese literary tradition, they had no choice but to present their story in Japanese, the only language in which they had been trained to express themselves. Writing in this colonial language, they could not help assuming the subject position of converted "citizens" of the empire. Estranged from their natal culture within their own homeland, they were first forced to assimilate to the culture of their colonial overlords and then were demonized by their own people.

I do not want to dwell here on the uniformly negative treatment of this body of work in Taiwanese literary history.[3] The binary scheme of evaluating these texts based on a litmus test that insists on a single national identity oversimplifies the complexity of identity formation among the colonized subjects and thus is not a productive way of (re)reading these texts. The texts are valuable for what they reveal about the cultural and political conditions of the times in which they were written. Instead I want to examine the texts and contexts of two writers, Zhou Jinpo and Chen Huoquan, who are considered representative of the genre. As we shall see, the texts themselves reveal the contradictory inner voices that coexist in their fiction. Many of the literary creations of this new generation of writers deal with the conflicts between an ethnic self and the collective national self—a theme that we also find in the works of the native writers discussed previously. What distinguishes the imperial-subject writers from the "genuine" native writers is the solutions these writers proposed in order to break through the aporia of the entanglement of native ethnicity and imposed colonial culture. They sought to survive in a cultural environment that was at once foreign and indigenous.

A Stranger at Home: Zhou Jinpo

Born in 1920, Zhou Jinpo spent the early years of his childhood in Tokyo, while his father studied to become a dentist at Nihon University. The Kantō Earthquake of 1923 took the family back to Taiwan. Zhou reminisced that his Taiwanese playmates used to bully him because, initially, he did not know any Taiwanese. He returned to Tokyo in 1934 to attend high school, and later he too enrolled in Nihon University to become a dentist. Unlike Yang Kui or Zhang Wenhuan, who lived the life of impoverished students in Tokyo, Zhou was well financed by his family and thoroughly enjoyed his stay there. He was a member of the Seven Luminaries group (Shichiyōkai 七曜会) and trained with the prestigious

Literary Theater group (Bungakuza 文学座).[4] His interest in theater continued in his later life, prompting him to create the Blue Sky Taiwanese Language Theater Group (Qingtian Taiyu Jushe 青天台語劇社) in 1953. By all accounts, his ten-year stay in Tokyo was an exciting time for Zhou.

Early Works

One of Zhou's friends, Zhang Minghui (who later served as the model for the protagonist Chō Meiki in "Volunteer Soldier"), sent Zhou the first issue of the magazine *Bungei Taiwan*. Zhou was greatly impressed and wrote his first short story, "Water Cancer" ("Suigan" 水癌, 1941), for the magazine while he was still living in Tokyo. Based on what he saw and experienced during a visit home, the piece is a harsh indictment of the backwardness of Taiwanese society. The protagonist has just opened a dental practice after a decade of living and studying in Japan. At first he does not feel comfortable in his estranged homeland. But after remodeling his traditional bedroom into a tatami room, he feels at ease and is confident that he can raise the level of culture of the natives in no time. Imbued with a feeling of superiority and a sense of mission, he implores his patients to "destroy the old, corrupt customs and burn off superstitions like a wildfire in a dry field" (Nakajima and Kawahara 1998: 108). The protagonist's passionate enthusiasm, however, is soon frustrated by the indifference of the islanders—exemplified by his encounter with a woman who would rather sacrifice her daughter's medical treatment than rein in her own gambling impulse. Nevertheless, the story ends with the protagonist even more determined to lead the island out of its quagmire:

> So this is the current situation in Taiwan. But precisely for this reason, because of this situation, I shall not be defeated. The blood that flows through the body of that kind of woman is the same blood that circulates in my body. I cannot remain silent. I will purify my blood, too. I am not merely a doctor; I must also be a doctor for the hearts of my people. [p. 110]

"Water Cancer" (the title refers to an oral disease) was well received, and in the fall of the same year, immediately after his return to Taiwan, Zhou wrote "Volunteer Soldier" ("Shiganhei" 志願兵).[5] The story, written only a couple of months after the conscription system was instituted on the island, became Zhou's signature piece and has often been hailed as one of the three representative works of imperial-subject literature, together with Chen Huoquan's "The Way" ("Michi" 道, 1943)[6] and Wang Changxiong's "Wild Current" ("Honryū" 奔流, 1943).[7]

The protagonist, Zhang Minggui, has just finished his studies in Japan and returned home for the summer vacation. He has difficulty communicating with his parents, who, he feels, are too traditional and too Taiwanese. (For example, they are dead set against the young people's desire to adopt Japanese names.)[8] The only person he can discuss this frustration with is his brother-in-law, who also was educated in Japan. Their conversation is full of the discontent and disillusionment concerning the cultural backwardness of Taiwan. Minggui has a best friend from childhood, Gao Jinliu, who is now working as a clerk for a Japanese business. Gao expresses his desire to join the Patriotic Youth Brigade (*Hōkoku Seinentai* 報国青年隊) in order to achieve the Japanese spirit that represents a union of the gods with human beings (*shinjin itchi ni yoru Nihon seishin* 神人一致による日本精神). Minggui, however, argues that to become an imperial subject has nothing to do with the gods; instead the priority should be raising the level of culture in the colony to match that of Japan. The narrative thus consists of conversations—and hotly debated disagreements—concerning the best way to become an imperial subject. Even though both men agree that the essential goal is to become Japanese, they diverge on the purpose and proper course of the conversion. Gao represents the hot-blooded young man of action, a man who quits smoking and makes pilgrimages to Shinto shrines every morning to achieve a spiritual unification with the Japanese gods. Zhang, having lived in Japan himself, is more skeptical and hesitant. He finds it irrational that one must clap hands or enter into a trance before a Shinto *kami* in order to become a Japanese. Gao counters that becoming an imperial subject is not merely a matter of culture *(bunka mondai)* but hinges on spiritual issues *(seishin mondai)*:

> By clapping our hands we members [of the Patriotic Youth Brigade] are able to come into contact with the heart of Yamato (*Yamatogokoro* 大和心). We are trying hard to embody the heart of Yamato. . . . But injecting a Japanese spirit is not the sort of spirit possession you are thinking of. You, I, or anyone else who has received a Japanese education can become Japanese. I can speak for my own case; I am certain that I have completely turned into a Japanese. Is it that difficult to be a Japanese? I do not think so. Is it not enough to be able to kowtow in front of Nijūbashi in gratitude for its serene majesty? Is one not a Japanese when one cannot help but be moved when one

kowtows before the Yasukuni Shrine? [Nakajima Toshio and Kawa-hara Isao 1999, 5:346–347]

When his brother-in-law remarks that the two men's aims are essentially the same, Zhang points out a distinction:

> I am fully aware that we have to become Japanese. But I don't want to be like him—to become simply a horse that pulls the carriage. First I have to figure out why we must become Japanese. I was born in Japan and brought up receiving a Japanese education since I was little. I can speak only Japanese. I cannot even write a letter without using the Japanese kana. Therefore, my life would be totally meaningless if I did not become a Japanese. [p. 349]

Zhang's intellectualized reasoning contrasts with Gao's belief in the efficacy of symbolic acts in and of themselves; this difference epitomizes the chasm separating the reception of Japanization by the elite class of intellectuals and everyday working folks. The elite class, mostly educated in Japan and often enjoying a quasi-equality with the Japanese in social status (most of them were professionals such as lawyers and doctors), justified their assimilation into the empire through rational discourses on the Japanese character of their own lives. To common folks like Gao, lacking privilege and opportunities for career advancement, becoming an imperial subject meant taking a leap of faith manifested through concrete actions.

Gao affirms this conviction through another sudden leap of faith. Ten days after their conversation, Gao informs Minggui that he has sent out an application, written in his own blood, to enlist voluntarily in the army. Minggui is greatly moved by Gao's action. He tells his brother-in-law: "[Gao] Jinliu is the kind of person who will truly move Taiwan forward. I am powerless. I cannot do anything for Taiwan. . . . There is no way I could do what he has done. My hat is off to him" (p. 350). It is precisely this sort of enthusiasm for the institution of conscription that earned Zhou Jinpo an unsavory reputation as an imperial-subject writer. The success of "Volunteer Soldier," which was awarded the first *Bungei Taiwan* Award, established Zhou's reputation as an author. He served on the board of directors of the theatrical section of the Writers and Artists Association (Bungeika Kyōkai 文芸家協会) and attended the second Greater East Asian Writers Conference as a Taiwanese delegate. From the postcolonial, nationalist point of view, however, speaking and writing the colonizer's language, changing one's own ancestral name, and dressing in a foreign costume constituted abandonment of one's true ethnic identity. And nothing could be worse than the action lionized in this story: voluntarily joining the military forces to fight for the conquering enemy. This sort of twenty-twenty hindsight was not available to these writers. Placing this story in its social and historical context helps us to understand its significance at the time.

As part of its policy of "enriching the country and strengthening the military" (*fukoku kyōhei* 富国強兵), the Meiji government instituted a conscription ordinance (*chōheirei* 徴兵令) in 1873. Up until that point, the army had consisted of unremunerated members of the aristocratic (*shizoku* 士族) class. With the first Sino-Japanese war (over interests in Korea) and, later, the Russo-Japanese War (over conflicts in Manchuria), military service was made compulsory for all adult males. The conscription ordinance was the result of modernization and the consequent drive for external expansion. It is through these military activities that the ordinary citizens (*kokumin* 国民) of Japan participated in the building of their nation. If the *jomin* 常民 concept proposed by Yanagita Kunio refers to the common folk of a nostalgically remembered agrarian, premodern Japan, the modern citizen was defined through the collective, egalitarian (though highly gendered) infrastructure of taxation, conscription, and education. After Japan entered into a full-fledged war with China in 1937—and, in particular, after embarking upon the Pacific War with the United States in the early 1940s—the imperial forces experienced shortages of both manpower and matériel. As a consequence, the last bastion of segregation, the military, was finally opened to its colonial subjects. (All other social institutions, such as education, employment, and taxation, were at least nominally equal.) The military government first instituted a conscription system in Korea in 1940, followed shortly by Taiwan in June 1941.[9] Initially the system was promoted as strictly voluntary. But as war dragged on and manpower shortages became more acute, it took on the characteristics of a compulsory conscription system. For colonial subjects in both Taiwan and Korea, a failure to "volunteer" meant automatic expulsion from school and assignment to forced labor in factories supporting the war effort. Ironically, to the segment of the Taiwanese population that was eager to assimilate and chose to volunteer, thus avoiding the coercion suffered by their more reluctant compatriots, service in the Japanese military was an honor shared with the Japanese native population. Such military service was, in fact, considered a major step forward in the realization of the slogan of "Japan and Taiwan as one" (*nai-Tai ichijo* 内台一如). Zhou Jinpo himself recorded in his diary the excitement he felt upon hearing the announcement:

> I have never felt so self-confident and joyful as today. Finally I am able to emerge from the shell of my long loneliness. My actual experience in Taiwan is altogether less than ten years. When we returned from Tokyo after the big earthquake I was four and knew only a limited amount of Japanese. When I returned to Tokyo at fourteen, I had to relearn the language. As my Japanese improved, I gradually forgot my Taiwanese. As a consequence, I am always excluded from Taiwanese society. Even if there are contacts, they are rarely intimate. I can never show my real face. My Japanese is half-baked and so is my Taiwanese. I am not really in a position to write, and whatever I write draws no real response; the masses are totally silent.[10]

The Imperial Subject movement culminated in the inauguration of a conscription system for the Taiwanese. The opportunity to shed one's blood for the empire finally eradicated the last barrier between colonizer and colonized. Zhou elaborated on the significance of this development for transcending the dynamic of unequal power—for becoming one of the masters: "There is a belief that the reason we are discriminated against in Taiwan is because we are not shedding our blood. Everyone, in their own heart, knows that only when they bleed can they speak out. Fulfill your obligations, then you can make demands" (Shimomura et al. 1995: 445).

The voluntary conscription covenant established between the empire and its colony served as a symbolic link guaranteeing a theoretical shared equality (whatever the reality). For Zhou Jinpo, who felt alienated from both cultures, the advent of this system held a dual promise: the end of his alienation from his own people and the attainment of formal equality in status between the islanders and the Japanese in the homeland. The "joy" he records in his diary is reflected in the enthusiasm voiced by his character, Gao. The somewhat masochistic yet nevertheless real desire to be acknowledged as a legitimate part of the empire, a subject of the spiritual imperial realm, was not unique to Zhou Jinpo and the characters he created. As we shall see, in Chen Huoquan's "The Way" ("Michi") the protagonist follows a similar course of action and arrives at a similar resolution, albeit via a rather different logic. The personal desire of Zhou inadvertently colluded with the imperial discourse of its time and branded him forever an imperial-subject writer.

Zhou Jinpo and Chen Huoquan were not the only two writers whose works echoed the dominant propaganda of the day. Many writers, both Japanese and native, wrote stories incorporating the idea of becoming an imperial subject. Many harbored the (perhaps mistaken) impression that the voluntary enlistment campaign offered hope of a truly equal standing that would bring the two ethnic groups together. The semi-official Imperial Subject Public Service Association (Kōmin Hōkōkai 皇民奉公会)—the most powerful organization dedicated to promoting the imperial-subject campaign—offered a major monetary incentive for film scripts advancing the cause. After the formal announcement of the volunteer enlistment campaign on June 20, 1941, newspapers daily carried hyperbolic stories filled with praise for patriotic native youth who enlisted. It is not surprising that Zhou's story and Kawaai Sanryō's "Birth" ("Shussei" 出生), which dealt with the same subject, were published in the same issue of *Bungei Taiwan* and the following year shared the first *Bungei Taiwan* Award.[11]

Zhou's work was, to be sure, wedded to the larger discourse of its time. What sets him apart from many others writing in this genre was that he refused to limit his literary explorations to the official propaganda rhetoric. Zhou consistently sought to explore contradictory and ambivalent elements in his tales—in particular the cultural and religious chasms that confronted the natives as they rushed to embrace the dominator's cultural identity. In their reading of Zhou Jinpo's stories, both Nakajima Toshio and Hoshina Hironobu reach the interesting conclusion that whereas most analyses of imperial-subject writers situate native identity and colonial identity in a binary polarity, Zhou's adoption of the imperial-subject discourse did not result in a conflict with his love for his native land.[12] That is, Zhou's advocacy of cultural assimilation with Japan did not necessarily entail the abandonment of his native Taiwan. One might even say that the imperial ultimatum to display loyalty toward Japan and Zhou's goal of achieving a higher cultural state for the island were at cross-purposes.

Zhou Jinpo's "Volunteer Soldier" is often compared to the story "The Torrent" ("Honryū" 奔流, 1943),[13] by Wang Changxiong 王昶雄 (1916–2000), who is sometimes considered an imperial-subject writer.[14] This story too juxtaposes two characters with divergent views on what it means to become an imperial subject. One is a schoolteacher, Zhu Chunsheng, who has changed his name to Itō Haruo and is such a devotee of the Imperial Subject movement that he is even willing to forsake his ties with his parents. The other, his cousin Lin, agrees with the rationale for transforming the natives into imperial subjects but still believes that "the more one wants to be an outstanding Japanese, the more one must be an outstanding Taiwanese." Wang's "Torrent" is often hailed as superior to "Volunteer Soldier" in that Wang proposes an alternative way of looking at identity politics.[15] Zhu Chunsheng, like the characters created by Zhou Jinpo, views the identity question in a binary manner requiring the debasement of the indigenous culture and the idealization of the colonial culture. Wang, through his character Lin, proposes a dual identity that brokers the harmonious coexistence of a Japanese identity and a native one—thus transcending the cultural absolutism that so often tormented the imperial-subject writers. Many of Zhou's works treat this issue of the coexistence of Japanese and Taiwanese identities, but he is ultimately pessimistic about the possibility of maintaining this precarious balance.

Later Works

The two short stories "Water Cancer" and "Volunteer Soldier" established Zhou as one of the most celebrated imperial-subject writers. But the focus on these two early works, one written when Zhou was still in Japan, the other finished shortly after his return to Taiwan, has meant that his later, more nuanced works have been largely ignored. Both early stories are full of enthusiasm for the Japanization of his native culture and people. In later essays and stories, Zhou seems to be reevaluating his initial dogmatic stance. The real gap between the empire and its colonial subjects was enormous, and Zhou was haunted by alienation, loneliness, and an unsettling feeling of being trapped between the two cultures. In subsequent, lesser-known stories, we can see pained, thoughtful deliberations on cultural hybridity—a concern that is masked by upbeat optimism in his two early works.

The typical protagonist in Zhou Jinpo's narratives is a young, elite Taiwanese male who has lived and studied in Japan and is well schooled in the finer aspects of metropolitan culture. "Birth of a Ruler" ("Monosashi no tanjō" ものさしの誕生) is a rare case in which the story is told through the eyes of a young boy.[16] The protagonist, Wu Wenxiong, comes from a privileged family background; his father is a local village councilman.[17] Like every twelve-year-old boy who attends public school (kōgakkō 公学校),[18] he loves to be the leader when playing war games with his buddies, but he yearns for a chance to attend the elementary school (shōgakkō 小学校) in his town, which is reserved for Japanese children. His curiosity and strong desire to be close to the Japanese are evident in the following passage. One day the teacher calls upon him using the name "Fumio" 文雄 instead of the usual Taiwanese pronunciation:

> He was surprised. This was the first time he was accepted [under this name] and he felt a current of warmth flow through his body; his blood began to surge.
>
> After school, he went with his buddies to see the warships. There they met an officer and he walked with them to the main street, holding his hand.
>
> The officer held his hand as if Wenxiong were his younger brother or the son of a relative. He glanced up to look at the officer's face several times to see if he could read the same sentiment in the officer's face. But his daydreaming dissipated whenever a *shōgakkō* pupil walked by. When their eyes met, he searched the [Japanese student's] face eagerly.
>
> They played in the sea with the officer.
>
> Wu Wenxiong was really happy. Everyone was naked, even the schoolchildren from the *shōgakkō*. It was hard to tell who was whom. Anyway, it did not matter even if someone could discern their differences; everyone was naked—all the same. [Huang Yingzhe 1944: 74–75]

In this poignant account of a young boy's urgent desire to be recognized as a Japanese, we see his equally tense anxiety not to be exposed as a Taiwanese. The desire to be the "same" was first rewarded with the naming (or renaming) by the teacher—a figure who, together with the police and government bureaucrats, counted among the three most important colonial civil authorities. The boy was exhilarated to be able to "role-play" the subordinate position of a younger brother/nephew. Even a boy of twelve instinctively understands the mechanism of superiority/inferiority inherent in a colonial society. Unlike Gao in "Volunteer Soldier," Wenxiong has no grand theory to rationalize his "voluntary" assimilation to Japanese religious beliefs and culture. By being seen with a Japanese navy officer, the most potent symbol of the expansionist empire, Wenxiong is passing as a Japanese by association. He is anxious that his passing not be discovered by the real Japanese schoolboys from the *shōgakkō* and is happily relieved when they all take off their clothes and play together naked. The temporary stripping off of the cultural insignia marking their racial and cultural differences is a blissful moment for the boy.

A while later, the boy is told that his father has made special arrangements with the local government and he will be attending the *shōgakkō*. The reaction of the protagonist is mixed and complicated:

> When he heard the word *"shōgakkō,"* he discovered a sense of joy that instantly crept into his face—a joy hidden in the deepest part of his heart that he never knew existed. So many different thoughts assaulted him. Just as he thought he had reached the light, he felt he was in a dark shadow. Was it anxiety, unnecessary wariness, or his attachment and nostalgia toward the *kōgakkō?* He was totally confused. [p. 76]

Somehow the fulfillment of his long-held desire is not accompanied by the expected joy. Instead he faces a much more complex choice. To resolve his confusion, he goes to the Japanese schoolyard and joins with the Japanese pupils in making fun of an elderly Taiwanese woman. When he returns to his own school, feeling that they can see through his pretension, he cannot play the usual war games with his classmates anymore:

> He felt they were all looking at him with cynical eyes; he no longer dared to claim he was the "great general." He had lost his gumption for being the leader of the [Taiwanese] group. All he could do was watch attentively from afar the war game being played by the Japanese school kids, standing by the fence that he had been growing accustomed to all this time. [p. 76]

Wenxiong is always conscious of the gaze of others—whether that of the Japanese pupils when he is with the naval officer or that of his own buddies in school. Unlike the characters in "Water Cancer" and "Volunteer Soldier," so sure of their vision, Wenxiong is tortured by ambivalence. Zhou Jinpo can be seen to use the guilt felt by this little boy when he joins the Japanese pupils in taunting the old Taiwanese woman as a critique of the hypocritical protagonist in "Water Cancer," who felt only contempt for his native culture. In this story, becoming Japanese comes with a full range of contradictory emotions.

Zhou revisits the theme of religious belief, first broached in "Volunteer Soldier," in "Weather, Belief, and Chronic Disease" ("Kikō to shinkō to jibyō to" 気候と信仰と持病と; hereafter referred to simply as "Weather").[19] Here Zhou uses the theme of religious belief to continue his exploration of cultural determinism. "Weather" is a more complex story in terms of its structure and characterization. The major character, Cai Dali, is head of a financial company and a devoted practitioner of Shintoism. Cai suffers from neuralgia, and the damp monsoon season aggravates the condition. All the people around him speculate that he is cursed with this chronic illness because of his participation in the colonial government's campaign to eliminate the custom of burning paper money as offerings to the gods. Cai's wife is a traditional woman who adheres to the indigenous religion and disapproves of her husband's actions. His good friend Guo is a Christian, but after being introduced to Saigenji Daizo, Cai's Shinto mentor who has made a pilgrimage from the port city of Jilong to the Taiwan Shrine in Taipei on foot, he decides to convert to Shinto because he wants to find a religion "that one can hold onto as a Japanese no matter what happens" (Shimomura et al. 1995: 436). Cai's son Qingdu, a young man who has just returned from studying in Japan, views his father's fanatic practice with amazement and disdain. The "weather" in the title refers to the succession of rainy days that keep Cai in excruciating physical pain and a depressed mental state. His suffering is reflected in the gloomy environment. His treasured Taima talisman (issued by the Ise Shrine and symbolizing the sun goddess, Amaterasu no Ōmikoto) on the unpainted wooden shelf makes the room look desolate and lifeless.

The short story reflects two central themes of the early stage of the Imperial Subject movement (1936–1937): the campaign was then focused on promoting thrift through drastic reductions in consumption (the primary justification for the prohibition of burning paper money; see Garon 2000) and the purging of corrupt traditional customs and practices (such as native folk beliefs). As part of the campaign to limit consumption in anticipation of the intensified war effort and to speed up the assimilation process, Governor-General Kobayashi issued two policies intended to rein in local religious practice and encourage conversion to Shintoism. First, the pavilions housing furnaces for burning paper money that existed in every local temple were prohibited in the Gold Pavilion Abolition Campaign (*Kintei haishi undō* 金亭廃止運動); second, the ritual accoutrements of the main hall of the traditional Taiwanese home were ordered changed. The offering of paper money to gods and ancestors is one of the most basic rituals of Chinese popular religion, but it was never transmitted to Japan and must have seemed curious if not sacrilegious to the Japanese. The main hall of a traditional home is its most important public space and its ritual center. It is here that the ancestral tablets share an altar with the deities the family has chosen as its protectors. The Main Hall Reconfiguration Movement (正庁改善運動) decree stipulated that a Japanese *kamidana*, a Shinto altar to the Japanese *kami*, should replace the traditional Chinese altar, ancestral tablets, and god statues. All families were encouraged to install the Taima talisman *(ofuda)* from Ise Shrine. The worship of this talisman was considered to have the same efficacy as a personal pilgrimage to the shrine (Nakamura Takashi 1988: 354). In the Cai family,

> the most resplendent icon in the main hall had been that of the Heavenly Sacred Mother Mazu. Ever since the inauguration of the Gold Pavilion Abolition Campaign, it had been sent to the neighborhood Mazu temple. The hall suddenly felt lonesome without the incense burning every morning and evening. Only the ancestral tally and a tiny statue of the bodhisattva Kannon [Guanyin] remained. [Shimomura et al. 1995: 437]

Note that the statue removed from the house was that of Mazu, the patron goddess of fishermen that originated in Fujian province; for centuries her cult has been the most popular in Taiwan and along the southeastern Chinese coast.[20] Ancestor veneration and the worship of the bodhisattva of mercy, Guanyin (Japanese Kannon), were elements of Taiwanese religious life shared by the Japanese, but the distinctively Chinese Mazu had no role in Japanese religious practice. By removing Mazu, Cai was making the ritual center of his home at least plausibly Japanese. When he renovated the room into a Japanese-style *washitsu* and installed a Shinto altar, he bifurcated the house in a way that suggests a more fundamental division:

> The renovation unexpectedly divided the house into two separate parts. The glass shoji doors in the Japanese-style room opened to the kitchen. The kitchen, main hall, and several other darker rooms that remained in the old style were to the rear of the Japanese room. [p. 437]

The partition of the physical environment of the Cai family echoes a psychological division. On the anniversary of the death of his grandfather, Cai wants a simple, spare ceremony that can express his respect tastefully. But his wife, A-jin, insists that they do it the way they always have, as colorfully and elaborately as possible. For the first time in their marriage, the wife has gone against her husband's will, hoping that a return to traditional rituals might restore Cai's health. On her own initiative, she livens up the main hall with a colorful ceremonial tablecloth, hanging scrolls, and an altar for the gods; the bright colors, reflected even in the vermilion chopstick boxes, contrast sharply with the spare, restrained plainness of the Japanese room. A-jin tries to teach her son the proper, traditional way to offer prayers to the ancestors, but the young man is indifferent to these matters; listening to the difficult Taiwanese, looking at all the sacrificial food lining the table, he wonders how long this tradition can continue and questions his own ability to carry out this duty when the time comes. Cai is surprised and rather impressed by his wife's determination to maintain their religious traditions; he withholds comment on her patronage of diviners and Taoist priests as well as her frequent visits to the Mazu temple. When his ailment becomes severe, he agrees to consult a traditional healer. Miraculously he is cured, and Cai gradually distances himself from his Shinto beliefs and friends.

The story has a dramatic ending. When the son comes down with pneumonia around the day of the goddess Guanyin's ascension to heaven, the family decides to host a major ritual. Cai displays a grand Guanyin statue that his grandfather had purchased many years ago and reminisces about his childhood when he burned incense to the sacred icon every morning and night:

> The sky was filled with sparkling stars. The flicker of the candlesticks burning red and the sacrificial animals piled high. God, ancestors, wife, children—how many years had it been since all of their hearts had united together as a family? When he gazed at the image of Guanyin, tears of gratitude welled up in his eyes. [p. 440]

Just as he has finally attained a measure of peace and satisfaction, with his family again united in one religious practice, his friend Guo rushes in to accuse him of betraying Shinto. Cai is left standing, lost, not knowing what to say.

The story reflects the tug of war between the modern mindset of the author Zhou Jinpo—a physician who saw the world through the prism of science—and the seductive power of the age-old traditions of his youth, which he had long ago forsaken. The harsh voice of criticism directed by the protagonist of "Water Cancer" toward the brash, ignorant countrywoman, a symbol of the backwardness of Taiwanese society, is absent from this tale. Zhou's typical protagonist, the young, ambitious, Japan-trained professional, is assigned a lesser role here as simply an observer on the periphery of the action. Instead the tension between the new, colonial values and the old, traditional values is resolved by members of the older generation, usually the focus of criticism and source of frustration in Zhou's stories.

Nishikawa Mitsuru presents a rather peculiar reading of this tale. In a review of this story, Nishikawa expounds on his dissatisfaction with it and, in particular, what he considers a weak ending:

> Zhou Jinpo is still experimenting 模索 [in his writing] and that's a good thing. If he stopped [experimenting] and settled down, that would be the end of it. Though I call it searching, it is a searching process oriented toward an already decided direction, so there is nothing to worry about. Zhou always jumps for anything that is Japanese. . . . He is so infatuated with Japan that he attacks the old customs of Taiwan. Yet he sometimes worries unduly that this spirit of denunciation is too obvious; this blurs what he wants to say and the ending becomes weak. [p. 440]

This passage indicates Nishikawa's unease that Zhou's seeking will turn into backsliding toward nativism—in this case, in the triumph of the indigenous beliefs over the national religion of Japan. What Nishikawa characterizes as Zhou's "already decided direction" is based on the staunchly imperial-subject rhetoric of "Water Cancer" and "Volunteer Soldier." Nishikawa recognizes in "Weather" Zhou's usual critical attitude toward old Taiwanese customs (that is, superstitions); in previous stories he had denounced them vehemently. In this story, however, Zhou introduces a counterdiscourse supporting native belief, which results in an ambiguous ending. Reading from the postcolonial point of view, we can see an amplification of the ambivalent state of the in-between-ness that was discerned in Zhou's first two stories and explored further in "Birth of a Ruler"; in "Weather" this ambiguity approaches resolution. It is interesting that Nishikawa, a progressive Japanese colonialist and modernist, perceives the threat inherent in the mythical healing powers of native superstition and its significance as a reactionary retreat from Zhou's modernist position and his earlier stance in support of the imperial-subject discourse. But Nishikawa seems ignorant of—or at least unwilling to acknowledge—the highly politicized myth-making surrounding the position of the emperor during wartime. Nishikawa's reading juxtaposes native beliefs (the old, the mythical) and Shinto (the new, the political) as two mutually exclusive entities, though in fact neither discourse can lay claim to scientific objectivity.

In this story, Zhou Jinpo for the first time ponders the possibility that there might indeed be no grounds for reconciliation—no way for the two cultures to integrate fully with each other. No longer can he naively believe that all Taiwan needs is to overhaul its cultural landscape. The weather, a natural force not susceptible to human manipulation, has a great impact on human life (by fostering disease, for example). More-over, certain aspects of the cultural environment (architecture, aesthet-ics, religion) cannot be separated from the natural environment. Religious beliefs and practices, in particular, have their roots in a specific land and people; they cannot easily be transplanted to a new re-gion and translated into a new cultural language. The story thus ac-knowledges the limits of cross-cultural fertilization.

The bliss Cai finds in a return to his native religion was fleeting; soon he must confront the doubts expressed by his friend concerning his loyalty to both Shinto and his friends. In Zhou's writings there is no longer the simple triumph of "Volunteer Soldier."

The Ambivalence of Modernism

The pendulum of Zhou Jinpo's cultural ambivalence swings back and forth in his next story, "Nostalgia" ("Kyōshū" 郷愁).[21] The protagonist is a Taiwanese who has just returned from a long stay in Tokyo and is try-ing to settle back into life on the island. For the protagonist, Taiwanese society is distant, cold, even frightening, and he longs for the familiar skies of Tokyo. He decides to take a break by visiting an old hot springs. There he chances upon two groups of gangsters who have been archrivals since the early days of Taiwanese history but have on this very day decided to make peace so they might cooperate in "completion of the sacred war" 聖戦完遂. The two rival gangs, referred to as the Xipi 西皮 and the Fulu 福禄, have their origins in the ethnic clans from differ-ent parts of South China that first colonized Taiwan. In the early years of the Japanese occupation, they were part of the armed rebels that the colonial government branded as "bandits." These groups fought con-stantly among themselves for territorial power and profit. The prota-gonist has happened upon an old-fashioned truce ceremony in which the weapons are submitted to the gods:

> It was purely by chance that he visited this red brick town that re-mains the last bastion of old Taiwanese customs. Today will be the last day of the last citadel. The men who guard this lone fortress are about to march heroically into a new era and a new world. All the villagers who had left to work and make a living in the cities and other regions have returned. The ancient, blood-splattered history of war between the Xipi and Fulu, whether stupid or inno-cent, will leave only two or three pages in the history books. . . .
> The group song was sung with low, dispirited voices. Sadly,

helplessly, yet earnestly they sang. My chest tightened while I listened to it. [Nakajima Toshio and Kawahara Isao 1999: 365]

The protagonist is deeply moved by this tragic yet sublime ceremony, which marks the end of an old (native) way of life. The clan-based communal unit of the traditional Chinese social structure can no longer be sustained in the colonial world; slowly but surely it is being absorbed into the Japanese hegemony. The narrative concludes with one of the most agonizing endings in all colonial fiction. After the ceremony, the protagonist gropes his way in the darkness back to his *ryokan* (Japanese-style inn) in a town that is unfamiliar to him:

> All of a sudden I start running. As if grasping something empty I run, crying out loud. How can I reach the *ryokan* where I will stay tonight, where there are brightly lighted human dwellings? I can only hear the sound of my own footsteps. Keep running, keep running, I tell myself. The sound of my footsteps, despite my anxiety, take on a certain rhythm like the music played by idiots, repeating itself monotonously.
>
> Perhaps I will never get there. This is indeed a long dark road. A labyrinth. I am getting dizzy, yet my two legs move about back and forth on their own like two sticks. [p. 366]

As in "Weather," a communal ritualized act of devotion (to the indigenous spiritual power) plays a central role in the narrative. But whereas the rite in "Weather" marks a return to traditional social structure, in "Nostalgia" it marks their dissolution. Despite the doubts expressed at the end of "Weather" about the appropriateness of this affirmation of traditional Taiwanese belief, the story is on the whole positive about the continuing value of Taiwanese culture. "Nostalgia," by contrast, is pessimistic. The solemn, ancient ritual turns the traditional community groups away from their own tradition and toward increasing integration into the Japanese empire. The protagonist is left groping, in the dark, cut loose from the moorings of tradition but unable to reach the comforting light of his Japanese lodging.

The protagonists in Zhou's stories can be seen to have evolved from a rather straightforward faith in the modernism represented by the Japanese imperial state to a certain ambivalence about modernity and a reluctance to abandon traditional Taiwanese society and its intellectual underpinnings. The author's uncertainty about modernity and technology is expressed at the beginning of "Nostalgia." On a train to the hot springs resort, the protagonist ponders the relationship between technology and civilization:

> There is nothing that brings to mind the ephemerality of mechanical civilization more than the panting of a steam engine as it climbs a slope. As inventors of these machines, we might expect that we would be able to travel in them at utmost ease. Instead we are confined in this small space where we share its burdens. . . . In any case, so long as we are trapped in this long narrow box, we should just resign ourselves to our helplessness. [p. 351]

This transformation of opinion was rapid—from the confident, Japan-trained physician of "Water Cancer," whose primary concern is to release his patients from their benighted superstitions through the wonders of modern science, to the Doubting Thomas of "Nostalgia," trapped in a modern world that eats away inexorably at the traditional life he knew while offering only an "ephemeral" promise, a remote refuge of light somewhere out there in the darkness. All these stories were written within a span of less than two years. What Hoshino refers to as a gradual progression from optimism to pessimism is, in fact, this deepening sense of ambiguity and conflict that stubbornly haunts his characters and, perhaps, Zhou himself (Huang Yingzhe 1994: 59–86).

Focusing exclusively on Zhou's first two short stories has resulted in a stereotyped characterization of him as the epitome of colonial complicity. Later stories reveal a much more complex writer with a more nuanced view of the relationship between Japanese and Taiwanese culture. In these narratives we see the ambivalence that is a typical product of cultural hybridity—a continual fluctuation between wanting one thing and wanting its opposite. Adapted into colonial discourse by the critic Homi Bhabha, ambivalence describes the complex mix of attraction and repulsion that often characterizes the relationship between colonizer and colonized. Zhou's writing displays an evolution from early complicity in the colonial discourse to the cultural and ethnic ambiguity of his later writings. This indeterminacy undercut his earlier faith in the authority of the colonial discourse of modernization and civilization.

The nostalgic sentiment embedded in the story reminds us of the nostalgic melancholy that was so effectively employed as a central trope in Zhang Wenhuan's oeuvre. Still, unlike Zhang's characters, who found a sense of peace and resignation in their pastoral utopia, Zhou Jinpo's "Nostalgia" results in a sense of loss, disorientation, and fear. The story opens with the protagonist waxing nostalgic about Taiwan; by the end of the story, however, the focus has shifted to a nostalgia for traditional Taiwanese culture and apprehension about the future as part of Japan. In "Weather," and especially in "Nostalgia," Zhou comes to the realization that the process of (colonial) modernization is not so clearly beneficial and not so clear-cut a choice as the character Zhang Minggui in "Volunteer Soldier" thought. Installing the new means eliminating the old. But in these later stories Zhou expresses a reluctance to abandon the society and culture of traditional Taiwan. "Nostalgia" can be seen as a eulogy to this traditional world, but its gut-wrenching end reflects the inevitability of its disappearance. The ideal of assimilation so eagerly pursued in "Water Cancer" and "Volunteer Soldier" founders on the reality of the profound differences in history, society, and custom that separate the divine Japan and Taiwan.

Unlike two other noted imperial-subject writers, Chen Huoquan and Wang Changxiong, after the war Zhou Jinpo stopped writing almost completely. Amid a purge of cultural traitors (those who had promoted Japanese ideology), Zhou changed his surname and used his mother's surname, Yang, for ten years or so to avoid persecution. He was twice arrested during the February 28 Incident, a bloody conflict between the native Taiwanese and the ruling Nationalist government. Though peripherally involved in theater and tanka writing, he mostly concentrated on his dental practice.[22] Zhou was considered the quintessential imperial-subject writer; his works were taboo and rarely discussed in public. Even though some of his stories were translated into Chinese as early as 1979, they were never published. The editor of the multivolume *Complete Collection of Taiwanese Literature During the Colonial Period* (*Guangfuqian Taiwan wenxue quanji* 光復前台湾文学全集), Yang Ziqiao, disclosed that Zhou's works were originally to be included in the project. Typeset and ready for printing, they were withdrawn at the last moment with this explanation: "As an editorial principle, selections of works reflect our critical view of that particular literary work. As for writings that carry heavy overtones of imperial-subject inspiration to serve the official ideology, we chose not to include them to subtly indicate our silent and forbearing criticism" (Yang Ziqiao 1993: 231).

As late as 1992, when the writer and president of the Taiwan Pen Club, Zhong Zaozheng, mentioned Zhou in a column in a daily newspaper, only his surname was printed and his given name was blacked out.[23] Shortly thereafter, however, interest in the writer was rekindled in Taiwan. The journal *Wenxue Taiwan* put out a special issue on Zhou Jinpo.[24] Japan followed suit with invitations for him to address the Taiwan Bungaku Kenkyūkai and Chūgoku Bungei Kenkyūkai.[25] He was, moreover, treated at length in Tarumi Chie's monograph on Japanese-language literature in Taiwan (Tarumi 1995a).

The Way to Become an Imperial Subject: Chen Huoquan

Zhou Jinpo disappeared completely from the literary world of postwar Taiwan, but another representative imperial-subject writer, Chen Huoquan (a.k.a. Takayama Bonseki 高山凡石), traversed a very different postcolonial path. Chen continued his writing activities in the postcolonial period as an active essayist and novelist, and in 1980 he won the Union Press Award for "supporting Chinese culture under the extremely difficult environment of the Japanese occupation." Two years later, with the Nationalist government's conferral of an Award for Special Contributions to the Creation of a National Literature (*Guojia wenyi chuangzuo teshu gongxian jiang*), the rehabilitation of Chen Huoquan was complete.

Chen is most famous for his tale "The Way" ("Michi" 道),[26] in which the theoretical core of the Imperial Subject movement is put to a rigorous test. The story is a simple and straightforward tale with a standard plot for imperial-subject fiction. Set in the midst of the Imperial Subject movement, this work represents one person's take on the identity politics of Japaneseness; its subsequent treatment by critics reveals the complicated machinations of postcolonial textual politics.

The protagonist of "The Way" is a low-level technician working for a Japanese camphor company in Taipei. He always thinks of himself as an "outstanding Japanese" (*rippa na Nihonjin* 立派な日本人) and is determined not to let his being an "islander" (*hontōjin* 本島人) impede his career in the company. He writes haiku and acquires the pen name Seinan (Green Camphor 青楠). An innovation he introduces to improve the factory's productivity wins praise from his superiors and he is assigned to write a treatise, "The Way to Become an Imperial Subject" ("Kōmin e no michi" 皇民への道). He is quite gung-ho—to use a term from this same period—about becoming a model *kōmin*. He believes that "it is not because one has Japanese blood that one is a Japanese. It is those who are imbued with traditional Japanese spirit from an early age and always manifest in themselves that spirit who are true Japanese" (Nakajima Toshio and Kawahara Isao 1999, 5:40).

When promotion time comes around, however, he is passed over for the engineer position he so fervently covets. And when he hears his trusted superior uttering contemptuous comments such as "Taiwanese are not human beings,"[27] Seinan experiences an identity crisis. He laments: "A chrysanthemum is a chrysanthemum and a cherry blossom (*sakura*) is a flower (*hana*). Alas, a peony can never be a flower!"[28] This collapse of his cherished values sends him into a deep depression. One day, lying in bed wallowing in self-pity, he realizes that at this moment of physical and mental weakness he is nursing his bruised ego in his mother tongue, Taiwanese. Springing back from his depression, he realizes that he has merely been passing as a Japanese while all along thinking as a Taiwainese in the Taiwanese language. The only way to become a real Japanese, he resolves, is to think, speak, and write in Japanese (*kokugo de omoi, kokugo de katari, kokugo de kaku;* note the use of "*kokugo*" here rather than "*Nihongo*"). Soon voluntary military enlistment is instituted in all the colonies and, leaving behind his wife, four kids, and several farewell haiku, he eagerly joins the army to fight in the South Pacific.

The novella was published in *Bungei Taiwan* in 1943. Despite the paper shortage, the novel was published in full and took up almost an entire issue. Hamada Hayao and Nishikawa Mitsuru, in essays appended to the end of the novella, expressed great enthusiasm for the work. Hamada remarked that he had read it three times and each time was moved to tears: "I have never before been so moved by a piece of Taiwanese literature. . . . Is there any work that better depicts the passion in the heart of an imperial subject? Could there be any other work that reveals so vividly the agony experienced by an imperial subject?"[29] Despite having made extensive corrections to Chen's Japanese grammar, Hamada nevertheless praised the work as "something not previously seen in Taiwanese literature, a unique kind of imperial-subject literature that reflects the current situation in Taiwan" and went so far as to proclaim that "I foresee a new kind of Taiwanese literature in this work. In this sense, I am totally infatuated with it." Nishikawa Mitsuru's initial skepticism about the piece also gave way to an extremely positive response. Fondly he reminisced about a previous encounter when Chen had come to ask for some draft paper (*genkō yōshi*) for his writing and Nishikawa had encouraged him to publish something in *Bungei Taiwan*.

Accompanied by laudatory recommendations from two leading lights of the local literary scene, "The Way" attracted attention from a diverse segment of the population. Chen published another short story, "Teacher Zhang" ("Chō sensei" 張先生),[30] in a subsequent issue and went on to publish many essays under his newly acquired Japanese name, Takayama Bonseki. "The Way" and "Teacher Zhang," reprinted together, comprised the first volume of the Imperial Subject Series (*Kōmin sōsho* 皇民叢書). The volume was graced by an introduction by Nishikawa Mitsuru, who signed himself as "a colleague of the Imperial Subject Literary Studio" 皇民文学塾同人.

The setting of the story, a camphor factory, came from Chen's own life experience. After graduating from technical school, Chen found employment in the colonial government's Monopoly Bureau and was, in fact, recognized by the prime minister of Japan for his contribution to improving camphor distilling technology. But the setting came to take on a larger meaning within colonial economic policy, particularly after the war with China intensified and hostilities broke out with the United States. Camphor was used at the time not only for creating fragrances and medicine but also for military purposes such as making smokeless bombs. Natural camphor was produced only in China and Japan, but when Germany began to manufacture synthetic camphor after World War I, the Japanese colonial government decided to develop the colony's resource for the global market. In 1930, Taiwan became the biggest provider of natural camphor in the world.[31] With the military buildup, the need for all wartime matériel, including camphor, increased dramatically. This pressing economic situation and the pressures of the imperial-subject movement form the context for the emergence of Chen Huoqian's *Michi*.

The protagonist thought he had both fronts covered: responding to the call for increased production to aid the war effort and converting to an imperial subject in his heart:

> He had thought he was an outstanding Japanese. The nuance of the terms *"naichijin"* [Japanese homelander] and its counterpart *"hontōjin"* [islander] made him uneasy. He thought it idiotic, the way people would assume that *naichijin* would act in such a way while *hontōjin* would act in another. [Nakajima Toshio and Kawahara Isao 1999, 5:32]

The protagonist is described as someone "with a devout soul." He looks at his obsession to invent a new machine not only as a scientific endeavor but also very much in accordance with the Japanese spirit to which he aspires:

> Ordinarily, inventing a machine and improving on mechanical operations is a job for scientific brains. But in the Orient, especially in Japan, there is an ancient tradition against considering anything

simply an exercise for the hands or the brain; rather, they value the training of the gut *(hara)* and the spirit. Japanese swordfighting, often said to embody the essence of Japanese spirit, is certainly one example, but so too are all other art forms, such as painting, sculpture, tea ceremony, and flower arrangement. The same attitude is manifest in fasting, purifying oneself, or performing Zen meditation before carrying out one's job. Of course, in the West they have this saying too: "Life is short but art is forever." But art is not just a solitary endeavor like painting or literature. When one puts all his soul into his work, pouring everything into it, only then is there true skillfulness, only then will a masterpiece of the gods be born. [p. 12]

Here the protagonist considers a third element in the construction of a model imperial subject: the elusive "Japanese spirit" that must accompany the perceptible acts of hands and mind. The irony is that although the protagonist through relentless effort has been able to attain his physical and intellectual goals, acquiring a Japanese spirit proves even harder. Certainly it is not for lack of trying. The protagonist is well versed in various Japanese poetic traditions. In the opening of the narrative, he encounters a stranger in a bar where they share drinks and carry on a lively conversation. When Seinan quotes from Bashō, the famous poet of the Edo period, the Japanese is ignorant of the poem. Instead the Japanese lectures him on the essence of being a Japanese. Half drunk, he tells him that "the Japanese spirit is to die . . . to die for one's motherland happily. . . . Isn't it grand. . . . Isn't it glorious?" (p. 15).

This statement shatters the protagonist's positivist understanding that one can become an imperial subject through physical actions, the transformation of the mind, and the cultivation of a "Japanese spirit." The process is much more brutal than he was willing to admit. Ultimately Seinan comes to understand that it all boils down to a matter of blood and one's willingness to shed it. Blood ties at birth are beyond the control of the protagonist, who was born a non-Japanese. But by shedding his blood for the empire, as the Japanese were asked to do for their country, he could perhaps circumvent the unbridgeable gorge of ethnicity. His final gesture toward a Japanese identity is enlisting in the Japanese army and heading out to the front. The predicament encountered by the colonial subject—the protagonists in "Voluntary Soldier" or "The Way," for example, who want to be Japanese but are not recognized as such by the Japanese masters—represents a dilemma inherent in Japanese colonialism. The ideological foundation of the war was the

Greater East Asian Coprosperity Sphere (*dai Tōa kyōeiken*), which posited a commonality of interest among the inhabitants of East Asia and an ultimate goal of assimilation (*dōka* 同化) and Japanization.[32] But the empire itself was centered on the figure of the emperor and his descendents, the Japanese people. How could colonial subjects, who shared no genetic link (fictive or real) with the emperor, ever truly become part of the clan that is the Japanese people? Although some liberals did see the subjects of the areas influenced by Confucian culture, in particular, as "not quite Japanese but capable of becoming Japanese," the Japanese government, Mark Peattie argues, "intended from the outset that the enlightenment and progress of the indigenes were to be consistent with the limited and distinctly inferior position which they were to occupy in the empire."[33] Open warfare with its Asian neighbors, requiring the mobilization of the colonial populations in the war effort, exacerbated the internal contradictions of this position, as did the increasingly strident demands by colonial subjects to be accepted as citizens of the empire equal to ethnic Japanese. A similar contradiction was found in colonial language policy, which promoted a racially based national language, Kokugo, as the common language of a Greater East Asia 大東亜共通語. As a result, though the colonial subjects were promised a position with the "same claims to liberties and economic opportunities as the citizens of metropolitan Japan," Jennifer Robertson points out that becoming an imperial subject "was by no means a straightforward matter of becoming Japanese" (Robertson 1998: 92).

Physical differences are often crucial in the construction of the Other and might be expected to play a role in the differentiation of the Japanese from their colonial subjects (Fanon 1961; Glissant 1989). The body is typically a central site for the construction of the colonial subjectivity. Indeed the idea of chromatism—differentiation on the basis of skin color—was central to the Western colonial experience. The inhabitants of Japan's Asian colonies did not, on the whole, differ markedly from the Japanese in terms of skin color, hair type, or facial features. Lacking this sort of external differentiation, the Japanese discourse on differences between the colonizer and colonized came to focus instead on the concept of "purity of the blood." Miura Nobutaka (2000: 454–456) identifies a "blood right" (*chi no kenri* 血の権利) that automatically trumped the claims of the rhetoric of assimilation. In fact, dissonance between the two theories gave rise to policy disputes; Oguma Eiji (1995) points out that in its advocacy of this doctrine of blood purity, the Health Department (which was strongly influenced by eugenics) ran into opposition from the colonial administration, which saw it as a threat to the imperial-subject campaign and the conscription system.

Chen Huoquan struggles with this question of how to become a Japanese in *Michi*, much as Zhou Jinpo did in "Volunteer Soldier." Chen's Seinan tries both material contributions—in the form of a technological innovation that would advance the war effort—and spiritual cultivation—by immersing himself in Japanese literature and culture. But neither is sufficient. Given the ideological justifications advanced for the superiority of the Japanese over their colonial subjects, it is not surprising that both Chen and Zhou resolve their dilemmas by having their characters enlist in the Japanese military. Only by shedding their blood in the service of the empire can they make a claim against the "blood right" of Japanese identity. Seinan, foreseeing his own death as he goes off to war, asks that his tombstone be engraved: "Layman Seinan was born as a Taiwanese and raised in Taiwan, but he died having become a Japanese citizen" (Nakajima Toshio and Kawahara Isao 1999, 5:63).

As one might imagine, the fanatical, over-the-top rhetoric of this story (and many other imperial-subject tales like it) proved embarrassing both to the postwar Japanese, who found the righteousness of colonial rhetoric discomforting, and to Taiwanese exponents of postcolonial nativism. Many scholars relegate writers like Chen Huoquan to the category of collaborator and deem his works politically untouchable; others view them as pedestrian authors of broad caricature unworthy of study. Both groups prefer writings characterized by an ambivalent mixture of deference and disobedience—by writers such as Lü Heruo and Zhang Wenhuan, for example. Critics like Tarumi Chie think that the protagonist's unabashed desire to be subjugated makes Chen merely a mouthpiece for the Imperial Subject movement. She contrasts his seeming lack of self-reflection on his native identity with the subtle ambivalence of Zhou Jinpo and Wang Changxiong, concluding that he is the lesser writer among the three, and argues against reading any trace of "resistance" into the narrative (Huang Yingzhe 1994: 93–97). Lin Ruiming maintains that "The Way" had the potential to become a piece of resistant literature if it had ended at the point when Chen realized he could never become a true Japanese (1993b: 238–244).

Hoshina Hironobu (1994a: 45–47) believes that "The Way" is both imperial-subject literature and protest literature at the same time. He argues there is a significant divergence between authorial intent and textual effect in the story, making it a much more revealing work than the typical example of imperial-subject dogma. Hoshina also stresses an aspect that most critics ignore: class background. Comparing Chen Huoquan to Zhou Jinpo, Hoshina points out that Zhou came from a privileged, elite background, living and studying among Japanese in Tokyo since his teens. Chen, by contrast, never left Taiwan during the colonial period (a rarity among colonial authors, most of whom were educated in Japan) and came from a poor, working-class family. His direct contact with the Japanese was limited to his colleagues and superiors at work. For Chen, being Japanese meant social mobility. And, in fact, publication of "The Way" made Chen famous overnight; the story was nominated for the Akutagawa Award, the most distinguished literary prize in Japan.[34] Ironically both the writer Chen and the protagonist Seinan achieved their goals through the text. The element of social class is too often ignored in discussions of imperial-subject literature. Although it is not a popular topic—it disrupts the neat dichotomies established among writers on the basis of resistance to the colonial discourse—it is useful in explaining variation within groups.

Not all colonial texts are anticolonial. Chen's protagonist is a product of his environment, born and raised in a Taiwan that was part of a greater Japanese empire. Though he might speak Taiwanese at home, his schooling was entirely in Japanese and Japanese was his intellectual language. The hybrid identities generated in such an environment have been the subject of considerable discussion in postcolonial scholarship, but the bearers of such identities are not always given the respect due them as writers. To Chen, Japaneseness equals modernity. His native colloquial Taiwanese has no written expression, and he was never educated in Mandarin, the official Kokugo of China. One possible reading of the story, then, is as the tale of an ambitious young man who takes seriously the discourse of the Japanese empire being open to all the peoples of Asia and actively pursues a place in the modern world that Japan has promised. This surface reading of the text was validated by the rave reviews it received from the Japanese literary establishment in Taipei.

A different reading of the text was implicit in the shroud of silence that fell over the Japanese-language literature of the colonial era after the Pacific War both in Japan and in the ex-colony. In the late colonial period, the term "imperial-subject literature (and writer)" came with certain cachet and status. After the war, Taiwan reverted back to become part of China; and when China fell to the Communists in 1949, it became to the Nationalist government the sole remaining sliver of true China. Chen Huoquan adapted to the new environment by learning Mandarin and writing in his new language. His pro-Japanese past, however, was never wholly forgotten or forgiven. Finally, in 1982, he was formally rehabilitated when the Nationalist literary establishment granted him an award in recognition of his long and prolific career. This did nothing, however, to endear him to the rising generation of nativist, postcolonial scholars who were just beginning to rediscover occupation-era Taiwan and incorporate the literature of that period into a new Taiwanese literary history. Chen Huoquan has been systematically excluded from recent collections of literature dating to this period. Moreover, it is interesting to note that these collections make available to modern readers only Chinese translations of the original *Nihongo bungaku*. There is still considerable ambiguity about Taiwan's Japanese heritage.[35] Works that can be seen to represent nativist resistance to foreign domination are valorized.

The Way can, however, be read as a subversive text belonging in the canon of *Nihongo bungaku*. The host of creative anxieties, the conflicting desires, and the sense of displacement manifested in Chen's text are genuine and worthy of consideration. One might even see the text as kindred in spirit to Lu Xun's "True Story of Ah-Q" ("A-Q zheng zhuan" 阿Q正伝, 1921). Like Chen's protagonist, the submissive, self-deluding Ah-Q is at the center of a masochistic satire that resonates with Homi Bhabha's account of "colonial mimicry." Colonial mimicry designates the gap between the normative metropolitan vision of grand discourse and its distorted colonial (mis)imitation. It is this unsettling sense of "almost the same, but not quite" that sustains the irony of Chen's work (Bhabha 1944: 95). In Shakespeare's *Tempest*, there is a well-known altercation between Miranda, daughter of Prospero, and Caliban, a dispossessed (ab)original inhabitant of Prospero's island. When Miranda chastises Caliban's ingratitude for her efforts in teaching him language, he responds that the prime benefit of her instruction has been that now he can communicate his curses. This is what Leela Gandhi (1998: 148–149) refers to as the "Caliban paradigm"— when the empire talks back. One often assumes, in the colonial context, that adopting the master's language is a sign of subjugation. But this ignores the immense empowerment that may come with this act. Read as a comic parody, Chen's story symbolically illustrates the logic of protesting "from," rather than "against," the cultural vocabulary of colonialism. Although in postwar articles Chen claimed to have been writing satire, we can never really know his intentions in composing *Michi*. Both straight and ironic readings of the work are possible; perhaps both are valid. The shifting assessment of this work, however, can tell us much about the influence of politics on the reception of *Nihongo bungaku.*

The two imperial-subject writers treated here followed similar paths. The fervent imperial-subject rhetoric in Zhou Jinpo's first two works, "Volunteer Soldier" and "Water Cancer," established him as the quintessential writer of this genre despite his later attempt to distance himself from it.[36] Chen Huoquan, once "The Way" had established him as an imperial-subject writer, began using a Japanese name and participated enthusiastically in the imperial-subject campaign.[37] Zhou stopped writing altogether after the war whereas Chen remained productive and eventually rehabilitated his reputation. The critical evaluation of these two authors is still ongoing and may not be resolved for some time. The history of anticolonialism has too often been confused with a history of nationalism—leading to the rejection of imperial-subject literature on the grounds that it is not nationalistic. The texts may not appeal to critics and historians with a nationalist agenda, but this is precisely what makes them interesting to a postcolonial reader. Unlike the nativist writers treated in the previous chapter, whose allegiance to their native identity is firm, the imperial-subject writers exemplify the cultural indeterminacy and multiple affiliations that characterize their historical moment. Their self-conscious manipulation of cultural difference and ambiguity in the construction of a new identity seems at times somewhat desperate, even pitiful. But the contemporary reader, aware of the multivocality of culture and the complexity of the subjectivity, should be able to find a productive interpretation of this atopic state.

Japanese Expatriates: Modernism Unquestioned

The discussion of imperial-subject literature has so far centered on Taiwanese writers, but Japanese expatriate writers in Taiwan participated in the discourse as well. Together they created a highly charged ideological literature that is uniquely bound to a geographic location and thus different from the wartime literature (*sensō bungaku* 戦争文学) that circulated in the metropolis.[38]

The imperial-subject campaign began in 1937 and by the early 1940s had become the dominant cultural discourse on the island. No writer could ignore it. Even the colonial literature of men like Nishikawa Mitsuru, Hamada Hayao, and Shimada Kinji, which had emphasized romantic portrayals of the colony, went through a process of redirection called "self-reformation" (*jiko kaizō* 自己改造) (Ide Isamu 1999: 97–100).

In a patriotic poem, "A Decision" ("Hitotsu no ketsui" 一つの決意),[39] written after Japan's attack on Pearl Harbor, Nishikawa essentially declared his personal war with the West and vowed to make his literature contribute to the war effort. This "self-reformation"—with its echoes of the "reorientation" (*tenkō* 転向) process many proletarian writers went through a decade earlier in order to disavow the Marxist elements of their earlier works—was intended to mobilize all writers in the colony to promote the assimilation of the imperial-subject campaign. Although Nishikawa did not totally abandon his romantic writing, he did embark on a series of works tailored to the social surroundings of the time, turning from romance and poetry to history. His "Record of Mining" ("Sairyūki" 採硫記, 1942) was written under the auspices of the conscripted writers' project;[40] here he outlined the precolonial and colonial history of sulfur mining on the island to emphasize the importance of sulfur in the national defense. He also wrote about the history of the railroad in his longest modern historical novel, *Taiwan Cross-Island Railway*, using it as a metaphor for colonial modernization.

Other writers examined the issue of assimilation on a more personal level. Niigaki Kōichi's 新垣広一 series of stories—"City Gate"("Jōmon" 城門, 1942),[41] "Engagement" ("Teimei" 訂盟, 1942), and "Dust" ("Shachin" 砂塵, 1944)—focuses on changes in the social life of the natives as a result of the imperial-subject campaign. "City Gate" criticizes natives who still could not break free of traditional ways in order to make the transition into a new (imperial) way of life. "Engagement" deals with a traditional marriage in Taiwan, indirectly indicting the feudalistic family system. "Dust" depicts the generation gap between the newly educated (in Japanese) youths and their parents. In these stories, the imperial-subject campaign is portrayed as a movement for modernization—its mission noble and its modus operandi unquestioned. The same can be said of Hamada Hayao's "Rough Beginning" ("Sōsō" 草創, 1943),[42] in which a modern sugar factory drives out the indigenous sugar farm at the turn of the century. Whereas native writers of imperial-subject literature were obsessed with ethnic and cultural identity, these Japanese writers from the *Bungei Taiwan* camp stressed the achievement of modernity and rarely questioned the wisdom of the assimilation policy. The rival *Taiwan Bungaku* camp eschewed this type of writing. But according to Ide Isamu's study (1999: 108–109) Japanese writers in this group, such as Nakayama Susumu 中山侑 (1909–1959), were still influenced by nationalist sentiments that manifested as a desire for Japan to be strong and invincible.

All of these writers, with the exception of Chen Huoquan, experienced a dislocation of cultural identity due to a change in geographic location. Their responses to this dislocation are varied. The imperial-subject literature, seen in the context of its time and the colonial circumstances, does not reflect a single agenda or worldview. Instead it confirms that there is neither "a monolithic imperial project nor a monolithic subaltern reaction, but rather that there are different historical trajectories of contest and change with lags and disjunctures along the way" (Breckenridge and van der Veer 1993: 10).

Conclusion:
A Voice Reclaimed

THE MEIJI RESTORATION of 1868 marked Japan's reentry into the increasingly interconnected international world from which it had withdrawn in the early seventeenth century. Suddenly Japan realized that it must confront the European colonial powers making inroads across Asia and assert its own prerogatives or risk becoming a colonial backwater governed by a remote European power. Japan would have to modernize its economy and military, train a corps of experts with knowledge of the outside world, and establish itself as a modern power that dominated its region. It set to this task energetically, sending abroad a group of talented individuals who came back from all corners of the modern world with a vision of the modern colonial empire.

Advised by these experts, Japan set upon an aggressive path of modernization and expansion. First it consolidated power by bringing the northern regions, inhabited by the Ainu, and the Ryukyu Islands, populated by the Okinawans, under direct governmental control. Casting its imperial eye over Asia, the Japanese developed plans to expand further to the west, onto the Asian continent, and south, into the islands of the Pacific Rim and the South Pacific. The Ryukyus pointed to a route of expansion through Taiwan to the Philippines and Southeast Asia. The Bonin (Ogassawara) Islands, annexed in 1876, led the Japanese to Micronesia. Dreams of the southward advance loomed large in plans for an expanding Japanese empire—contributing to an image of the South as composed of lush, bountiful landscapes populated by primitive but friendly natives with quaint customs and picturesque folk art. It was a canvas upon which it seemed dreams of empire could be drawn.

The South, in fact, referred to a vast territory of great diversity encompassing rich agricultural lands, trackless jungles, isolated atolls, and bustling trading centers. The population of the South did include uncivilized tribes, but the primitives proved to be more complex than originally thought. Micronesia supplied the utopian images of bare-breasted maidens serving up the bounty of the sea. But true savagery was to be found closer to hand, among the aborigines who inhabited the mountains of Japan's first colony, Taiwan. These headhunters, who would periodically kill Japanese sailors or traders who had the misfortune to encounter them, came to represent to the urban Japanese masses the primitive in its most pure, undiluted form. They shared the island with ethnic Chinese, heirs to an ancient culture that had once transformed Japan, who were everything the aborigines were not: urban, settled, educated, and sure of their cultural identity.

The challenge that faced Japan throughout the colonial period was how to meld the various peoples and regions that comprised the empire into a single, internally coordinated whole. This task had significant parallels to the creation of a Japanese state out of the disparate feudal domains that constituted premodern Japan, though in constructing the empire they did not have the advantage of a common language or a shared history. Still, some of the same ideological tools were brought to bear on the new problem. The foundation was military conquest—creating political unification and suppressing any overt opposition to the empire. The symbolic capital of the emperor was mobilized—providing a single focus of loyalty with a potent symbol that functioned rather like the British monarchy in the British Empire. The Shinto religion with the emperor at its center had been recently revived—providing a theological justification for the universal rule of the Japanese state. Next a common language, the recently formulated standard language of Japan, was taught throughout the empire to peoples at all socioeconomic and cultural levels—creating a common means of communication and a common idiom in which to express key ideological terms like "loyalty" and "sacrifice for the common good." Finally, the discourse on Japanese identity at this time promoted an image of Japan as one among a number of Asian nations with a common racial and cultural heritage—all joining in solidarity against the West.

Japan's colonial administration sought to transform the empire into Japan. There was a sizable investment in the infrastructure of modernity, including modern transport and communication networks that facilitated rapid economic growth. Although much of the empire was outside the formal legal network of Japan and subject to the decrees of resident governors-general, still the principles of Japanese law, concepts of impartial justice and individual rights, and a system of courts staffed by honest judges were implemented throughout the empire. Improvements in public health were dramatic, too, as Japanese standards for sanitation and modern Western medicine were brought to all corners of the Japanese realm, lengthening lifespans and reducing or eliminating many communicable diseases. Improvements in medical care also fostered the growth of a modern, scientific understanding of the world that was inimical to traditional superstitions. And an elaborate educational apparatus promoted a Japanese view of the world, though it was more successful in regions with a tradition of literacy and scholarship.[1]

Although Japanese colonialism was not founded upon immigration prompted by population pressures, many farmers did emigrate to areas like Manchuria, and a much more diverse group of industrialists, traders, businessmen, teachers, grifters, prostitutes, and laborers visited or settled in the colonies. They created a Japanese expatriate community in the colonies that was typically quite insular and maintained a Japanese lifestyle through the regular importation of Japanese foodstuffs, books, newspapers, and other items of daily life. More rarely, there were men like Hijikata Hisakatsu, who "went native" in the South Seas, took a native wife, learned the local language, and tried to fit in.

Although the dominant impulse in Japanese colonialism was to remake the colonies into replicas of a modern Japan, some expatriates favored incorporating the local cultures of the colonies into a new, more inclusive Japan. Nishikawa Mitsuru was one such figure. His orientalist fascination with the culture of the Taiwanese prompted him to devote his life to capturing it on paper with the ultimate goal that it be transmitted back to Japan and win favor there. Nishikawa was a nationalist and supported assimilation through the Imperial Subject movement; all the citizens in Taiwan should, in his view, learn the Japanese language, adopt Japanese customs, and recognize the unique position of the emperor. But he also saw value in the local traditions and envisioned Taiwanese culture becoming a new regional variant of Japanese culture, not unlike the local culture of Aizu Wakamatsu, his home, or the Provençal culture of southern France.

The Japanese empire and its policies of forced assimilation posed a problem for its colonial subjects. How should they respond to demands to abandon their own culture and adopt a new one? For the aborigines of Taiwan, assimilation offered many advantages—especially inclusion in a modern international world—but for most the leap from a tribal lifestyle founded on a hunting-gathering economy was too great. In Nakamura Chihei's "The Mist-Enshrouded Village," we see the aborigines struggle with these issues; but Nakamura's faith that they would soon accept assimilation was perhaps too optimistic. The paroxysms of violence such as the Saramao and Musha incidents are a better indication of the unbridgeable cultural gap between the aborigines and the Japanese.

The ethnically Chinese Taiwanese majority responded to the Japanese occupation in a number of ways over the half-century of its duration. The initial response was armed rebellion, but this was largely suppressed by 1915. The 1920s saw two types of response. Men like Zhang Wojun, steeped in Chinese tradition with ties to the mainland, advocated the adoption of North China Mandarin—the national language (Guoyu) promoted by the Nationalist government—as a way of maintaining Taiwan's Chinese heritage and creating a modern vernacular language that could be disseminated widely and used in the creation of modern fiction. Interestingly Zhang was an expert in Japanese literature and was inspired by the Japanese *genbun itchi* (union of spoken and written languages) movement.

A contemporary movement with a very different goal was the home-rule campaign. Composed primarily of local Taiwanese elites, it was led by the wealthy landowner Lin Xiantang (Rin Kendō) and sought a secure place for elites within the Japanese empire by pressing for autonomy and the right to make their own laws. There was no provision in the Meiji constitution supporting their position, however, and their efforts were consistently foiled by Taiwan's governor-general, who had considerable independent power. Although this was not a literary movement, its position did imply that Taiwanese people would continue to live and function in a Japanese world.

The 1930s saw the emergence of a new generation of Taiwanese intellectuals—wholly educated in the Japanese system and with few ties to their Chinese past. Some sought to create a literature in Taiwanese by developing an orthography for the hitherto unwritten language, but this first Nativist *(xiangtu)* Literature movement was choked off by Japanese government restrictions and bore little fruit.

Another group of writers, educated in Japan and inspired by the Proletarian Literature movement, accepted Japanese rule but demanded social justice. Yang Kui began his career with "Newspaper Boy," a story about a Taiwanese lad working to eke out a living in Tokyo. Although his family suffered exploitation in Taiwan, the focus of the novel is on the protagonist's struggle to survive in Japan, and it was meant to have significance for all the downtrodden. Yang's later stories, such as "Water Buffalo" and "Native Chicks," focus exclusively on Taiwan, and while they point out the exploitation of the working class by the Japanese colonial administration, they also contain withering criticism of traditional Chinese society. Lü Heruo too engaged in social criticism in stories like "The Oxcart," but his most compelling pieces, such as "Neighbors" or "Magnolia," focus on the dynamic of personal interactions between Japanese and Taiwanese people.

As political pressures intensified along with the expanding war, much of the previous activity, including stories with leftist themes and experimentation with writing in the Taiwanese language, was banned. The imperial-subject writers emerged in the early 1940s, writing about the difficulties of reconciling their Taiwanese roots with the Japanese intellectual world in which they lived. These writers accepted that they lived in the Japanese empire and an increasingly Japanized society, but they wanted full membership in that society with all its attendant rights and privileges. Their identification with Japan led these writers to denigrate their own culture and ponder incessantly on how to raise its "cultural level" to equal that of the metropolis—a sort of self-hatred well known from other colonial settings. Among these aspirants to full citizenship in the Japanese empire a debate arose, captured eloquently in Zhou Jinpo's "Volunteer Soldier" and Chen Huoquan's "Way," concerning whether citizenship was justified because one lived fully in a Japanese intellectual world or whether actions expressing devotion and subservience were the best qualifications for claiming a Japanese identity. Ultimately, ethnocentric Japanese notions of a racial basis for Japanese identity frustrated these aspirations, leaving the sole option of shedding one's blood in service to the empire as a demonstration of one's identity.

National identities are created by a combination of culture and history and are resistant to change. Yet they can change over time as the result of long-term, typically government-orchestrated, changes in culture and society. Taiwan during the first half of the twentieth century was a nation in the throes of such an identity shift. Taiwanese society—comprising an aboriginal population only a small portion of which had been influenced by Chinese culture and a much larger population of ethnic Chinese immigrants who owed nominal allegiance to China but had enjoyed much autonomy—was cast into the Japanese empire in 1895, beginning a fifty-year odyssey that culminated in the 1940s in a society on the verge of turning Japanese. Reversion to Chinese control in 1945 slammed this process in reverse, turning upside down the values and worldview of a generation and reversing the judgment of history on many politicians, writers, and thinkers.

The literature of the Japanese colonial empire is a reflection of this turbulent period. Writings by Japanese authors and critics reveal the attitudes of the colonizers to the diverse peoples then under their control. The fascination of Japanese writers and readers with the primitive and exotic shaped their view of the aborigines. But the ethnic Chinese (and Koreans) were apprehended through a romantic prism that delighted in the aesthetics of half-remembered legends and simple folk arts while dismissing the political achievements and literary and artistic masterpieces of its history.

The literature of Japan's colonial subjects in Taiwan, by contrast, presents a cross section, frozen in time, of a culture in transition wrestling with questions of identity, ethnicity, and nation. Postcolonial critics, writing from the position of one or the other of the two national cultures that vied for the allegiance of the Taiwanese during this period, have been quick to fault the Taiwanese for making the transition to a Japanese identity too readily, or too thoroughly, or for failing to abandon this identity once Chinese suzerainty was restored—for "colonial nostalgia." Such critiques are essentialist in nature: they see two pure forms—Chinese and Japanese—that exhaust the possibilities of identity for the Taiwanese. But this denies any agency to the Taiwanese. They were, to be sure, molded by the Japanese educational, legal, political, and economic systems during the occupation period, just as they were shaped by the Qing imperial rule that preceded it and the Nationalist regime that followed. It was the responsibility of the Taiwanese people alone to choose from among the various ethnic signifiers those that were most relevant to them and most appropriate to the society and times in which they lived. They created a rich body of literature that reflected their dual cultural heritage and confronted the basic questions of identity, modernity, and tradition which their unique historical circumstance inevitably raised. One aim of this book has been to let their voices speak—and to react to them as objective but sympathetic readers, aware of the forces that influenced their writing but unwilling to reduce their creations to mere reactions to external pressures.

This segment of literary history has significance for the larger field of postcolonial studies. There the model has all too often been a native culture that represents the subjugated colonized populace and a foreign culture that represents a dominating colonizer. The South within the Japanese empire presents a more complex picture. First, the colonial history of the region is complex and multilayered. Taiwanese aborigines were colonized first by the Portuguese and Dutch, then by Chinese immigrants, then by the Japanese, and finally by the Chinese Nationalists. In the South Pacific and Indochina, too, the comparatively late-arriving Japanese empire had to contend with the social and cultural remnants of previous colonizers. Second, the colonized peoples were internally diverse: some mountain aborigines followed a very traditional lifestyle while assimilated plains aborigines and ethnic Chinese lived settled, urban lives with all the trappings of civilization. Finally, the historic relations of the cultures—specifically the dominant position of China and Chinese culture with regard to Japan for many centuries—inevitably colored the relationship of enlightened colonizer and benighted colonized that Japan tried to establish with its colonial subjects. This anxiety is particularly evident in the realm of education, where Japanese educators were often reluctant to teach Chinese characters and the Chinese classics, essential elements of Japanese culture, to their ethnically Chinese subjects because it called into question the primacy of their own culture.

The implications of this study for the broad field of postcolonial studies are far-reaching with significance for our understanding of race, gender, and social class. Karatani is, on the whole, justified in claiming that Japanese colonialism was unique because it viewed the colonized peoples as essentially the same as the colonizers. There was no racial gulf among the peoples involved—which greatly facilitated the promotion of Asian solidarity in the face of Western aggression. Here racial identity rather than difference was made to serve the colonial enterprise. Nonetheless we have seen with the imperial-subject writers, in particular, that there was still a gulf separating even the most assimilated colonial subject and the colonizer.

The genderized nature of the colonial relationship, with the colonizer playing the role of the dominant male, is borne out by colonial encounters between Japanese men and native women in Taiwan—whether it be the aboriginal wives of Japanese policemen or the courtesan lover of Nishikawa's "Spring on the Rice River." But in Hayashi Fumiko's recollection of wartime colonial life, it was the Japanese women who were empowered while the colonial ambition and libido of the Japanese men were, ultimately, frustrated. Colonized females like Niu are still simply sexual partners to be discarded, but war and life in the colonies allowed some Japanese women to break free of the restrictions of gender and class.

Finally there is social class. Class is the great silent participant to all we have said about Japanese colonial literature. The writers in this study, on the whole, have been from bourgeois or even elite backgrounds, both the Japanese and the Taiwanese. Chen Huoquan and, perhaps, Yang Kui are the exceptions. Almost all, regardless of background, write with great empathy for the poor and downtrodden. But for writers like Zhou Jinpo the discourse is condescending: they write as representatives of the metropolis ready to aid and guide the poor, benighted peasants. Yang Kui made it to Japan but lived hand to mouth and learned there a socialist view of the world; he came to distrust the Japanese as a colonial power but actively tried to inject himself into the circles of Japanese writers and wrote as a representive of a metropolitan idea: proletarian literature. There is, however, in his writings a genuine empathy for his characters that comes from having shared their hardships. Chen Huoquan alone among these writers never made it to Japan, but he was the most determined to become Japanese. For Chen, Japanization was the key to social mobility, a way out of poverty. His willing abandonment of his Taiwanese identity is understandable once the class implications are understood. Hayashi Fumiko actually had the most deprived upbringing, and her fiction tells of the struggle of women from lower-class backgrounds. In her wartime reportage we also see an identification and sympathy with the Japanese conscripts fighting at the front, but a strange silence about the sufferings of the Chinese.

To these three canonical standards of modern social criticism I would add one more category: language. Language may be superfluous to many, but it is the writer's lifeblood and central to the problems of identity formation that are at issue in the colonial condition. The creation of a national language, Kokugo, was important in the construction of a modern national identity for the Japanese, and the transmission of this language to the colonized was central to the civilizing, assimilating project of Japanese colonialism. To the colonized, the Japanese language provided access to Japanese media, literature, and the arts—and, through the burgeoning number of translations, to world literature as well. The Japanese empire arose at a time when classical Chinese was no longer a viable medium of expression and the Japanese language filled a gap for the Taiwanese, who could not write vernacular Taiwanese and did not know the vernacular language of North China, Mandarin. Despite attempts to create a literature in either Taiwanese or Mandarin, Japanese became the dominant means of written expression and provided a common language for Taiwanese authors that brought them to the notice of the arbiters of taste in the metropolis. Through colonial mimicry, some of the subalterns were able to claim the fame and fortune normally reserved for the colonizer and were able to talk back to the empire. In this sense Japanese-language education was empowering and opened new worlds to the colonized. We should not, however, ignore the resistance reflected in efforts to find a different medium of expression, whether through a written vernacular Taiwanese or the adoption of Mandarin. Nowhere do we see so clearly the blurring of lines of ethnic identity as in the struggles of the Taiwanese to find a means of written expression that can accommodate their mixed Chinese-Taiwanese-Japanese heritage.

In his study of Japanese literary prizes like the Akutagawa Award, Kawamura Minato points out that the major recipients of these awards in the 1930s were often writers who were from the colonies or who wrote about the colonies.[2] Like the Greater East Asian Writers Conference or the Pen Brigades, these literary awards are part of a larger cultural apparatus that promoted an imperial cultural identity. Writers repatriated from Japan's colonies constituted a significant segment of the postwar Japanese literary world.[3] Colonialism and the colonial landscape are deeply embedded in modern Japanese literature, particularly the literature of the Shōwa era, but the postwar reformulation of Japanese social, racial, and cultural identities that followed decolonization erased this textual legacy from orthodox literary history.

In this book, I have tried to recuperate the colonial literature that has been excluded from the canon of modern Japanese literature and to show how elements of geography, culture, and history have influenced the creation of this literature, producing an alternative to the dominant metropolitan point of view. I have emphasized, in particular, a body of work by native writers whose writing is an integral part of their self-definition as colonial subjects. The lively heterogeneity of styles and speaking positions adopted in their quest for a reliable personal and cultural identity has resulted in rich, multilayered texts. Whether resistant to or complicit with the occupying culture, these works are infused with an urgency to fill the space left empty by a missing mother tongue. They also fill a gap in the history of Japanese literature and add a page of unique experiences to the global record of the colonial condition.

Epilogue:
Postcolonial Refractions

ALTHOUGH THERE WERE some in Japan and Taiwan who foresaw Japan's defeat, the bombing of Hiroshima and Nagasaki brought the war to a sudden, jolting end. Japanese for the first time heard their emperor's voice, announcing Japan's defeat and setting Japan on a new path with his resolution "to pave the way for a grand peace for all generations to come." This speech brought to a close a half-century of Japanese expansion and ended dreams of a greater Japanese empire in Asia. Throughout East Asia, Japanese troops laid down their weapons and Japanese expatriates packed their bags, uncertain of how they would be treated or when if ever they would see Japan again. The dissolution of the Japanese empire was equally unsettling for its non-Japanese residents.

The end of the war was a chaotic time that saw Japan withdraw from the colony in 1945, the Nationalists take over, and eventually, in 1949, move the center of their government to the island. The whirlwind of political change was accompanied by wrenching transformations in the linguistic and cultural spheres. The official language was changed from Japanese to Mandarin—though not without some contentious debates among intellectuals, educators, and newspaper editors.[1] The inculcation of the Japanese language among the colonized populace had been a long and tumultuous process; the linguistic decolonization process, as might be expected, was neither quick nor clear-cut. In fact, the four-year period from 1945 to 1949—that is, from the withdrawal of the Japanese to the consolidation of Nationalist power on Taiwan after their defeat on the mainland by the Communists—was a rare break in authoritarian domination that permitted a broader, more wide-ranging discourse. On the language question, multiple voices were heard and a variety of positions considered. For many Taiwanese intellectuals, Japanese was their sole intellectual language, their only means of expressing their ideas freely and with confidence. The initial reaction of many was to embrace the standard language of the motherland into which they were about to be reintegrated. But there was also a nativist movement of those who sought independence for Taiwan and wanted Taiwanese to be the official language of the island. Positions on the language issue mirrored those of an earlier debate concerning political and cultural allegiances and the ultimate unification with or independence from China.[2] A half-century of Japanese colonial rule and an imposed foreign language had merely suppressed this debate; with the departure of the Japanese, it surfaced again.

The debate cannot be reduced to two polarized stances. Many sought a middle ground advocating a transitional period during which Japanese would be used alongside Chinese. The writer Wu Zhuoliu 吳濁流 (1900–1976) urged a bolder course of action.[3] In an article titled "My Humble Opinion on Abolishing Japanese" ("Nichibun haishi ni taisuru kanken" 日文に対する管見),[4] Wu made a passionate plea for the continued publication of newspapers and magazines in Japanese. (He conceded that official government publications and announcements should be in Chinese.) He argued that the six and a half million Taiwanese who knew Japanese could make a great contribution to China's modernization because "a disarmed Japan can fulfill an important role in introducing culture. Almost all the world's literature has been translated into Japanese. As long as one has a knowledge of Japanese, one will come into contact with the cultures of all countries." China should take advantage of the abilities of these educated Taiwanese, he said, viewing them as six and a half million exchange students just returned from studies in Japan.

Many authors, such as Zhou Jinpo, chose to remain silent in the new environment. Others, however, with varying degrees of success, attempted to continue their creative endeavors in colloquial Mandarin. Long Yingzong was one who attempted the transition but failed. Chen Qianwu wrote in Japanese for a time immediately after the war but was able to switch successfully to Chinese. Other authors who succeeded in transforming themselves include Wu Yongfu, Ye Shitao, and Zhong Zaozheng, all of whom were still active in the year 2000. Acquiring another language at midlife is a daunting task, but Japanese had become a dangerous political liability. To strengthen the sense of national identity and purge the residual memories of the Japanese colonial era, the Nationalist government implemented a draconian language policy that banned not only Japanese but also the native Taiwanese (Fujian) dialect in public. Anyone who violated the edict did so at his or her peril.[5] The political tension stifled many writers, whose only means to continue their literary endeavors was deemed politically unacceptable.

Yang Kui lamented the difficulty of switching from writing in Japanese to Chinese and suggested that the government should permit a transitional period of three to five years during which newspapers could publish in a mixture of Japanese and Chinese. Lü Heruo, by contrast, embraced the new national language with enthusiasm. He published three short stories in Chinese (in new magazines such as *Xingxing* and *Zhengjingbao*) before his mysterious death in 1950 at the age of thirty-seven.[6] Chen Huoquan had the most active postwar career in Chinese-language literature. He is a prolific author and was fully rehabilitated from the demeaned status of imperial-subject writer through his 1981 award. Most colonial writers who wrote in Japanese, however, chose silence over the new, politically imposed mother tongue.

The legacy of Japanese-language literature in Taiwan never died out completely. The verse tradition, in particular, still thrives, though it is limited to a small community. Beginning in the late 1960s, there was a revival of the tanka form by the elder generation that had been educated in Japanese. At the center of this small but dynamic movement was Kohō Banri 孤蓬万里 (a.k.a. Dr. Wu Jiantang, 1926–1999), a typical member of the "Nihongo generation," men who were about twenty years old when Japan lost the empire. While he was in high school, Wu studied the *Manyōshū* with the famous *Manyō* scholar Inukai Takeshi.[7] After the war he was trained as a medical doctor both in Taiwan and Japan. In 1968 he founded the tanka magazine *Taipei Kadan* 台北歌壇, which regularly sponsored poetry gatherings and competitions, fostering a community of interest in the Japanese poetic tradition. Kohō Banri is typical of many intellectuals educated in colonial Taiwan: not only was he adept at Chinese poetry and Japanese *waka*,[8] but he was also an excellent swordsman.[9] The part-time poet once lamented that "the *waka* style of Taiwan is often considered old fashioned," but he took pride in the fact that his unadorned and unpolished *waka* style was appreciated by the poet Ōoka Shinobu, who included it in his prestigious *Asahi shinbun* column, "Oriori no uta" 折々の歌 (A poem for every season), nineteen times (see Kohō 1994: 8–11). In 1994, a major publishing house, Shūeisha, published a two-volume collection of his *waka* titled *Taiwan Manyōshū* 台湾万葉集; for this work Kohō was awarded the Kikuchi Kan

Award.[10] The collection comprises about fourteen hundred tanka with short explanatory notes on each poem.

In the area of fiction, the publication of Zhang Wenhuan's *The Earth Crawler* (*Chi ni hau mono* 地に這うもの) in Japan in 1975 merits note. Zhang was one of those writers who failed (or refused) to switch from writing in Japanese to Chinese. After the war he dabbled briefly in politics and was elected a member of the Taizhong County Council. He later quit politics and worked as a banker. Soon Zhang gave up writing altogether. He was to take up the pen again only after thirty years had passed. *The Earth Crawler* is a novel set in colonial Taiwan with peasants as the main characters. Zhang was able to look at the colonial period with a certain detached objectivity. The narrator is careful to explain to readers various features (the policy on adopting Japanese names, the system of collective responsibility) that were unique to colonial Taiwan. The novel is more critical of the colonial government than anything Zhang published before the end of the war. Since there was practically no chance for this novel to be published in Taiwan (other than self-publishing), Zhang's intended audience seems to have been the postwar generation of Japanese. Writing in Japanese in postwar Taiwan itself was a defiant political act. Thirty years after the war, Zhang felt the need to call attention to the colonial memories that were gradually fading amidst Japan's rapid growth and unprecedented prosperity. The Zhang family at the center of the novel, the poor villagers, and the peasants struggling to live a decent human life under harsh colonial rule offered an unforgiving contrast with the glossy, gilded age of Japan in the 1970s. The Japanese Library Association chose the novel as a special selected book *(sentei tosho)* for the year, but it garnered little public attention.

Several other writers who wrote in Japanese during the postwar era shed light on the historical and social contexts of the postwar Nihongo literary scene. Qiu Yonghan 邱永漢 (a.k.a. Qiu Bingnan 邱柄南, b. 1924) is well known as a stock market genius, an expert on financial and economic affairs, and a successful venture capitalist who preaches to Japanese corporations the benefits of business opportunities throughout Asia. His entrepreneurial success gained him the nickname "the God of Stock" *(kabu no kamisama)* in Japan, but few are aware that he originally came from Japan's ex-colony and that in his previous incarnation he was a budding writer active in the Taiwanese independence movement during the period immediately following the war.[11]

Qiu Yonghan cut his literary teeth at Nishikawa Mitsuru's *Literary Taiwan*, publishing poetry and plays written in Japanese, but embarked in earnest on his writing career only after the end of colonial rule. After graduating from Tokyo University with a degree in economics, his return to Taiwan was impeded by the February 28 Incident in which the Nationalist regime consolidated its rule through the violent suppression of nativist demonstrations, resulting in widespread arrests, the killing or execution of tens of thousands of native Taiwanese, and the purging of left-leaning intellectuals.[12] Because of the imposition of martial law in Taiwan, Qiu was forced to detour to Hong Kong, where he joined the budding Taiwanese independence movement. Later he went into self-imposed exile in Japan and began writing seriously. The first work he published in Japan was "Memoir of an Illegal Immigrant" ("*Mitsu nyūkokusha no shuki*" 密入国の手記, 1954), a short story written in a confessional style about an illegal alien in Japan who is apprehended and put on trial.[13]

The short story tells of the precarious existence of many people like the protagonist, Yu Tentoku (You Tiande). Educated at an elite university in Japan, Yu finds the oppressive political climate of Nationalist-ruled Taiwan unbearable. As a participant in the February 28 Incident, he is now on the run from the Nationalist police. Escaping from Taiwan, he seeks refuge in his second motherland, Japan, but is dismayed to discover he is no longer considered a Japanese national and thus is deemed an illegal immigrant. In a final attempt to avoid deportation, the protagonist pleads with the judge to allow him to stay in Japan. In his defense he submits a rich and detailed chronicle of his life and that of his brother, Yu Buntoku (You Wende).

The straightforward, I-novelistic account closely parallels the life of Qiu and echoes the experiences of many of that generation. Born in the 1920s, a decade after authors such as Lü Heruo and Wang Changxiong, this generation was the best-educated so far, with many members graduating from elite Japanese universities. (Both the protagonist Yu Tentoku and his brother Buntoku attended Tokyo Imperial University studying law and economics.) But they were also the most estranged from traditional Chinese culture and suffered the most in the transition from a Japanese to a sinicized world. Unlike their parents and grandparents, who either experienced or maintained ties to precolonial Taiwanese society, this generation knew only the "Japanese way." It was they who offered the strongest resistance to the sudden, forced shift of politics and culture in the immediate postwar period. The newly installed Chinese regime was equally suspicious of them, characterizing these trouble-making youths as "led astray by the evil poison of the slavish Japanese education" (Kurokawa Sō 1966, 1:274). This mutual distrust was a key factor in the largest violent conflict of the period, the February 28 Incident, in which this generation was most deeply involved. Older members of society were able to see the imposition of Chinese rule as a return to a previous, if vaguely remembered, lifestyle, and the memories of the occupation period gradually faded for those who were still young at the end of the war—however these members of what I call the "nostalgic generation" had to reconcile an established colonial sense of self with a new cultural identity imposed against their will by an external power with which they did not identify. In this story, Qiu relates the greatest tragedy of this generation—that they have never been able to determine for themselves who they are:

> Because I was born in Taiwan, a colony of Japan, my fate was always in the hands of others. The awareness that my fate is controlled by others always stirs up my rebellious spirit, which, in turn, makes me feel even less free. . . . In the fall, voluntary enlistment was instituted for Taiwanese and Koreans. Even though they said it was voluntary, it was actually a compulsory measure. If we students from the colonies did not volunteer, we would be expelled from school and soon we would receive notification that we were conscripted for heavy labor. They controlled our every move. Of course, we did not have any freedom of choice. What we had was the freedom to enlist, if you call that freedom. [pp. 262 and 265]

When the initial euphoria of being liberated from colonial rule subsided and the reality set in of being ruled by a power that claimed to be ethnically the same—yet still treated the Taiwanese as second-class citizens—the sense of betrayal was deep. This and many other stories written by Qiu Yonghan at this time eloquently articulate the confusion, dismay, and alienation of the nostalgic generation. The sense of dislocation in stories from this period is both metaphorical and psychological; for many, like Qiu, it was also geographic.

This story of the predicament of a stateless individual from Japan's ex-colony had a profound resonance for many others. In fact, Qiu's story was submitted as evidence in the trial of the Taiwanese independence activist Wang Yude, who was seeking political asylum at the time. Whether Qiu's story truly influenced the judge is unknown, but Wang was granted Japanese residency and escaped being deported back to Taiwan. Qiu later reminisced about this period in his and Wang's life with deep emotion:

Back in the colonial period, both Wang and I, though people from the colony, nevertheless were Japanese. With the defeat of Japan, we were made foreigners against our will. Then Wang and I were wanted by the Nationalist government. We were not asking the Japanese government to provide for our livelihood—all we wanted was for them to give us a tiny space in a corner of Japan where we could survive. . . . [1994: 8]

Qiu's literary activities were concentrated in the period 1954–1956, when he published a flurry of short stories including "Old Garden" ("Koen" 故園), "Wife of the Defeated" ("Haisentsuma" 敗戦妻), and "The Prosecutor" ("Kensatsukan" 検察官) in 1955 and "The Rock" ("Ishi" 石) in 1956. His novel *Hong Kong* (1955) won the Naoki Award; this sister to the Akutagawa Award, also established by Kikuchi Kan and awarded twice a year to works of popular fiction, established him as a popular writer. At the time, Japan was eager to emerge from the shadow of its imperial past and reenter the global community on the basis of its new economic prowess. Hailing from a former colony and writing in Japanese, Qiu's efforts to map his personal narrative onto the colonial memory that most Japanese readers wanted desperately to forget met with a cool reception. Qiu grew despondent: "The function of literary awards is that once one receives an award, he is established; but at least in my case, it did not work that way. Because the editors of major magazines and newspapers held the unconscious prejudice that novels with no Japanese characters would never be accepted in Japanese living rooms, I was never given any substantial commissions" (Marukawa Tetsushi 2000b: 94–95). Qiu moved into the financial consulting field and became a successful entrepreneur. He became a naturalized Japanese citizen in 1980 and ran, unsuccessfully, for a senate seat in the same year. Later he came to shuttle between Japan, Hong Kong, and other locations in Asia, maintaining his boundary-crossing, diasporic mobility.

Qiu's exile in Japan, marked by a successful career as a writer and an even more successful role as a member of the Japanese financial establishment, contrasts starkly with the career of Huang Lingzhi 黄霊芝 (a.k.a. Huang Tianji 黄天驥, b. 1928), another Nihongo writer who, like Qiu, began writing seriously only after the war.[14] Through private publishing, Huang managed to assemble an impressive body of work that has been largely ignored by both Japanese and Taiwanese critics. Huang stands out because, unlike Yang Kui or Wu Zhuoliu, who eventually shifted to writing in Chinese, he resolutely wrote only in Japanese yet never once set foot in Japan.[15] Rejecting the view that Japanese was just a transitional medium in the decolonization process, Huang voluntarily maintained a colonial linguistic identity, knowing full well that, given the political climate and market realities, by doing so he was committing literary suicide. In this sense he is similar to the poets of the *Taiwan Manyōshū*, who viewed language as primarily an instrument for literary expression and made a clear choice to use the language that best suited their artistic expression.

Huang Lingzhi self-published his own fourteen-volume collected works, *Huang Lingzhi sakuhin shū* 黄靈芝作品集, which included six volumes of fictional writings, as well as haiku, tanka, *shi* (Chinese poetry), critical writings, essays, and translations. The great majority of his works were written in Japanese, a few in Chinese and French.[16] Thanks to the tireless efforts of Okazaki Ikuko (1998; 1999a; 1999b; 2000a; 2000b), a fuller picture of this heretofore unknown writer is gradually emerging and further studies of Huang's oeuvre will surely appear in the near future. Okazaki points out three characteristics of Huang's writings: first, the highly polished style of his fictional works; second, the flawless, elegant Japanese; and finally, the apolitical nature of his work. The true essence of Huang Lingzhi's literary endeavor is, Okazaki insists, "to give a picture of the everyday life and thoughts of the anonymous common folk who happened to be living in the land called Taiwan" (1998: 8–9).

Like Wu Zhuoliu's pragmatic view that designating Japanese as an official language would provide Taiwan easy access to world culture, Huang's conscious choice of Japanese as his artistic language reflects his belief that the language is most appropriate for his own writing. Huang writes occasionally in French and Chinese as well, indicating that his choice of creative languages is less bound by borders and nationalities than by the imperative of artistic expression. In this sense, both Wu Zhuoliu and Huang Lingzhi, though at times criticized by nationalistic critics and writers, share a globalized vision of what language is and how it can be employed to empower its users.

The decision of writers like Huang to write in the language of Taiwan's former colonial overlord baffles many. In a roundtable *(taidan)* between the literary critic Kawamura Minato, the historian Narita Ryūichi, and the Korean-Japanese linguist Lee Yeounsuk, all three agreed that postwar Japanese-language literature in Taiwan reveals another aspect of colonial literature: its use by Taiwanese nativists to promote their struggle against the authoritarian rule of the Nationalists while glossing over the colonial heritage (Kawamura Minato et al. 1999: 140–150).

They also cautioned that some Japanese might take comfort in this fact and read it as a sign of nostalgia for Japanese rule—or even interpret the birth of Taiwanese nationalism as an unexpected by-product of Japanese colonialism.

One must remember, however, that the use of Japanese in literature after the conclusion of the war, within the context of Nationalist rule by continental Chinese who did not speak Taiwanese, had a significance different from that of the creation of Japanese-language literature during the colonial period. Taiwanese is not Mandarin and its common designation as a dialect of Chinese can be misleading. In his discussion of the relationship between dialects and officially designated standard languages, Tanaka Katsuhiko stresses the arbitrary character of such relationships, pointing out that "the discourse on whether a certain language is an independent language or a dialect comprising a subordinate element of another language is decided by the political status and aspirations of the speakers of that language" (Tanaka 1981: 9). During the fifty years of Japanese rule, Japanese grew from a language spoken by the colonizer and a small class of privileged, elite natives to a common tongue shared by more than two-thirds of the island's inhabitants.[17] After the war—especially after the Nationalist government moved to the island in 1949—Mandarin Chinese was granted primacy and the use of Taiwanese was discouraged, though it survived in the private sphere and as a language of commerce. It was not until the democratization process took hold in the 1990s that the native dialect began to make inroads into the public sphere.[18] Moreover, the lack of a standard orthography for Taiwanese meant that authors could choose to write only in the traditional, largely forgotten, medium of classical Chinese, the Japanese they learned in their youth, or colloquial Mandarin. The current creolization of the local language, mixing Mandarin, Taiwanese, Japanese, and some English, is the result of a process of acculturation and interculturation among these cultures.[19] The ebb and flow of the overlapping linguistic landscapes indicates that language is not a fixed code; it is intimately related to ethnic and cultural identities and strongly influenced by the "political status and aspirations" of its speakers.

As a Japanese citizen of Korean descent, Lee Yeounsuk was particularly puzzled by the decision of writers such as Huang to write in Japanese. But the comparison with postcolonial Korea implicit in Lee's comments is not necessarily appropriate. Although postwar Korea was divided into two political entities, there was never a split in terms of ethnic or cultural identity comparable to native Taiwanese and mainlanders—

and both Koreas speak the same language. Politically Taiwan as the Republic of China was one part of a divided China. But the superficial parallels to Korea (capitalist, Western-oriented South Korea and Taiwan versus communist North Korea and People's Republic of China) are again misleading. South Korea after World War II was ruled, however autocratically, by Koreans, and use of the imposed master tongue of the colonial period would have been a betrayal of the ideal of self-rule. The new masters of Taiwan, with their government-in-exile and their shadow administration for every province of their imagined empire, no doubt also saw authors like Huang Lingzhi as traitors to the Chinese nation. But Huang and the other authors who chose to write in Japanese considered themselves Taiwanese, and the Japanese language was part and parcel of their Taiwanese identity. In fact, this aspect of their cultural identity held special significance precisely because it was not shared by the newfound "brothers" and overlords from the mainland.

The significance of writing in Japanese long after the end of the Japanese era no doubt varied from person to person. To members of the generation of Taiwanese who grew up in a Japanese colonial environment, the Japanese language still holds powerful symbolism. Some may use it out of a sense of nostalgia, others because they never really made the transition to Mandarin as an intellectual language or because Japanese remains the medium in which they can best express their creative impulses. But for some, at least, it is also a strategic choice—an expression of resistance toward the continental, Mandarin culture that has been imposed on Taiwan over the last half-century. This act should be viewed—pace Lee Yeounsuk—as an assertion of the writer's subject position: a brave, defiant self-identification that voluntarily puts the writer in the position of an "interpellated" subject. Japan's colonial legacy in Taiwan is to be found not merely in the railway system and the neocolonial architecture of the Presidential Palace; it survives in cultural features such as food and customs, in elements of the self-definition of the Taiwanese people, and in linguistic hybridism. A recent example of this hybridity is a best-selling biography by the feminist writer Li Ang based on the adventurous life of the occupation-period woman writer Xie Xuehong. The novel's title, *The Novel of My Autobiography* (*Zizhuan no xiaoshuo* 自傳の小説, 1999), is a mixture of Chinese ideographs and Japanese phonographic (kana) symbols.

The question of a fixed linguistic identity was not limited to writers; everyone educated under colonial rule faced it in some fashion or other.[20] Nor was the experience unique to Taiwan—as is attested by the equally wrenching experiences imposed by the process of decolonization on the Third World writers of the French and English colonies in Africa and the Caribbean. But the existence of this genre of writing during the postwar period does make evident the evolving connection between colonial history and its postcolonial appropriations. These Japanese-language writers suffered over the second half of the twentieth century from lack of a fixed geopolitical affinity and a sustained crisis of cultural identity. One should not let the illusion of colonial nostalgia cloud the underlying reality; the victims of this linguistic violence bear the scars of colonization.

Marukawa Tetsushi is rightly alarmed about the potential for misinterpreting the colonial nostalgia that still prevails among a certain generation of Taiwanese.[21] He warns that some Japanese, ignorant of the labyrinthine identity politics that informs this attitude, might naively assume that Japan has atoned for the misdeeds of its colonial past. Shiba Ryōtarō's account of his trip to Taiwan is a prime example of this type of misreading.[22] Certainly Shiba was not unaware of the ethnic politics that simmered beneath the surface during his visit to the island; yet he seems to have taken what he heard at face value and accepted the colonial nostalgia he encountered without reflection. Kobayashi Yoshinori's recent *manga* work, *A New Declaration of Arrogance: A Discourse on Taiwan* (*Shin gōmanizumu sengen: SP Taiwan ron*, 2000), is even more blatant in exploiting this nostalgia and marrying it to the revisionist neoconservatism that Kobayashi first advocated in *Shin gōmanizumu sengen* (1998) and in serialized comic strips published in *Sapio* and other magazines.

Sentiments toward Japan, the Japanese people, and the Japanese language have recently been captured in a trio of related terms: "*meirizu*" 媚日族 (fawners on Japan), those (mostly Taiwanese) who feel nostalgia for the good old colonial times; "*henrizu*" 恨日族 (Japan haters), those (mostly mainlanders) who despise Japan; and "*harizu*" 哈日族 (Japan fans), members of the younger generation (mostly teenagers) who grew up with no burden of colonial memory and regard all things Japanese—from technology and fashion to popular culture such as *manga, anime,* and J-pop songs—as superior to both their Western and native counterparts.[23] The statue erected by a group of physicians in 1999 in the southern city of Tainan of Gotō Shinpei (1857–1929), the first civilian head of the Japanese colonial administration under General Kodama (from 1898 to 1906) and the person credited with introducing modern medicine to Taiwan, attests to the ambivalent attitudes that still prevail among many concerning the colonial legacy on the island.

I end this book with a tanka, taken from *Taiwan Manyōshū* (Kohō Banri 1944: 38), which conveys the forlorn state of poets writing in a land where their chosen language of expression has been largely forgotten. The postcolonial age will not truly begin until all members of the Japanese-educated generation have passed away, taking with them the last strands of colonial memory, its language, and its poetry.

Nihongo no	日本語の	Living in
sudeni horobishi	すでに滅びし	a country where Japanese
kuni ni sumi	国に住み	has already perished
utayomitsuzugeru	短歌読み継げる	how many are there—
hitoya ikunin	人や幾人	those who continue to
		compose *uta?*

Notes

Introduction

1. The Taiwanese delegation consisted of two Japanese expatriate colonial writers, Nishikawa Mitsuru and Hamada Hayao, and two native writers, Zhang Wenhuan and Long Yingzong, who are discussed in detail in later chapters.

2. Educated in Japan (1905–1907 and 1915–1919), Yi started out as an activist in the nationalist Korean independence movement. In 1919 he drafted the Independent Proclamation of February 8, which resulted in a warrant for his arrest. With the Japanese authorities in pursuit, he escaped to Shanghai, joined the Korean government-in-exile, and wrote the novel *Unfeeling* (*Mujō* 無情) and short stories such as "Sadness of a Young Boy" ("Shōnen no hiai" 少年の悲哀), which are considered to be Korea's earliest modern fiction. After his return from Shanghai, Yi published the controversial "Minzoku kaizō ron" (Thesis on reforming the race) and was attacked as an antinationalist. After 1930, he began to collaborate with the colonial government, changed his name to Kōyama Mitsuo 香山光郎, and became the most outspoken collaborative writer of the colonial period.

3. See the essay by Hamada Hayao, a delegate from Taiwan, titled "Impressions on the Conference" ("Taikai no inshō" 大会の印象) in *Bungei Taiwan* 5(3) (December 1942): 17–21. Essays by the three other Taiwanese delegates, in the same issue, are also informative. A special issue on the conference was published; see pp. 5–38 in the same issue. The conference seemed to be a big event for the writers from the colony, a sentiment shared by writers both in the colonial camp (Nishikawa, Hamada, Long) and in the native camp (Zhang). Detailed reports can also be seen in the rival journal *Bungei Taiwan;* Zhang Wenhuan's own *Taiwan Bungaku* had a special section on the conference the following month. See *Taiwan Bungaku* 3(1) (January 1943): 62–71.

4. Kawamura points to the significant overlap with the list of writers who attended the International Pen Club conference in Tokyo in 1957. The continuing postwar dominance of writers deeply enmeshed in the colonial enterprise

has seldom been addressed in the scholarly literature. See Kawamura (1997a: 23–24).

5. See, for example, Peattie and Myers (1984), Beasley (1987), Brooks (2000), Tsurumi (1977), and Young (1998).

6. I follow Kurokawa Sō (1996) in adopting this threefold division of colonial literature.

7. For a feminist analysis of gender, sexuality, and nationalism see the authors cited in Chapter 3.

8. I follow common practice in Taiwan in reading the author 周金波 as Zhou Jinpo, rather than the Zhou Jinbo favored in modern China.

Chapter 1: The Genealogy of the "South"

1. Yano Tōru indicates that *"nanyō"* was the most common prewar usage; during the war, *"nanpō"* or *"nanpōken"* became dominant; after the war, the region became known as Southeast Asia or *"tōnan ajia."* See Yano Tōru (1975: 6–7).

2. Though the development of colonial policy paralleled the Sino-Japanese and Russo-Japanese wars, the first application of the term "colonial" *(shokumin)* was with reference to Hokkaido. The first experiments in Japanese colonialism were conducted there, where the founder of colonial studies, Nitōbe Inazō, offered courses such as Colonial History *(shokuminshi)* and Colonial Theory *(shokuminron)* to students in Sapporo Agricultural School. See Murai Osamu (1995: 92–119).

3. Yanagita used the term *"dōhōshuzoku"* 同胞種族 ("ethnic groups sharing the same womb") to refer to the Okinawan people in *Kaijō no michi* 海上の道. A certain ambivalence about the proper place of the island in the Japanese empire is reflected in the fact that, after the Taiwan Incident, Japan considered splitting the islands with Qing China. China would have gotten the Miyako and Yaeyama Islands, located at the southern end of the chain, while Japan would exercise control over the rest. See Gotō Sōichirō (1992: 210–211).

4. On political novels of the period see Keene (1984: 76–93); for the works discussed here see Iwao Sei'ichi (1996; 1987) and Peattie (1988: 14–15).

5. This was hardly the only inaccuracy in Suzuki's often retold and frequently shifting account of his mission. See Peattie (1988: 9–14).

Chapter 2: Taming the Barbaric

1. For a detailed discussion of *Bōken Dankichi* see Yano Tōru (1979: 154–155) and Kawamura Minato (1994b: 21–26 and 87–90).

2. Introduction in the reissue of *Bōken Dankichi* (Tokyo: Kōdansha, 1967).

3. Kawamura Minato (1994b: 26). Tomiyama Ichirō makes a similar point in "Tropical Science and Colonialism" ("Nettai kagaku to shokuminchi shugi" 熱帯科学と植民地主義), in Sakai Naoki et al. (1996: 59–60).

4. Kawamura Minato (1944b: 88) points out that the music already existed in the Taishō period; Ishida wrote new lyrics and updated the arrangement and made it into a hit. Peattie (1988: 338, n. 37), in discussing this song, gives the title as "Sonchō no musume" 村長の娘.

5. Private sources include Itō Hisaaki's *Taiwan senki* (1874), Honda Masatatsu, ed., *Hanchi shozoku ron* (1874), and Matsui Junji, ed., *Ryūkyū jiken* (1880); official documents include records such as *Shohan shushisho* by the Bureau of Indigenous Peoples Management. See Yano Tōru (1979: 11).

6. Inō conducted fieldwork among the Taiwanese aborigines for a decade, beginning in 1895. He was a close friend of Yanagita Kunio, father of Japanese ethnology, who wrote the preface for the posthumous edition of Inō's massive *Taiwan bunkashi* 台湾文化史.

7. For the circumstances of Torii's four Taiwan expeditions see Nakazono Eisuke (1995: 29–54). For Torii's writings on the aboriginal culture in the serialized *Letters from Taiwan* (*Taiwan tsūshin* 台湾通信) see Torii Ryūzō (1996).

8. There are different theories on how the term *"takasago"* came to be used for the indigenous people. Tokutomi Sohō, in his *Taiwan yūki* 台湾遊記 (1929), indicated that Japan used to refer to Taiwan as Takasago (高砂) or Takasan (高山) due to its tall mountains. Another theory claims that when Japanese first arrived in Taiwan, they marveled at the beautiful seacoast, which reminded them of the Takasago beach in Banshū, and they consequently adopted the term "Takasago" to refer to Taiwan. Yet another explanation assumes a mispronunciation of the name of the mountain *"Táⁿ-káu-soaⁿ"* 打狗山 (Mandarin Dagoushan) in southern Taiwan. (The name of the second-largest city in Taiwan, Gaoxiong, derives from a Japanese transcription of this Taiwanese term as Takao, using the Japanese reading of the characters 高雄). In postwar Taiwan, the various indigenous tribes were collectively referred to as Gaoshanzu 高山族 (high mountain tribes) or Shandi tongbao 山地同胞 (compatriots of the mountain regions). Recently, it has become common to refer to them as *yuanzhumin* 原住民, or "original inhabitants," a term devoid of derogatory associations with backward mountain areas and one that acknowledges their status as the earliest inhabitants of the island.

9. On the representation of the aborigines under Japanese rule see Ching (1998).

10. See *Shōjo no tomo* 8(6) (May 1915); reprinted in Nakajima Toshio and Kawahara Isao (1998, 6:7–17).

11. This story was labeled as a children's tale (*dōwa* 童話) and published in the magazine *Friends for Young Girls (Shōjo no tomo)*, but the same theme is found in many stories written for an adult audience. See my discussion of Oshika Taku, Nakamura Chihei, and Satō Haruo's writing on the Takasago theme later in this chapter.

12. Kaneko Mitsuharu was adopted into the Kaneko family—thus the different surname.

13. In *Sakuhin* (December 1931); reprinted in Kawahara Isao (2000b, 18:59–90).

14. See *Chūō kōron* 50(2) (February 1935): 67–101; reprinted in Nakajima Toshio and Kawahara Isao (1998, 6:355–390).

15. On September 18, 1920, warriors of the Saramao tribe attacked the local Japanese police station in Musha, killing nineteen policemen.

16. Satō Haruo first published his travelogue in *Kaizō* (March 1925), several years after returning from the colony; Ōshika's *The Barbarians* was first published in *Chūō kōron* (February 1935). In 1936, both were published in book form. See Kawahara Isao (1997: 78 and 84).

17. The edition reprinted in Nakajima Toshio and Kawahara Isao (1998, 5:355–390) was first published in *Chūō kōron* with the censored passages blank. A collection of short stories by Ōshika under the title *"Yabanjin"* was reprinted twice by two different publishers after the war. Both the Hyakuhō shiin edition (1949) and Gengensha edition (1955) restored the censored passages.

18. Ōshika is also known for novels that deal with the mining issue. His *Mining Diary* (*Tankō nikki* 探鉱日記) was nominated for the sixth Akutagawa Literary Prize.

19. Komagome Takeshi (1991; 1996). Ching (2000: 797) concurs that one function of the story was to "intensify the preexisting antagonism between the Taiwanese-Chinese and the aboriginal population during the early years of aboriginal subjugation."

20. For the transformation in content of colonial textbooks see Sai Kindō's article "Nihon tōchiki Taiwan kōgakkō 'shūshin' kyōkasho no ichikōsatsu" in Ōhama Tetsuya (1999: 299–311).

21. For a detailed study of the construction of the Wu Feng legend see Komagome Takeshi (1991; 1996: 166–190).

22. Often these plans involved manipulating the untamed aborigines, the more assimilated "tamed" aborigines, and the ethnically Chinese Taiwanese for the benefit of the empire. For an example of a triadic relationship between colonial Japanese, Han Taiwanese, and the Takasago people see Ōshika Taku's short story "The Desire of Sō" ("Sō no Yokubō" 荘の欲望, 1935) in Ōshika Taku (1936: 247–274).

23. See Tamura Shizue (2000: 172); Ching (2000). Kerr (1974: 152) gives the chief's name as Moldanao.

24. The uprising was clearly well planned and targeted only Japanese; Taiwanese were spared except for two schoolchildren, one of whom was dressed in Japanese attire. For more details on the incident see Tamura Shizue (2000: 169–182). The Hanaoka brothers later joined three hundred other aborigines, including many children, in committing group suicide. Their status was controversial well into the postcolonial period, with disagreements over whether they should be honored in the Shrine for the Loyal and Ardent (Zhonglieci 忠烈祠), the equivalent of the Yasukuni Shrine in Japan, where those who died for the

country were honored. For many years they were considered traitors who sold out to the Japanese (through name changing and imperialization) and were banned from the ranks of anti-Japanese national heroes. In April 2001, however, the Taiwanese government minted new coins with the two brothers' images and officially proclaimed them anticolonial heroes.

25. There have been a number of studies of the Musha Incident. See, for example, Morita Shunsuke (1976), Nakagawa Kōichi et al. (1980), Dai Guohui (1981), Qiu Ruolong et al. (1993), and, more recently, Mukōyama Hirō (1999).

26. For example, "Telling the Truth of the Musha Incident" (Musha jiken no shinsō o kataru), published in *Kaizō* 13(3) (March 1931) by Kawakami Jōtarō and Kōno Hisoka, is a thoughtful assessment of the incident. Kawakami, a politician of the National Mass Party 全国大衆党, and Kōno went to the colony to investigate the incident at the request of the Taiwanese People's Party 台湾民衆党. They also published "A Sketch of Taiwanese Rule" (Taiwan tōji sobyō) in *Hihan* (February 1931) and "Exposing the Truth of the Musha Incident" (Musha jiken no shinsō o abaku) in *Chūō kōron* (March 1931). These reports contradicted the official report "Details of the Musha Incident" (Musha jiken no tenmatsu, December 1930) issued by the Governor-General's Office. Kōno Hisoka, incidentally, was married to Ōshika Taku's sister and Ōshika might have learned about the rebellion through his brother-in-law. See Kawahara Isao (2000b, 18:kaisetsu 2–4; 1997: 81–84 and 106–120).

27. Nakamura Chihei's "Kiri no bansha" 霧の蕃社 in *Bungakkai* (December 1939); Sakaguchi Reiko's 坂口䙥子 "Tokeisō" 時計草 in *Taiwan bungaku* 2(1) (February 1942); Nishikawa Mitsuru's "Banka" 蕃歌 in *Omoshiro kurabu* 4(4) (April 1951); and Yoshiya Nobuko's 吉屋信子 "Bansha no rakujitsu" 蕃社の落日 in *Bessatsu Bungeishunjū* 71 (March 1960) are just a few examples. The works range from the early 1930s well into the postwar period, the latest work being Terada Tsutomu's 寺田勉 novel *Anger of the Sun: Rebellion of the Takasago-zoku* (*Taiyō no ikari Takasagozoku no hanran* 太陽の怒り高砂族の反乱; Tokyo: Hyakuteisha, 1986). See Kawahara Isao (1997: 62–63 and 69–105).

28. Nakamura's personal name is sometimes given as Jihei.

29. Nakamura Chihei studied in Taipei High School from 1926 to 1930. He returned more than a decade later in 1939 to research his novel, *The Adventure to the Long Ear Country* (*Chōjikoku hyōryūki* 長耳国漂流記, 1940–1941), about the 1871 Taiwan Incident. The same trip also yielded "Woman in the Barbaric Realm" (Bankai no onna 蕃界の女, 1939), "The Mist-Enshrouded Barbarian Village" (Kiri no bansha 霧の蕃社, 1939), and "Conquering the Sun" (Taiyō seibatsu 太陽征伐, 1939), a story based on a Takasago myth.

30. In *Bungei* 9 (1939); reprinted in Nakajima Toshio and Kawahara Isao (1998, 6:237–266); see also a reissued version (*fukoku*) of his short story anthology *Taiwan shōsetsushū* (Tokyo: Bokusui shobo, 1941) in Kawahara Isao (2000b, 20:199–244).

31. In *Bungakkai* 12 (1939); reprinted in the reissued version *(fukoku)* of his short story anthology *Taiwan shōsetsushū* (Tokyo: Bokusui shobo, 1941) in Kawahara Isao (2000b, 20:1–66).

32. Nakamura Chihei's writings set in Taiwan do not all involve the aborigines. "The Seeds of the Tropical Willow" (Nettaiyanagi no tane 熱帯柳の種子, 1932), based on his experiences as a student, depicts the friendship of a native Taiwanese girl with three Japanese students. In "Ruined Seaports" (Sutareta minato 廃れた港, 1941), inspired by Satō Haruo's "aestheticism of the ruined," Nakamura pays homage to two ancient but now abandoned seaports, Anping and Tamsui. He also presents a moving portrayal of a Japanese woman and her unfortunate marriage to a dentist in the colonies in "On the Road" (Tabisaki nite 旅先にて, 1934). See Nakamura Chihei (1941).

33. Meisen is a cheap fabric, half silk in content, often used for everyday kimonos.

34. Takano Rokurō, *Jikō mondai* 4(4) (1942): 22; quoted in Sakai Naoki et al. (1996: 66–67).

35. These troupes are depicted in *The Puppetmaster* (*Ximeng rensheng* 戲夢人生, 1993), a movie by Hou Xiaoxian recounting the life of the famed puppeteer Li Tianlu 李天禄. The film includes a funeral ceremony for an aborigine who has died as a Japanese soldier.

36. A multitalented actress, Li was an ethnic Japanese raised in Manchuria and Beijing who passed as a native Chinese throughout her prewar movie career. Her typical role was as a sweet, obedient Chinese girl who initially harbored anti-Japanese sentiments but by the end of the film had been converted through her love for a young, handsome, brave Japanese man. She also played more exotic roles as a Takasago or Korean girl. After the war, she barely escaped being tried as a war criminal. In the 1950s she went to Hollywood and starred in such roles as the bride in *Japanese War Bride* (1952). In the 1970s, she was the first in Japan to succeed in interviewing Yasser Arafat and the Japanese Red Army in Palestine. She also ran successfully for the Diet. Li's turbulent life story made her a legend in her own time. A musical based on her life was a big hit not only in Japan but also in China. See Yomota (2000: 119–120).

37. "Musha" was originally published in *Kaizō* (March 1925) four and a half years after his return from the colony. Later it was included in the essay collection under the same title (Tokyo: Shōshinsha, 1936); reprinted in Nakajima Toshio and Kawahara Isao (1998, 5:21–54).

38. Those who died in battle were referred to as "military gods" (*gunshin* 軍神). On this process of canonization see Yamashiro Kentoku (1999).

39. Quoting from the *Journal of the Archipelago* (*Guntō nisshi* 群島日誌), one of three travel records included in his *Journal of Red Insect Island* (*Akamushijima nisshi* 赤虫島日誌). Because Ishikawa visited in an official capacity, these diaries were censored by the Navy Ministry. See Ishikawa Tatsuzō (1972: 403–446).

40. First published in *Chūō kōron* (October 1923); later included in *Bijin* (Tokyo: Shinchosha, 1924). Contemporary editions include *Satō Haruo zenshū*, vol. 6 (Tokyo: Kōdansha, 1967). The discussion here uses the version in Kurokawa Sō (1996, 1:39–52).

41. This is a reference to the persecution of socialists and other leftists, such as the anarchist Ōsugi Sakae 大杉栄 (1885–1923), who were arrested and executed following the earthquake.

42. Note that Satō makes no mention of the resident Koreans who fell victim to governmental and mob violence after the earthqake.

Chapter 3: Writers in the South

1. A similar cultural conscription was carried out in Taiwan during the war. See Fix (1995; 1998).

2. Others include Abe Tsuyako, Mikawa Kiyo, Mizuki Yōko, Kawakami Kikuko, and Koyama Itoko; see Kamiya Tadataka and Kimura Kazunobu (1996: 8–9).

3. Twenty-three of Yuasa's stories have been republished in a collected volume; see Yuasa Katsuhiko, ed., *Kannani* (Tokyo: Inpakuto shuppankai, 1995).

4. For Nakajima's creative life in Korea see Nihon shakai bungakukai (1993: 88–89).

5. Published in the alumni magazine *Kōyūkai zasshi* of the premier prep school Ichikō, (November 1927).

6. *Kōyūkai zasshi* (June 1929).

7. *Kōyūkai zasshi* (January 1930).

8. The title actually uses a native Samoan word, Tusitala, which means "teller of tales."

9. *Hikari to kaze to yume* competed fiercely with Ishitsuka Tomoji's *Matsukase* for the prize, but no winner was declared for that cycle (second half of 1942).

10. In a letter to Fukada Hisaya, Nakajima wrote about the economic pressure and his illness as the reasons for his decision to head south.

11. See the "Sakka annai" by Sagi Tadao in Nakajima Atsushi, *Hikari to kaze to yume / Waga saiyūki* (Tokyo: Kōdansha bungei bunko, 1997), p. 240.

12. Ibid.

13. *Gojō shussei* (1942), *Sangetsuki* (*Bungakkai*, February 1942), *Deshi* (*Chūō kōron*, Feburary 1943), *Ri Ryō* (*Bungakkai*, July 1943).

14. See the chronology edited by Gunji Katsuyoshi in Nakajima Atsushi (1979: 239–249).

15. At one point Stevenson makes fun in his diary of some writers' confessional tendency, echoing Nakajima's own disdain for the I-novel genre; see Nakajima Atsushi (1992: 139).

16. Letter to his wife dated January 9, 1942, in Nakajima (1979: 247).

17. Letter to his wife dated November 9, 1942, in Kawamura Minato (1994b: 151).

18. Peattie (1984: 187) notes that in the early stages of the mandate over Micronesia, education was entrusted to "uniformed naval officers, swords at their sides." Apparently the substitution of civilian teachings did not completely alter the character of education there.

19. Quoted in *Kaisetsu* by Kawamura Minato in Nakajima Atsushi (1992: 211–212).

20. Okuno Masamoto (1996: 18) refers to Nakajima's quiet and dignified style as an "artistic resistance" in a dark period of Japanese modern history. See also Kawamura Minato's discussion of Nakajima's use of the orthographic system as an allegorical reference to civilization; Kawamura Minato (1994a: 154–166; 2000a: 34–46).

21. Hayashi traveled to Taiwan in 1930, China in 1931, and Europe in 1931–1932, visited Manchuria and China in 1936, was sent to Nanjing as a special correspondent for *Mainichi shinbun* in 1937, was sent to Shanghai and Hankou as part of the Pen Brigades in 1938, visited Manchuria and Korea in 1940, went to Manchuria again in 1941, and followed the army into French Indochina and Singapore as a special correspondent in 1942–1943. See Fessler (1998: 73ff, 183, n. 12); "*Nenpu*" in Hayashi Fumiko (1964: 497–503).

22. *Ukigumo* was serialized in two parts—running in *Fūgetsu* from November 1949 to August 1950 and in *Bungakukai* from September 1950 to April 1951—and then was reprinted as a book by Shinchōsha in 1953. I cite the 1964 reprint in *Hayashi Fumiko*, Nihon no Bungaku series 47, pp. 237–474.

23. Mizuta (1996: 329). Fessler (1998: 42) concurs that it is "her best work."

24. Mizuta (1996: 337) identifies Sugio as Yukiko's uncle; Fessler (1998: 144) says "brother-in-law"; but the text is clear on his relationship to her. Mizuta is certainly correct, though, in saying that Yukiko was entrusted to Sugio's care, and there was an expectation that he would protect rather than exploit her. See Hayashi Fumiko (1964: 244–245).

25. For many, of course, especially those women who remained in Japan throughout the war, the gender hierarchy became, if anything, more rigid as the fascist regime marshaled women to serve the nation and support their men on the front lines. For studies of the role of Japanese women during wartime see Kanō Mikiyo (1987; 1995a; 1995b; 2000).

26. Ching speaks here of Japan's colonial experience as a whole, but the comment is particularly appropriate for regions where Japanese rule succeeded that of Western powers.

27. Hayashi records a conversation she overheard between soldiers on the campaign calmly discussing how they would execute a captured member of the resistance, she then praises their decision to simply cut his head off as reflecting the "pure mind of a soldier." Fessler comments: "She was not spared the sight of illness and death on that journey, but it did not seem to move her unless it was suffered by Japanese troops." See Fessler (1998: 133–34) and Ericson (1997: 80).

28. Fessler (1998: 135). Fessler characterizes the postwar era as her "dark" period.

29. Mizuta (1996: 339). She also remarks: "Tomioka and Yukiko were able to meet because of the extraordinary circumstances of the war, which created a moment of connection in an 'other' world far removed from their previous lives."

30. See Mizuta (1996: 330), who, puzzlingly, claims that Yukiko's escape to the colonies "leads to her descent to the margins of society."

Chapter 4: Nishikawa Mitsuru and *Bungei Taiwan*

1. Nishikawa's stature as the preeminent colonial writer in Taiwan is attested by the two volumes of his selected works in the five-volume *Taiwanese Literature Under the Japanese Rule: Collection of Works by Japanese Writers and Works* (Tokyo: Rikuin Shobo, 1998).

2. On the Xilaian revolt 西來庵事件, which sought to establish a Great Ming Compassionate State, see Takenaka Nobuko (1995: 94).

3. Nishikawa Mitsuru's father, Nishikawa Jun 西川淳, was head of the Shōwa Coal Company, which operated a coal mine outside of Taipei, and a member of the Taipei City Council. Nevertheless, at one point the coal company went bankrupt and the family had to move temporarily into a row house. Bibliographic information on Nishikawa is based on the chronology in Nakajima Toshio and Kawahara Isao (1998, 2:415–484).

4. The poetry collections include the following: *Higure no machi* (1928), *Le japonisme* (1928), *Itten shikai no haru* (1929), *AMANTE* (1929), *Yuganda kantaragai no chishio* (1929), and *Chibbai* (1932).

5. See the "Abridged Biography of Nishikawa Mitsuru" in Nakajima Toshio and Kawahara Isao (1998, 2:509–512).

6. One of the most influential political magazines published by the burgeoning democratic movement during that period was *Meilidao* 美麗島, a variation on the title of Nishikawa's poetry magazine. This term came to represent nativist Taiwanese sentiment as distinct from the mainland-oriented view of the Nationalist government. I do not claim that Nishikawa had anything to do with the nativist democratic movement during the 1970s and 1980s, but there is a strategic echoing in the use of this particular term and the images associated with it. We will return to this issue of the continuity of coloniality and postcoloniality later.

7. For a discussion of literacy in the Japanese language in colonial Taiwan see Chapter 4.

8. Nishikawa's *Bungei Taiwan* and Zhang's *Taiwan bungaku* were closed in 1944 and 1943 respectively by order of the colonial government. In May 1944 they were consolidated into *Taiwan bungei*, published by the government-sanctioned organization, Taiwan Bungaku Hōkōkai, with Nagasaki Hiroshi as managing editor. There were two main reasons for the consolidation: a desire to control information more tightly as the war became more intense and a desire to

limit the consumption of resources such as newsprint through the Newspaper Restriction Ordinance (*shinbun yōshi seigenrei* 新聞用紙制限令) of 1938.

9. First published in Tokyo (Shomotsu tenbōsha, 1942); also included in Nakajima Toshio and Kawahara Isao (1998, 1:201-235).

10. *Kaishinki* 会真記 (Tokyo: Ōgiku shoin, 1948) was later reissued by Nigen no hoshisha in 1976 in commemoration of Nishikawa's seventieth birthday.

11. Nakamura Tetsu (b. 1912), critic and scholar of the constitution and political science, graduated from Tokyo Imperial University in 1934 and taught at Taipei Imperial University from 1937 to 1945. After the war he became professor and later president of Hōsei University in Tokyo. He published most of his critical articles in *Taiwan bungaku*, the rival journal run by Zhang Wenhuan.

12. See *Bungei Taiwan* 1(4) (July 1940): 262-265. All references to *Bungei Taiwan* are to the reprints in *Xinwenxue zazhi congkan fukeben* 新文学雑誌叢刊 復刻版 (Taipei: Dongfang wenhua shuju, 1979). Page numbers refer to the continuous pagination of the reprint, not to the original page numbers.

13. *Bungei Taiwan* 1(4) (July 1940): 263-264.

14. After the war, Zhang stopped his writing activities. In 1975, however, he published his first novel: *Chi ni hau mono* (The crawler; Tokyo: Gendai bunmeisha). He also visited Japan in 1978 and reconciled with Nishikawa Mitsuru.

15. See, for example, Yang Qianhe's memoir *Jinsei no purizumu* (The prism of life, 1993), Wu Xinrong's diary *Wu Xinrong riji* (1981), and Zhang Wenhuan's article "Zasshi *Taiwan bungaku* no tanjō" (The birth of the magazine *Taiwan bungaku*) in *Taiwan kindaishi kenkyū* (Study of Taiwanese modern history, no. 2, August 1979).

16. See the *Chōdan* (Three-way dialogue) in *Bungei Taiwan* 4(3) (July 1942).

17. Yang Kui's zealous attempts to gain moral and financial support from activists (such as Tokunaga Sunao) in the Japanese proletarian literary movement were frustrated by indifference or, worse, criticism for not producing literature up to Japanese standards. See Zhang Jilin (2000).

18. For more details on the relationship between the two literary magazines see Fujii Shōzō (1998: 36-54).

19. Fujii Shōzō estimates more than half of the population (51 percent in 1940 and 57 percent in 1941 roughly translates into 3 million people, almost doubling the 24.5 percent in 1933) could understand Japanese. The statistic is based on research conducted by the Government General in 1940. But these numbers do not tell us the level of proficiency. For details see Shimomura et al. (1995: 73-96).

20. See, for example, Furukawa Shinji, "Rōman no ōji," in *Taishūbungei* (March 1948) and Tomida Eizō, "Shin Tokyo bundan chizu Nishikawa Mitsuru shi," in *Shinfū* (June 1948).

21. In particular, there was a surge in Taiwanese research on this topic during the 1980s, probably related to the termination of martial law and the increasing democratization during a period when the discussion of Japanese colonial rule was no longer taboo. For a complete bibliography of studies on

Nishikawa see appendix 2, Nishikawa Mitsuru kenkyū bunken mokuroku 西川満研究文献目録 , in Nakajima Toshio and Kawahara Isao (1998, 2:491–507).

22. See, for example, "Senzen no Taiwan ni okeru Nihon bungaku: Nishikawa Mitsuru o rei to shite" in *Andromeda* 125 (March 1980); see also "Xichuang Man xiansheng zhuzuo shuzhi" in *Taiwan wenyi* (May 1984).

23. *Wenji* 1(6) (March 1984); reprinted in Chen Yingzhen (1988: 49–64).

24. There were two nativist literary movements in Taiwanese literary history. The first occurred in the 1930s, when some writers reacted against writing in colloquial Mandarin Chinese *(baihua)* and Japanese and attempted to write in their native Taiwanese language. This native language movement quickly turned into a sociocultural movement with the founding of the journal *Formosa* in Tokyo in 1933. The magazine proclaimed its mission to be the creation and nurture of "traditional Taiwanese culture and literature." Its activities soon had an impact on the island itself, and in 1934 a cross-island organization, the Taiwan Literary Alliance, was founded in Taichung. Here, however, I am referring to the second *xiangtu wenxue yundong,* which occurred mainly between 1976 and 1979 with reverberations through the mid-1980s.

25. See Nishikawa Mitsuru, "Taiwan bungeikai no tenbō" (Outlook for the Taiwanese culture scene), in Nakajima Toshio and Kawahara Isao (1998, 1:461–468).

26. See Yanagi Sōetsu (1981, 6:145–150).

27. See Yanagi Sōetsu (1981, 15:501–503).

28. Oguma Eiji points out (rather cynically) that Yanagi's anti-Western orientation and his taste for things Asiatic developed only after his contact with Europeans. Consequently he regards this artistic reassessment as merely an extension of his fixation with the West. See Oguma (1998: 394–395).

29. Yanagi Sōetsu (1981, 15:501–503, 525, 564, 606).

30. See Yanagi Sōetsu (1981, 15:574 and 602).

31. See Yanagi Sōetsu (1981, 6:24–43).

32. Nishikawa was forced to limit his extravagant book productions due to shortages, particularly of paper, after the outbreak of the Pacific War. Perhaps due to his extensive connections in government and the business sector, Nishikawa and his private publishing company seem to have fared better than most. The imperial-subject writer Chen Huoquan recalled that during his first visit Nishikawa not only encouraged him to write but gave him a thick fold of blank manuscript paper, which, Chen remarked, was extremely difficult to obtain at the time.

33. For issues related to collecting see Brandt (2000).

Chapter 5: Gender, Historiography, and Romantic Colonialism

1. In early 1920, Satō Haruo, then an up-and-coming romantic poet and writer, was suffering a bout of depression. He returned to his home, Shingu, Wakayama, for a rest and there met his childhood friend Higashi Kiichi, who was

at the time practicing medicine in Takao (now Gaoxiong), Taiwan. At Higashi's invitation, Satō accompanied him on his return to Taiwan. They left Wakayama in June and arrived in the colony on July 5. Satō returned on October 15 of the same year, extending a short trip to more than three and a half months. His arrival was reported in the local newspaper and he was treated as a VIP by the colonial government throughout his stay. Some suggest the trip was prompted by the frustration he felt about the nascent romantic affair with Tanizaki Junichirō's wife Chiyo and the subsequent discord with his live-in lover, the actress Maiya Kayoko. In fact, after his return from the trip he quickly separated from Maiya Kayoko and the next year openly severed his ties with Tanizaki. For details of his trip to Taiwan see Fujii Shōzō (1998: 79–87) and Shimada Kinji (1976: 214–218); for the relationship with Tanizaki, see Oketani Hideaki (1987: 279–281).

2. Soseki traveled to Manchuria and returned to Japan via Korea in 1910. The six-week sojourn was recorded in "Mankan tokorodokoro," which was serialized in *Asahi Shinbun* shortly after his return. A decade after Soseki's expedition, Akutagawa took a four-month jaunt to China as an overseas observer for *Osaka Mainichi Shinbun* in 1921.

3. See *Kaizō* 3(3) (March 1921); reprinted in Satō Haruo (1998, 4:33–53). "Hoshi" includes a story published separately in the January issue titled "Fifth Daughter Huang" (Kō Gojō 黄五娘).

4. See *Chūō kōron* 38(9) (August 1923); reprinted in Satō Haruo (1998, 19:165–167).

5. See *Dōwa* 2(9) (September 1921); reprinted in Satō Haruo (1998, 4:67–70).

6. See *Kaizō* 7(3) (March 1925): 2–34.

7. See *Chūō kōron* 47(9) (September 1932): 92–132 and 47(10) (October 1932): 1–14.

8. For further discussion on "Journey to the Colony" see Kawahara Isao (1997: 3–23).

9. The name means "person outside the world" and clearly is something like a pen name or "fancy name" (*hao* 號). In fact, several articles were published under this name in various literary journals, leading to speculation about the true identity of the author. The prevailing theory is that it is the pen name of the writer Qiu Yonghan, but Qiu has denied it.

10. Satō Haruo, like Tanizaki and other Taishō writers, had a keen interest in the newly imported genre of detective stories. He wrote many essays on this genre, such as "Tantei shōsetsu shōron" 探偵小説小論 and "Tantei shōsetsu to geijutsumi" 探偵小説と芸術味. See Satō Haruo (1998, 19:273–276 and 340–345).

11. On Ban Zhao 班昭 (ca. 48–ca. 116) and her precepts see Swann (1932) and Yu-shih Chen (1996).

12. A high-class courtesan, similar to the geisha in Japan, who entertains men as they eat and drink. Although sexual services were not openly conducted

at the workplace, there was an understanding that the woman was available for such liaisons if agreeable terms could be reached.

13. The Lantern Festival is the fifteenth of the first lunar month, on the first full moon after Chinese New Year. Xuantanye 玄壇爺, "Lord of the Mysterious Altar," is Zhao Gongming 趙公明, an ancient figure renowned as a demon queller and guardian of contracts. Typically he is portrayed with a black face and body, astride a tiger, carrying a metal whip. Although his birthday is celebrated on the fifteenth of the third month, on the day of the Lantern Festival his statue is paraded through the community while the inhabitants toss firecrackers at it. See Noguchi Tetsurō et al. (1994: 401).

14. Located in the southern part of Taipei near the river, Banka 萬華 was originally developed as a river port.

15. Although he garnered fame for his traditional poetry, Lian is best known as the author of the first comprehensive history of Taiwan.

16. For more information on the ideology of motherhood used in the wartime context see Sakuramoto Tomio (1995: 121–126) and Kimura Kazuaki (2000: 88–123). See also my discussion of Lü Heruo's story "Neighbor" in Chapter 7.

17. "Sekikanki" was first published in Nishikawa's journal, *Bungei Taiwan* 1(6) (December 1940), and then was printed in an independent edition of 705 copies. In 1942 a publisher in Tokyo, Shomotsu tenbōsha, included it in a collection of short stories that took this story as its title. The collection won the Taiwan Culture Award the next year and came to be identified as the author's representative work.

18. Hamada Yahei was the captain of Tokugawa Hideyoshi's ship, which was captured by the Dutch for interfering with trade between Holland and Taiwan.

19. From the essay "Rekishi no aru Taiwan" in *Taiwan jihō* (February 1938): 65–67; reprinted in Nakajima Toshio and Kawahara Isao (1998, 1:449–451).

20. Chen Yonghua was an important retainer of Zheng Chenggong who came to control all civil affairs. Chenggong's son, Zheng Jing, married his son Kezang to Chen's daughter in an attempt to cement his loyalty. See Wills (1999: 95–102).

21. *Taiwan waiji* was written by Jiang Risheng (fl. 1692) and is devoted solely to the history of Zheng Chenggong and his heirs.

22. The full quote, which makes clear the link between male and female conduct, is from the *Record of the Historian* (ca. 100 B.C.E.): "A loyal vassal does not serve two lords, a chaste woman does not change to a second husband." See *Shiji* (Beijing: Zhonghua shuju), 82:2457.

23. Satō Haruo also wrote a number of historical tales involving Zheng Chenggong. These no doubt were consulted by Nishikawa in composing his own tale of the Red Fort. See Satō Haruo (1998, 30:191–224).

24. *Ikoku bungaku* 異国文学, or "exotic literature," refers to literature written by Japanese about foreign subjects or landscapes; literature written by foreign

writers is referred to as *gaikoku bungaku* 外国文学, "foreign literature." Mori Ōgai's "Maihime" (The dancer) might be considered a masterpiece within the genre of exotic literature. Satō Haruo's "Tale of the Fan" has been referred to as *ikoku bungaku* since its first publication and is included in anthologies of *ikoku bungaku*.

25. See *Bungei Taiwan* 2(6) (September 1941): 24–25. This is one of the many overtly political poems by Nishikawa Mitsuru. Others commemorate military victories, such as "Poem for the Occupation of Amoy," "Singapore Falling," and "Dutch Indonesia Surrenders Unconditionally."

26. Yasuda Yojirō, founder of the nationalistic Japanese romantic school, accompanied Satō Haruo to China when Satō served as a special correspondent for the journal *Bungei shunjū*. In Beijing they met with Takeuchi Yoshimi, who was studying there. Takeuchi took them sightseeing to the Marco Polo Bridge, where Satō Haruo composed his famous "Poem Composed Standing by the Marco Polo Bridge" (Rokōkyōhan ni tachite utaeru 蘆溝橋に立ちて歌へる), dedicating it to Yasuda and Takeuchi. Yasuda was inspired by the trip to write *Mongolia and Xinjiang*. The quote was taken from Yasuda Yojurō's essay collection *Mōkyō;* see Oketani Hideaki (1987: 298–302).

27. Another member of the Japanese romantic school discussed in this book is Nakamura Chihei.

28. The group's journal *Nihon Rōman ha* was published from 1935 to 1938, when it ceased publication due to financial difficulties. Yasuda, Nakatani Takao, and Asano Kō joined Hayashi Fusao in the New Japan Culture Group (Shin Nippon bunka no kai 新日本文化の会) and Kageyama Masaji's right-wing Great Eastern Academy (Daitōjuku 大東塾), thereby confirming the group's fascist tendencies.

29. See Doak (1999) for a thorough and thought-provoking study on the Japanese romantic school, especially the development of its nationalistic tendency and its relation with Yanagita Kunio's cultural specificism, historiography, and German romanticism.

Chapter 6: Language Policy and Cultural Identity

1. It is unclear when the indigenous populace of Taiwan became a minority in their own land, but the situation is probably of long standing. In 1942, the breakdown of the three groups of inhabitants in the colony was as follows: Han Taiwanese numbered about 6 million; the aboriginals were around 160,000; and there were approximately 380,000 Japanese colonial expatriates. Currently there are about 370,000 indigenous people living among the 22 million Han Taiwanese.

2. On *kotodama*, see Konishi (1984: 203–212).

3. Mark Peattie, approaching the question from a slightly different angle, has also pointed out differences in Japanese and French colonial rule. He insists

that the Japanese assimilation policy was characteristic of Asian traditions of rule and developed into something rather different from French pragmatism. See Peattie (1996: 134–140).

4. For a detailed discussion of Yanaihara's colonial theory see Asada Jyōji (1990: 315–518).

5. For an overview of Japanese colonial language policy in Korea, see Yasuda Toshiaki (1998); in China, Xu Minmin (1996); in Korea and Manchuria, Lee Yeounsuk (1996); in Taiwan, Manchuria, and China, Shi Gang (1993); and in Taiwan and the South Pacific islands, Tani Yasuyo (2000).

6. Ueno Chizuko highly praises Oguma's provocative book but questions his uncritical adoption of such terms as "ethnicity" *(minzoku)* and "nation-state" *(kokka)*. She also faults him for his proposed solution, which, she claims, falls into the trap of the "multiethnic state" *(taminzoku kokka)*. See Ueno (1998: 11–96).

7. See also the enlightening article by Brooks (1998) on the legal status of Korean colonial subjects.

8. Oguma followed up this study with an even more ambitious project: *The Boundaries of the Japanese People* (*Nihonjin no kyōkai* 日本人の境界, 1998) in which he explores how these theories of ethnicity affected the non-Japanese living throughout the empire, focusing on the Okinawans, the Ainu people, and the inhabitants of Japan's two major colonies: Taiwan and Korea.

9. See *Gekkan Nihongo Ron* 2(6) (June 1994).

10. For detailed discussion of the formation of *kokubungaku* see Suzuki Sadami (1998) and Suzuki Tomi (1999: 85–127).

11. From a speech given by Ueda Kazutoshi in October 1894. It was later included in *Kokugo no tame ni* (Tokyo: Fuku sanbō, 1895). See also Lee Yeounsuk (1996: 151) and Koyasu Nobukuni (1996: 121). This (in)famous quote was omitted when the speech/article was included in the multivolume collectanea of Meiji literature *Meiji bungaku zenshū* (vol. 44).

12. Ueda Kazutoshi left for Europe in 1891 and returned in June 1894 on the eve of the Russo-Japanese War. Upon his return he was immediately appointed professor at Imperial University. It was in a series of public talks, such as "Kokugo to kokka to" (The national language and the nation, October 1894) and "Kokugo kenkyū ni tsuite" (On the study of the national language, November 1894), later included in the collection *Kokugo no tame ni*, that he began to outline the ideology of the organic relationship between languages and nation-states. See Lee Yeounsuk (1996: 118–124).

13. For an in-depth study of Tokieda Motoki's activities at Keijō Imperial University see Yasuda Toshiaki (1998).

14. Starting in the late 1920s, the term "*gaichi*" 外地 (literally "external territory") was used officially by the Japanese government to avoid the term "*shokuminchi*" (colony).

15. On Japanese education in Taiwan during the colonial period see Tsurumi (1977; 1984).

16. For more information on Izawa Shūji see Shi Gang (1993: 28–50), Komagome Takeshi (1996: 42–74), and Uenuma Hachirō (1962).

17. *Taiwan tsūshin,* vol. 2 (Kokka kyōiku), no. 41.

18. This is only one of the many attacks on the Japanese army and governmental facilities in Taipei during the early stages of the Japanese occupation. For a discussion of the various armed incidents see Takenaka Nobuko (1995: 13–31).

19. Izawa was removed from his position *(hishoku)* because his aggressive education policy differed significantly from that of Governor-General Nogi Maresuke. In accordance with the standard length of elementary education for Japanese children in Japan, for example, he advocated a six-year public school education *(kōgakkō)* for the natives instead of the four years favored by Nogi and the colonial government. He also proposed that the Taiwan supervisory council *(hyōgikai),* responsible for overseeing the governor-general's legislative process, should include more than two Taiwanese natives to be chosen from those "who are well educated, with good reputations, and who pay more than ten yen of property tax or business tax." See Komagome Takeshi (1996: 44).

20. His position was summarized in the phrase *"isshidōjin"* 一視同仁, literally "viewing them as the same and according them the same benevolence."

21. From the "Sixth Regular Meeting Lecture of the National Education Association" (*Kokka kyōikusha dairokkai teikai enzetsu*), in Izawa Shūji (1958: 593).

22. *Taiwan kyōiku enkakushi* (Taiwan kyōikukai, 1939), p. 166.

23. For a detailed list of qualifications for students and future teachers of Japanese see Osa Shizue (1998: 187–200).

24. Thomas Barclay was born in Glasgow in 1849. In 1877, he took up residence in Taiwan as a missionary for the Presbyterian church, running an elementary school and a seminary in Tainan. A translator of the New Testament into the Amoy dialect, Barclay was sympathetic to Liu Yongfu's armed rebellion and critical of Japanese colonial policies. Izawa accompanied the first governor-general, Kabayama, to visit Barclay in October 1895. See Shi Gang (1993: 30–31), Ozaki Hotsuki (1971: 256–257), and Osa Shizue (1998: 192–196).

25. For details on the debates surrounding the romanization of the Japanese syllabaries (*kokuji kairyō undō* 国字改良運動) that occurred during the 1870s see Lee Yeounsuk (1996: 26–46).

26. This group, dedicated to an enlightenment movement in the early Meiji period, was founded by Mori Arinori (1847–1889) in the fall of 1873 and takes its name from that year, the sixth in the reign of the Meiji emperor. Having just returned several months earlier from a stay in the United States, Mori gathered thirty of his friends, including Nishi Amane 西周, Fukuzawa Yukichi 福沢諭吉, Nakamura Masanao 中村正直, and Nishimura Shigeki 西村茂樹, to form a group that would discuss topical issues concerning Japan's modernization. In the following year the organization published *Meiroku zasshi* as a forum for members to disseminate their ideas to a wide audience in government and society. The jour-

nal, which treated politics, orthography, education, natural science, religion, the economy, and women's issues, made important contributions to the national dialogue on the Meiji modernization process. In 1875 the Meiji government clamped down on criticism and the editors decided that, free expression being no longer possible, the journal should cease publication. After forty-three issues, *Meiroku zasshi* and Meirokusha were officially defunct. Members of Meirokusha formed the basis of the Academia of Japan (Nihon gakushiin 日本学士院, previously known as Teikoku gakushiin 帝国学士院), the highest national academic organization. See Braisted (1976).

27. Compare the translation of oxygen as *suine* すいね, hydrogen as *midumi* みづみ, atmosphere as *honoke* ほのけ, and carbon dioxide as *suminosu* すみのす in the all-kana chemistry book *Monowari no hashigo* (1874) to Fukuzawa Yukichi's adaptations of Sinitic character compounds for translating these terms: *sanso* 酸素, *suiso* 水素, *kūki* 空気, and *tanso* 炭素; these latter terms remain the standard translations to this day. See Lee Yeounsuk (1996: 34–35).

28. For detailed information on these debates in the 1870s and 1890s see Lee Yeounsuk (1996: 26–46).

29. Although this document is frequently cited in accounts of the *kokugo* and *kokuji* issue, recently scholars such as Noguchi Takehiko and Yasuda Toshiaki have questioned its authenticity and suggest that its true purpose was political rather than linguistic. See Osa Shizue (1998: 57) and Yasuda Toshiaki (1997: 35).

30. He debated with the Christian philosopher Uchimura Kanzō, for example, arguing that the spirit of the Imperial Rescript on Education and the spirit of Christianity, which claims that all men are sons of God, are incompatible. See Komagome Takeshi (1996: 55–70). Even a purist like Inoue was later forced to alter his views. In 1919, as chair of the East Asian Association 東亜協会 and founder of the magazine *Light of East Asia* (*Tōa no hikari* 東亜の光), he published a series of editorials; one, in particular, questioned whether the Imperial Rescript on Education could be taught in Taiwan without alteration. See *Light of East Asia* (May 1919): 1–2.

31. Inoue was an important proponent of German philosophy.

32. This first council was primarily a survey and research body with a primary mission to adopt a phonetic script. Initial moves toward replacing the historical kana orthography *(rekishiteki kanazukai)* still used in textbooks with a system that reflected current phonology were thwarted, however, through organized resistance from traditionalists. The council was disbanded in an administrative reorganization in 1913. Its successor was the Interim National Language Research Council (1921–1934), which saw increasing interest in script reform (limiting the number of kanji in use) from the newspapers. See Lee Yeounsuk (1996: 70) and Gottlieb (1995: 11–17).

33. The speech was given on February 17, 1901, at the Conference for the Study of Kokugo. It was later published in the magazine *Taiwan kyōiku kai zasshi* 1 (February 1901): 4.

34. In an 1895 speech titled "Taiwan kyōiku dan." See Izawa Shūji (1958: 571).

35. In a 1904 article titled "Iwayuru saikin no kokugo mondai ni tsukite." See Izawa Shūji (1958: 727).

36. The Five Classics are the *Book of Documents* (*Shujing* 書経), *Book of Odes* (*Shijing* 詩経), *Book of Changes* (*Yijing* 易経), *Record of Rites* (*Liji* 禮記), and *Spring and Autumn Annals* (*Chunqiu* 春秋). The Four Books, the core curriculum of the Song Neo-Confucian Zhu Xi 朱熹 (1130–1200), are the *Analects* (*Lunyu* 論語), *Mencius* (*Mengzi* 孟子), *Greater Learning* (*Daxue* 大學), and *Doctrine of the Mean* (*Zhongyong* 中庸).

37. "Taiwan kyōiku dan." See Izawa Shūji (1958: 570).

38. In a speech titled "Taiwan kōgakkō setchi ni kansuru iken." See Izawa Shūji (1958: 618).

39. The first four years of instruction in Chinese texts followed the traditional Chinese approach; but beginning in the fifth grade, students learned the Japanese *kanbun kundoku* 漢文訓読 way of reading Chinese through Japanese. See Tsurumi (1977: 20).

40. For a description of education in Taiwan before the occupation see Tsurumi (1977: 9–10). Under the Qing dynasty there had also been publicly funded prefectural and district academies, but enrollment was limited to those drawn from the ranks of the literati.

41. Many such examples of cross-cultural misunderstanding and misappropriation in the early days of Japanese-language education are documented in Ozaki Hotsuki (1971: 251–265).

42. For a detailed discussion and helpful diagram of the polarized positions advocated by these figures see Komagome Takeshi (1996: 72–74).

43. Izawa also specified why he believed that the "self-determinism" model was inappropriate. He argued that it had failed in Alsace-Lorraine because the Prussians had refused to admit the similarity between the Prussian and French peoples; it had succeeded in Hawaii only because of the great disparity in levels of culture between the two peoples. Taiwan and Japan were like France and Prussia, not Hawaii and the United States.

44. *Taiwan kyōikukai zasshi* 6 (August 1902): 15.

45. See, for example, stories such as Long Yingzong's "Papaya no aru machi." See Ozaki Hotsuki (1971: 252–254).

46. Minami Maho, "Nokosareta kokugo mondai," *Taiwan kyōiku* 439 (1939): 35; see Osa Shizue (1998: 46).

47. For example, a section chief (*kachō*) would be fined ten yen; an infraction would cost an appointed official (*hanninkan*) five yen; all others would pay three yen. Considering that day laborers in Japan were making only one yen a day on average and there was a considerable wage gap between Japan and the colony, these fines were substantial. See Shi Huiran (1999: 59–69).

48. See the "Introduction" to Anderson (1991).

49. See Inoue Tetsujirō (1891: 1–5); see also Gottlieb (1995: 75–85 and 17–25) for details on postwar language policy.

50. Typical examples emphasizing the role of language are *Nihongo no sahō* (1979) by Tada Michitarō, *Kotoba to bunka* (1973) and *Tozasareta gengo—Nihongo no sekai* (1975) by Suzuki Takeo, *Nihongo no ronri* (1973) and *Nihongo no kosei* (1976) by Toyama Shigehiko, *Nihonjin no gengohyōgen* (1975) and *Nihonjin no gengoseikatsu* (1979) by Kindaichi Haruhiko, *Kango to Nihonjin* (1978) by Suzuki Shūji, and Itasaka Gen's *Nihongo no hyōjō* (1978), just to name a few. See the appendix in Nishikawa Nagao (1999: 1–24).

51. In later chapters I discuss the current status of Japanese-language literature overseas in more detail.

52. Language acquisition was the cornerstone of the colonial cultural policy and was predicated on the understanding of Japanese culture, but the current global consumption of Japanese popular culture does not require knowledge of the Japanese language. The difference certainly has to do with issues of First World and Third World cultural circulation, the transcultural nature of postmodern pop culture, and above all, the ability of postcolonial agency to initiate action in engaging, selecting, (re)constructing, and even resisting the First World cultural force. For a discussion of related issues see Leo Ching, "Imaginings in the Empires of the Sun," in Treat (1996: 169–196).

53. Though Phillipson mainly discusses the global commodification of English, the implications of his work can be applied to other colonial and postcolonial contexts. See Phillipson (1992: 109–136).

54. On the tradition of blood feuds among communities in Taiwan see Shepherd (1993: 308ff.).

55. Interpretations of the New Literature movement vary. Huang Qichun (1995) suggests that from 1920 to 1926 the emphasis was on language reform but after 1926 the focus shifted to proletarian literary activities. Peng Ruijin (1995) denies that the movement had anything to do with literature and language reform; he views it as a nationalist social movement. Perhaps it is best seen as a movement for linguistic and literary reform that was inspired by nationalist, anticolonial sentiments and an accompanying sense of urgency concerning modernization. Although earlier activities centered on issues of language and representation, these concerns do not disappear after 1926.

56. For details of the life of Taiwanese intellectuals in the metropole see Rubinstein (1999: 230–234).

57. For details on the New People's Society, Taiwanese Youth Association, and Taiwanese Cultural Association see Kawahara Isao (1997: 132–145).

58. There is no record of Taiwanese students studying abroad prior to the 1920s. At the end of 1920 there were only 19 students studying in China as opposed to 273 students three years later. Although this number is still minuscule compared to those who were studying in Japan, the dramatic increase in a short period of three years illustrates an increasing awareness of the colonial

condition on the part of native youth inspired by Woodrow Wilson's idea of self-determination, by the May Fourth movement, and by the emergence of citizen's rights advocacy groups such as the Association of Taiwanese Culture (Taiwan bunka kyōkai 台湾文化協会). See Kawahara Isao (1997: 132–149).

59. "Riyongwen guchui lun" 日用文鼓吹論 , *Taiwan Qingnian* 4(1) (January 1922); cited in Kawahara Isao (1997: 149).

60. "Lun puji baihuawen de xinshiming" 論普及白話文的新使命, *Taiwan* 4(1) (January 1923); cited in Kawahara Isao (1997: 150–151).

61. "Hanwen gaige lun" 漢文改革論, *Taiwan* 4(1–2) (January/February 1923); cited in Kawahara Isao (1997: 151).

62. For Zhang's activities in Beijing and Tokyo see Kawahara Isao (1997: 156–169).

63. "Qing heli chaixia zhezuo baicaocongzhong de puojiu diantang" 請合力拆下這座敗草叢中的破舊殿堂, *Taiwan minbao* 3(1) (January 1, 1925); cited in Kawahara Isao (1997: 160–161).

64. "Juewujinyou de jibuoyin de yiyi" 絕無僅有的擊鉢吟的意義, *Taiwan minbao* 3(2) (January 11, 1925).

65. For details on this and many other debates of the new and old schools see Kawahara Isao (1997: 156–169).

66. "Shiti de jiefang" 詩体的解放 , *Taiwan minbao* 3(7–9) (March 1, 14, 21, 1925).

67. "Xin wenxue yundong de yiyi" 新文学運動的意義 , *Taiwan minbao*, 67, special issue (August 26, 1925).

68. "Guanglin" 光臨, *Taiwan minbao* 86 (January 1, 1926): 19–20.

69. "Zheyuan de huanghun" 蔗園的黃昏, *Taiwan minbao* 124 (September 26, 1926): 13–14.

70. "Jialifan" 加里飯, *Taiwan minbao* 138 (January 2, 1927): 21–22.

71. For Zhang's involvement in new-style vernacular poetry from 1920 to 1932 see Xu Junya (1997a: 163–208). For comments made by Chinese literary critic Wu Zhichun on the authenticity of his Chinese style see Zhang Henghao (1990: 136).

72. On Hu's "Eight-Don't-Ism" and Chen's "Three Great Principles" see Chow Tse-tsung (1960: 273–277).

73. Zhang is also the author of eight Japanese-language textbooks for Chinese learners and wrote many introductory essays on Japanese literature. See the chronology of Zhang Wojun's works in Zhang Henghao (1990: 159–164).

74. From an essay in Lu's essay collection *Eryiji* titled "Xiezai 'laodong wenti' zhiqian"; included in *Lu xun quanji*, vol. 3 (Beijing: Renmin Wenxue Chubanshe, 1981).

75. In the preface written for the book *Wuwan Taiwan* edited by Zhang Xiaozhe and Yang Zhicheng (1926). See also Matsunaga Masayoshi (1993: 219–220).

76. This feeling of mutual distrust was not resolved with the end of colonial

rule. Instead it formed a backdrop to postcolonial conflicts between the Nationalist government and nativist Taiwanese, leading to such violent encounters as the February 28 Incident. This feeling of being betrayed by both China and Japan is best captured in Wu Zhuoliu's *Orphan of Asia* (*Ajia no koji*, 1973).

77. For Zhang Wojun's fictional writings see the short stories collected in Zhang Henghao (1990: 85–128).

78. For an interesting discussion of how Taiwanese perceptions of the signifier "China" evolved during the Japanese colonial period see Xu Junya (1997a: 109–140).

79. Linguists have compared the difference between Taiwanese (a dialect of the Southern Min regional language) and Mandarin to that between English and Dutch or French and Spanish. The crucial distinction between a dialect and a language is mutual intelligibility. Thus today there are two main dialects of Taiwanese reflecting disparate origins in the Southern Min dialects of Zhangzhou and Quanzhou. A native speaker of either dialect could communicate with a speaker of any other dialect of Southern Min with only the occasional misunderstanding that might occur when an Australian speaks to an American—but could not, without further training, converse with someone who only spoke a dialect of Mandarin, Cantonese, or Wu. See DeFrancis (1984: 39), Y. R. Chao (1976: 24, 87, 97, 105), and Norman (1988: 187).

80. *Taiwan minbao* 2(19) (October 1, 1924): 14.

81. See "Taiyü zhengli shi touxu" 台語整理史頭緒 and "Taiyü zhengli zhi zeren" 台語整理之責任, published in *Taiwan minbao* (1929). See Xu Junya (1997a: 151–152).

82. Guo played a particularly important role in fashioning a Taiwanese written language *(Taiwanhuawen)*. See Kawahara Isao (1997: 182–191) and Xu Junya (1997a: 152–156).

83. The serialized article "Zenyang butichang xiangtu wenxue" 怎樣不提倡鄉土文學 was banned by the colonial government and only three installments ever appeared; see *Wurenbac* 伍人報, vols. 9–11 (August–October 1930). See also Kawahara Isao (1997: 180–181).

84. Quoted in Xu Junya (1997a: 152–153).

85. *Wurenbao* 9 (August 1930); cited in Li Xianzhang (1986: 157–158). See also Fix (1998: 8).

86. The best source for information on Huang Shihui's early articles is, in fact, a postwar article by Liao Yuwen, who was an opponent of Huang's ideas in the 1930s. See Liao Yuwen, "Taiwan wenzi gaige yundong shilue" 臺灣文字改革運動史略, in *Taiwan wenwu* 3(3) (December 1954) and 4(1) (May 1955): 99–100.

87. Quoted in an article by Furen (Zhuang Chuisheng), "Taiwan huawen zabo IV," *Nanyin* 1(4) (February 22, 1932): 10–11.

88. See Kawahara Isao (1997: 182–185). In *Nanyin* Guo published two columns: one gave detailed instructions on how to represent Taiwanese; the

other presented an actual example of this theory written in the orthography he advocated.

89. *Nanyin* 9(10) (joint issue, July 1931): 36.

90. See "Jianshe 'Taiwan huawen' yiti'an" 建設臺灣話文一提案, *Taiwan xinminbao* 379 (August 29, 1931): 11; cited in Fix (1998).

91. *Taiwan xinminbao* was founded in January 1932; *Formosa* published its first issue in July 1933.

92. "*Yige tongzhi de pixin*" 一個同志的批信, *Taiwan xinwenxue* 1 (December 1935): 67.

93. Political problems exacerbated the difficulties he encountered in writing. He was forced to suspend his medical practice in 1938 and was jailed for almost two months in 1941, which left him sick and weak. In jail he composed his last, unfinished work, "Prison Diary," and died a year after his release.

94. For example, besides terms for everyday objects like the radio (*rajio* ラジオ) that were introduced by the Japanese and never had indigenous names, abstract words such as "*tsugō*" 都合 (*to-háp* in Taiwanese) and "*saisoku*" 催促 (*chhui-chhiok* in Taiwanese) remain part of the native dialect to this day.

Chapter 7: The Nativist Response

1. In *Bungaku hyōron* 1(8) (October 1934): 199–233.

2. See Shimomura (1994: 12–13). For a detailed discussion of the process of selection and the comments of individual reviewers see Zhang Jilin (2000: 57–76).

3. Lai later became a writer in his own right. He was one of the founding members of the Taiwanese Literary Federation (Taiwan wenyi lianmeng) and a contributing member of its organizational journal, *Taiwan wenyi*. See Kawahara Isao (1997: 207–222).

4. Chō Kakuchu debuted two years earlier with his "Gakidō" 餓鬼道 (Way of the Hungry Ghosts), which was awarded a literary prize in a contest sponsored by the magazine *Kaizō* (April 1932). Chō became the first Korean writer from the colony to publish in a major *naichi* journal. For general information on Korean writers during the colonial period see Ōmura Masuo and Hotei Toshihiro (1997). For studies on Chō Kakuchu, see Hayashi Kōji (1997), Nin Tenkei (1994), Shirakawa Yutaka (1995), and Nakane Takayuki (1999).

5. These ideological and methodological debates are reflected in the writings of Wang Tuo and Song Zelai and their quarrel with writers who opposed the Nativist Literature *(xiangtu wenxue)* movement, such as Wang Wenxing (who advocated abstract avant-gardism) and the poet Yu Guangzhong (a proponent of modernism).

6. In 1921, the elementary school attendance rate—100 percent for Japanese residents—was only 30 percent for the Taiwanese. For middle and high schools, the gap was even larger, owing to government-mandated quotas. Yang

Kui himself failed the middle school entrance examination. See Yamaguchi Mamoru (1992: 130).

7. On the Taiwanese Cultural Association see Kerr (1974: 128–129).

8. See Yang Kui (1985). For a detailed discussion of Yang's views on literature in the context of Japanese realism and naturalism see Zhang Jilin (2000: 120–125).

9. He left Tainan Second High School (today called Tainan First High School). During the colonial period, the First High School (Ikkō) was usually reserved for Japanese residents. Few native Taiwanese were allowed to enter. High schools were the equivalent of prep schools for universities. In Taiwan, a good high school education was possible for Taiwanese with an appropriate background, but applicants to the only university on the island, Taihoku Imperial University (Taihoku Teikoku Daigaku 台北帝国大学), faced stiff competition from applicants from the Japanese homeland. As a result, many families with resources sent their sons (and, rarely, daughters) to Japan to enroll in private universities. For education in Taiwan during the colonial period see Tsurumi (1977; 1984: 279-294).

10. Yang wrote about the harsh reality facing day laborers in an article titled "Profile of the Life of a Free Laborer, or How Not to Die of Starvation" in *Gōgai* 1(3) (September 1927). Yang characterized this work as documentary-style literature *(hōkoku bungaku)* and in many ways his "Newspaper Boy" is a fictionalized version of the article; there are many similarities in the depiction of a laborer's daily life. For a comparison of the two works see Kawahara Isao's "Yō Ki 'Shinbun haitatsufu' no seiritsu haikei" in Shimomura et al. (1995: 287–300).

11. In *Shanling: Chaoxian Taiwan duanpian xiaoshuoji* 山靈朝鮮臺灣短編小説集 (Mountain spirits: Anthology of Korean and Taiwanese short stories; Shanghai: Wenhua shenghuo chubanshe, 1936) and in *Ruoxiao minzu xiaoshuo xuan* (Selected stories from powerless ethnic groups; Shanghai: Shenghuo shudian, 1936).

12. For Chinese views on Taiwanese and Korean colonial literature see Shimomura (1994: 16–20).

13. *Taiwanese New Literature* 2(1) (January 1937). Hayashi Fusao was active as a proletarian writer in the 1920s but reoriented *(tenkō)* his proletarian leaning to "return to Japan" *(Nihon kaiki)* in 1934, when he was jailed. In 1936 he published his "Proclamation Renouncing Proletarian Writings."

14. The term first appeared in Hirabayashi Hatsunosuke's article "Dialectical Historical View and Literature" (Yuibutsu shikan to bungaku) in *Shinchō* (December 1921). For further information see Yamada Seizaburō (1966: 276-279).

15. For detailed information see Yuchi Asao (1991: 9–30) and Satō Shizuo (1989: 59–70).

16. *Senki* 2(5) to 2(6) (May–June 1929).

17. *Senki* 2(6) to 2(9) and 2(11) (June–September and November 1929).

18. For information on major proletarian magazines published in Taiwan during the late 1920s through 1930 see Kawahara Isao (1997: 169–178).

19. For further reading on the history of Taiwanese communism see Yamabe Kentarō (1971), Lu Xiuyi (1990), Liang Mingxiong (1996), Jian Jiongren (1997), Kawahara Isao (1997), and Chen Fangming (1998).

20. Published in the founding issue of *Taiwan shinbungaku* (September 1935): 14–18.

21. In *Bungaku annai* 2(6) (June 1936); reprinted in Nakajima Toshio and Kawahara Isao (1999: 93–98).

22. This visceral dislike carried over into his private life; he named his first-born son Zibeng 資崩—literally, "capitalism crumbles."

23. In *Taiwan jihō* 268 (April 1942); reprinted in Nakajima Toshio and Kawahara Isao (1999: 137–148).

24. Consider Confucius' famous statement that all he required for happiness was simple food, water, and a crooked elbow for a pillow whereas wealth and riches unjustly attained were as distant from his ideals as "floating clouds" (*Analects* 7:16).

25. The tension also existed between Japanese expatriate writers who lived and wrote in the colonies and the Japanese homeland or *naichi* writers, as in the case of Nishikawa Mitsuru.

26. For a detailed study of Yang's relationships with Numakawa and Nyūta see Zhang Jilin (2000: 29–56 and 148–173).

27. In 1949, a "Peace Proclamation" drafted by Yang Kui was published in the Shanghai newspaper *Dagongbao* and he was subsequently arrested on April 6. In October of the same year, the Chinese Communists proclaimed the founding of the People's Republic of China and in December the Nationalist government began its retreat to the island. The next year, Yang was sentenced to twelve years in the harshest political prison.

28. Edited by Peng Xiaoyan of the National Center for Preservation of Cultural Resources.

29. See *Bungaku hyōron* 2(1) (January 1935); reprinted in Nakajima Toshio and Kawahara Isao (1999, 2:9–38).

30. See *Taiwan bungaku* 2(4) (October 1942): 40–56; reprinted in Nakajima Toshio and Kawahara Isao (1999, 2:183–200).

31. See *Taiwan bungaku* 2(2) (March 1942): 2–37; reprinted in Nakajima Toshio and Kawahara Isao (1999, 2:133–168).

32. See *Taiwan bungaku* 3(2) (April 1943): 47–73; reprinted in Nakajima Toshio and Kawahara Isao (1999, 2:215–242).

33. See *Taiwan bungaku* 3(3) (July 1943): 169–188; reprinted in Nakajima Toshio and Kawahara Isao (1999, 2:243–262).

34. See *Taiwan bungei* 3(7) and 3(8) (August 1936): 11–36; reprinted in Nakajima Toshio and Kawahara Isao (1999, 2:77–102).

35. See *Taiwan jihō* 272 (August 1942): 177–190; reprinted in Nakajima Toshio and Kawahara Isao (1999, 2:169–182).

36. "Seishū" in *Seishū* (Tokyo: Shimuzu shoten, 1944): 245-336; reprinted in Nakajima Toshio and Kawahara Isao (1999, 2:277-370).

37. See *Taiwan kōron* 82 (October 1942): 81-93.

38. First published in *Taiwan bungaku* 4(1) (December 1943): 119-131. References are to the reprinted version in Nakajima Toshio and Kawahara Isao (1999, 2:263-275).

39. See, for example, the stories cited later in this chapter.

40. For an overview of this scholarship see Ueno Chizuko (1995; 1998).

41. See Wakakuwa Midori (1995). Soldiers who died in battle were enshrined at the Yasukuni Shrine and became gods.

42. First published in *Taiwan bungaku* 4(1) (December 1943): 119-131; text quoted from reprint in Nakajima Toshio and Kawahara Isao (1999, 2:263-275).

43. "Golden paper" 金紙 is a type of spirit money used for offerings to gods and spirits. It fulfills a variety of functions. See Hou (1975).

44. The ritual of summoning the soul is recorded in *Songs of the South* (*Chuci* 楚辭), an anthology of South Chinese poetry dating as early as the third or fourth century B.C.E. See Hawkes (1985).

45. See *Bungei Taiwan* 1 (May 1944): 12-35; reprinted in Lü Heruo (1995: 470-497).

46. Zhou Jinpo, discussed in the following chapter, dealt with the issue of nature and cultural colonialism in the short story "Weather, Belief, and Chronic Disease."

47. For a detailed account of the conscription of writers by the Kōmin hōkō-kai see Fix (1998).

48. See *Taiwan jihō* 295 (August 1944): 83-95; reprinted in Nakajima Toshio and Kawahara Isao (1999, 2:371-383).

49. See Ye Shitao (1982: 21-26). For an extensive analysis of this story, including its historical and political context, see Fix (1998: 35-40).

50. Tarumi Chie (2000) offers the most detailed study so far of Lü Heruo's life in Japan and his activities from his return to 1943.

51. See *Seishū* (Taipei: Shimizu shoten, 1943). The collection includes the title short story "Clear Autumn" and the following six stories: "Fortune, Children, and Longevity"; "Temple Courtyard"; "Neighbor"; "Moonlit Night"; "A Happy Family"; and "Pomegranate." Other than "Clear Autumn" all stories were first published in Zhang Wenhuan's *Taiwan bungaku*.

52. The other four members of the executive committee were Nishikawa Mitsuru, Hamada Hayao, Takemura Takeshi, and Nagasaki Hiroshi. See Nakajima Toshio and Kawahara Isao (1999, 2:411).

53. Lü Heruo got the job at the recommendation of *Bungei Taiwan* writer Long Yingzong, a protégé of Nishikawa Mitsuru's *Bungei Taiwan*—evidence that despite the official ideological difference between *Bungei Taiwan* and *Taiwan bungaku*, private friendships and communications existed between members. In the essay "Some Thoughts" ("Omou mama ni" 思ふままに) Lü talked about his affection for Long. See *Taiwan bungaku* 1 (June 1941): 106-109.

54. Serialized in *Zhengjingbao* 2(3) (February 1946) and 2(4) (March 1946); reprinted in Lü Heruo (1995: 519–524).

55. See *Xinxin* 7 (October 1946); reprinted in Lü Heruo (1995: 525–532).

56. See *Taiwan wenhua* 2(2) (February 1947); reprinted in Lin Shuangbu (1989: 4–20).

57. See *Kaizō* 19(4) (April 1937): 1–58; reprinted in Nakajima Toshio and Kawahara Isao (1999, 4:11–68).

58. Weng's obsessive fascination with Japanese femininity was a source of controversy among nationalistic readers and critics. See the excerpt on Weng Nao's life in Tokyo in Yang Yizhou's autobiography, *Bukan huishou hua dangnian* 不堪回首話當年, in Weng Nao (1991: 139–142).

Chapter 8: Imperial-Subject Literature and Its Discontents

1. For details on the movement see Zhou Wanyao (1994).

2. For the progress of the movement to cut off the queue (*duanfa* 斷髮) and free bound feet (*fangzu* 放足) see Wu Wenxing (1992: chaps. 5–6). For a comparative study of the Imperial Subject movement in Taiwan and Korea see Zhou Wanyao (1994: 117–156).

3. See, for example, Ye Shitao (1987: 66); Xu Junya (1994: 297–303; 1995: 476–495); and Huang Chongtian et al. (1992: 27–29).

4. Founded by Sawada Mikiko, Shichiyōkai was an elite theater appreciation group that gathered together many theater lovers, including the actress Kahara Natsuko. For more information on Zhou's life in Tokyo see Tarumi Chie (1995a: 54–56).

5. See *Bungei Taiwan* 2(6) (September 1941): 8–21; reprinted in Nakajima Toshio and Kawahara Isao (1999, 5:337–350).

6. See *Bungei Taiwan* 6(3) (July 1943): 87–141; reprinted in Nakajima Toshio and Kawahara Isao (1999, 5:9–64).

7. See *Taiwan bungaku* 3(3) (July 1943): 104–129; reprinted in Nakajima Toshio and Kawahara Isao (1999, 5:93–120).

8. The campaign to change names commenced in 1940. All Taiwanese were allowed to change their indigenous family names providing that the family was a "Kokugo family" (meaning that Japanese was adopted as its principal language), that they could prove they possessed the qualities appropriate to imperial subjects, and that they contributed to the public good. The name-changing campaign in Taiwan was not so widely accepted as in Korea. By 1943, of the 6.5 million members of the native population only 100,000 had signed up. See Yamamoto Yūzo (1991: 47).

9. For the relationship between the Imperial Subject movement and military conscription of the colonized see Kondō Masami (1996).

10. See "Watashi ga ayunda michi," in *Yasō* 54 (August 1994); see also Shimomura Sakujirō et al. (1995: 444).

11. See *Bungei Taiwan* 2(6) (September 1941). By this time *Bungei Taiwan* could no longer survive as simply a magazine of literature and the arts. Beginning in the second half of 1941, it put out several special issues promoting the sacred war for the Great East Asian Coprosperity Sphere. See Huang Yingzhe (1994: 62).

12. See Nakajima Toshio's "Shū Kinpa shinron" in Nakajima Toshio and Noma Nobuyuki (1998: 105–127) and Hoshina Hironobu's "'Kikō to shinkō to jibyō' ron" in Nakajima Toshio et al. (1995: 433–450).

13. *Taiwan bungaku* 3(3) (July 1943): 104–129; see also Nakajima Toshio and Kawahara Isao (1999, 5: 93–120).

14. For more information on Wang Changxiong see *Wenxue Taiwan* 34 (April 2000): 68–134.

15. See Huang Yingzhe (1994: 87–107). The fact that Wang's narrative was published in *Taiwan bungaku*, which is understood to have been a forum for nativist literary sentiment, has no doubt influenced later readings. If the three representative stories of imperial-subject literature are compared, independent of the magazine they were published in, their rhetorical stances and discourses on the imperial-subject campaign share amazing similarities.

16. See *Bungei Taiwan* 1(5) (January 1942).

17. After the attack on Pearl Harbor, when Japan declared war on the United States, the implementation of imperial-subject policies was less strict. The colonial government worried that high-pressure methods of forced imperialization might foster sympathy among the natives toward America and facilitate U.S. intelligence gathering on the island. The administration rewarded local gentry by opening low-level positions to them in exchange for their support of the war. See Lü Shaoli (1998: 85–87) and Chen Yisong (1994: 234).

18. For a description of life in a *kōgakkō*, see Xu Shikai (1992: 7–8).

19. See *Taiwan jihō* (January 1943). This text has not been reprinted. I rely here on the summary and extensive excerpt in Shimomura Sakujirō et al. (1995: 435–441).

20. On the Mazu cult see Bosco and Ho (1999) and Ruitenbeek (1999). For a treatment of Mazu in modern Taiwan and relations with the continental cult see Rubinstein (1995).

21. See *Bungei Taiwan* 5(6) (April 1943): 23–38; reprinted in Nakajima Toshio and Kawahara Isao (1999, 5:351–366).

22. He created the Blue Sky Taiwanese Language Theater Group (Qingtian Taiyu jushe) in 1953 and produced the film *Sharong* 紗蓉 in 1956 (which opened in 1958). He also participated in tanka composition circles. His tanka were published in *Taipei Kadan* and *Taiwan Manyōshu* (vol. 2, 1988). See Hoshina Hironobu, "'Kikō to shinkō to jibyō' ron," in Nakajima Toshio and Kawahara Isao (1995: 434) and Tarumi Chie (1995a: 62–63).

23. See "Bihui yuebao" in *Ziliwanbao* (5.31.1992) in which he was mentioned as "Zhou XX."

24. *Wenxue Taiwan* 8 (October 1993).

25. Zhou broke his long-held silence in two speeches presented in 1993. The first, before the Taiwan bungaku kenkyūkai (October 9, 1993, at Tenri University), was titled "Watashi no bungaku o kataru" (Speaking about my literature); the second, before the Chūgoku bungei kenkyūkai (December 25, 1993, at Ritsumeikan University, Kyoto), was titled "Watashi no ayunda michi" (The path I have walked). The texts of both speeches were included in *Yasō* 54 (August 1994) and represent an important source for understanding the writer Zhou Jinpo.

26. *Michi* was first published in *Bungei Taiwan* 6(3) (July 1943): 87–141. My citations refer to the reprint in Nakajima Toshio and Kawahara Isao (1999, 5:9–89).

27. The word "human" was blanked out when the story was first published. After the war, when Chen translated the story into Chinese himself, he filled in the blank.

28. In Japanese poetry, "*hana*" typically refers to the cherry blossom. The peony is associated with China and here represents his Chinese identity.

29. See "Shōsetsu *Michi* ni tsuite" in Nakajima Toshio and Kawahara Isao (1999, 5:64).

30. See *Bungei Taiwan* 6(6) (November 1943): 53–62.

31. For a brief history of the camphor industry during the colonial period see Shi Huiran (1999: 71–74).

32. On the assimilation policy see Peattie and Myers (1984: 39–41, 96–104), and Lamley (1970–1971).

33. See Peattie and Myers (1984: 40). Peattie points out the significance of ideas of eugenics and social Darwinism in the development of this view.

34. According to an article on the eighteenth Akutagawa Award in *Bungei shunju* 22(3) (March 1943), four finalists made the final selection out of the ten nominations. Although "Michi" was not among the four finalists, one of the judges (Kishida Kunio) mentioned it as one of the ten works. See Lin Ruiming (1993b: 259).

35. The ambivalence can be seen in the recent controversy over Kobayashi Yoshinori's *manga* of Taiwanese colonial history, *Taiwan ron,* in which he valorized the colonial legacy—particularly the "Japanese spirit" *(Nippon seishin)* that had been preserved in the colony while lost in the younger generation of Japanese. See Kobayashi Yoshinori (2000).

36. In "A Fabricated 'Imperial Subject Writer' Zhou Jinpo" つくられた「皇民作家」周金波, Nakajima Toshio (1999) argues that Zhou Jinpo should not be categorized as an imperial-subject writer at all.

37. See, for example, his speech "On Imperial Subject Literature" given several months after the publication of "Michi" at the Conference on Taiwanese War Literature 台湾決戦文学 (November 13, 1943), which repeated the sentiments seen in his fiction. See Huang Yingzhe (1994: 33–34).

38. Like many literary terms, the category "imperial-subject literature" was only assigned to this group of works after the genre was well established. In his study of the genre, Ide Isamu points out that the first use of the term *"kōmin bungaku"* occurred in an article in *Taiwan kōron* (May 1943) by Tanaka Yasuo. Initially the application of the term was rather loose, but it gained currency as the war progressed. Chen Huoquan's *The Way* was the first work to be explicitly identified as imperial-subject literature. See Ide Isamu (1999: 100–103).

39. See *Bungei Taiwan* 5(3) (December 1942): 10–12.

40. Three installments in *Bungei Taiwan* 3(6) (March 1942): 76–95; 4(1) (April 1942): 68–87; and 4(2) (May 1942): 108–131; reprinted in Nakajima Toshio and Kawahara Isao (1998, 1:359–422).

41. See *Bungei Taiwan* 3(4) (January 1942): 58–70.

42. Originally published in eight installments in *Bungei Taiwan* from April 1943 to June 1944; reprinted in Nakajima Toshio and Kawahara Isao (1998, 4:249–396).

Conclusion: A Voice Reclaimed

1. Recall, for example, the criticism of Satō Haruo cited earlier about the difficulty in conveying concepts like metropolis and emperor to primitive aborigines.

2. Kawamura notes the special relationship with the Asian region of Kikuchi Kan's publishing house, Bungeishunjūsha, which sponsors the Akutagawa Award. Writers nominated for the award who wrote about the colonies include Ishikawa Tatsuzō (China), Takami Jun (Southeast Asia), Miyauchi Kanya (Sakhalin), Ōshika Taku (Taiwan), Ushijima Haruko (Manchuria), and Nakajima Atsushi (South Pacific). See Kawamura Minato (1996: 139–160).

3. Here Abe Kōbo, Haniya Yutaka, and Yoshida Tomoko come to mind. See also the introduction in Kawamura Minato (1995).

Epilogue: Postcolonial Refractions

1. For an account of the transition from Japanese to Mandarin during the period 1945–1949 and the creolization of the spoken language see Marukawa Tetsushi (2000b: 30–44).

2. See my discussion of the New Literature movement, the first Nativist Literature movement, and the *Taiwan huawen yundong* in Chapter 6.

3. Although Wu was of the same generation as Yang Kui and Lai He and wrote predominately in Japanese, he is not usually considered a colonial-period writer because most of his works were written and published after the war. Rather than devoting himself to causes of social justice and liberation, Wu spent the first part of his life in education. After graduating from the Colonial Government Normal School (Sōtokufu kokugo gakkō shihanbu) founded by Izawa

Shūji, he taught Japanese language and literature in public schools for nineteen years. In 1940 he quit his job after being publicly humiliated by a school superintendent. Moving to Nanjing, he worked for a time as an editor for the Japanese-language newspaper *Continental News* (*Tairiku shinpō* 大陸新報) but ultimately became disillusioned with the collaborationist regime of Wang Jingwei and returned to Taiwan where he worked as a reporter for a number of newspapers. Wu was a reporter for *Nichinichi shinpō*, where he overlapped briefly with Nishikawa Mitsuru, as well as for *Taiwan shinbun* 台湾新聞, *Minpō* 民報, and *Shinseipō* 新生報; he remained at *Shinseipō* long after the war and published many of his novels and short stories there. His most famous novel, *The Orphan of Asia* (*Ajia no koji* アジアの孤児) delineates the protagonist Hu Taiming's struggle to exist in three cultural spheres: Taiwanese, Japanese, and Chinese.

4. See *Xinxin* 新新 (October 17, 1946): 12.

5. Michiue (2000), describing the fascist control of literary production in Taiwan during the 1950s, points out that even writing in Chinese at this time was a perilous enterprise. Works in Japanese were viewed with suspicion regardless of their content.

6. Lü's death remains shrouded in mystery. The official story is that he was hiding in a cave outside of Taipei, working for the Communist Party, when he was bitten by a poisonous snake and died. After his death, his family destroyed his diary and other writings. In 1996, a surviving portion of his diary (mainly written when he was studying in Tokyo) was discovered and will be useful in reexamining Lü's musical and literary activities in Tokyo.

7. Inukai Takeshi taught Japanese literature in Taiwan from 1942 to 1945. He also wrote the preface for a Taiwanese edition of the book. The preface for the Japanese version was written by the poet Ōoka Shinobu.

8. His unusual pen name was taken from Li Po's famous "Seeing a Friend Off"

　　青山黄北部　　白水遶東城
　　此地一為別　　孤蓬万里征

9. He held the eighth *dan* rank in kendo and placed third in the Third World Championship individual competition.

10. The work was first published as a three-volume collection in 1981, 1988, and 1993 respectively in Taiwan. Shūeisha reissued them as a two-volume set in 1994.

11. For an extensive discussion of Qiu Yonghan see Okazaki Ikuko (1996a) and Marukawa Tetsushi (2000b: 147–180).

12. It has been estimated that the victims of the political purge numbered some thirty thousand.

13. First published in *Taishū bungei* (January 1954), the story was included in a collection with the same title (Gendaisha, 1956) and also in the more recent *Kyū Eikan tanpen shōsetsu kessaku sen—mienai kokkyōsen* (Shinchōsha, 1994). Here the discussion is based on the text in Kurokawa Sō (1996, 1:261–283).

14. Huang was born into an elite family in Tainan. His father, Huang Xin, was educated in Japan and was a successful businessman active in the local political scene. Huang Xin was well versed in *kanshi* (Chinese poetry) and also wrote a number of fictional works and plays in Japanese. Huang Lingzhi was educated in the education system for the Japanese colonizers *(shōgakkō)*, and though he was always interested in literature, his first love was art. Even when enrolled in Taipei Imperial University, he spent most of his time studying sculpture in private studios and won awards in an art contest held in France.

15. Huang wanted to go to Japan in the early 1950s for medical treatment but was denied an exit visa. See Okazaki Ikuko (1998: 14–15).

16. For details of Huang's works in various genres see Okazaki Ikuko (1998: 7–9).

17. For demographic changes in the Japanese-language population of the colony see Fujii Shōzō (1998: 31–36).

18. For the prewar generation, their primary language was Taiwanese and their secondary language Japanese. For the first postwar generation, the primary language was still Taiwanese and then Mandarin Chinese. For the second postwar generation, with the high concentration and saturation of the *Guoyü* (national language) movement, Mandarin became the first language and Taiwanese was relegated to secondary status.

19. The creolization of local language is particularly evident in the youth culture. See Marukawa Tetsushi (2000b: 34–40; 62–76).

20. For the personal dimension of the struggle over linguistic identity see Kleeman (2000b: 286).

21. See Marukawa Tetsushi (2000b: 10–22).

22. See Shiba Ryōtarō, *Taiwan kikō kaidō o yuku* (Tokyo: Asahi shinbunsha, 1997). This is one installment in a series of travelogues, started in the early 1980s by Shiba, nostalgically recording journeys he made to many parts of Japan and reminiscences about its people and history. The series was later expanded to foreign countries such as Ireland, Holland, and Taiwan. The series is extremely popular and was constantly reissued throughout the 1990s; a new edition with videos was published in 2000.

23. The use of *"zu"*族, originally "tribe," in the sense of a generation or social group sharing certain likes and dislikes is itself based on the Japanese use of the corresponding term *"zoku,"* which arose among the Japanese mass media during the 1960s to refer to groups such as the *taiyōzoku* 太陽族, or "sun tribe," that is, surfers. In the name of the third group, *harizu*, the *"ha"*哈 is a phonetic representation of English "hot," in the sense that they consider all things Japanese to be "hot." The terms themselves testify to Taiwan's postcolonial linguistic hybridity.

Bibliography

Abe Kōbō 安部公房. 1972. *Kemonotachi wa kokyō wo mezasu* けものたちは故郷を
めざす. *Abe Kōbō zensakuhin*, vol. 3. Tokyo: Shinchōsha.

Akasaka Norio 赤坂憲雄. 2000. *Tōzai nanboku kō* 東西／南北考. Tokyo: Iwanami Shoten.

Anderson, Benedict. 1991. *Imagined Communities: Reflections on the Origin and
Spread of Nationalism*. London: Verso.

Aoki Tamotsu 青木保. 1990. *"Nihonbunkaron" no henyō—sengo nihon no bunka to
aidentitii* 「日本文化論」の変容一戦後日本の文化とアイデンティティー
Tokyo: Chūōkōronsha.

Asada Jyōji 浅田喬二. 1990. *Nihon shokuminchikenkyūshi ron* 日本植民地研究史
論. Tokyo: Miraisha.

———. 1993. *Teikoku Nihon to Ajia* 「帝国」日本とアジア. Tokyo: Yoshikawa
Kōbunkan.

Asahi shinbunsha, ed. 1991–1992. *Onnatachi no taiheiyō sensō* 女たちの太平洋
戦争. 3 vols. Tokyo: Asahi shinbunsha.

Ashcroft, Bill, Gareth Griffiths, and Helen Tiffin. 1989. *The Empire Writes Back:
Theory and Practice in Post-Colonial Literatures*. London: Routledge.

Ashiya Nobukazu 芦屋信和 et al., eds. 1992. *Sakka no Ajia taiken* 作家のアジア
体験. Tokyo: Sekai Shisōsha.

Ayyappa Paniker, K., ed. 1991. *Indian English Literature Since Independence*. New
Delhi: Indian Association for English Studies.

Bao Hengxin 包恒新. 1988. *Taiwan xiandai wenxue jianshu* 台湾現代文学簡述.
Shanghai: Shanghai Shehuikexueyuan Chubanshe.

Baskett, Michael Dennis. 1993. "The Japanese Colonial Film Enterprise 1937–
1945: Imagining the Imperial Japanese Subject." M.A. thesis, UCLA.

Bassnett, Susan, and Harish Trivedi, eds. 1999. *Post-colonial Translation: Theory
and Practice*. London: Routledge.

Baucom, Ian. 1999. *Out of Place: Englishness, Empire, and the Locations of Identity*.
Princeton: Princeton University Press.

Beasley, William G. 1987. *Japanese Imperialism, 1894–1945*. Oxford: Oxford University Press.

Behdad, Ali. 1994. *Belated Travelers Orientalism in the Age of Colonial Dissolution*. Durham: Duke University Press.

Bewell, Alan. 1999. *Romanticism and Colonial Disease*. Baltimore: Johns Hopkins University Press.

Bhabha, Homi. 1994. *The Location of Culture*. London: Routledge.

Boehmer, Elleke. 1995. *Colonial and Postcolonial Literature: Migrant Metaphors*. Oxford: Oxford University Press.

Bongie, Chris. 1998. *Islands and Exiles*. Stanford: Stanford University Press.

Bosco, Joseph, and Puay-Peng Ho. 1999. *Temples of the Empress of Heaven*. Hong Kong: Oxford University Press.

Braisted, William Reynolds, trans. 1976. *Meiroku zasshi: Journal of the Japanese Enlightenment*. Cambridge, Mass.: Harvard University Press.

Brandt, Kim. 2000. "Objects of Desire: Japanese Collectors and Colonial Korea." *positions* 8(3) (Winter): 711–746.

Breckenridge, Carol, and Peter van der Veer. 1993. *Orientalism and the Postcolonial Predicament*. Philadelphia: University of Pennsylvania Press.

Brooks, Barbara. 1998. "Peopling the Japanese Empire: The Koreans in Manchuria and the Rhetoric of Inclusion." In Minichiello (1998: 25–44).

———. 2000. *Japan's Imperial Diplomacy: Treaty Ports, Consuls, and War in China, 1894–1938*. Honolulu: University of Hawai'i Press.

Cai Jintang 蔡錦堂. 1994. *Nihon teikokushugika Taiwan no shūkyō seisaku* 日本帝国主義下台湾の宗教政策. Tokyo: Tōseisha.

———. 1999. "Nihon tōchi shoki Taiwan kōgakkō 'shūshin' kyōkasho no ichikōsatsu" 日本統治初期台湾公学校「修身」教科書の一考察. In Ōhama Tetsuya (1999: 299–312).

Cai Maofeng 蔡茂豐. 1989. *Taiwan ni okeru Nihongo kyōiku no shiteki kenkyū* 台湾における日本語教育の史的研究. Taipei: Soochow University Japanese Culture Research Center.

Cai Peihuo 蔡培火 et. al, eds. 1983. *Taiwan minzu yundongshi* 台湾民族運動史. Taipei: Ziliwanbaoshe.

Castle, Kathryn. 1996. *Britannia's Children: Reading Colonialism Through Children's Books and Magazines*. Manchester: Manchester University Press.

Chang, Sung-sheng Yvonne. 1993. *Modernism and the Nativist Resistance: Contemporary Chinese Fiction from Taiwan*. Durham: Duke University Press.

———. 1997. "Beyond Cultural and National Identities: Current Re-evaluation of the Kominka Literature from Taiwan's Japanese Period." *Xiandai Zhongwen wenxue xuebao* [Journal of modern literature in Chinese] (Hong Kong) 1(1) (July): 75–107.

———. 1999a. "Taiwanese New Literature and the Colonial Context." In Rubinstein (1999: 261–274).

———. 1999b. "Literature in Post-1949 Taiwan, 1950–1980s." In Rubinstein (1999: 403–418).

Chao, Yuen Ren. 1976. *Aspects of Chinese Sociolinguistics.* Stanford: Stanford University Press.

Chen, Ai-li. 1991. "The Search for Cultural Identity: Taiwan 'Hsiang-t'u' Literature in the Seventies." Ph.D. dissertation, Ohio State University.

Chen Fangming 陳芳明. 1995. *Zuoyi Taiwan: Zhimindi zhishifenzi de dikang yu cuozhe* 左翼台湾：殖民地知識分子的抵抗與挫折. Taipei: Shibao Wenhua Chubanshe.

———. 1998. *Zhimindi Taiwan zuoyi yundong shilun* 殖民地台湾左翼政治運動史論. Taipei: Maitian Chubanshe.

———. 1999. "Zhiminzhuyi yu minzuzhuyi—Taiwan zuojia Ye Shitao de yige kunjing, 1940–1950" 殖民主義与民族主義台湾作家葉石濤的一個困境. In Peng Xiaoyan 彭小妍 ed., *Wenxue lilun yu tongsu wenhua* 文学理論与通俗文化. Taipei: Institute of Chinese Literature and Philosophy, Academia Sinica.

Chen Haoyang 陳浩洋. 1992. Translated by Jiang Qiuling 江秋玲. *Taiwan sibainian shuminshi* 台湾四百年庶民史. Taipei: Ziliwanbao Wenhua Chubanshe.

Chen, Kuan-hsing. 1998. "The Decolonization Question." In Kuan-hsing Chen et al., eds., *Trajectories: Inter-Asia Cultural Studies.* London: Routledge.

———. 2001. "Why Is 'Great Reconciliation' Im/Possible? De–Cold War/Decolonization, or Modernity and Its Tears" 為什麼大和解不／可能？〈多桑〉與〈香蕉天堂〉殖民／冷戦効應下省籍問題的情緒結構. In *Inter-Asia Cultural Studies: Movements.* Website.

Chen Mingtai 陳明台. 1999. "Zhanqian he zhanhou Taiwan guoce wenxue zhi bijiao yanjiu" 戰前和戰後台湾国策文学之比較研究. *Wenxue Taiwan* 文学台湾 29 (January): 109–133.

Chen Peifeng 陳培豊. 1996. *Shokuminchi Taiwan no kokugo kyōiku seisaku to iminzoku tōchi kokutai ideorogi o chūshin ni* 植民地台湾の国語教育政策と異民族統治国体イデオロギーを中心に. Tokyo: Fuji Zerokusu Kobayashi Setsutarō Kinen Kikin.

Chen, Robert L. 1994. "Language Unification in Taiwan." In Murray A. Rubinstein, ed., *The Other Taiwan: 1945 to the Present.* New York: Sharpe.

Chen Wanyi 陳萬益. 1995. "Yume to genjitsu: Ō Chōyū 'Honryū' shiron" 夢と現実—王昶雄試論. In Shimomura Sakujirō et al. (1995: 389–406).

Chen Yingzhen 陳映真. 1988. *Xichuang Man yu Taiwan wenxue* 四川満與台湾文学. Taipei: Renjian Chubanshe.

Chen Yisong 陳逸松. 1994. *Chen Yisong huiyilu* 陳逸松回憶録. Recorded by Wu Junying 呉君瑩 and edited by Lin Zhongsheng 林忠勝. Taipei: Qianwei Chubanshe.

Chen Yixiong 陳逸雄. 1988. *Taiwan Kōnichi shōsetsusen* 台湾抗日小説選. Tokyo: Genbun Shuppan.

Chen, Yu-shih. 1996. "The Historical Template of Pan Chao's *Nü chieh.*" *T'oung Pao* 82: 229–297.

Chen Zaoxiang 陳藻香. 1995. "Riju shidai Riren zai Tai zuojia: Yi Xichuan Man
wei zhongxin" 日據時代日人在台作家－以西川滿為中心. Ph.D disserta-
tion, Soochow University, Taipei.

———. 1996. "Nishikawa Mitsuru no haishi shōsetsu 'Sekikanki' kō" 西川滿の
稗史小説「赤嵌記」考. *Tenri Taiwan kenkyūkai nenpō* 天理台湾研究会年報
5 (June): 7-24.

Chin Shukubai 陳淑梅. 1997. "Bungakusha ga mita kindai Chūgoku (2)—No-
gami Ayako *Watashi no chūgoku ryokō* ron" 文学者が見た近代中国（二）─
野上弥生子「私の中国旅行」論 . *Meiji daigaku Nihon bungaku* 明治大学日
本文学 6(25): 34-43.

Ching, Leo. 1994. "Tracing Contradictions: Interrogating Japanese Colonialism and Its Discourse." Ph.D. dissertation, University of California, San Di-
ego.

———. 1995. "Imaginings in the Empire of the Sun." In Rob Wilson et al., eds.,
Asia/Pacific as Space of Cultural Production. Durham: Duke University Press.

———. 1998. "Yellow Skin, White Masks: Race, Class, and Identification in Japanese Colonial Discourse." In Kuan-hsing Chen et al., eds. *Trajectories: Inter-
Asia Cultural Studies.* London: Routledge.

———. 2000. "Savage Construction and Civility Making: The Musha Incident
and Aboriginal Representations in Colonial Taiwan." *positions* 8(3) (Winter):
795–818.

———. 2001. *Becoming "Japanese": Colonial Taiwan and the Politics of Identity Formation.* Berkeley: University of California Press.

———. Forthcoming. "From Identity to Consciousness: Colonial Historiography in *The Orphan of Asia.*" In Germaine Hoston, ed., *Competing Modernities in
20th-Century Japan.* Pt. 2: *Empires, Cultures, Identities, 1930–1960.*

Chiu Yen Liang [Fred]. 1995. "From the Politics of Identity to an Alternative
Cultural Politics: On Taiwan Primordial Inhabitants' A-Systematic Move-
ment." In Rob Wilson et al., eds., *Asia/Pacific as Space of Cultural Production.*
Durham: Duke University Press.

Chow, Eileen Cheng-yin. 1999. "A Peach Blossom Diaspora: Negotiating Nation Spaces in the Writing of Taiwan." *South Atlantic Quarterly* 98: 143–162.

Chow Tse-tsung. 1960. *The May Fourth Movement: Intellectual Revolution in Modern China.* Stanford: Stanford University Press.

Christy, Alan S. 1997. "The Making of Imperial Subjects in Okinawa." In Tani
Barlow, ed., *Formations of Colonial Modernity in East Asia.* Durham: Duke University Press.

Dai Guohui 戴国輝 , ed. 1981. *Taiwan Musha hōki jiken: kenkyū to shiryō* 台湾霧
社蜂起事件－研究と資料－ . Tokyo: Shakaishisōsha.

Darby, Phillip. 1998. *The Fiction of Imperialism: Reading Between International Relations and Postcolonialism.* London: Cassell.

DeFrancis, John. 1950. *Nationalism and Language Reform in China.* Princeton:
Princeton University Press.

———. 1984. *The Chinese Language: Fact and Fantasy*. Honolulu: University of Hawai'i Press.

Denoon, Donald, et al., eds. 1996. *Multicultural Japan: Palaeolithic to Postmodern*. Cambridge: Cambridge University Press.

Dikotter, Frank, ed. 1997. *The Construction of Racial Identities in China and Japan: Historical and Contemporary Perspectives*. London: Hurst.

Dissanayake, Wimal, ed. 1994. *Colonialism and Nationalism in Asian Cinema*. Bloomington: Indiana University Press.

Dixon, Robert. 1995. *Writing the Colonial Adventure*. Cambridge: Cambridge University Press.

Doak, Kevin Michael. 1994. *Dreams of Difference: The Japan Romantic School and the Crisis of Modernity*. Berkeley : University of California Press.

———. 1999. *Nihon romanha to nashonarizumu* 日本浪漫派とナショナリズム. Tokyo: Kashiwa Shobō.

———. 2001. "Building National Identity Through Ethnicity: Ethnology in Wartime Japan and After." *Journal of Japanese Studies* 27(1) (Winter): 1–40.

Donaldson, Laura E. 1992. *Decolonizing Feminisms: Race, Gender, and Empire-Building*. Chapel Hill: University of North Carolina Press.

Du Quoqing 杜國清. 1997. "Taiwan wenxue yanjiu de guoji shiye" 台湾文学研究的国際視野. In *Taiwan wenxue yu shehui* 台湾文学與社會. Taipei: Shifan Daxue Chubanshe.

Durix, Jean-Pierre. 1998. *Mimesis, Genres, and Post-Colonial Discourse: Deconstructing Magic Realism*. New York: St. Martin's Press.

Eagleton, Terry, Fredric Jameson, and Edward Said. 1990. *Nationalism, Colonialism, and Literature*. Minneapolis: University of Minnesota Press.

Ericson, Joan E. 1997. *Be a Woman: Hayashi Fumiko and Modern Japanese Women's Literature*. Honolulu: University of Hawai'i Press.

Ezaki Jun 江崎淳. 1989. "Shokuminchi shihai o kokuhatsu shita sakuhin" 植民地支配を告発した作品. *Minshū bungaku* 285: 121–126.

Fanon, Frantz. 1961. *The Wretched of the Earth*. Translated by Constance Ferrington. New York: Grove Weidenfield.

———. 1967. *Black Skin, White Masks*. Translated by Charles L. Markmann. New York: Grove Weidenfield.

Fessler, Susanna. 1998. *Wandering Heart: The Work and Method of Hayashi Fumiko*. Albany: State University of New York Press.

Fix, Douglas L. 1995. "Chōyō sakkatachi no 'sensō kyōryoku monogatari': Kessenki no Taiwan bungaku katsudō" 徴用作家たちの「戦争協力物語」―決戦期の台湾文学. Translated by Kanetsuki Yuki 金築由紀. In Shimomura Sakujirō et al. (1995: 131–166).

———. 1998. "Conscripted Writers, Collaborating Tales? Taiwanese War Stories." *Harvard Studies on Taiwan: Papers of the Taiwan Studies Workshop* 2: 19–41.

———. Forthcoming. "From 'Taiwanese Experience' to the Traveling Doctor's Subaltern Tales: Colonial Modernity and Its Radical Vernacular Critique."

In Germaine Hoston, ed., *Competing Modernities in 20th-Century Japan.* Pt. 2: *Empires, Cultures, Identities, 1930–1960.*

Fogel, Joshua A. 1994. *The Cultural Dimension of Sino-Japanese Relations: Essays in the Nineteenth and Twentieth Centuries.* Armonk, N.Y.: Sharpe.

———. 1996. *The Literature of Travel in the Japanese Rediscovery of China 1862–1945.* Stanford: Stanford University Press.

Fujii Shōzō 藤井省三. 1998. *Taiwan bungaku kono hyakunen* 台湾文学この百年. Tokyo: Tōhō Shoten.

———. 1999. *Gendai Chūgoku bunka tanken: Yottsu no toshi no monogatari* 現代中国文化探検 —— 四つの都市の物語. Tokyo: Iwanami Shinsho.

———. 2000. "Satō Haruo '*Musha*' kaisetsu" 佐藤春夫『霧社』解説. In Satō Haruo, *Musha* 霧社, ed. Kawahara Isao 河原功, Nihon shokuminchi bungaku seisenshū: Taiwan hen series 5 日本植民地文学精選集台湾編 5. Tokyo: Yumani Shobō.

Fulford, Tim, and Peter J. Kitson, eds. 1998. *Romanticism and Colonialism: Writing and Empire, 1780–1830.* Cambridge: Cambridge University Press.

Gandhi, Leela. 1998. *Postcolonial Theory.* New York: Columbia University Press.

Garon, Sheldon. 2000. "Luxury Is the Enemy: Mobilizing Savings and Popularizing Thrift in Wartime Japan." *Journal of Japanese Studies* 26(1) (Winter): 41–78.

Gikandi, Simon. 1996. *Maps of Englishness: Writing Identity in the Culture of Colonialism.* New York: Columbia University Press.

Glissant, Edouard. 1989. *Caribbean Discourse: Selected Essays.* Translated by J. Michael Dash. Charlottesville: University Press of Virginia.

Gong Zhong 公仲 and Wang Yisheng 汪义生, eds. 1989. *Taiwan xinwenxueshi chubian* 台湾新文学史初編. Nanchang: Jiangxi Renmin Chubanshe.

Gotō Ken'ichi 後藤乾一. 1995. *Kindai Nihon to Tōnan Ajia nanshin no 'shōgeki' to 'isan'* 近代日本と東南アジア: 南進の「衝撃」と「遺産」. Tokyo: Iwanami Shoten.

———. 1996. "Indonesia Under the 'Greater East Asia Co-Prosperity Sphere.'" In Denoon et al. (1996: 160–173).

Gotō Sōichirō 後藤総一郎. 2000. *Yanagita Kunio no "shokuminchishugi" o haisu* 柳田國男の＜植民地主義＞を排す. Tokyo: Meijidaigaku Seijikeizai Gakubu Gotō Sōichirō Zeminaaru.

Gotō Sōichirō et al., eds. 1992. *Shin bungei dokuhon Yanagita Kunio* 新文芸読本柳田国男. Tokyo: Kawade Shobō Shinsha.

Gottlieb, Nanette. 1995. *Kanji Politics: Language Policy and Japanese Script.* London: Kegan Paul International.

Gu Zitang 古継堂. 1989. *Taiwan xiaoshuo fazhanshi* 台湾小説発展史. Taipei: Wenshizhe Chubanshe.

Haddon, Rosemary M. 1992. "Nativist Fiction in China and Taiwan: A Thematic Survey." Ph.D. dissertation, University of British Columbia.

———. 1996. *Oxcart: Nativist Stories from Taiwan, 1934–1977.* Dortmund: Projekt Verlag.

Hanazaki Kōhei. 1996. "Ainu Moshir and Yaponesia: Ainu and Okinawa Identities in Contemporary Japan." In Denoon et al. (1996: 117–134).

Hariu Ichirō 針生一郎. 1998. "Nihon no posuto koroniarizumu" 日本のポスト・コロニアリズム. *Shin Nihon bungaku* 新日本文学 53(2): 11–17.

Hashikawa Bunzō 橋川文三. 1998. *Nihon rōmanha hihan josetsu* 日本浪漫派批判序説. Tokyo: Kōdansha Bungei Bunko.

Hasumi Shigehiko 蓮実重彦. 1989. *Shōsetsu kara tōku hanarete* 小説から遠く離れて. Tokyo: Nihon Bungeisha.

Hata Kōhei 秦恒平. 1997. *Sakka no hihyō* 作家の批評. Tokyo: Shimizu Shoin.

Hawkes, David. 1985. *The Songs of the South*. 2nd ed. New York: Penguin.

Hayashi Fumiko 林芙美子. 1964. *Ukigumo* 浮雲. In *Hayashi Fumiko* 林芙美子, *Nihon no bungaku*, vol. 47. Tokyo: Chūōkōronsha.

Hayashi Kōji 林浩治. 1997. *Sengo hinichi bungakuron* 戦後非日文学論. Tokyo: Shinkansha.

Hayashi Mariko 林真理子. 1998. *Onnabunshi* 女文士. Tokyo: Shinchōsha.

He Yilin 何義麟. 2000. "'Guoyü' zhuanhuan guochengzhong Taiwanren zuqun tezhi zhi zhengzhihua" 「国語」転換過程中臺灣人族群特質之政治化. In Wakabayashi Masatake and Wu Micha (2000: 449–479).

Hershatter, Gail. 1997. *Dangerous Pleasures: Prostitution and Modernity in Twentieth-Century Shanghai*. Berkeley: University of California Press.

Heylen, Ann. 2000a. "The Chinese Language in Colonial Taiwan." *Ricci Bulletin* 3: 75–76.

———. 2000b. "A Re-examination of Taiwan's Colonial Past." *Ricci Bulletin* 3: 77–78.

Higashi Shigemi 東茂美. 2000. *Higashi Ajia Manyō shinfūkei* 東アジア万葉新風景. Osaka: Nishi Nippon Shinbunsha.

Hijikata Hisakatsu 土方久功. 1984. *Mikuroneshia=satewanutō minzokushi* ミクロネシア＝サテワヌ島民俗誌. Tokyo: Miraisha.

———. 1991–1993. *Hijikata Hisakatsu chosakushū* 土方久功著作集. 8 vols. Tokyo: San'ichi Shobo.

Hijikata Keiko 土方敬子. 1992. "Otto Hijikata Hisakatsu no koto" 夫土方久功のこと. In *Geppō* 月報 1, *Kindai Nihon to shokuminchi* 近代日本と植民地, vol. 1. Tokyo: Iwanami Shoten.

Hikage Jōkichi. 日影丈吉. 1975. *Kareitō shiki* 華麗島志奇. Tokyo: Bokushisha Shuppan.

———. 1997. *Hikage Jōkichi shū* 日影丈吉集. Tokyo: Riburio Shuppan.

Hisamatsu Sen'ichi 久松潜一, ed. 1968. *Ochiai Naobumi, Ueda Kazutoshi, Haga Yaichi, Fujioka Sakutarō shū* 落合直文上田万年芳賀矢一藤岡作太郎. Meiji bungaku zenshū 44. Tokyo: Chikuma Shobō.

Hisamatsu Sen'ichi and Yoshida Seiichi 吉田精一, eds. 1954. *Kindai Nihon bungaku jiten* 日本近代文学辞典. Tokyo: Tōkyōdō.

Hong Yanqiu 洪炎秋. 1977. *Laoren laohua* 老人老話. Taizhong: Zhongyang Shuju.

Hoshina Hironobu 星名広修. 1994a. "'Dadongya gongronquan' de Taiwan zuojia 1: Chen Huoquan zhi huangmin wenxue xingtai" 「大東亜共栄圏」的台湾作家 (一)：陳火泉之皇民文学型態. In Huang Yingzhe (1994: 33–58).

———. 1994b. "'Dadongya gonronquan' de Taiwan zuojia 2: Ling yizhong 'huangmin wenxue': Zhou Jinpo de wenxue xingtai" 「大東亜共栄圏」の台湾作家(二) 另一種「皇民文学」－周金波的文学型態. In Huang Yingzhe (1994: 59–86).

———. 1995. "'Kikō to shinkō to jibyō to' ron: Shū Kinpa no Taiwan bunka-kan" 「気候と信仰と持病と」論－周金波の台湾文化観. In Shimomura Sakujirō et al. (1995: 433–450).

Hoston, Germaine A. 1994. *The State, Identity, and the National Question in China and Japan.* Princeton: Princeton University Press.

Hou, Ching-lang. 1975. *Monnaies d'offrande et la notion de trésorie dans la religion chinoise.* Paris: Collège de France.

Howell, David L. 1996. "Ethnicity and Culture in Contemporary Japan." *Journal of Contemporary History* 31: 171–190.

Huang Chongtian 黄重添 et al., eds. 1992. *Taiwan xinwenxue gaiguan* 台湾新文学概観. Taipei: Daohe Chubanshe; reprint of Xiamen: Lujiang Chubanshe, 1986.

Huang Chunming 黄春明. 1993. *Senryo to bungaku* 占領と文学. Tokyo: Orijin Shuppan Sentā.

Huang Qichun 黄琪椿. 1995. "Sakaishugi shichō no eikyōka ni okeru kyōdo-bungaku ronsō to Taiwanwabun undō" 社会主義思潮の影響における郷土文学論争と台湾話文運動. Translated by Sawai Noriyuki 澤井律之. In Shimomura Sakujirō et al. (1995: 47–71).

Huang Yingzhe 黄英哲, ed. 1994. *Taiwan wenxue yanjiu zai reben* 台湾文学研究在日本. Translated by Tu Cuihua 塗翠花. Taipei: Qianwei Chubanshe.

——— [Kō Eitetsu] 黄英哲. 1999. *Taiwan bunka saikōchiku 1945–1947 no hikari to kage* 台湾文化再構築 1945-1947 の光と影. Tokyo: Sōtosha.

Ide Isamu 井出勇. 1999. "Senjika no zaitai Nihonjin sakka to 'Kōmin bungaku.'" 戦時下の在台日本人作家と「皇民文学」. In Taiwan bungaku ronshū kankō iinkai 台湾文学論集刊行委員会, ed., *Taiwan bungaku kenkyū no genzai Tsukamoto Terukazu sensei koki kinen* 台湾文学研究の現在塚本昭和先生古稀記念. Tokyo: Rikuin Shobō.

Ihara Yoshinosuke. 1988. "Taiwan no Kōminka undō Shōwa jyūnendai no Taiwan, part 2" 台湾の皇民化運動—昭和十年代の台湾 (二). In Nakamura Takashi (1988: 271–386).

Iijima Kōichi. 1997. *Nihon no beru epokku* 日本のベル・エポック. Tokyo: Rippū Shobō.

Ikeda Hiroshi 池田浩士. 1983. *Taishū shōsetsu no sekai to hansekai* 大衆小説の世界と反世界. Tokyo: Gendai Shokan.

———, ed. 1995. *Yuasa Katsuhiko shokuminchi shōsetsushū Kan'nani* 湯浅克衛植民地小説集カンナニ. Tokyo: Inpakuto Shuppankai.

———. 1997. *Kaigai shinshutsu bungaku ron josetsu* 海外進出文学論序説. Tokyo: Inpakuto Shuppankai.

Imaizumi Yumiko 今泉裕美子. 1998–1999. "'Nanyō guntō' o meguru hitobito"「南
洋群島」をめぐる人々. *Gekkan Tokyo* 月刊東京 180–181 (April–July/August).

Inō Kanori 伊能嘉矩. 1928. *Taiwan bunkashi* 台湾文化誌. 3 vols. Tokyo: Tōkō
Shoin; reprinted Tokyo: Tōsui Shoin, 1965.

———. 1992. *Inō Kanori no Taiwan tōsa nikki* 伊能嘉矩の台湾踏査日記. Taipei:
Taiwan Fengwu Zazhishe.

Inose Kumie 井野瀬久美恵. 1998. *Onnatachi no daieiteikoku* 女たちの大英帝国.
Tokyo: Kōdansha.

Inoue Tetsujirō 井上哲次郎. 1891. *Chokugo engi* 勅語衍義. Tokyo: Keigyōsha.

Ishii Kōsei. 2000a. "Kyōto gakuha no tetsugaku to Nihon bukkyou: Takayama
Iwao no baai" 京都学派の哲学と日本仏教－高山岩男の場合. *Kikan Buk-
kyou: Nihon bukkyou no kadai* 季刊仏教：日本仏教の課題 49 (February):
111–119.

———. 2000b. "Dai Tou-a kyōeiken no gōrika to Kegon tetsugaku: Kihira
Masami no yakuwari wo chūshin to shite" 大東亜共栄圏の合理化と華厳哲
学－紀平正巳の役割を中心として. *Bukkyōgaku* 仏教学 42: 1–26.

Ishikawa Tatsuzō 石川達三. 1972. *Ishikawa Tatsuzō sakuhinshū* 石川達三作品集,
vol. 23. Tokyo: Shinchōsha.

Ishimitsu Masakiyo 石光真清. 1994. *Jōka no hito Ishimitsu Masakiyo shuki* 城下の
人石光真清手記. Tokyo: Chūōkōronsha.

Itamoto Hiroko 板元ひろ子. 1998. *"Fukusūbunka" no tame ni* ＜複数文化＞の
ために. Tokyo: Jinbunshoin.

Itō Yuzuru 伊東譲. 1993. *Taisenchū ni okeru Taiwan no bungaku* 大戦中における
台湾の文学. Tokyo: Kindaibungeisha.

Ivy, Marilyn. 1995. *Discourses of the Vanishing: Modernity, Phantasm, Japan.* Chicago:
University of Chicago Press.

Iwamoto Yoshiteru 岩本由輝. 1993. "Shokuminchi seisaku to Yanagita Kunio
Chōsen Taiwan" 植民地政策と柳田国男－挑戦・台湾. *Kokubungaku* 国文
学 38(8) (July): 46–54.

Iwao Seiichi 岩生成一. 1966. *Nanyō Nihonmachi no kenkyū* 南洋日本町の研究.
Tokyo: Iwanami Shoten.

———. 1987. *Zoku Nanyō Nihonmachi no kenkyū* 続南洋日本町の研究. Tokyo:
Iwanami Shoten.

Izawa Shūji 伊沢修二. 1958. *Izawa Shūji senshū* 伊沢修二選集. Nagano: Shinano
Kyōikukai.

Jian Jiongren 簡炯仁. 1997. *Taiwan gongchanzhuyi yundongshi* 臺灣共産主義運
動史. Taipei: Qianwei Chubanshe.

Jian Yuezhen 簡月真. 2000. "Taiwan no Nihongo" 台湾の日本語. *Kokubungaku
kaishaku to kanshō* 国文学解釈と鑑賞 65(7) (July): 113–121.

Jin Zhiyang 靳治揚. 1989. *Taiwan Fuzhi* 臺灣府志. 11 vols. Taipei: Chengwen
Chubanshe.

Jinno Morimasa 陣野守正. 1992. *Tairiku no hanayome: "Manshū" ni okurareta onnatachi* 大陸の花嫁―「満州」に送られた女たち. Tokyo: Nashinoki Sha.

Ka, Chih-ming. 1995. *Japanese Colonialism in Taiwan*. Boulder: Westview.

Kamiya Tadataka 神谷忠孝 and Kimura Kazunobu 木村一信, eds. 1992. "Jawa no chōyō bungakusha: Mofutaru Rubisu no hōkoku wo jikuni" ジャワの徴用文学者－モフタル・ルビスの報告を軸に. *Shōwa bungaku kenkyū* 昭和文学研究 25 (September): 129–141.

———. 1996. *Nanpō chōyō sakka* 南方徴用作家. Kyoto: Sekai Shisōsha.

Kaneko Naokazu 金子尚一. 2000. "Dainihonteikoku to Taiwan to nihongo nado" 大日本帝国と台湾と日本語など. *Kokubungaku kaishaku to kanshō* 国文学解釈と鑑賞 65(7) (July): 122–132.

Kang Sanjung 姜尚中. 1996. *Tabunkashugi no kigoron* 多文化主義の記号論. Tokyo: Tokai Daigaku Shuppansha.

———. 1999. *Orientarizumu no mukō e* オリエンタリズムの彼方へ. Tokyo: Iwanami Shoten.

Kanō Mikiyo 加納実紀代. 1987. *Onnatachi no "jūgo"* 女たちの＜銃後＞. Tokyo: Chikuma Shobō.

———, ed. 1995a. *Bosei fashizumu* 母性ファシズム. Tokyo: Gakuyō Shobō.

———. 1995b. *Sei to kazoku* 性と家族. Tokyo: Shakai Hyōronsha.

———. 2000. "Daitōa kyōeiken no onnatachi" 大東亜共栄圏の女たち. In Kimura Kazunobu 木村一信, ed., *Bungakushi o yomigaeru* 文学史をよみがえる. Tokyo: Inpakuto Shuppankai.

Kaplan, Caren. 1996. *Questions of Travel: Postmodern Discourses of Displacement*. Durham: Duke University Press.

Karatani Kōjin 柄谷行人. 1980. *Nihon kindai bungaku no kigen* 日本近代文学の起源. Tokyo: Kōdansha.

———. 1990. *Shūen o megutte* 終焉をめぐって. Tokyo: Fukutake Shoten.

———. 1993a. "Nihon no shokuminchi shugi no 'kigen'" 日本の植民地主義の「起源」. *Geppō* 月報 5, Iwanami kōza kindai nihon to shokuminchi 岩波講座近代日本と植民地, vol. 4. Tokyo: Iwanami Shoten.

———. 1993b. *Hyūmoa to shite no yuibutsuron* ヒューモアとしての唯物論. Tokyo: Chikuma Shobō.

———. 1994. *Simpojium [I]* シンポジウム [I]. Tokyo: Ōda Shuppan.

———. 1997a. *Simpojium [III]* シンポジウム [II]. Tokyo: Ōda Shuppan.

———. 1997b. *Kindai Nihon no hihyō I (Shōwa hen, jyō)* 近代日本の批評 I（昭和編上）. Tokyo: Fukutake Shoten.

———. 1997c. *Kindai Nihon no hihyō II (Shōwa hen, ka)* 近代日本の批評 II（昭和編下）. Tokyo: Fukutake Shoten.

Kasahara Masaji 笠原政治 and Ueno Hiroko 植野弘子, eds. 1997. *Taiwan Dokuhon* 台湾読本. Translated by Wang Ping. Taipei: Qianwei Chubanshe.

Kashiwagi Takao 柏木隆雄 and Yamaguchi Osamu 山口修, eds. 1996. *Ibunka no kōryū* 異文化の交流. Osaka: Osaka Daigaku Shuppansha.

Katō Norihiro 加藤典洋. 1995. *Kono jidai no ikikata* この時代の生き方. Tokyo: Kōdansha.

———. 1997a. *Haisengo ron* 敗戦後論. Tokyo: Kōdansha.

———. 1997b. *Mijikai bunshō hihyōka to shite no kiseki* 短い文章批評家としての軌跡. Tokyo: Goryū Shoin.

———. 1997c. *Sukoshi nagai bunshō: Gendai Nihon no sakka to sakuhinron* 少し長い文章現代日本作家と作品論. Tokyo: Goryū Shoten.

———. 1998. "Jihei to sakoku Murakami Haruki *Hitsuji o meguru bōken*." "自閉と鎖国村上春樹羊をめぐる冒険." In *Murakami Haruki* 村上春樹, *Nihon bungaku kenkyū ronbun shūsei 46* 本文学研究論文集 46. Tokyo: Wakagusa Shobō.

Kawahara Isao 河原功. 1995. "Yōki 'Shinbun haitatsufu' no seiritsu haikei" 楊逵「新聞配達夫」の成立背景. In Shimomura Sakujirō et al. (1995: 287–312).

———. 1997. *Taiwan shinbungaku undō no tenkai nihonbungaku to no setten* 台湾新文学運動の展開 日本文学との接点. Tokyo: Genbun Shuppan.

———. 2000a. "Sakka Hamada Hayao no kiseki" 作家濱田隼雄の軌跡. *Seikei ronsō* 成蹊論叢 38 (March): 307–320.

———, ed. 2000b. *Nihon shokuminchi bungaku seisenshū: Taiwan hen* 日本植民地文学精選集台湾編. Vols. 13–20. Tokyo: Yumani Shobō.

Kawamoto Saburō 川本三郎. 1990. *Taishō gen'ei* 大正幻影. Tokyo: Shinchōsha.

Kawamura Minato 川村湊. 1989. *Ajia to iu kagami: kyokutō no kindai* アジアという鏡－極東の近代. *Shōwa no kuritikku* series. Tokyo: Shinchōsha.

———. 1990. *Ikyō no Shōwa bungaku: "Manshū" to kindai Nihon* 異郷の昭和文学：満州と近代日本. Tokyo: Iwanami Shoten.

———. 1992a. *Rinjin no iru fūkei* 隣人のいる風景. Tokyo: Kokubunsha.

———. 1992b. "Mumojishakai no sasoi: Nakajima Atsushi to Ajia teki na mono" 無文字社会の誘い－中島敦と＜アジア＞的なもの. In Katsumata Hiroshi 勝又浩 and Kimura Kazunobu 木村一信, eds., *Nakajima Atsushi* 中島敦. Tokyo: Sōbunsha.

———. 1993a. "Kim Shiryou to Chō Kakuchū—shokuminchijin no seishin kōzō" 金史良 と張赫宙－植民地人の精神構造 *Kindai Nihon to shokuminchi* 近代日本と植民地, vol. 6. Tokyo: Iwanami Shoten.

———. 1993b. "Taishū orientarizumu to ajia ninshiki" 大衆オリュンタリズムとアジア認識. *Kindai Nihon to shokuminchi* 近代日本と植民地, vol. 7. Tokyo: Iwanami Shoten.

———. 1994a. *Umi o watatta Nihongo: Shokuminchi no "kokugo" no jikan* 海を渡った日本語－植民地の国語の時間. Tokyo: Seidōsha.

———. 1994b. *Nanyō Karafuto no Nihon bungaku* 南洋樺太の日本文学. Tokyo: Chikuma Shoten.

———. 1995. *Sengo bungaku o tou: Sono taiken to rinen* 戦後文学を問う－その体験と理念. Tokyo: Iwanami Shoten.

———. 1996. *"Dai Tōa minzokugaku" no kyojitsu* 「大東亜民俗学」の虚実. Tokyo: Kōdansha.

———. 1997a. *Manshū hōkai daitōa bungaku to sakka tachi* 満州崩壊：大東亜文学と作家たち. Tokyo: Bungei Shunju.

———. 1997b. "Shokuminchishugi to minzokugaku/minzokugaku: Yanagita minzokugaku no mienai shokuminchishugi o toinaosu" 植民地主義と民俗学・民族学：柳田民俗学の見えない植民地主義を問い直す. In Ōmori Chiaki (1997: 136–140).

———. 1998a. *Sengo hihyō ron* 戦後批評論. Tokyo: Kōdansha.

———. 1998b. *Bungaku kara miru "Manshū": "Gozoku kyōwa" no yume to genjitsu* 文学から見る満州－＜五族協和＞の夢と現実. Tokyo: Yoshikawa Kobunkan.

———. 2000a. *Sakubun no naka no dainippon teikoku* 作文のなかの大日本帝国. Tokyo: Iwanami Shoten.

———. 2000b. *Sōru toshi monogatari: Rekishi・bungaku・fūkei* ソウル都市物語：歴史・文学・風景. Tokyo: Heibonsha shinsho.

Kawamura Minato et.al., eds. 1999. *Sensō wa dono yō ni katararete kita ka* 戦争はどのように語られてきたか. Tokyo: Asahi Shinbunsha.

Keene, Donald. 1980. *Yokomitsu Riichi Modernist*. New York: Columbia University Press.

———. 1981. "The Sino-Japanese War of 1894–95 and Japanese Culture." In *Appreciations of Japanese Culture*. New York: Kōdansha International.

———. 1984a. "Sensō bungaku" 戦争文学. In Tokuoka Takao 徳岡孝夫 and Tsunochi Yukio 角地幸男, trans., *Nihon bungakushi kindai gendai hen 4* 日本文学史近代・現代編四. Tokyo: Chūōkōronsha.

———. 1984b. *Dawn to the West: Japanese Literature of the Modern Era, Fiction.* New York: Holt.

———. 1998. *Modern Japanese Diaries*. New York: Columbia University Press.

Kerr, George H. 1974. *Formosa: Licensed Revolution and the Home Rule Movement, 1895–1945*. Honolulu: University of Hawai'i Press.

Kimura Kazuaki 木村一信. 1992. "Nanyōkō—aratana ninshiki to no deai" 南洋行―新たな認識との出会い. In Katsumata Hiroshi 勝又浩 and Kimura Kazunobu 木村一信, eds., *Nakajima Atsushi* 中島敦. Tokyo: Sōbunsha.

———. 1996. "Geijutsuteki teikōha Nakajima Atsushi" 芸術的抵抗派 中島敦. In *"Sensō" e no manazashi Mō hitotsu no bungakushi* 「戦争」へのまなざしもうひとつの文学史. Shizuoka: Zōshinkai Shuppansha.

———. 1997. "Kieta 「Niji」 Satō Haruo no Kantō daishinsai" 消えた「虹」佐藤春夫の関東大震災. In Kurihara Yukio 栗原幸夫, ed., *Bungakushi o yomikaeru 1* 文学史を読みかえる. Vol. 1: *Haikyo no kanousei* 廃虚の可能性. Tokyo: Inpakuto Shuppankai.

———. 2000. *Bungakushi o yomikaeru 1* 文学史を読みかえる. Vol. 4: *Senjika no bungaku kakudai suru sensōkūkan* 戦時下の文学 拡大する戦争空間 Tokyo: Inpakuto Shuppankai.

King, Anthony. 1997. *Culture, Globalization, and the World System: Contemporary Conditions for the Representation of Identity*. Minneapolis: University of Minnesota Press.

Kitagawa Katushiko 北川勝彦 and Hirata Masahiro 平田雅博. 1999. *Teikoku ishiki no kaibōgaku* 帝国意識の解剖学. Tokyo: Sekai Shisōsha.

Kitagawa Tsuneo 喜多川恒男 et al., eds. 1995. *Nijyūseiki no nihonbungaku* 二十世紀の日本文学. Kyoto: Hakujisha.

Kiyooka Takayuki 清岡卓行. 1988. *Akashiya no Dairen* アカシヤの大連. Tokyo: Kōdansha.

Kleeman, Faye Yuan. 2000a. "Amerika ni okeru posutoshokuminchi kenkyū no shōkai—nihonnhen" アメリカにおけるポスト植民地研究の紹介―日本編. *Shuka* 朱夏 14 (April): 113–117.

―――. 2000b. "Kattō suru gengo" 葛藤する言語. *Eureka* ユリイカ 32(14) (November): 286.

―――. 2001a. "The Boundary of Japaneseness: Between Nihon bungaku and Nihongo bungaku." *Proceedings of the Association for Japanese Literary Studies* 8: 377–388.

―――. 2001b. "Colonial Ethnography and the Writing of the Exotic: Nishikawa Mitsuru in Taiwan." *Proceedings of the Association for Japanese Literary Studies* 9: 355–377.

―――. 2001c. "Xichuang Man he *Wenyi Taiwan*: Dongfang zhuyi de shixian" 四川満和《文藝臺灣》―東方主義的視線. *Zhongguo wenzhe yanjiu tongxun* 中國文哲研究通訊 11(1) (March): 135–146.

Kobayashi, Hideo. 1995. *Literature of the Lost Home: Kobayashi Hideo—Literary Criticism, 1924–1939.* Translated by Paul Anderer. Stanford: Stanford University Press.

Kobayashi Yoshinori. 1998. 小林よしのり *Shin gōmannizumu sengen* 新ゴーマンニズム宣言. Tokyo: Shogakkan.

―――. 2000. *Shin gōmannizumu sengen supesharu: Taiwan ron* 新ゴーマンニズム宣言スペシャル：台湾論. Tokyo: Shōgakkan.

Kobayashi Yoshinori 小林よしのり and Tahara Sōichirō 田原総一郎. 1999. *Sensōron sōsen* 戦争論争戦. Tokyo: Bunkasha.

―――. 2000. *Taiwan ron* 台湾論. Tokyo: Shōgakkan.

Kohō Banri 孤蓬万里, ed. 1994. *Taiwan Manyōshū* 台湾万葉集. Tokyo: Shūeisha.

Komagome Takeshi 駒込武. 1991. "Shokuminchi kyōiku to ibunka ninshiki: 'Gohō densetsu' no hen'yō katei" 植民地教育と異文化認識―「呉鳳伝説」の変容過程. *Shisō* 思想 802 (April): 104–126.

―――. 1996. *Shokuminchi teikoku Nihon no bunka tōgō* 植民地帝国日本の文化統合. Tokyo: Iwanami Shoten.

Komagome Takeshi et al. 2000. "Taiwan: Sekai shihonshugi to teikoku no kioku" 台湾―世界資本主義と帝国の記憶. *Impaction* 120: 6–33.

Komori Yōichi 小森陽一 et al., eds. 1988. *Kōzō to shite no katari* 構造としての語り. Tokyo: Shinyōsha.

―――. 1996. *Dekigoto to shite no yomukoto* 出来事としての読むこと. Tokyo: Tokyo University Press.

———. 1997. *Media hyōshō ideorogi: Meiji sanjyū nendai no bunka kenkyū* メディ
ア・表象・イディオロギー：明治三十年代の文化研究. Tokyo: Ozawa
Shoten.

———. 1998. *Yuragi no Nihon bungaku* ゆらぎの日本文学. Tokyo: Nihon Hōsō
Shuppan Kyōkai.

Komota Nobuo 古茂田信男 et al., eds. 1994. *Nihon ryūkōkashi* 日本流行歌史. 2
vols. Tokyo: Shakai Shisōsha.

Kondō Masami 近藤正巳. 1981. *Nishikawa Mitsuru sakki* 西川満札記. Tokyo:
Ningen no Hoshi Sha.

———. 1992. "Taiwan sōtokufu no 'rihan' seisaku to Musha jiken" 台湾総督
府の『理蕃』政策と霧社事件. In Iwanami Kōza, *Kindai Nihon to shokuminchi* 岩波講座近代日本と植民地, vol. 2. Tokyo: Iwanami Shoten.

———. 1996. *Sōryokusen to Taiwan: Nihon shokuminchi hōkai no kenkyū* 総力戦と
台湾：日本植民地崩壊の研究. Tokyo: Tōsui shobō.

Konishi Jin'ichi. 1984. *A History of Japanese Literature.* Vol. 1: *The Archaic and Ancient Ages.* Translated by Aileen Gatten and Nicholas Teele. Princeton:
Princeton University Press.

Kosaku, Yoshino. 1992. *Cultural Nationalism in Contemporary Japan: A Sociological
Enquiry.* London: Routledge.

Koyasu Nobukuni 子安宣邦. 1996. *Kindai chi no arukeorojii: Kokka to sensō to chi-
shikinin* 近代知のアルケオロジー国家と戦争と知識人. Tokyo: Iwanami
Shoten.

Kurasawa Aiko 倉沢愛子. 1997. *Nanpō tokubetsu ryūgakusei ga mita senjika no nihonjin* 南方特別留学生が見た戦時下の日本人. Tokyo: Sōshisha.

Kurokawa Sō 黒川創. 1996. *"Gaichi" no Nihongo bungaku sen* 「外地」の日本語
文学選. 3 vols. Tokyo: Shinjuku Shobō.

———. 1998a. "Hyōryū to kokkyō—Ibuse Masuji no shiya kara" 漂流と国境－
井伏鱒二の視野から. In Kawai Hayao 河合隼雄 and Tsurumi Shunsuke 鶴
見俊輔, eds., *Gendai Nihon bunkaron*, vol. 9: *Rinri to dōtoku* 現代日本文化論,
vol. 9: 倫理と道徳. Tokyo: Iwanami Shoten.

———. 1998b. *Kokkyō* 国境. Tokyo: Metalogue.

Kyodai jōhō shisutemu o kangaerukai 巨大情報システムを考える会. 1998.
<*Chi>no shokuminchi shihai* 「知」の植民地支配. Tokyo: Shakai Hyōronsha.

Lamley, Harry. 1970–1971. "Assimilation Efforts in Taiwan: The Fate of the
1914 Movement." *Monumenta Serica* 29: 496–520.

Lazarus, Neil. 1999. *Nationalism and Cultural Practice in the Postcolonial World.*
Cambridge: Cambridge University Press.

Lee Yeounsuk イ・ヨンスク（李妍淑）. 1992. *Ekkyō suru bungaku* 越境する文学.
Tokyo: Kawade Shobō Shinsha.

———. 1996. *Kokugo to iu shisō: Kindai Nihon no gengo ninshiki* 国語という思
想－近代日本の言語認識. Tokyo: Iwanami Shoten.

———. 2000. "'Nihongo' to 'kokugo' no hazama" 「日本語」と「国語」のは
ざま. *Kokubungaku kaishaku to kanshō* 国文学解釈と鑑賞 65(7) (July): 86–93.

Lestringant, Frank. 1994. "Travels in the Eucharitia: Formosa and Ireland from George Psalmanzar to Jonathan Swift." *Yale French Studies* 86: 109–125.

Levy, Hideo. 1992. *Seijouki no kikoenai heya* 星条旗の聞こえない部屋. Tokyo: Kōdansha.

———. 1998. *Kokumin no uta* 国民のうた. Tokyo: Kōdansha.

Li Ang. 1999. *Zizhuan no xiaoshuo* 自傳の小説. Taipei: Huangguan Wenhua Chubanshe.

Li, Lincoln. 1996. *The China Factor in Modern Japanese Thought: The Case of Tachibana Shiraki, 1881–1945*. Albany: State University of New York Press.

Li Xiangzhe 李相哲. 2000. *Manshū ni okeru Nihonjin keiei shinbun no rekishi* 満州における日本人経営新聞の歴史. Tokyo: Kaifūsha.

Liang Mingxiong 梁明雄. 1996. *Rijushiqi Taiwan xinwenxue yundong de yanjiu* 日據時期台灣新文學運動的研究. Taipei: Wenshizhe Chubanshe.

Liao, Xianhao. 1995. "From Central Kingdom to Orphan of Asia: The Transformation of Identity in Modern Taiwanese Literature in the Five Major Literary Debates." *Literature East and West* 28: 106–126.

Lin Ruiming 林瑞明. 1993a. *Taiwan wenxue yu shidai jingshen: Lai He yanjiu lunji* 台灣文學與時代精神—賴研究論集. Taipei: Yunchen Wenhua Chubanshe.

———. 1993b. "Kessenki Taiwan no sakka to kōmin bungaku: Kumonsuru tamashi no rekitei" 決戦期台湾の作家と皇民作家－苦悶する魂の歴程. Translated by Matsunaga Masayoshi 松永正義. In *Kindai Nihon to shokuminchi* 近代日本と植民地, vol. 6. Tokyo: Iwanami Shoten.

———. 1996a. *Taiwan wenxue de lishi kaocha* 台湾文学的歴史考察. Taipei: Yunchen Wenhua.

———. 1996b. *Taiwan wenxue de bentu guancha* 台湾文学的本土観察. Taipei: Yunchen Wenhua.

———. 1996c. "Saodong de linghun: Juezhan shiqi de Taiwan zuojia yu huangmin wenxue" 騒動的霊魂－決戦時期的台湾作家与皇民文学. In Dai Baochun 戴寶村 et al., eds., *Taiwanshi lunwen jingxuan* 台湾史論文精選, vol. 2. Taipei: Yushanshe.

Lin Shuangbu 林雙不, ed. 1989. *Ererba Taiwan xiaoshuo xuan* 二二八臺灣小説選. Taipei: Ziliwanbao Wenhua Chubanbu.

Liu Jianhui 劉健輝. 1992. "Kindai no chōkoku to 'Manshū' bungaku: Zasshi *Geibunshi* dōjin o chūshin ni" 近代の超克と「満州」文学－雑誌『芸文誌』同人を中心に. *Shōwa bungaku kenkyū* 昭和文学研究 25: 69-78.

———. 1997. "Sōseki to 'Manshū': 'Getō yūmin' hakken no tabi" 漱石と「満州」－「下等遊民」発見の旅. *Kokubungaku kaishaku to kanshō* 国文学解釈と鑑賞 6(62) (June): 17-23.

———. 2000. *Mato Shanhai: Nihon chishikijin no "kindai" taiken* 魔都上海—日本知識人の「近代」体験. Tokyo: Kōdansha.

Liu Shuqin 柳書琴. 1995. "Sensō to bundan Rokōkyō jihen go no Taiwan bungaku katsudō no fukkō" 戦争と文壇－蘆溝橋事変後の台湾文学活動の復興. In Shimomura Sakujirō et al. (1995: 109-130).

Loomba, Ania. 1998. *Colonialism/Postcolonialism*. London: Routledge.

Low, Gail Ching-Liang. 1996. *White Skins/Black Masks: Representation and Colonialism*. London: Routledge.

Lü Heruo 呂赫若. 1991. *Lü Heruo ji* 呂赫若集. Edited by Zhang Henghao 張恒豪. Taipei: Qianwei Chubanshe.

———. 1995. *Lü Heruo xiaoshuo quanji* 呂赫若小説全集. Translated by Lin Zhijie 林至潔. Taipei: Lianhe Wenxue Chubanshe.

Lü Shaoli 呂紹理. 1998. *Shuiluo xiangqi: Rizhi shiqi Taiwan shehui de shenghuo zuoxi* 水螺響起：日治時期台湾社会的生活作息. Taipei: Yuanliu Chubanshe.

Lu Xiuyi 盧修一. 1990. *Rijushidai Taiwan gongchandangshi* 日據時代台灣共産黨史 (1928–1932). Taipei: Qianwei Chubanshe.

Lu Xun 魯迅. 1981. *Lu Xun quanji* 魯迅全集. 3 vols. Beijing: Renmin Wenxue Chubanshe.

MacDonald, Robert H. 1994. *The Language of Empire: Myth and Metaphors of Popular Imperialism, 1880–1918*. Manchester: Manchester University Press.

McClintock, Anne. 1995. *Imperial Leather: Race, Gender, and Sexuality in the Colonial Contest*. London: Routledge.

McClintock, Anne, Aamir Mufti, and Ella Shohat, eds. 1997. *Dangerous Liaisons: Gender, Nation, and Postcolonial Perspectives*. Minneapolis: University of Minnesota Press.

Martin, Daniel. 1996. "A Glimmer of Light Between the Clouds: The Vision That Formosan Military Personnel Serving in the Japanese Army Held for Post-War Reconstruction in Formosa as Seen Through the Mei Tai Hō" (Unkan no shokō—"Meitaihō" ni mirareru Taiwanseki Nihonhei no sengo Taiwanzō) 雲間の曙光 ― 「明台報」に見られる台湾籍日本兵の戦後台湾像. *Journal of Asian and African Studies* 東京外国語大学アジア・アフリカ言語文化研究 51: 151–170.

Martin, Helmut. 1996. "The History of Taiwanese Literature: Towards Cultural-Political Identity: Views from Taiwan, China, Japan, and the West." *Hanhsüeh Yen-chiu* 14(1): 1–51.

Marukawa Tetsushi 丸川哲史. 2000a. "Posuto Taiwan nyūshinema to gurōbarizēshon" ポスト台湾ニューシネマとグローバリゼーション. *Gendai shisō* 現代思想 (June): 172–184.

———. 2000b. *Taiwan posutokoroniarizumu no shintai* 台湾ポストコロニアリズムの身体. Tokyo: Seitosha.

Matakichi Morikiyo 又吉盛清. 1992. "Taiwan shokuminchi to Okinawa no kakawari" 台湾植民地と沖縄の関わり. In *Geppō* 月報 2, *Kindai Nihon to shokuminchi* 近代日本と植民地. Tokyo: Iwanami Shoten.

Matsumoto Ken'ichi 松本健一. 2000. *Takeuchi Yoshimi Nihon no ajia shugi seidoku* 竹内好「日本のアジア主義」. Tokyo: Iwanami Gendai Bunko.

Matsumoto Naoji 松本直治. 1993. *Daihon'ei hakken no kisha tachi* 大本営派遣の記者たち. Tokyo: Katsura Shobō.

Matsumura Gentarō 松村源太郎. 1981. *Taiwan: Mukashi to ima* 台湾一昔と今. Tokyo: Jijitsushisha.

Matsumura Tomomi 松村友視 1992. "Chūō to chihō no hazama: Meiji bungaku o shiza toshite" ＜中央＞と＜地方＞のはざま：明治文学を視座として. In *Nihonbungakushi o yomu*, vol. 5: *Kindai* 日本文学史を読む、5近代. Tokyo: Yūseitō.

Matsunaga Masayoshi 松永正義. 1993. "Taiwan no bungaku katsudō" 台湾の文学活動. In *Kindai Nihon to shokuminchi* 近代日本と植民地, vol. 7. Tokyo: Iwanami Shoten.

Michiue Tomohiro 道上知弘. 2000. "Gojū nendai Taiwan ni okeru bungaku jōkyō" 五十年代台湾における文学状況. *Geibun kenkyū* 芸文研究 78 (June): 87–105.

Minatoya Yumekichi 湊谷夢吉. 1988. *Kōryū imon* 虹龍異聞. Tokyo: Hokutō Shobō.

Minichiello, Sharon A. 1998. *Japan's Competing Modernities: Issues in Culture and Democracy 1900–1930*. Honolulu: University of Hawai'i Press.

Miura Masashi 三浦雅士. 1991. *Shōsetsu to iu shokuminchi* 小説という植民地. Tokyo: Fukutake Shoten.

Miura Nobutaka 三浦信孝. 2000. *Gengo teikoku shugi to wa nani ka* 言語帝国主義とは何か. Tokyo: Fujiwara Shoten.

Miyashita Kyōko 宮下今日子. 1992. "Shokuminchijin sutaiiru: Nihonjin no nanpō keiken, pt. 3" 植民地人スタイル (3). *Shuka* 朱夏 4: 28–37.

———. 2000. "Taiwan no haiku: Nihon no ichichihō toshite no Taiwan" 台湾の俳句―日本の一地方としての台湾. *Shuka* 朱夏 14: 36–41.

Mizuta Noriko 水田宗子. 1995. "Hōrō suru onna no ikyō e no yume to tenraku: Hayashi Fumiko *Ukigumo*" 放浪する女の異郷への夢と転落―林芙美子『浮雲』. In Iwabuchi Hiroko 岩淵広子 et al., eds., *Feminizumu hihyō e no shōtai* フェミニズム批評への招待. Tokyo: Gakugei Shorin.

———. 1996. "In Search of a Lost Paradise: The Wandering Woman in Hayashi Fumiko's Drifting Clouds." In Paul Gordon Schalow and Janet A. Walker, eds., *The Woman's Hand: Gender and Theory in Japanese Women's Writing*. Stanford: Stanford University Press.

Momokawa Takahito 百川敬仁. 2000. *Nihon no erotishizumu* 日本のエロティシズム. Tokyo: Chikuma Shinsho.

Moore, David Chinoi. 2001. "Is the Post- in Postcolonial the Post- in Post-Soviet? Toward a Global Postcolonial Critique." *Proceedings of the Modern Language Association* 116(1) (January): 111–128.

Morgan, Susan. 1996. *Place Matters: Gendered Geography in Victorian Women's Travel Books About Southeast Asia*. New Brunswick: Rutgers University Press.

Morita Shunsuke 森田俊介. 1976. *Taiwan no Musha jiken* 台湾の霧社事件. Tokyo: Shinkyōsha.

Morris-Suzuki, Tessa. 1996. "A Descent into the Past: The Frontier in the Construction of Japanese History." In Denoon et al. (1996), pp. 81–94.

———. 1998a. "Unquiet Graves: Katō Norihiro and the Politics of Mourning." *Japanese Studies* 18(1) (May): 21–30.

———. 1998b. *Re-inventing Japan: Time, Space, and Nation*. New York: Sharpe.

Mukōyama Hirō 向山寛夫. 1999. *Taiwan Takasagozoku no kōnichi hōki* 台湾高砂族の抗日蜂起. Tokyo: Chūō Keizai Kenkyūjo.

Murai Osamu 村井紀. 1995. *Nantō ideorogi no hassei: Yanagita Kunio to shokuminchi shugi* 南東イデオロギの発生：柳田國男と植民地主義. Tokyo: Ōta Shuppan.

Myrsiades, Kostas, and Jerry McGuire, eds. 1995. *Order and Partialities: Theory, Pedagogy, and the "Postcolonial."* Albany: State University of New York Press.

Nagumo Michio 南雲道雄. 1983. *Gendai bungaku no teiryū: Nihon nōmin bungaku nyūmon* 現代文学の底流日本農民文学入門. Tokyo: Orijin Shuppansha.

Nakagawa Kōichi 中川浩一 et al., eds. 1980. *Musha jiken* 霧社事件. Tokyo: Sanseidō.

Nakajima Atsushi 中島敦. 1962. *Light, Wind, and Dreams: An Interpretation of the Life and Mind of Robert Louis Stevenson*. Translated by Akira Miwa. Tokyo: Hokuseido.

———. 1979. *Ri Ryō, Deshi, Meijin den* 李陵・弟子・名人伝. Tokyo: Kadokawa Bunko.

———. 1992. *Hikari to kaze to yume: Waga saiyūki* 光と風と夢・わが西遊記. Tokyo: Kōdansha Gakujutsu Bunko.

Nakajima Kuni 中嶌邦. 1992. *Kindai Nihon ni okeru onna to sensō* 近代日本における女と戦争. Tokyo: Daikūsha.

Nakajima Toshio 中島利郎, ed. 1994. *Riju shiqi Taiwan wenxue zazhi* 日據時期台灣文學雜誌. Taipei: Qianwei Chubanshe.

———. 1995. "Nishikawa Mitsuru to Nihon tōchiki Taiwan bungaku: Nishikawa Mitsuru no bungakukan" 西川満と日本統治期台湾文学－西川満の文学観. In Shimomura Sakujirō et al. (1995: 407–432).

———. 1997. "Nihon tōchiki Taiwan no Nihonjin sakka: Nishikawa Mitsuru bungaku no fukken" 日本統治期台湾の日本人作家―西川満文学の復権 201 (November): 37–40.

———. 1999. "Tsukurareta 'Kōmin sakka' Shū Kinpa" つくられた「皇民作家」周金波. In Taiwan bungaku ronshū kankō iinkai 台湾文学論集刊行委員会, ed., *Taiwan bungaku kenkyū no genzai Tsukamoto Terukazu sensei koki kinen* 台湾文学研究の現在 塚本昭和先生古稀記念. Tokyo: Rikuin Shobō.

Nakajima Toshio and Kawahara Isao 河原功, eds. 1998. *Nihon tōchiki Taiwan bungaku Nihonjin sakka sakuhinshū* 日本統治期台湾文学：日本人作家作品集. 6 vols. Tokyo: Ryokuin Shobō.

———. 1999. *Nihon tōchiki Taiwan bungaku Taiwanjin sakka sakuhinshū* 日本統治期台湾文学：台湾人作家作品集. 6 vols. Tokyo: Ryokuin Shobō.

Nakajima Toshio and Noma Nobuyuki 野間信幸, eds. 1998. *Taiwan bungaku no shosō* 台湾文学の諸相. Tokyo: Ryokuin Shobō.

Nakamura Chihei 中村地平. 1941. *Taiwan shōsetsushū* 台湾小説集. Tokyo: Bokushuo Shobo.

Nakamura Kokyō 中村古峡. 1916. "Banchi kara" 蕃地から. *Chūō kōron* 中央公論 31 (8) (July): 209–235.

Nakamura Takashi 中村孝志. 1988. *Nihon no nanpō kan'yo to Taiwan* 日本の南方関与と台湾. Nara: Tenrikyō Dōyūkai.

Nakane Takayuki 中根隆行. 1999. "Bungaku ni okeru shokuminchi shugi: 1930 nendai zenhan no zasshi media to Chōsenjin sakka Chō Kakuchū no tanjō" 文学における植民地主義――九三〇年代前半の雑誌メディアと朝鮮人作家張赫宙の誕生. In Tsukuba Daigaku bunkahihyō kenkyūkai 筑波大学文化批評研究会, ed., *Shokuminchishugi to Ajia no hyōshō* 植民地主義とアジアの表象. Tsukuba: Tsukuba Daigaku Bunka Hihyō Kenkyūkai.

Nakanishi Susumu 中西進 and Yan Shaotang 厳紹湯, eds. 1995. *Nitchū bunka kōryū shi sōsho,* vol. 6: *Bungaku* 日中文化交流史叢書「6」文学. Tokyo: Taishūkan.

Nakanō Kyōtoku 中濃教篤. 1976. *Tennōsei kokka to shokuminchi dendō* 天皇制国家と植民地伝道. Tokyo: Kosshō Kankōkai.

Nakazono Eisuke 中薗英助. 1995. *Torii Ryūzō den: Ajia o sōhashita jinruigakusha* 鳥居竜蔵伝：アジアを走破した人類学者. Tokyo: Iwanami Shoten.

Namikata Tsuyoshi 波潟剛. 1999. "Suna toshite no taishū, sabaku to shite no shokuminchi: Hanada Kiyoteru no 'Manshū'" 砂としての大衆、砂漠としての植民地―花田清輝の「満州」. In Tsukuba Daigaku bunkahihyō kenkyūkai 筑波大学文化批評研究会, ed., *Shokuminchishugi to Ajia no hyōshō* 植民地主義とアジアの表象. Tsukuba: Tsukuba Daigaku Bunkahihyō Kenkyūkai.

Nan Bujin 南富鎮. 1999. "Tanaka Hidemitsu no Chōsen to bokuyō to iu kagami" 田中英光の朝鮮と牧洋という鏡. In Tsukuba Daigaku bunkahihyō kenkyūkai 筑波大学文化批評研究会, ed., *Shokuminchishugi to Ajia no hyōshō* 植民地主義とアジアの表象. Tsukuba: Tsukuba Daigaku Bunkahihyō Kenkyūkai.

Ningen no Hoshi Sha 人間の星社, ed. 1999. *Keibo kaiseirō shujin Nishikawa Mitsuru sensei* 敬慕魁星楼主人西川満. Tokyo: Ningen no Hoshi Sha.

Nihon Shakai Bungakukai 日本社会文学会, ed. 1993. *Shokuminchi to bungaku* 植民地と文学. Tokyo: Orijin Shuppan Sentā.

Nin Tenkei 任展慧. 1994. *Nihon ni okeru Chōsenjin no bungaku* 日本における朝鮮人の文学の歴史. Tokyo: Hōsei University Press.

Nishi Masahiko 西成彦. 1997. *Mori no gerira Miyazawa Kenji* 森のゲリラ宮沢賢治. Tokyo: Iwanami Shoten.

Nishihara Kazuumi 西原和海. 1992. "Manshū bungaku kenkyū no mondaiten" 満州文学研究の問題点. *Shōwabungaku kenkyū* 昭和文学研究 25 (September): 93–101.

Nishikawa Mitsuru 西川満. 1940. *Rika fujin* 梨花夫人. Tokyo: Tōto Shoseki.

———. 1942. *Sekikanki* 赤嵌記. Tokyo: Shomotsu Tenbō Sha.

———, ed. 1943. *Taiwan ehon* 台湾絵本. Taipei: Tōa Ryokōsha Taihoku Shisha.

———. 1981a. *Jiden Nishikawa Mitsuru* 自伝西川満. Tokyo: Nigen no Hoshi Sha.

———, ed. 1981b. *Bungei Taiwan* 文芸台湾. Taipei: Dongfang Wenhua.

———. 1983. *Wagakoeshi ikusanga* わが越えし幾山河. Tokyo: Ningen no Hoshi Sha.

———. 1997a. *Xichuan Man xiaoshuoji* 1 西川満小説集 1. Translated by Ye Shi-tao 葉石濤. Kaohsiung: Chunhui Chubanshe.

———. 1997b. *Xichuan Man xiaoshuoji* 2 西川満小説集 2. Translated by Chen Qianwu 陳千武. Kaohsiung: Chunhui Chubanshe.

———. 1999. *Kareitō kenpūroku* 華麗島顕風録. Taipei: Zhiliang Chubanshe.

Nishikawa Mitsuru and Ikeda Yoshio 池田敏雄. 1942. *Kareitō minwashū* 華麗島民話集. Taipei: Nikō Sanbō; reprinted Taipei: Zhiliang Chubanshe, 1999.

Nishikawa Nagao 西川長夫. 1999. *Chikyū jidai no minzoku = bunka riron: Datsu "kokuminbunka" no tame ni* 地球時代の民族＝文化理論：脱「国民文化」のために. Tokyo: Shinyōsha.

Noguchi Tetsurō 野口鉄郎 et al., eds. 1994. *Dōkyō jiten* 道教事典. Tokyo: Hirakawa Shuppansha.

Norman, Jerry. 1988. *Chinese*. Cambridge: Cambridge University Press.

Nozaki Rokusuke 野崎六助. 1997. *Fukuin bungakuron* 復員文学論. Tokyo: Inpakuto Shuppankai.

Ōba Minakao 大庭みな子. 1992. *Yawarakai feminizumu e: Ōba Minako taidanshū* やわらかいフェミニズムへ大庭みな子対談集. Tokyo: Seitōsha.

Ōe Shinobu 大江志乃夫 et al., eds. 1993. *Iwanami kōza Kindai Nihon to shokuminchi* 岩波講座近代日本と植民地. 8 vols. Tokyo: Iwanami Shoten.

———. 1998. *Nihon shokuminchi tanpō* 日本植民地探訪. Tokyo: Shinchōsha.

Oguma Eiji 小熊英二. 1995. *Tan'itsu minzoku no kigen* 単一民族の起源. Tokyo: Shinyōsha.

———. 1997. "Yanagita Kunio to「uikkoku minzokugaku」「sōzō no kyōdōtai」Nihon o kanseisaseta gakumon" 柳田國男と「一国民俗学」「想像の共同体」日本の完成させた学問. In Ōmori Chiaki 大森千明, ed., *Minzokugaku ga wakaru* 民俗学がわかる. Tokyo: Asahi Shinbunsha.

———. 1998. *Nihonjin no kyōkai* 日本人の境界. Tokyo: Shinyōsha.

Ogura Mushitarō 小倉虫太郎 [Marukawa Tetsushi]. 1998. "Meta <nantō>bungakuron" メタ・「南島」文学論. *Eureka* ユリイカ 407 (August): 170–181.

Ōhama Tetsuya 大濱徹也 1999. *Kindai Nihon no rekishiteki isō kokka minzoku bunka* 近代日本の歴史的位相－国家・民族・文化. Tokyo: Tōsui Shoin.

Ohnuki-Tierney, Emiko. 1993. *Rice as Self: Japanese Identities Through Time*. Princeton: Princeton University Press.

Okaya Kōji 岡谷公二. 1990. *Nankai hyōhaku Hijikata Hisakatsu no shōgai* 南海漂泊　土方久功の生涯. Tokyo: Kawade Shobō Shinsha.

Okazaki Ikuko 岡崎郁子. 1992. "Taiwan bungaku no naka no Shōwa to iu jidai" 台湾文学のなかの昭和という時代. *Shōwa bungaku kenkyū* 昭和文学研究 25 (September): 193–197.

———. 1996a. *Taiwan bungaku: Itan no keifu* 台湾文学―異端の系譜. Tokyo: Tabata Shoten.

———. 1996b. "'Meitaihō' zenbun"「明台報」全文. *Journal of Asian and African Studies* 東京外国語大学アジア・アフリカ言語文化研究 51: 151–170.

———. 1998. "Kō Reishi ron, sono ichi" 黄霊芝論その 1. *Journal of Kibi Inter-*

national University School of International and Industrial Studies 吉備国際大学
社会学部研究紀要 8: 7–21.

———. 1999a. "Kō Reishi ron" 黄霊芝論. In Taiwan bungaku ronshū kankō iinkai 台湾文学論集刊行委員会, ed., *Taiwan bungaku kenkyū no genzai Tsukamoto Terukazu sensei koki kinen* 台湾文学研究の現在塚本昭和先生古稀記念.
Tokyo: Rikuin Shobō.

———. 1999b. "Kō Reishi ron, sono san" 黄霊芝論その三. *Journal of Kibi International University School of International and Industrial Studies* 9: 1–18.

———. 2000a. "Kō Reishi ron, sono 4: Shakai to ningen o egaku shiten" 黄霊
芝論その四―社会と人間を描く視点. *Journal of Kibi International University
School of International and Industrial Studies* 8: 69–87.

———. 2000b. "Kō Reishi ron, sono go: Ren'ai shōsetsu 'Ajisai' no shūhen" 黄
霊芝論その五―恋愛小説「紫陽花」の周辺. *Journal of Kibi International
University School of International and Industrial Studies* 吉備国際大学社会学部
研究紀要 10: 1–17.

Oketani Hideaki 桶谷秀昭. 1987. *Bunmei kaika to Nihonteki sōzō* 文明開化と日
本的想像. Tokyo: Fukutake Shoten.

———. 1992. *Shōwa seishinshi* 昭和精神史. Tokyo: Bungeishunjū.

Ōkubo Akio 大久保明男. 2000. "*Taiwan Manyōshū* no omomi to kanōsei" 『台
湾万葉集』の重みと可能性. *Shuka* 14 (April): 65–67.

Okuno Masamoto 奥野政元. 1993. *Nakajima Atsushi zenshū* 中島敦全集. 3 vols.
Tokyo: Chikuma Shobō.

———. 1996. "Nakajima Atsushi to sono jidai" 中島敦とその時代. In Fukuoka
yunesuko kyōkai, ed., *Sekai ga yomu Nihon no kindai bungaku* 世界が読む日
本の近代文学. Tokyo: Maruzen Kabushiki Kaisha.

Ōmori Chiaki 大森千明, ed. 1997. *Minzokugaku ga wakaru* 民俗学がわかる. Tokyo: Asahi Shinbunsha.

Ōmura Masuo 大村益男 and Hotei Toshihiro 布袋敏弘, eds. 1997. *Chōsen bungaku kankei Nihongo bunken mokuroku* 朝鮮文学関係日本語文献目録. Tokyo:
Rikuin Shobō.

Osa Shizue 長志珠絵. 1998. *Kindai Nihon to kokugo nashonarizumu* 近代日本と国
語ナショナリズム. Tokyo: Yoshikawa Kōbunkan.

Oshika Taku 大鹿卓. 1936. *Yabanjin* 野蛮人. Tokyo: Sōrin Shobō.

Oshino Takeshi 押野武志. 1993. "Nantō orientarizumu e no teikō: Hirotsu
Kazuo no 'sanbun seishin'" 南島オリエンタリズムへの抵抗―広津和郎
の＜散文精神＞. *Nihon kindai bungaku* 日本近代文学 49: 27–38.

Oson, Gary A., and Lynn Worsham, eds. 1999. *Race, Rhetoric, and the Postcolonial.*
Albany: State University of New York Press.

Osterhammel, Jürgen. 1997. *Colonialism: A Theoretical Overview.* Translated by
Shelley L. Frisch. Princeton: Weiner.

Ōtsuka Eiji 大塚英志 and Mori Yoshinatsu 森美夏. 1999a. *Hokushin denki* 北神
伝綺. 2 vols. Tokyo: Kadokawa Shoten.

———. 1999b. *Kijima nikki* 1 木島日記. Tokyo: Kadokawa Shoten.

Ozaki Hotsuki 尾崎秀樹. 1971. *Kyū shokuminchi bungaku no kenkyū* 旧植民地文学の研究. Tokyo: Kinsō Shobō.

———. 1991. *Kindai Bungaku no shōkon: Kyū shokuminchi bungaku ron* 近代文学の傷痕. Tokyo: Iwanami Shoten.

Ozawa Yūsaku 小沢有作, ed. 1998. *Shokuminchi kyōikushi nenpō daiichigō tokushū shokuminchi kyōikushi no saikōsei* 植民地教育史年報　第一号　特集植民地教育史の再構成. Tokyo: Kōseisha.

Peattie, Mark R. 1984. "The Nan'yō: Japan in the South Pacific." In Peattie and Myers (1984: 172–212).

———. 1988. *Nan'yō: The Rise and Fall of the Japanese Empire in Micronesia, 1885–1945*. Honolulu: University of Hawai'i Press.

———. 1996. *Shokuminchi: Teikoku 50 nen no kōbō* 植民地：帝国 50 年の興亡. Tokyo: Yomiuri Shinbunsha.

Peattie, Mark R., and Ramon H. Myers, eds. 1984. *The Japanese Colonial Empire, 1895–1945*. Princeton: Princeton University Press.

Peattie, Mark R., Ramon H. Myers, and Peter Duus, eds. 1989. *The Japanese Informal Empire in China, 1895–1937*. Princeton: Princeton University Press.

———. 1996. *The Japanese Wartime Empire, 1931–1945*. Princeton: Princeton University Press.

Pek Nakchong 白楽晴, I Sune 李順愛, and So Kyonsik 徐京植, trans. 1991. *Chie no jidai no tameni* 知恵の時代のために. Tokyo: Orijin Shuppan Sentā.

Peng Ruijin 彭瑞金. 1982. *Lishi de touying: Riju shidai Taiwan xinwenxue zuojia zuopin xuandu* 歷史的投影：日據時代台灣新文學作家作品選讀 Kaohsiung: Hepan Chubanshe.

———. 1991. *Taiwan xinwenxue yundong sishinian* 台灣新文學運動四十年. Taipei: Zili Wanbao Chubanshe.

———. 1995. "Senzen Taiwan shakai undō no hassei to shinbungaku undō no hajimari" 戦前台湾社会運動の発生と新文学運動の始まり. Translated by Kai Masumi 甲斐ますみ. In Shimomura Sakujirō et al. (1995: 21–45).

———. 1998. "Yongli qiaodachulai de Taiwan lishimuqing: Lun Xichuan Man xie 'Cailiuji'" 用力敲打出来的台湾歷史慕情－論西川満寫＜採硫記＞. In Chen Yizhi 陳義芝, ed., *Taiwan xiandai xiaoshuo zonglun* 台湾現代小説綜論. Taipei: Lianjing Chubanshe.

Peng Xiaoyan 彭小妍 et al., eds. 1998–2000. *Yang Que quanji* 楊逵全集. Taipei: Guoli Wenhuazican Baocun Yanjiu Zhongxin Choubeichu.

Phillips, Richard. 1997. *Mapping Men and Empire: A Geography of Adventure*. London: Routledge.

Phillipson, Robert. 1992. *Linguistic Imperialism*. Oxford: Oxford University Press.

Pincus, Leslie. 1996. *Authenticating Culture in Imperial Japan: Kuki Shūzō and the Rise of National Aesthetics*. Berkeley: University of California Press.

Pratt, Mary Louise. 1992. *Imperial Eyes: Travel Writing and Transculturation*. London: Routledge.

Qiu Ruolong 邱若龍 et al., eds. 1993. *Musha jiken* 霧社事件. Tokyo: Gendai Shokan.

Qiu Yonghan 邱永漢. 1994. *Kyū Eikan tanpen shōsetsu kessaku sen: Mienai kokkyōsen* 邱永漢短編小説傑作選－見えない国境線. Tokyo: Shinchōsha.

——. 1996. "Mitsunyūkokusha no shuki." In Kurokawa Sō 黒川創, ed, *"Gaichi" no Nihongo bungaku sen* 「外地」の日本語文学選, vol. 1: *Nanpō・nanyō/Taiwan* 南方・南洋/台湾. Tokyo: Shinjuku Shobō.

Rimer, Thomas J. 1990. *Culture and Identity: Japanese Intellectuals During the Interwar Years.* Princeton: Princeton University Press.

Robertson, Jennifer. 1998. *Takarazuka: Sexual Politics and Popular Culture in Modern Japan.* Berkeley: University of California Press.

Rubinstein, Murray. 1995. "The Revival of the Mazu Cult and of Taiwanese Pilgrimage to Fujian." *Harvard Studies on Taiwan: Papers of the Taiwan Studies Workshop* (Fairbank Center for East Asian Research) 1: 89–125.

——, ed. 1999. *Taiwan: A New History.* New York: Sharpe.

Ruitenbeek, Klaas. 1999. "Mazu, the Patroness of Sailors, in Chinese Pictorial Art." *Artibus Asiae* 58(3–4): 281–329.

Said, Edward. 1978. *Orientalism.* New York: Vintage.

Sagi Tadao 鷺只雄. 1997. "Sakka annai: Nakajima Atsushi" 作家案内：中島敦. In *Hikari to kaze to yume* 光と風と夢. Tokyo: Kōdansha Bunko.

Sakai, Cecile セシル・サカイ. 1997. *Nihon no taishū bungaku* 日本の大衆文学. Translated into Japanese by Asahina Kōji 朝比奈弘次. Tokyo: Heibonsha.

Sakai Naoki 酒井直樹. 1994. "'Tōyō' no jiritsu to daitōa kyōeiken" 「東洋」の自立と大東亜共栄圏. *Jōkyō* 状況 12: 6–20.

—— et al., eds. 1996. *Nashonariti no dakkōchiku* ナショナリディの脱構築. Tokyo: Kashiwa Shobō.

Sakuramoto Tomio 桜本富雄. 1993a. *Bunkajintachi no Dai Tōa sensō* 文化人たちの大東亜戦争. Tokyo: Aoki Shoten.

——. 1993b. *Bunkajintachi no Dai Tōa sensō: PK butai ga yuku* 文化人たちの大東亜戦争：PK部隊が行く. Tokyo: Aoki Shoten.

——. 1995. *Nihon bungaku hōkokukai Dai Tōa sensōka no bungakushatachi* 日本文学報国会　大東亜戦争下の文学者たち. Tokyo: Aoki Shoten.

Sanada Shinji 真田信治. 1991. *Hyōjungo wa ika ni seiritsu shita ka* 標準語はいかに成立したか. Tokyo: Sōtakusha.

Satō Haruo 佐藤春夫. 1936. *Musha* 霧社. Tokyo: Shōshinsha.

——. 1966. "Jokaisen kidan" 女誡扇綺譚. In *Satō Haruo* 佐藤春夫, Nihon bungaku zenshū, vol. 31. Tokyo: Chūōkōronsha.

——. 1994. *Satō Haruo* 佐藤春夫. In Torii Kuniaki 鳥居邦朗, ed., *Sakka no jiden* 作家の自伝, vol. 12. Tokyo: Nihon Tosho Sentā.

——. 1996. "Machō" 魔鳥. In Kurokawa Sō (1996, 2:39–52).

——. 1998. *Teihon Satō Haruo Zenshū* 定本佐藤春夫全集. 35 vols. Kyoto: Rinsen Shoten.

——. 2000. *Musha* 霧社. Edited by Kawahara Isao 河原功, Nihon shokuminchi bungaku seisenshū: Taiwan hen 日本植民地文学精選集台湾編. Tokyo: Yumani Shobō.

Satō Shizuo 佐藤静夫. 1989. *Shōwa bungaku no hikari to kage* 昭和文学の光と影. Tokyo: Ōtsuki Shoten.

Sears, Laurie J. 1996. *Shadow of Empire: Colonial Discourse and Javanese Tales.* Durham: Duke University Press.

Senryō to bungaku henshū iinkai 「占領と文学」編集委員会, ed. 1993. *Senryō to bungaku* 占領と文学. Tokyo: Orijin Shuppan Sentā.

Sharpe, Jenny. 1993. *Allegories of Empire: The Figure of Woman in the Colonial Text.* Minneapolis: University of Minnesota Press.

Shepherd, John Robert. 1993. *Statecraft and Political Economy on the Taiwan Frontier, 1600–1800.* Stanford: Stanford University Press.

Shiba Ryōtarō 司馬遼太郎. 1990. *Higashi to Nishi* 東と西. Tokyo: Asahi Shinbunsha.

Shi Gang 石剛. 1993. *Shokuminchi shihai to Nihongo* 植民地支配と日本語. Tokyo: Sangensha.

Shi Huiran 石輝然. 1999. *Mingzhi Dazheng Zhaohe Taiwan kaifa shi* 明治・大正・昭和台湾開発史. Taipei: Xinkeji Shuju.

Shi Shu 施淑, ed. 1992. *Riju shidai Taiwan xiaoshuo xuan* 日據時代台灣小説選. Taipei: Qianwei Chubanshe.

Shimada Kinji 島田謹二. 1976. "Gaichiken bungaku no jissō" 外地圏文学の実相. In *Nihon ni okeru gaikoku hikaku bungaku kenkyū* 日本における外国文学—比較文学研究, vol. 2. Tokyo: Asahi Shinbunsha.

———. 1995. *Kareitō bungakushi: Nihon shijin no Taiwan taiken* 華麗島文学史：日本詩人の台湾体験. Tokyo: Meiji Shoin.

Shimomura Sakujirō 下村作次郎. 1994. *Bungaku de yomu Taiwan* 文学で読む台湾. Tokyo: Tabata Shoten.

Shimomura Sakujirō 下村作次郎 et al., eds. 1995. *Yomigaeru Taiwan Bungaku* よみがえる台湾文学. Tokyo: Tōhō Shoten.

Shinozawa Hideo 篠沢秀夫. 1992. *Nihon kokka ron* 日本国家論. Tokyo: Bungeishunjūsha.

Shirakawa Yutaka 白川豊. 1995. *Shokuminchiki Chōsen no sakka to Nihon* 植民地朝鮮の作家と日本. Tokyo: Daigaku Kyōiku Shuppan.

Shirane Haruo. 1999. "'Nihon bungaku' kōchiku no rekishiteki kentō: Gurōbaru nashonarizumu no shiten kara" 「日本文学」構築の歴史的検討—グローバル・ナショナリズムの視点から. *Nihon bungaku* 日本文学 48 (January): 13–22.

Shirane Haruo ハルオ・シラネ and Tomi Suzuki 鈴木登美, eds. 1999. *Sōzōsareta koten* 創造された古典. Tokyo: Shinyōsha.

Shōji Hajime 庄司肇. 1994. *Yoshida Tomoko Ron* 吉田知子論. Tokyo: Chūsekisha.

Shōji Sōichi 庄司総一. 1944. *Chin fujin* 陳夫人. Tokyo: Tsūbunkaku; reprinted Taipei: Hongrutang, 1992.

———. 1999. *Chen furen* 陳夫人. Translated by Huang Yuyen 黄玉燕. Taipei: Wenyingtang Chubanshe.

Shōju Satoshi 松寿敬. 2000. "Shanhai"「上海」. *Kokubungaku kaishaku to kanshō* 国文学解釈と鑑賞「横光利一の世界」65(6) (June): 113-121.

Shufelt, John. 1998a. "Appropriating Formosa: Two Eighteenth-Century European Accounts of Taiwan." *Studies in English Literature and Linguistics* (Taiwan) 24 (June): 257-275.

———. 1998b. "Enduring Memories of False Formosa: An Assessment of Psalmanazar's Fraudulent Description of Formosa of 1704." Paper presented to the Fourth Annual North America Taiwan Studies Conference, University of Texas at Austin, May 29 to June 1.

———. 1998c. "Formosa as the Center of the Periphery in the Writings of Psalmanazar and Benyowsky." Paper presented to the Third Annual Conference of the Research Group for Taiwanese History and Culture, Columbia University, August 20-23.

Smith, Vanessa. 1998. *Literary Culture and the Pacific: Nineteenth-Century Textual Encounters.* Cambridge: Cambridge University Press.

Spivak, Gayatri Chakravorty. 1999. *A Critique of Postcolonial Reason.* Cambridge, Mass.: Harvard University Press.

Suga Hidemi 絓秀実, Shimizu Yoshinori 清水良典, Chiba Kazumiki 千葉一幹, and Yamada Junji 山田潤治. 1999a. "Zadankai: 90 nendai Nihon bungaku kessan hōkokusho: 'Riaru' wa torimodoseta ka" 座談会90年代日本文学決算報告書「リアル」は取り戻せたか. *Bungakukai* (December): 176-199.

———. 1999b. *Shōburu kyūshinshugi hihan sengen: 90 nendai, bungaku, kaisetsu* 小ブル急進主義批判宣言─90年代・文学・解読. Tokyo: Yotsuya Round.

Suzuki Sadami 鈴木貞美. 1994. *Nihon no "bungaku" o kangaeru* 日本の「文学」を考える. Tokyo: Kadokawa Shoten.

———. 1998. *Nihon no "bungaku" gainen* 日本の「文学」概念. Tokyo: Sakuhinsha.

———. 1999. "'Gaichi' to Shōwa bungaku"「外地」と昭和文学. In Hoshō Masao 保昌正夫 et al., eds., *Shōwa bungaku no fūkei* 昭和文学の風景. Tokyo: Shōgakkan.

Suzuki Tomi 鈴木登美. 1999. "Janru jenda bungakushi Kijutsu: 'Joryū nikki bungaku' no kōchiku o chūshin ni" ジャンル・ジェンダー・文学史記述─「女流日記文学」の構築を中心に. In Shirane Haruo and Suzuki Tomi, eds., *Sōzōsareta koten* 創造された古典. Tokyo: Shinyōsha.

Suzuki Tsunenori 鈴木経勲. 1892. *Nanyō tanken jikki* 南洋探険実記. Tokyo: Hakubunkan; reprinted Tokyo: Heibonsha, 1980, and Tokyo: Sōzō Shobo, 1983.

Suzuki Yūko 鈴木裕子. 1995. "Bosei sensō heiwa: Nihon no 'bosei' to feminizumu" 母性・戦争・平和─日本の「母性」とフェミニズム. *Nyū feminizumu rebyū* ニュー・フェミニズム・レビュー (New feminism review) 6: 68-73.

———. 1997a. *Feminizumu to sensō: Fujin undōka no sensō kyōryoku* フェミニズムと戦争─婦人運動家の戦争協力. Tokyo: Maruju Sha.

———. 1997b. *Sensō sekinin to jenda* 戦争責任とジェンダー. Tokyo: Miraisha.

Swann, Nancy Lee. 1932. *Pan Chao: Foremost Woman Scholar of China*. New York: Russell.

Tai, Eika. 1999. "Kokugo and Colonial Education in Taiwan." *positions* 7(2): 503–540.

Taiwan bungaku ronshū kankō iinkai 台湾文学論集刊行委員会, ed. 1999. *Taiwan bungaku kenkyū no genzai Tsukamoto Terukazu sensei koki kinen* 台湾文学研究の現在 塚本昭和先生古稀記念. Tokyo: Rikuin Shobō.

Takahashi Tetsuya 高橋哲哉. 1999. *Sengo sekinin ron* 戦後責任論. Tokyo: Kōdansha.

Takazawa Shūji 高澤秀次. 1998. *Hyōden Nakagami Kenji* 評伝中上健次. Tokyo: Shūeisha.

Takeda Seiji 竹田青嗣. 1995. *"Zainichi" to iu konkyo* ＜在日＞という根拠. Tokyo: Chikuma Shobō.

Takenaka Nobuko 竹中信子. 1995. *Shokuminchi Taiwan no Nihon josei seikatsushi*, vol. 1: *Meijihen* 植民地台湾の日本女性生活史, 明治編 Tokyo: Tabata Shoten.

——. 1996. *Shokuminchi Taiwan no Nihon josei seikatsushi*, vol. 2: *Taishōhen* 植民地台湾の日本女性生活史, 大正編. Tokyo: Tabata Shoten.

Takeuchi Yasuhiro 竹内泰広. 1974. *Ajia no naka no Nihon bungaku* アジアのなかの日本文学. Tokyo: Chikuma Shobō.

Tal, Kali. 1996. *Worlds of Hurt: Reading the Literatures of Trauma*. Cambridge: Cambridge University Press.

Tamura Shizue 田村志津枝. 2000. *Hajime ni eiga ga atta shokuminchi Taiwan to Nihon* はじめに映画があった植民地台湾と日本. Tokyo: Chūōkōronsha.

Tān, K. T. 1978. *A Chinese-English Dictionary: Taiwan Dialect*. Taipei: Southern Material Center.

Tanabe Yukinobu 田鍋幸信. 1992. "Nakajima to Yōroppa narumono" 中島とヨーロッパなるもの. In Katsumata Hiroshi 勝又浩 and Kimura Kazunobu 木村一信, eds., *Nakajima Atsushi* 中島敦. Tokyo: Sōbunsha.

Tanaka Katsuhiko 田中克彦. 1981. *Kotoba to kokka* 言葉と国家. Tokyo: Iwanami Shinsho.

Tanaka Keizō 田中敬三. 1995. "Kyū shokuminchi no bungaku: Wasurerareta sakka gunzō" 旧植民地の文学—忘れられた作家群像. In Nakanishi Susumu and Yan Shaotang (1995: 429–435).

Tanaka Masuzō 田中益三. 1992. "Henreki・ikyō—Chōsen・Chūgoku taiken no imi" 遍歴・異郷—朝鮮・中国体験の意味. In Katsumata Hiroshi 勝又浩 and Kimura Kazunobu 木村一信, eds., *Nakajima Atsushi* 中島敦. Tokyo: Sōbunsha.

Tani Yasuyo 多仁安代. 2000. *Dai Tōa kyōeiken to Nihongo* 大東亜共栄圏の日本語. Tokyo: Keisō Shobō.

Tarumi Chie 垂水千恵. 1992. *Sannin no "Nihonjin" sakka: Wang Changxiong, Zhou Jinpo, Chen Huoquan* 三人の「日本人」作家：王昶雄・周金波・陳火泉. In *Ekkyoosuru sekai bungaku* 越境する世界文学. Tokyo: Kawade Shuppansha, 1992.

———. 1994. "Zhanqian 'Ribenyǔ' zuojia: Wang Changxiong yǔ Chen Huo-quan, Zhou Jinpo zhi bijiao" 戦前「日本語」作家－王昶雄与陳火泉、周金波之比較. In Huang Yingzhe (1994: 87–108).

———. 1995a. *Taiwan no Nihongo bungaku* 台湾の日本語文学. Tokyo: Goryū Shoten.

———. 1995b. "'Seishu' sono chien no kōzō" 「清秋」その遅延の構造. In Shimomura Sakujirō et al. (1995: 371–388).

———. 1996. "Sen kyūhyaku yonjū nendai no Taiwan bundan to tabunkashugi" 一九四〇年代の台湾文壇と多文化主義. In *Tabunkashugi no kigoron* 多文化主義の記号論. Tokyo: Tokai Daigaku Shuppansha.

———. 1999. "Nakajima Atsushi wa enoken o mitanoka?: 'Waga Saiyūki' no ura/omotegawa" 中島敦はエノケンを見たのか？―「わが西遊記」の裏 / 表側. *Nihon bungaku* 日本文学 48 (January): 23–31.

———. 2000. "Ro Kakujaku kenkyū: 1943 nen made no bunseki o chūshin toshite" 呂赫若研究―1943年までの分析を中心として. Ph.D. dissertation, Ochanomizu University.

———. 2002. *Rokakujaku kenkyū: 1943 nen made no bunseki o chūshin toshite* 呂赫若研究―1943 年までの分析を中心として. Tokyo: Kazama Shobō.

Tatsumi Takayuki 巽孝之. 1998. *Nihon henryū bungaku* 日本変流文学. Tokyo: Shinchōsha.

Teng, Emma Jinhua. 1993. "A Search for the Strange and a Discovery of the Self: Yu Yung-ho's Small Sea Travelogue as a Work of Self-Representation." *Harvard Papers on Chinese Literature* 1 (Spring).

———. 1997. "Travel Writing and Colonial Collecting: Chinese Travel Accounts of Taiwan from the Seventeenth Through Nineteenth Centuries." Ph.D. dissertation, Harvard University. [DAI 1997 58(5): 1715–A. DA9733198]

———. 1998. "An Island of Women: The Discourse of Gender in Qing Travel Writing About Taiwan." *International History Review* 20(2) (June): 353–370.

———. 1999. "Taiwan as a Living Museum: Tropes of Anachronism in Late-Imperial Chinese Travel Writing." *Harvard Journal of Asiatic Studies* 59(2): 445–484.

Terasaki Hiroshi 寺崎浩. 1974. *Sensō no yokogao* 戦争の横顔. Tokyo: Taihei Shuppansha.

Tierney, Robert. 2001. "Anti-Colonialism and the Colonial Novel: Nakajima Atsushi's *Light Wind and Dreams*." Paper presented at the annual meeting of the Association of Asian Studies, Chicago, March.

Tiffin, Chris, and Alan Lawson. 1994. *De-Scribing Empire*. London: Routledge.

Tobin, Beth Fowkes. 1999. *Picturing Imperial Power*. Durham: Duke University Press.

Tomiyama, Ichirō. 1997. "Colonialism and the Sciences of the Tropical Zone: The Academic Analysis of Difference in the 'Island People.'" In Tani Barlow, ed., *The Formation of Colonial Modernity in East Asia*. Durham: Duke University Press.

Torgovnik, Marianna. 1990. *Gone Primitive: Savage Intellects, Modern Lives.* Chicago: University of Chicago Press.

Torii Ryūzō 鳥居龍蔵. 1996. *Tanxian Taiwan* 探險台湾. Translated by Yang Nanjun 楊南郡. Taipei: Yuanliu Chubanshe.

Treat, John William, ed. 1996. *Contemporary Japan and Popular Culture.* Honolulu: University of Hawai'i Press.

Trivedi, Harish. 1995. *Colonial Transactions: English Literature and India.* Manchester: Manchester University Press.

Tsuji Yoshio 辻義男. 1993. "Zhou Jinpo lun" 周金波論. Translated by Liu Shuqin 柳書琴. *Wenxue Taiwan* 文学台湾 8 (October): 237–247.

Tsukamono Terukazu 塚本照和. 1995. "Yō Ki no 'Den'en shōkei' to 'Mohanson' no koto" 楊逵の「田園小景」と「模範村」のこと. In Shimomura Sakujirō et al. (1995: 313–344).

Tsurumi, E. Patricia. 1977. *Japanese Colonial Education in Taiwan.* Cambridge, Mass.: Harvard University Press.

———. 1984. "Colonial Education in Korea and Taiwan." In Peattie and Myers (1984: 275–311).

Tsurumi Shunsuke 鶴見俊輔. 1991. *Tsurumi shunsuke shū* 鶴見俊輔集. Tokyo: Chikuma Shobō.

Ueda Hiroshi 上田博, Kimura Kazunobu 木村一信, and Nakagawa Shigemi 中川成美, eds. 1997. *Nihon kindai bungaku o manabu hito no tame ni* 日本近代文学を学ぶ人のために. Kyoto: Sekai Shisōsha.

Ueda Kazutoshi 上田万年. 1968. *Ochiai Naofumi, Ueda Kazutoshi, Haga Yaichi, Fujioka Sakutarō shū* 落合直史上田万年芳賀矢一藤岡作太郎集. Meiji bungaku zenshū 明治文学全集 44. Tokyo: Chikuma Shobō.

Ueno Chizuko 上野千鶴子. 1995. "Orientarizumu to jendā" オリエンタリズムとジェンダー. *Nyū feminizumu rebyū* ニュー・フェミニズム・レビュー (New feminism review) 6: 108–131.

———. 1998. *Nashonarizumu to jendaa* ナショナリズムとジェンダー. Tokyo: Seitosha.

Uenuma Hachirō 上沼八郎. 1962. *Izawa Shūji* 伊沢修二. Tokyo: Yoshikawa Kōbunkan.

Varadharajan, Asha. 1995. *Exotic Parodies: Subjectivity in Adorno, Said, and Spivak.* Minneapolis: University of Minnesota Press.

Wachman, Alan. 1994. *Taiwan: National Identity and Democratization.* Armonk, N.Y.: Sharpe.

Wakabayashi Masatake 若林正丈 and Wu Micha 呉密察. 2000. *Taiwan chongceng jindaihua lunwenji* 台湾重層近代化論文集. Taipei: Bozhongzhe Wenhua.

Wakakuwa Midori 若桑みどり. 1995. *Sensō ga tsukuru joseizō: dainiji sekaitaisenka no Nihon josei dōin no shikakuteki puropaganda* 戦争がつくる女性像－第二次世界大戦下の日本女性動員の視覚的プロパガンダ. Tokyo: Chikuma Shobō.

Wang, Ya-lun 王雄倫. 1997. *Anciennes Photographies de Taiwan: Collection de la*

Bibliotheque Nationale de France: Dialogue entre la photographie et l'histoire 法国
珍蔵早期台湾影像：撮影與歴史的對話. Taipei: Xiongshe Meishushe.

Watanabe Naomi 渡部直巳 and Komori Yōichi 小森陽一. 2000. "Taidan 'Shokuminchi' taiken toshite no tennōsei Nihon kindai shōsetsu 'Haiboku' no
rekishi" 台湾「植民地」体験としての天皇制 日本近代小説「敗北」の歴
史. *Sekai* 673 (April): 209–223.

Weng Nao 翁鬧. 1991. *Weng Nao, Wu Yongfu, Wang Changxiong heji* 翁鬧・巫永
福・王昶雄合集. Edited by Zhang Henghao 張恒豪. Taipei: Qianwei Chubanshe.

Willims, Patrick, and Laura Chrisman, eds. 1994. *Colonial Discourse and Post-colonial Theory: A Reader*. New York: Columbia University Press.

Wills, John E., Jr. 1999. "The Seventeenth-Century Transformation: Taiwan
Under the Dutch and the Cheng Regimes." In Rubinstein (1999: 84–106).

Wu, Shu-hui. 1998. "On Taiwanese Historical Poetry: Reflections on the Shimonoseki Treaty of 1895." *Journal of Asian History* (Germany) 32(2): 157–179.

Wu Wenxing 呉文星. 1987. "Riju shiqi Taiwan zongdufu tuiguang Riyu yundong chutan, pt. 1" 日據時期台湾総督府推廣日語運動初探(上). *Taiwan
Fengwu* 台湾風物 (Taiwan folkways) 37(1): 1–32.

———. 1992. *Rijushiqi Taiwan shehui lingdao jieceng zhi yanjiu* 日據時期台湾社
会領動階層之研究. Taipei: Zhengzhong Shuju.

Wu Zhuoliu 呉濁流. 1946. "Nichibun haishi ni taisuru kanken" 日文廃止に対
する管見. *Xinxin* 新新 (October 17): 12.

———. 1973. *Ajia no koji* アジアの孤児. Tokyo: Shinjinbutsu Ōraisha.

———. 1994. *The Fig Tree: Memoirs of a Taiwanese Patriot, 1900–1947*. Translated
by Duncan B. Hunter; edited by Helmut Martin. Edition Cathay, 1. Dortmund: Projekt Verlag.

Xu Junya 許俊雄. 1994. *Taiwan wenxue sanlun* 台湾文学散論. Taipei: Wenshizhe
Chubanshe.

———. 1995. *Riju shiqi Taiwan xiaoshuo yanjiu* 日據時期台灣小説研究. Taipei:
Wenshizhe Chubanshe.

———. 1997a. *Taiwan wenxuelun: Cong xiandai dao dangdai* 台湾文学論—從現
代至當代. Taipei: Nantian Shuju.

———. 1997b. *Taiwan xieshi shizuo zhi kangri jingshen yanjiu: 1895–1945 nian
zhi gudian shige* 台湾写実詩作之抗日精神研究：1895–1945 年之古典詩歌.
Taipei: Bianyiguan.

———. 1998. *Riju shiqi Taiwan xiaoshuo xuandu* 日據時期台灣小説選讀. Taipei:
Wanjuanlou.

Xu Minmin 徐敏民. 1996. *Senzen Chūgoku ni okeru Nihongo kyōiku* 戦前中国にお
ける日本語教育. Tokyo: Emuti Shuppan.

Xu Shikai 許世楷. 1992. "Kōgakkō seikatsu" 公学校生活. *Geppō* 月報 1, *Kindai
Nihon to shokuminchi* 近代日本と植民地, vol. 1. Tokyo: Iwanami Shoten.

Yamabe Kentarō 山辺健太郎. 1971. *Taiwan* 台湾. Gendaishi shiryō 現代史資料
21. Tokyo: Misuzu Shobō.

Yamada Keizō 山田敬三. 1995. "Kanashiki rōmanshugisha Nihon tōchi jidai no Ryū Eisō" 哀しき浪漫主義者—日本統治時代の龍瑛宗. In Shimomura Sakujirō et al. (1995: 345–370).

Yamada Seizaburō 山田清三郎. 1966. *Puroretaria bungakushi* プロレタリア文学史. Tokyo: Rironsha.

Yamada Yoshio 山田孝雄. 1941. *Kokugo gairon hen* 国語概論篇. *Kokugo bunka kōza* 国語文化講座 2. Tokyo: Asahi Shinbunsha.

Yamaguchi Mamoru 山口守. 1992. "Kamen no gengo ga shōshasuru mono: Taiwan sakka Yō Ki no Nihongo sakuhin" 仮面の言語が照射するもの—台湾作家楊逵の日本語作品. *Shōwa bungaku kenkyū* 昭和文学研究 25 (September): 129–141.

Yamashiro Kentoku 山室建徳. 1999. "Gunshinron" 軍神論. In Aoki Tamotsu 青木保 et al., eds., *Sensō to guntai* 戦争と軍隊, vol. 10: *Kindai Nihon bunkaron* 近代日本文化論. Tokyo: Iwanami Shoten.

Yamashita Shinji 山下晋司 and Yamamoto Matori 山本真鳥, eds. 1997. *Shokuminchi shugi to bunka jinruigaku no pāsupekutivu* 植民地主義と文化—人類学のパースペクディヴ. Tokyo: Shinyōsha.

Yanagi Sōetsu 柳宗悦. 1981. *Yanagi Sōetsu zenshū* 柳宗悦全集. Tokyo: Chikuma Shoten.

Yanagita Kunio 柳田国男. 1943. "Zadankai Yanagita Kunio o kakomite dai Tōa minzokugaku no kensetsu to 'Minzoku Taiwan' no shimei" 座談会柳田国男氏を囲みて 大東亜民俗学の建設と「民俗台湾」の使命. *Minzoku Taiwan* 民俗台湾 3(12) (December): 2–14.

Yanagita Setsuko 柳田節子. 1992. "Omoidasu koto nado" 思い出すことなど. In *Geppō* 月報 2: *Kindai Nihon to shokuminchi* 近代日本と植民地. Tokyo: Iwanami Shoten.

Yanaihara Tadao 矢内原忠雄. 1929. *Teikokushugika no Taiwan* 帝国主義下の台湾. Tokyo: Iwanami Shoten.

Yang Du 楊渡. 1994. *Riju shiqi Taiwan xinju yundong, 1923–1936* 日據時期台湾新劇運動 1923–1936. Taipei: Shibao Wenhua Chuban Shiye.

Yang Kui 楊逵 1985. *E mama yao chujia* 鵝媽媽要出嫁 Taipei: Qianwei Chubanshe.
———. 1991. *Yang Kui ji* 楊逵集. Edited by Zhang Henghao. Taiwan zuojia quanji rijushidai 台湾作家全集日據時代, series 7. Taipei: Qianwei Chubanshe.

Yang Qianhe 楊千鶴. 1998. *Jinsei no purizumu* 人生のプリズム. Taipei: Nantian Shuju.

Yang Yongbin 楊永彬. 2000. "Riben ling Tai chuqi Ri-Tai guanshen shiwen changhe" 日本領臺初期日臺官神詩文唱和. In Wakabayashi Masatake and Wu Micha (2000: 105–182).

Yang Ziqiao 羊子喬. 1993. "Lishi de beiju, rentong de mangdian: Du Zhou Jinpo 'Shuiai' 'Chi' de dansheng" 歷史的悲劇 忍同的盲点—讀周金波＜水癌＞＜『尺』の誕生＞. *Wenxue Taiwan* 文学台湾 8 (October): 231–236.

Yano Tōru 矢野暢. 1975. *Nanshin no keifu* 「南進」の系譜. Tokyo: Chūōkōronsha.

———. 1979. *Nihon no Nan'yō shikan* 日本の南洋史観. Tokyo: Chūōkōronsha.

Yasuda Toshiaki 安田敏朗. 1997. *Teikoku Nihon no gengo hensei* 帝国日本の言語編制. Tokyo: Seori Shobō.

———. 1998. *Shokuminchi no naka no "kokugogaku": Tokieda Motoki to Keisei teikoku daigaku o megutte* 植民地の中の「国語学」時枝誠記と京成帝国大学をめぐって. Tokyo: Sangensha.

———. 1999. *"Kokugo" to "hōgen" no aida: Gengo kōchiku no seijigaku* ＜国語＞と＜方言＞のあいだ：言語構築の政治学. Tokyo: Jinbun Shoin.

Ye Shitao 葉石濤. 1982. "Qingchiu: Weizhuang de huangminhua ouge" 清秋－偽装的皇民化謳歌. *Taiwan wenyi* 77: 21–26.

———. 1987. *Taiwan wenxue shigang* 台湾文学史綱. Kaohsiung: Chunhui Chubanshe.

———, ed. and trans. 1996. *Taiwan wenxue ji 1: Riwen zuopin xuanji* 台湾文学集 1：日文作品先週. Kaohsiung: Chunhui Chubanshe.

———. 1997. *Taiwan wenxue rumen* 台湾文学入門. Kaohsiung: Chunhui Chubanshe.

Yee, Angelina C. 1995. "Rewriting the Colonial Self: Yang Kui's Texts of Resistance and National Identity." *Chinese Literature, Essays, Articles, Reviews* 17: 111–132.

Yin Yunfan 段允芃, ed. 1996. *Taiwan no rekishi: Nichi-Tai kōshō no sanbyakunen* 台湾の歴史：日台交渉の三百年. Translated by Maruyama Katsu 丸山勝. Tokyo: Fujiwara Shoten.

Yomota Inuhiko 四方田犬彦. 1998. *Kokoro tokimekasu* 心ときまかす. Tokyo: Seibunsha.

———. 2000. *Nihon eigashi 100 nen* 日本映画史100年. Tokyo: Shūeisha Shinsho.

Yoshida Sumio 吉田澄夫 and Inoguchi Yūichi 井之口有一, eds. 1964. *Meiji ikō kokugo mondai shū* 明治以降国語問題集. Tokyo: Kazama Shoten.

Yoshino Kōsaku 吉野耕作. 1998. *Bunka nashonarizumu no shakaigaku: Gendai Nihon aidentiti no yukue* 文化ナショナリズムの社会学—現代日本アイデンティティの行方. Nagoya: Nagoya Daigaku Shuppankai.

Yoshiyasu Yukio 喜安幸夫. 1981. Taiwan tōchi hishi: Musha jiken ni itaru kō-Nichi no zenbō 台湾統治秘史—霧社事件に至る抗日の全貌. Tokyo: Hara Shobō.

You Peiyün 游珮芸. 1999. *Shokuminchi Taiwan no jidō bunka* 植民地台湾の児童文化. Tokyo: Akashi Shoten.

Young, Louise. 1998. *Japan's Total Empire: Manchuria and the Culture of Wartime Imperialism*. Berkeley: University of California Press.

Yuasa Katsuhiko 湯浅克彦. 1995. *Yuasa Katsuhiko shokuminchi shōsetsushū Kannani* 湯浅克衛植民地小説集 カンナニ. Tokyo: Inpakuto Shuppankai.

Yuchi Asao 湯地朝雄. 1991. *Puroretaria bungaku undō: Sono risō to genjitsu* プロレタリア文学運動. Tokyo: Banseisha.

Yui Masaomi 由井正臣. 2000. *Dai Nippon teikoku no jidai* 大日本帝国の時代. Nihon no rekishi series 日本の歴史, 8. Tokyo: Iwanami Shoten.

Yun Kenkil 尹建治. 1997. *Minzoku gensō no zatetsu: Nihonjin no jikōzō*. 民族の蹉
跌—日本人の自己像. Tokyo: Iwanami Shoten.

Yuri Hajime ゆりはじめ. 1987. *Sensō no seishun: Kakinokosareta Shōwa seishinshi*
戦争の青春—書き残された昭和精神史. Tokyo: Nihon Tosho Sentā.

Zhang Henghao 張恒豪, ed. 1990. *Yang Yünping, Zhang Wojun, Cai Qiutong heji*
楊雲萍張我軍蔡秋桐合集. Taiwan zuojiachuanji rijushidai 台湾作家全集
日據時代 2. Taipei: Qianwei Chubanshe.

Zhang Jilin 張季琳. 2000. "Taiwan puroretaria bungaku no tanjō: Yō Ki to Dai
Nippon teikoku" 台湾プロレタリア文学の誕生—楊逵と「大日本帝国」.
Ph.D. dissertation, University of Tokyo.

Zhang Liangze 張良澤. 1981. *Nishikawa Mitsuru sensei chosaku shoshi* 西川満先生
著作書誌. 2 vols. Tokyo: Nigen no Hoshi Sha.

Zhang Wenhuan 張文環. 1975. *Chi ni hau mono* 地に這うもの. Tokyo: Gendai
Bunkaisha.

———. 1994. *Zhang Wenhuan ji* 張文環集. Taipei: Qianwei Chubanshe.

Zhou Jinpo 周金波. 1993a. "<Chi> de dansheng" <尺>の誕生. Translated by
Chen Xiaonan 陳暁南. *Wenxue Taiwan* 文学台湾 8 (October): 248–260.

———. 1993b. "Shuiai" 水癌. Translated by Xu Bingcheng 許炳成. *Wenxue Taiwan* 文学台湾 8 (October): 261–269.

———. 1998a. "Michi." 道. In Nakajima Toshio and Kawahara Isao (1998, 5:9-
64).

———. 1998b. "Chō sensei" 張先生. In Nakajima Toshio and Kawahara Isao
(1998, 5:65–76).

Zhou Wanyao 周婉窈. 1994. "Cong bijiao de guandian kan Taiwan yǔ Hanguo
de huangminhua yùndong (1937–1945)" 徒比較的観点看台湾與韓国的
皇民化運動 (1937–1945). *Xinshixue* 新史学 5(2) (June): 117–156.

Index

Yuasa Katsuhiko, 46; *Honō no kiroku*, 46; *Kannani*, 46

Zhang Liangze, 79–80
Zhang Wenhuan, 5, 72, 76, 123, 161, 171, 174, 192, 196, 198–199, 215, 222, 240
Zhang Wojun, 148, 150–154, 158

Zheng Chenggong, 99–105, 140
Zhishanyan Incident, 131–132
Zhou Jinpo, 6, 120, 199, 202–208, 211–217, 222–225, 232, 235, 238; "Nostalgia," 213; "The Volunteer Soldier," 200–202, 205, 212–213, 216; "Water Cancer," 200

About the Author

Faye Yuan Kleeman attended Soochow University in Taiwan (B.A.), Ochanomizu University in Japan (M.A.), and the University of California, Berkeley, where she received a Ph.D. in 1991. She has taught at City College of New York, the College of William and Mary, and since 1998, the University of Colorado, Boulder, where she is associate professor of East Asian Languages and Civilizations.

Production Notes for Kleeman/UNDER AN IMPERIAL SUN

Interior design by Josie Herr

Composition by inari

Jacket design by Santos Barbasa Jr.

Text in New Baskerville; display type in Barbedor; Japanese and Chinese type in Meichō

Printing and binding by The Maple-Vail Book Manufacturing Group

Printed on 50 lb. Glatfeter Hi-Opaque, 440 ppi.